COUNTRY
Pubs & Inns of
WALES

By Barbara Vesey

© Travel Publishing Ltd.

Regional Hidden Places

Cornwall
Devon
Dorset, Hants & Isle of Wight
East Anglia
Gloucs, Wiltshire & Somerset
Heart of England
Hereford, Worcs & Shropshire
Lake District & Cumbria
Lancashire & Cheshire
Northumberland & Durham
Peak District
Sussex
Yorkshire

National Hidden Places

England
Ireland
Scotland
Wales

Hidden Inns

East Anglia
Heart of England
North of England
South
South East
West Country
Yorkshire

Country Pubs & Inns

Cornwall
Devon
Sussex
Wales

Country Living Rural Guides

East Anglia
Heart of England
Ireland
North East of England
North West of England
Scotland
South
South East
Wales
West Country

Published by: Travel Publishing Ltd, 7a Apollo House, Calleva Park, Aldermaston, Berkshire RG7 8TN

ISBN 1·904·43434·7

© Travel Publishing Ltd

Published 2005

Printing by: Scotprint, Haddington

Maps by: © Maps in Minutes ™ (2005)
© Crown Copyright, Ordnance Survey 2005

Editor: Barbara Vesey

Cover Design: jpbstudio, Whitchurch, Hampshire

Cover Photograph: Griffin Inn, Llyswen, Powys
© www.britainonview.com

Text Photographs: © www.britainonview.com

Foreword

The *Country Pubs & Inns of Wales* is the first title in a series of guides which will eventually cover the whole of the UK (the guides covering England will be published by county). This guide provides details of pubs and inns (including hotels which welcome non-residents) situated in the countryside of Wales. "Countryside" is officially defined by *The Office of National Statistics* as "settlements of less than 10,000 inhabitants".

There are of course many selectively-based pub guides covering the UK but each title in the Country Pubs & Inns series will provide the reader with the *most comprehensive* choice of pubs and inns in the countryside. The guide enables the reader to choose the pub or inn to visit based on his/her own criteria such as location, real ales served, food, entertainment etc.

The easy-to-use guide is divided into 22 chapters based on the counties of Wales which allows the reader to select the area of Wales being visited. Each chapter begins with a brief illustrated summary of the places of interest in the area and a map containing the numbered location of the pub or inn. By using the number the reader can then find more information on their choice of pub.

We do hope that you will enjoy visiting the pubs and inns contained in this guide. We are always interested in what our readers think of the pubs and inns covered (or not covered) in our guides so please do not hesitate to write to us using the reader reaction forms provided to the rear of the guide. Equally, you may contact us via our email address at info@travelpublishing.co.uk. This is a vital way of ensuring that we continue to provide a comprehensive list of pubs and inns to our readers.

Finally, if you are seeking visitor information on Wales or any other part of the British Isles we would like to refer you to the full list of Travel Publishing guides to be found at the rear of the book. You may also find more information about any of our titles on our website at www.travelpublishing.co.uk

Travel Publishing

How to use the guide

The *Country Pubs & Inns of Wales* provides details of pubs and inns (including hotels which welcome non-residents) situated in the countryside of Wales. "Countryside" is defined by *The Office of National Statistics* as "settlements of less than 10,000 inhabitants".

This guide has been specifically designed as an easy-to-use guide so there is no need for complicated instructions. However the reader may find the following guidelines helpful in identifying the name, address, telephone number and facilities of the pub or inn.

Finding Pubs or Inns in a Selected Location

The guide is divided into chapters each covering a specific Welsh county. Identify the county and page number you require from the table of contents at the front of the guide and turn to the relevant page.

At the beginning of each chapter there is a detailed map of the county. Select the specific area of the county you require. The numbered boxes in the area chosen represent each pub or inn in the area selected. Simply locate the same number within the chapter to find the name, address, telephone number and facilities of the pub or inn.

Finding a Specific Pub or Inn

If you know the name of the pub or inn then simply go to the relevant county chapter where the names of the pubs are listed in alphabetical order.

Pub and Inn Information

All pubs or inns in the guide give details of the name, address, telephone number and whether they offer real ales, food, accommodation and no smoking areas.

The advertising panels found in each chapter provide more comprehensive information on the pub or inn such as contact details, location, interior and exterior facilities, real ales, opening times, food, entertainment, disabled access, credit cards and places of interest.

Contents

ISLE OF ANGLESEY

■ Anglesey Reference Number - Detailed Information

▨ Anglesey Reference Number - Summary Entry

Ceredigion
Page 249 ▶ Adjacent area - refer to pages indicated

ANGLESEY, ISLE OF

HOLYHEAD • MENAI BRIDGE • AMLWCH

Anglesey (Welsh: *Ynys Môn*) is separated from the mainland by a narrow stretch of water called the Menai Strait. It is connected to the mainland by two bridges, the original Menai Suspension Bridge, built by Thomas Telford in 1826 as a road link, and the newer, twice-reconstructed Britannia Bridge, carrying the A55 and the North Wales Coast Railway line. Historically, Anglesey has long been associated with the Druids. Circa AD 60, the Roman general Suetonius Paullinus determined to break the power of the Druids by attacking the island and destroying the shrine and sacred groves there. In the centuries that followed the island was invaded by Vikings, Saxons, and Normans before falling to King Edward I of England in the 13th century.

Anglesey is fertile and relatively low-lying, and has, over the centuries, been known as 'the breadbasket of Wales' and, during the Middle Ages, as Anglesey Mother of Wales (Welsh: *Môn Mam Cymru*). It was of significant strategic importance during the struggles between the English kings and the Welsh princes.

Menai Bridge

The island's entire rural coastline had been designated an Area of Outstanding Natural Beauty and features many sandy beaches, especially along its northern coast between the towns of Menai Bridge and Amlwch. This accounts for the island's principal industry: tourism.

Anglesey has many small towns scattered all around the island, making it quite evenly populated. Beaumaris, to the south of the island, features Beaumaris Castle, built by Edward I as part of his campaign in North Wales. The town of Newborough, created when the townfolk of Llanfaes were relocated to make way for the building of Beaumaris Castle, houses the site of Llys Rhosyr, the court of the mediaeval Welsh princes, which features one of the oldest courtrooms in the United Kingdom. Beaumaris town also has a large marina, and acts as a yachting centre for the region. Llangefni is located in the centre of the island and is also the island's administrative centre. The town of Menai Bridge grew up when the first bridge to the mainland was being built, in order to accommodate workers and construction. A short distance from this town lies Bryn Celli Ddu, a Stone Age burial mound.

The island also has the village with the longest place name in the United Kingdom, the famous Llanfairpwllgwyngyllgogerychwyrndrobwllllantysiliogogogoch — which means 'St Mary's Church in a hollow of white hazel near a rapid whirlpool and St Tysilio's Church near the red cave' and is, thankfully, usually shortened to 'Llanfair PG'.

1 Adelphi Vaults

Quay St, Amlwch Port, Amlwch, Anglesey LL68 9HD

☎ 01407 830278

Real Ales

2 Anchorage Hotel

Four Mile Bridge, Holyhead, Anglesey LL65 2EZ

☎ 01407 740168

Real Ales, Bar Food, Restaurant Menu,
Accommodation, No Smoking Area

3 Benllech Hotel

Beach Road, Benllech, Isle of Anglesey LL74 8SW

☎ 01248 852374

Bar Food, Restaurant Menu, Accommodation,
No Smoking Area

Benllech Hotel is a friendly and convivial pub with
a good range of different ales on draught together
with lagers, cider, stout, wines, spirits and soft
drinks – something to quench every thirst.

The various menus and specials board provide
a choice of tempting traditional and creative
favourites. A new conservatory is under construction that will seat a further 50 diners. Children
and families very welcome.

🠖 6½ miles north of Menai Bridge on the
A5025

▌ 12-2.30 & 6-9.30

🛏 Self-catering cottages – please ring for details

⚓ Parking, garden, BBQ, disabled access

🕐 11.30-11 (Sun and Bank Holidays to 10.30)

🏛 Beach, Castell Mawr, Menai Bridge 6 miles

4 Bulkeley Hotel

19 Castle St, Beaumaris, Anglesey LL58 8AW

☎ 01248 810415

Real Ales, Bar Food, Restaurant Menu,
Accommodation

5 The Boathouse Hotel

Newrybeach, Holyhead, Anglesey LL65 1YF

☎ 01407 762094

Bar Food, Restaurant Menu, Accommodation,
No Smoking Area

6 The Bold Arms Hotel

6 Church Street, Beaumaris, Anglesey LL58 8AA

☎ 01248 810313

Real Ales, Bar Food, Restaurant Menu,
Accommodation, No Smoking Area

🠖 4 miles northeast of Menai Bridge off the
A545

🍺 Burtonwood

▌ Easter-end Oct 12-3 & 6-9 (and throughout
the year for residents)

🛏 4 en suite rooms

⚓ Parking, disabled access, patio

⚡ Not AMEX

🕐 Mon-Thurs 12-3 & 6-11, Fri-Sat 12-11, Sun
and Bank Holidays 12-10.30 (close Mon-
Thurs lunchtimes end Oct-Easter)

🏛 Beaumaris Castle, Museum of Childhood
Memories, Penmon 3 miles, Menai Bridge 4
miles, Pentraeth 8 miles

7 Breeze Hill Hotel

Benllech Bay, Anglesey LL74 8TN

☎ 01248 852308

Real Ales, Bar Food, Restaurant Menu,
Accommodation, No Smoking Area

8 Bull Hotel

Bulkley Square, Llangefni, Anglesey LL77 7LR

☎ 01248 722119

Real Ales, Bar Food, Restaurant Menu,
Accommodation, No Smoking Area

9 The Bull Hotel

London Rd, Valley, Holyhead, Anglesey LL65 3DP

☎ 01407 740351

Real Ales, Bar Food, Restaurant Menu,
Accommodation, No Smoking Area

10 The Bull Inn

33 High St, Llanerchymedd, Anglesey LL71 8EA

☎ 01248 470242

Real Ales, No Smoking Area

11 The Bull Inn

Pentraeth, Anglesey LL75 8LJ

☎ 01248 450232

Real Ales, Bar Food, Restaurant Menu

15 Church Bay Inn

Rhydwyn, Holyhead, Anglesey LL65 4ES

☎ 01407 730867

Bar Food, Accommodation, No Smoking Area

12 The California

Brynteg, Anglesey LL78 8JQ

☎ 01248 852360

Real Ales, Bar Food, Restaurant Menu, Accommodation, No Smoking Area

The California is a very pleasant and welcoming inn with a relaxed ambience and good food, drink and accommodation. Tenants Robert and Carys are the friendly hosts. Carys does all the cooking, creating an impressive and varied menu that offers a selection of delicious main courses including salmon fillet, home-made steak, mushroom and ale pie, home-made vegetable lasagne, lamb and home-made mushroom stroganoff, together with traditional lighter bites (cottage pie, scampi, sausage and mash, toasted sandwiches and more) and a tempting range of home-made desserts.

This spacious, welcoming inn has a separate restaurant and a conservatory for family meals. It also offers accommodation in five attractive and comfortable guest bedrooms – guests can stay on a B&B or B&B plus dinner basis.

🖝 Brynteg is north of Llangefri on A5025

🍺 Robinsons Unicorn and rotating brewery guest ale

🍴 12-3 & 6-9

🛏 5 en suite rooms

♫ Fri-Sat

🚗 Car park, disabled access, garden, children's play area

💳 All major cards

🕐 12.00-11 (Sun and Bank Holidays to 10.30)

🏛 Red Wharf Bay 5 miles, Din Lligwy 5 miles, Menai Bridge 10 miles

13 Carreg Bran Country Hotel

Ffordd Caergybi, Llanfairpwll, Anglesey LL61 5YH

☎ 01248 714224

Bar Food, Restaurant Menu, Accommodation, No Smoking Area

14 Cefn Glas

Llanfechell, Amlwch, Anglesey LL68 0PT

☎ 01407 710526

16 Crown Hotel

Bodedern, Holyhead, Anglesey LL65 3TU

☎ 01407 740734

Accommodation

17 Dinorben Arms Hotel

Dinorben Square, Amlwch, Anglesey LL68 9AL

☎ 01407 830358

Real Ales, Bar Food, Restaurant Menu, Accommodation, No Smoking Area

18 The Douglas Inn

Tregele, Cemaes Bay, Isle of Anglesey LL67 0DN
☎ 01407 710724
⊕ www.douglas-inn-anglesey.co.uk or
⊕ www.cemaes-bay.co.uk

Real Ales, Bar Food, Restaurant Menu,
Accommodation, No Smoking Area

Ongoing refurbishment has created, in The Douglas Inn, an attractive and welcoming 17th-century country inn that is spacious and modern while remaining cosy and traditional. Inside, this

Free House boasts an extended restaurant, 20 handsome and comfortable guest bedrooms and a gym, while outside there's a lovely landscaped garden.

The menu boasts a good choice of home-cooked food – everything from light bar snacks to hearty traditional favourites. The tasteful and attractive accommodation includes family rooms and suites.

Close to Cemaes Bay with its safe, sandy beaches and nature reserve, the inn makes a perfect base from which to explore this and the many other sights and attractions of the region. Lift access to rooms.

Children welcome.

- ☛ On the A5025 half a mile north of Cemaes
- 🍺 Tetleys Cask plus rotating guest ales
- ⫲ 12-10 (summer), 12-9 (winter)
- ⨝ 20 en suite rooms
- ⚒ Off-road parking, garden
- 💳 Not Amex
- 🕐 11.30-11 (Sun and Bank Holidays to 10.30)
- 🏛 Cemaes Bay 1 mile, Holyhead 8 miles

---

19 The Fourcrosses

Pentraeth Rd, Menai Bridge, Anglesey LL59 5RW
☎ 01248 712230
Real Ales, Bar Food, Restaurant Menu,
Accommodation, No Smoking Area

20 Gadlys Country Hotel

Cemaes Bay, Anglesey LL67 0LH
☎ 01407 710227
Bar Food, Restaurant Menu, Accommodation,
No Smoking Area

21 Gaerwen Arms

Chapel St, Gaerwen, Anglesey LL60 6DW
☎ 01248 421906
Real Ales, Bar Food, Restaurant Menu,
Accommodation, No Smoking Area

22 Gazelle Hotel

Glyngarth, Menai Bridge, Anglesey LL59 5PD
☎ 01248 713364
No Smoking Area

23 George And Dragon

Church St, Beaumaris, Anglesey LL58 8AA
☎ 01248 810491
Real Ales, Bar Food, No Smoking Area

24 Gwalchmai Hotel

Holyhead Rd, Gwalchmai, Holyhead,
Anglesey LL65 4PU
☎ 01407 720203

25 The Harbour Hotel

Harbour Lights, Cemaes Bay, Anglesey LL67 0NN
☎ 01407 710273
Real Ales, Bar Food, Restaurant Menu,
Accommodation, No Smoking Area

26 Holland Arms Hotel

Pentre Berw, Gaerwen, Anglesey LL60 6HY
☎ 01248 421651
Real Ales, Bar Food, Restaurant Menu,
Accommodation, No Smoking Area

27 The Joiners Arms
High St, Malltraeth, Bodorgan, Anglesey LL62 5AS
☎ 01407 840692
Real Ales, Bar Food, Restaurant Menu,
No Smoking Area

28 Kings Head Hotel
Salem St, Amlwch, Anglesey LL68 9BP
☎ 01407 831887
Bar Food, Accommodation

29 Kinmel Arms Hotel
Moelfre Bay, Moelfre, Anglesey LL72 8HH
☎ 01248 410231
Real Ales, Bar Food

30 Lastra Farm Hotel
Penrhyd Rd, Amlwch, Anglesey LL68 9TF
☎ 01407 830906
Real Ales, Bar Food, Restaurant Menu,
Accommodation

31 The Liverpool Arms
Machine St, Amlwch Port, Anglesey LL68 9HA
☎ 01407 839396
Real Ales, Bar Food, Restaurant Menu,
Accommodation, No Smoking Area

32 The Liverpool Arms Hotel
Castle St, Beaumaris, Anglesey LL58 8BA
☎ 01248 810362
Real Ales, Bar Food, Restaurant Menu,
Accommodation, No Smoking Area

33 Maelog Lake Hotel
Rhosneigr, Anglesey LL64 5JP
☎ 01407 810204
Bar Food, No Smoking Area

34 The Marilers
4 Salem St, Amlwch, Anglesey LL68 9BP
☎ 01407 830091
Real Ales

35 The Market Tavern
24-26 Mona St, Amlwch, Anglesey LL68 9AN
☎ 01407 839094
Real Ales

36 Meyrick Arms
Bodorgan, Anglesey LL62 5BL
☎ 01407 840933
Real Ales, Bar Food, Restaurant Menu,
No Smoking Area

37 Mostyn Arms
St George's Road, Menai Bridge,
Anglesey LL59 5EY
☎ 01248 713915
Real Ales, Bar Food, Accommodation, No Smoking Area

☛ At the junction of the A5, A5025 and A4080
🍺 Greene King IPA plus rotating guest ale
🍴 12-2 (to 6 p.m. on all-day openings)
🛏 2 en suite rooms
🎵 Weds quiz from 9; Thurs bingo
👪 Garden, children's play area, pool table, darts
🕐 winter: Mon-Thurs 11.30-2.30 & 5-11; Fri-Sat 11.30-11 (Sun and Bank Holidays to 10.30); summer: 11.30-11 (Sun and Bank Holidays to 10.30)
🏛 Menai Bridge, Llanfair PG 3 miles, Newborough 8 miles, Beaumaris 5 miles, Bangor 6 miles

38 The Mount Hotel
12/18 London Rd, Bodedern, Holyhead, Anglesey LL65 3TT
☎ 01407 765993
Real Ales, Bar Food, Restaurant Menu,
Accommodation, No Smoking Area

39 Old Foundry Vaults
High St, Llangefni, Anglesey LL77 7LT
☎ 01248 722139
Real Ales, Bar Food

40 Owain Glyndwr

Llanddona, Beaumaris, Anglesey LL58 8UF

☎ 01248 810710

Real Ales, Bar Food, Restaurant Menu, No Smoking Area

41 Panton Arms

The Square, Pentraeth, Anglesey LL75 8AZ

☎ 01248 450696

Real Ales, Bar Food, Restaurant Menu, No Smoking Area

42 The Parciau Arms

Marianglas, Anglesey LL73 8PH

☎ 01248 853766

Real Ales, Bar Food, Restaurant Menu, Accommodation, No Smoking Area

43 Penrhos Arms

Holyhead Rd, Ffordd Caergybi, Llanfairpwllgwyngyll, Anglesey LL61 5YQ

☎ 01248 714892

Real Ales, Bar Food, Restaurant Menu, Accommodation, No Smoking Area

44 Pilot Boat Inn

Dulas, Anglesey LL70 9EX

☎ 01248 410205

Real Ales, Bar Food, Restaurant Menu, No Smoking Area

45 The Queens Head

9 Queen St, Amlwch, Anglesey LL68 9AE

☎ 01407 832653

Real Ales

46 Queens Head Hotel

Ty Croes, Anglesey LL63 5RW

☎ 01407 810806

Real Ales

47 Railway Inn

High St, Llangefni, Anglesey LL77 7NA

☎ 01248 722166

Real Ales

48 The Ring Hotel

Rhosgoch, Anglesey LL66 0AB

☎ 01407 830720

Real Ales, Bar Food, Restaurant Menu, No Smoking Area

49 Royal Oak

High St, Malltraeth, Bodorgan, Anglesey LL62 5AS

☎ 01407 840015

Real Ales

50 Seacroft Hotel

Ravenspoint Rd, Ffraid Trearddur Bay, Holyhead, Anglesey LL65 2YU

☎ 01407 860348

Bar Food, Restaurant Menu, Accommodation, No Smoking Area

51 The Ship Inn

Red Wharf Bay, Pentraeth, Anglesey LL75 8RJ

☎ 01248 852568

Real Ales, Bar Food, Restaurant Menu, No Smoking Area

52 The Stag Inn

Cemaes Bay, Anglesey LL67 0EW

☎ 01407 710281

Real Ales, Bar Food, Restaurant Menu, Accommodation, No Smoking Area

53 Tafarn Y Bont

Telford Rd, Menai Bridge, Anglesey LL59 5DT

☎ 01248 716888

Real Ales, Restaurant Menu, No Smoking Area

54 Trearddur Bay Hotel

Trearddur Bay, Ffraid Trearddur Bay, Holyhead, Anglesey LL65 2UN

☎ 01407 860301

Real Ales, Bar Food, Restaurant Menu, Accommodation, No Smoking Area

55 Trecastell Hotel

Bull Bay, Amlwch, Anglesey LL68 9SA

☎ 01407 830651

Real Ales, Bar Food, Restaurant Menu, Accommodation, No Smoking Area

56 Tre-Ysgawen Hall
Capel Coch, Llangefni, Anglesey LL77 7UR

☎ 01248 750750

Bar Food, Restaurant Menu, Accommodation,
No Smoking Area

57 Ty Gwyn Hotel
8 Holyhead Rd, Llanfairpwll, Llanfairpwllgwyngyll,
Anglesey LL61 5UJ

☎ 01248 715599

Real Ales, Bar Food, Restaurant Menu,
No Smoking Area

58 Valley Hotel
London Rd, Valley, Holyhead, Anglesey LL65 3DU

☎ 01407 740203

Real Ales, Bar Food, Accommodation,
No Smoking Area

59 White Eagle Inn
Rhoscolyn, Holyhead, Anglesey LL65 2NJ

☎ 01407 860267

Real Ales, Bar Food, No Smoking Area

60 Woburn Hill Hotel
High St, Cemaes Bay, Anglesey LL67 0HU

☎ 01407 711190

Real Ales, Bar Food, Restaurant Menu,
Accommodation, No Smoking Area

61 Y Bedol
Penysarn, Anglesey LL69 9YR

☎ 01407 832590

Real Ales, Bar Food, No Smoking Area

62 Ye Olde Bulls Head Inn
Castle St, Beaumaris, Anglesey LL58 8AP

☎ 01248 810329

Real Ales, Restaurant Menu, Accommodation,
No Smoking Area

63 Ye Olde Vigour Hotel
Cemaes Bay, Anglesey LL67 0HH

☎ 01407 710205

Real Ales, Bar Food

BLAENAU GWENT
EBBW VALE • TREDEGAR • ABERTILLERY

The county borough of Blaenau Gwent borders the administrative areas of Monmouthshire and Torfaen to the east, Caerphilly to the west, and Powys to the north. Its main towns are Abertillery, Brynmawr, Ebbw Vale and Tredegar. The borough was formed in 1974 as a district in the new county of Gwent. This took the form of a merger of the Monmouthshire urban districts of Abertillery, Ebbw Vale, Nantyglo and Blaina and Tredegar, along with Brynmawr urban district and the parish of Llanelly in Brecknockshire. It was reconstituted in 1996 as a county borough, excluding Llanelli, which instead was transferred to the reconstituted Monmouthshire.

Hills and valleys dot this small borough, which laid claim to a great deal of wealth up until the decline of the iron and coal industries. In places such as Ebbw Vale, fine houses built by wealthy steel and coal magnates remain as a reminder of this prosperity. Occupying a crowded valley, Ebbw Vale's Festival Park occupies a site developed in 1992 and offering a community of houses, shops and various leisure activities. To the north lie the moorlands of the lower Brecon Beacons and beautiful countryside. The legacy of Aneurin Bevan, founder of the NHS and architect of much of the nationalising forces that helped postwar Britain, is felt throughout Blaenau Gwent. There's a monument to him in Ebbw Vale, and he was born

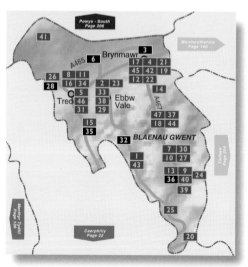

in Tredegar. At the time of his death, in 1960, his ashes were scattered in the hills above the town. Tredegar, too, served as the setting for Dr AJ Cronin's ground-breaking book *The Citadel*, about the life of a GP in the Welsh valleys during the 1930s.

The borough also boasts Bryn Bach Country Park, with its 600 acres of woodland, man-made lake and abundance of wildlife. Another attraction is the Elliot Colliery Winding House, now a museum of colliery where, once, over 2,000 people were employed.

■ Blaenau Gwent Reference Number - Detailed Information

▨ Blaenau Gwent Reference Number - Summary Entry

▶ Ceredigion Page 249   Adjacent area - refer to pages indicated

1   Bailey Arms

School Terrace, Cwm, Ebbw Vale,
Blaenau Gwent NP23 7QY
☎ 01495 370780
Bar Food, Restaurant Menu, Accommodation,
No Smoking Area

2   Bridgend Hotel

Pontygof, Ebbw Vale, Blaenau Gwent NP23 5AZ
☎ 01495 302171
Bar Food, Restaurant Menu

3   The Bridgend Inn

8 King Street, Brynmawr, Gwent NP23 4RE
☎ 01495 310721

Real Ales, Bar Food, Restaurant Menu,
Accommodation, No Smoking Area

The Bridgend Inn dates back nearly three
centuries and began life as three cottages and a
blacksmith's. The menus and specials board offer a
superb choice of delicious dishes including
Blacksmith's gammon – 12 ounces of gammon
with all the trimmings – as well as home-made
steak-and-ale pie and curry.

- ☛ Brynmawr is found where the A465 meets
  the A467, 5 miles west of Abergavenny
- 🍺 2 rotating guest ales
- 🍴 Tues-Sat 12-2 & 6.30-9, Sun 12-2
- 🛏 2 double rooms
- 🎵 Occasional food-themed evenings
- 🏛 Parking, disabled access
- 🚫 Not AMEX
- 🕐 Tues-Sat 12-3 & 6-11, Sun and Bank Holidays
  12-3 & 6-10.30
- 🏛 Brecon Beacons National Park 1 mile,
  Blaenavon 5 miles, Abergavenny 5 miles

4   The Bush Inn

1 Bailey St, Brynmawr, Ebbw Vale,
Blaenau Gwent NP23 4DN
☎ 01495 311411

5   The Cambrian Hotel

The Circle, Tredegar, Blaenau Gwent NP22 3PS
☎ 01495 711107
Bar Food

6   The Castle Inn

See panel on page 12

7   Clynmawr Hotel

Tybryn Rd, Abertillery, Blaenau Gwent NP13 1PH
☎ 01495 212323

8   Coach And Horses

Charles St, Tredegar, Blaenau Gwent NP22 4AE
☎ 01495 722414

9   The Commercial Hotel

Market St, Abertillery, Blaenau Gwent NP13 1AH
☎ 01495 212310
Real Ales, Restaurant Menu, No Smoking Area

10   Crown Inn

Victoria St, Abertillery, Blaenau Gwent NP13 1PG
☎ 01495 212896
Real Ales

11   The Crown Inn

Ashvale Nanty Bwch, Tredegar,
Blaenau Gwent NP22 4AQ
☎ 01495 722176
Bar Food, Restaurant Menu, No Smoking Area

12   Cymro Inn

22 Bailey St, Brynmawr, Ebbw Vale,
Blaenau Gwent NP23 4AN
☎ 01495 312088

13   The Dolls House

Alma St, Abertillery, Blaenau Gwent NP13 1QA
☎ 01495 213300
No Smoking Area

14   Ffosmaen Inn

Ffosmaen Rd, Nantyglo, Ebbw Vale,
Blaenau Gwent NP23 4PL
☎ 01495 310303

6 The Castle Inn

Nant-y-Croft, Rassau, Ebbw Vale,
Blaenau Gwent NP23 5DA
☎ 01495 302087
⊕ www.the-castleinn.co.uk

Bar Food, Restaurant Menu, Accommodation, No Smoking Area

Owner Paula Donoghue and her partner Keith have been at The Castle Inn since 1997, and have brought their impeccable taste and enthusiasm to

bear on making this inn one of the best in the area.

Well worth seeking out, the inn serves up a range of lagers, wines, spirits, stout, cider and soft drinks, while the superb restaurant brims with character and seats 44. Specialities include the home-made steak and Caffreys pie.

Paula is the cook, and creates a range of tempting delights including making all her own sauces and a mouth-watering selection of puddings. Booking essential at weekends.

The accommodation is also excellent – tastefully and comfortably decorated and furnished, with every amenity. To the rear of the inn there's a stunning Mediterranean-style garden.

☛ Just yards off the A465 2 miles north of Ebbw Vale

❚❚ 12-2 & 7-9 (except Sun eve)

⊢⊣ 3 en suite rooms

⚑ Parking, garden

🕐 12-3 & 7-11 weekdays & Sat (Sun to 10.30)

🏛 Ebbw Vale 2 miles, Tredegar 4 miles

---

15 Fir Tree Inn

Poplar Rd, Tredegar, Blaenau Gwent NP22 4LH
☎ 01495 718479
Bar Food, Restaurant Menu

16 The Glamorgan Tap

Club Row, Dukestown, Tredegar,
Blaenau Gwent NP22 4DW
☎ 01495 723161
Bar Food, Restaurant Menu, No Smoking Area

17 Gold Diggers Arms

122 King St, Brynmawr, Ebbw Vale,
Blaenau Gwent NP23 4SZ
☎ 01495 310787

18 Goodfellows

Blaina, Abertillery, Blaenau Gwent NP13 3BN
☎ 01495 292365

19 Gwesty Bach

Clarence St, Brynmawr, Ebbw Vale,
Blaenau Gwent NP23 4EH
☎ 01495 310245
Bar Food, Restaurant Menu, No Smoking Area

20 Hafodyrynys Inn

Crumlin, Newport, Blaenau Gwent NP11 5BE
☎ 01495 243010
Bar Food, Restaurant Menu, No Smoking Area

21 The Hobby Horse Inn

30 Greenland Rd, Brynmawr, Ebbw Vale,
Blaenau Gwent NP23 4DT
☎ 01495 310996
Real Ales, Bar Food

22 King William IV

41 Glamorgan St, Brynmawr, Ebbw Vale,
Blaenau Gwent NP23 4JY
☎ 01495 310643
Real Ales

23 Kings Arms
Newchurch Rd, Ebbw Vale,
Blaenau Gwent NP23 5BD
☎ 01495 352822
Bar Food, Restaurant Menu

24 Lianhilleth Top Hotel
High St, Abertillery, Blaenau Gwent NP13 1DD
☎ 01495 214267
Bar Food, Restaurant Menu, No Smoking Area

25 Mount Pleasant Inn
Mount Pleasant Estate, Brynithel, Abertillery,
Blaenau Gwent NP13 2HN
☎ 01495 214920
Real Ales

26 Mountain Air Inn
Llwynhelyg Nantybwch, Tredegar,
Blaenau Gwent NP22 3SD
☎ 01495 723116
Bar Food, Restaurant Menu

27 Mountain Pleasant Inn
Alma St, Abertillery, Blaenau Gwent NP13 1QD
☎ 01495 216987

28 The Nags Head
See below

29 The New Drysiog Inn
26 Commercial St, Ebbw Vale,
Blaenau Gwent NP23 6BS
☎ 01495 350571

30 Newbridge End Inn
Penybont Rd, Abertillery, Blaenau Gwent NP13 1JF
☎ 01495 213519

31 The Olympia
Morgan St, Tredegar, Blaenau Gwent NP22 3ND
☎ 01495 712910
Real Ales, Bar Food, Restaurant Menu,
No Smoking Area

28 The Nags Head
Tafarnaubach, Merthyr Road, Tredegar,
Gwent NP22 3AP
☎ 01495 722867

Bar Food, Restaurant Menu, Accommodation,
No Smoking Area

Dating back to the 1700s with later additions, The Nags Head is a supremely pleasant place to stop for a satisfying and relaxing drink or meal. Situated just a few minutes' drive from the centre of Tredegar, the inn is run by Michael and Mandy, ably assisted by Michael's parents Alan and Olive.

With a selection of three keg bitters, three lagers and cider on draught, together with wines, spirits and soft drinks, there's something to quench every thirst.

The menu boasts an impressive selection of expertly prepared dishes using the freshest locally-sourced ingredients. Mouth-watering desserts such as pear tartlet, chocolate or lemon tartufo and profiteroles are well worth leaving room for. During the lifetime of this edition there will be four en suite guest bedrooms available.

☛ From Tredegar, follow the signs for Bryn Bach, cross over the A465 via the new bridge

🍴 daily 12-2, Weds-Sat 7-8.30

🛏 3 en suite rooms

♫ Monthly live music and disco

♨ Parking, garden, disabled access, children's play area

🕐 Mon-Thurs 12-3 & 7-11, Fri-Sat 12-11, Sun 12-10.30, Bank Holidays 12-11

🏛 Tredegar 1½ miles, Ebbw Vale 3 miles, Brynmawr 5 miles, Merthyr Tydfil 12 miles

32 The Park Hotel

Station Road, Waunlwyd, Ebbw Vale,
Blaenau Gwent NP23 6TN

☎ 01495 371431

⊕ www.thepark-hotel.co.uk

Real Ales, Bar Food, Restaurant Menu,
Accommodation, No Smoking Area

Top of the range in every particular, The Park Hotel is a real gem. Elegant and distinctive, this fine hotel dates back to 1899 and offers great food, drink and accommodation. From morning coffee to lunch, afternoon tea and evenings meals, the hotel is renowned for its cuisine. Booking required Friday and Saturday evening and for Sunday lunch. Two of the guest bedrooms are decorated in Victorian style.

- ☛ 10 miles west of Abergavenny off the A465
- 🍺 Selection from the Brains Brewery
- ❙ Weds-Sun 12-2, Tues-Sat 7-9
- ▶ 9 en suite rooms
- ♿ Parking, disabled access
- 💳 Not AMEX
- 🏆 3 Stars Welsh Tourist Board
- 🕐 11.30-11 (Sun and Bank Holidays to 10.30)
- 🏛 Festival Park, Ebbw Vale, Abergavenny 10 miles

33 Picture House

Market St, Ebbw Vale, Blaenau Gwent NP23 6HP

☎ 01495 352382

Real Ales, Bar Food, Restaurant Menu, No Smoking Area

34 The Railway Tavern

Dukestown Rd, Sirhowy, Tredegar,
Blaenau Gwent NP22 4QD

☎ 01495 722616

Real Ales

35 Rhyd Hall

The Rhyd, Tredegar, Gwent NP22 4LY

☎ 01495 722615

Bar Food, Restaurant Menu, No Smoking Area

Rhyd Hall is an impressive Free House dating back to 1860. Once owned by the Tredegar Coal Company and later by the National Coal Board, it became a pub in 1955.

Proprietors Brian and Adeline Reynolds have been here for 20 years, providing excellent service and warm hospitality to all their guests. The food and drink are excellent. Booking required for Sunday lunch.

- ☛ Off the A465 on the outskirts of Tredegar, via the village of Georgetown
- ❙ Mon-Sat 6-9.30; Sun 12-2.30
- ♿ Parking, disabled access
- 🕐 12-3 & 6-11 (Sun and Bank Holidays to 10.30)
- 🏛 Bryn Bach Country Park (Tredegar), Ebbw Vale

36 Rolling Mill

16 Church Street, Abertillery, Gwent NP13 1DA

☎ 01495 212418

Bar Food, Restaurant Menu, No Smoking Area

Right in the centre of town, the Rolling Mill is run by husband-and-wife team Lionel and Delysia.

Lionel runs the bar whilst Delysia and her staff prepare your meal for the restaurant. She uses only the best fresh produce which is cooked to order.

Both they and their friendly staff offer a warm Welsh welcome to all their guests.

- ☛ Abertillery is 3 miles south east of Ebbw Vale
- ❙ Tues-Sun 12.30-2.30 & 6.30-9
- 🎵 Live music Fri/Sat/Sun
- ♿ Parking
- 🕐 11-11 (Sun and Bank Holidays to 10.30)
- 🏛 Tredegar, Ebbw Vale, Merthyr Tydfil

37 Royal Exchange

High St, Blaina, Abertillery,
Blaenau Gwent NP13 3AE
☎ 01495 291383

38 Seven Arches

62-64 Bethcar St, Ebbw Vale,
Blaenau Gwent NP23 6HG
☎ 01495 350135

39 Six Bells Hotel

Victoria Rd, Six Bells, Abertillery,
Blaenau Gwent NP13 2LX
☎ 01495 212568
No Smoking Area

40 Somerset Hotel

Somerset St, Abertillery, Blaenau Gwent NP13 1DJ
☎ 01495 212410

41 Tafarn Ty-Uchaf

Trefil, Tredegar, Blaenau Gwent NP22 4HG
☎ 01495 717690
Bar Food, Restaurant Menu, No Smoking Area

42 The Talisman

Market Square, Brynmawr, Ebbw Vale,
Blaenau Gwent NP23 4AJ
☎ 01495 312430
Real Ales, Bar Food, Restaurant Menu,
No Smoking Area

43 Victoria Arms Hotel

1 Mill Terrace, Cwm, Ebbw Vale,
Blaenau Gwent NP23 7SR
☎ 01495 370397

44 White Lion Inn

Queen St, Blaina, Abertillery,
Blaenau Gwent NP13 3JU
☎ 01495 291133

45 Wine Vaults And Restaurant

22 Beaufort St, Brynmawr, Ebbw Vale,
Blaenau Gwent NP23 4AQ
☎ 01495 315050
Real Ales

46 Ye Olde Red Lion Hotel

97 Queen Victoria St, Tredegar,
Blaenau Gwent NP22 3PX
☎ 01495 724449
Real Ales, Bar Food, Restaurant Menu

47 The Yew Tree

8 Railway Terrace, Blaina, Abertillery,
Blaenau Gwent NP13 3BU
☎ 01495 290008

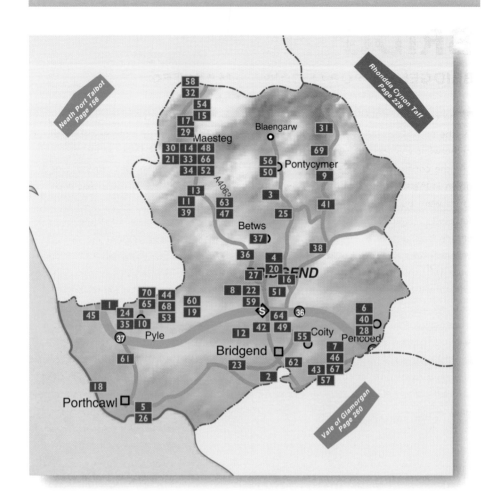

BRIDGEND

BRIDGEND • PORTHCAWL • MAESTEG

The county borough of Bridgend has a total population of 130,000 people, and contains the settlements of Bridgend, after which it is named, Maesteg, and the seaside town of Porthcawl. It was formed on April 1, 1996 from most of the former district of Ogwr.

At the confluence of the rivers Ogmore, Garw and Llynfi, the town of Bridgend itself is known in Welsh as Pen-y-bont Ar Ogwr. Once regarded as such a vital route that two castles were built either side of the River Ogmore: the remains of the 12th-century Newcastle Castle lie on the west riverside, while the more extensive ruins of the 14th-century Coity Castle lie on the eastern side. Originally built by the Norman Payn de Turberville and strengthened over the subsequent 300 years, Coity Castle was abandoned in the 16th century, after having withstood a siege by Owain Glyndwr 150 years earlier. Today this bustling market town is a centre of agriculture supporting the more industrial towns of the valleys.

The region also boasts Bryngarw Country Park, which throughout the year presents a variety of enchanting landscapes including woodland, grassland, water features and formal gardens, together with a helpful visitor centre with information on the many species of plants and birds found here. Delightful villages such as Merthyr Mawr, filled with thatched cottages, also grace the borough. Merthyr Mawr Warren is one of the largest areas of sand dunes in Europe, and a Site of Special Scientific Interest. Surrounded by the dune system are the remains of the 15th-century Candleston Castle. From the 1,000-foot summit of Mynydd y Gaer, four miles northeast of the town of Bridgend, there are superb views across the valleys to the north and the Bristol Channel to the south. Tondu Heritage Park occupies the site of the Tondu Ironworks and Parc Slip Nature Reserve.

Another lovely place to observe nature in all its glory can be found at Kenfig National Nature Reserve, amid the marvellous area of dunes to the northwest of the village of Kenfig, which boasts over 600 species of flowering plants including orchids, a freshwater lake and numerous birds, making it a haven for naturalists and ramblers. The borough is also home to Porthcawl, one of South Wales' most popular seaside resorts with its clean sandy beaches and handsome bays. Porthcawl Harbour has several historic buildings and, during the summer, two veteran steamships ply the journey along the Bristol Channel and across to Lundy Island.

Ogmore Castle

1 Angel Inn

Maudlam, Bridgend CF33 4PG

☎ 01656 740456

Real Ales, Bar Food, Restaurant Menu,
Accommodation, No Smoking Area

2 Heronston Hotel

Ewenny Rd, Ewenny, Bridgend, CF35 5AW

☎ 01656 668811

Bar Food, Restaurant Menu, Accommodation,
No Smoking Area

3 Braich-y-Cymmer

Pleasant View, Pont-y-Rhyl, Bridgend CF32 8BJ

☎ 01656 870215

Real Ales, Bar Food, Restaurant Menu,
No Smoking Area

4 Bryngarw House

Bryngarw Country Park, Brynmenyn,
Bridgend CF32 8UU

☎ 01656 729009

Bar Food, Restaurant Menu, Accommodation,
No Smoking Area

5 The Buccaneer Bar

Mackworth Rd, Porthcawl, Bridgend CF36 5BT

☎ 01656 785569

6 Chatterton Arms

2 Hendre Rd, Pencoed, Bridgend CF35 5NW

☎ 01656 860293

Real Ales, Bar Food, Restaurant Menu

7 Coed-Y-Mwstwr Hotel

Coychurch, Bridgend CF35 6AF

☎ 01656 860621

Real Ales, Bar Food, Restaurant Menu,
Accommodation, No Smoking Area

8 The Colliers Arms

52 Bridgend Rd, Aberkenfig, Bridgend CF32 9BA

☎ 01656 720493

Real Ales, Bar Food

9 Corbett Arms

Bridge St, Ogmore Vale, Bridgend CF32 7AL

☎ 01656 840386

10 The Cornelly Arms

Ffordd Yr Eglwys, North Cornelly,
Bridgend CF33 4HP

☎ 01656 740791

Bar Food, No Smoking Area

11 The Corner House Inn

Llangynwyd, Maesteg, Bridgend CF34 9SB

☎ 01656 732393

Real Ales, Bar Food

12 Court Colman Manor

Court Colman, Pen-Y-Fai, Bridgend CF31 4NG

☎ 01656 720212

Bar Food, Restaurant Menu, Accommodation,
No Smoking Area

13 Cross Inn

Maesteg Rd, Cwmfelin, Maesteg,
Bridgend CF34 9LB

☎ 01656 732476

Real Ales, Bar Food

14 Crown Hotel

Crown Row, Maesteg, Bridgend CF34 0LG

☎ 01656 732224

15 The Duffryn Restaurant

Coegnant Rd, Maesteg, Bridgend CF34 0TD

☎ 01656 732273

Real Ales, Bar Food, Restaurant Menu,
No Smoking Area

16 Dunraven Hotel

3 Blackmill Rd, Bryncethin, Bridgend CF32 9YW

☎ 01656 720231

Real Ales

17 Elderbush Inn

57 High St, Nantyffyllon, Maesteg,
Bridgend CF34 0BS

☎ 01656 731353

18 Esplanade Hotel

Porthcawl, Bridgend CF36 3YP

☎ 01656 788811

19 Farmers Arms

24 Cefn Rd, Cefn Cribbwr, Bridgend CF32 0BA

☎ 01656 743648

Real Ales, Bar Food, Restaurant Menu

20 Fox And Hounds

New Houses, Brynmenyn, Bridgend CF32 9LB

☎ 01656 720069

Bar Food, Restaurant Menu, No Smoking Area

21 The Garn Inn

1 Alma Rd, Maesteg, Bridgend CF34 9AN

☎ 01656 732516

22 The Golden Lion

103 Bridgend Rd, Aberkenfig, Bridgend CF32 9AP

☎ 01656 724098

23 Great House Hotel

High St, Laleston, Bridgend CF32 0HP

☎ 01656 657644

Bar Food, Restaurant Menu, Accommodation,
No Smoking Area

24 Green Acre Hotel

111 Heol Fach, North Cornelly,
Bridgend CF33 4LH

☎ 01656 743041

Real Ales, Bar Food, Restaurant Menu,
Accommodation

25 The Green Meadow Inn

Greenmeadow Terrace, Llangeinor,
Bridgend CF32 8PD

☎ 01656 870216

Bar Food, Restaurant Menu, No Smoking Area

26 The Hi-Tide Inn

Mackworth Rd, Porthcawl, Bridgend CF36 5BT

☎ 01656 782432

Bar Food, Restaurant Menu

27 Llynfi Arms

Maesteg Rd, Tondu, Bridgend CF32 9DP

☎ 01656 720010

Real Ales, Bar Food, Restaurant Menu,
No Smoking Area

28 The Maerdy Hotel

Coychurch Rd, Pencoed, Bridgend CF35 5NA

☎ 01656 860654

Bar Food, Restaurant Menu, Accommodation

29 Malsters Arms

52 Commercial St, Maesteg, Bridgend CF34 9HJ

☎ 01656 732231

30 Masons Arms

High St, Nantyffyllon, Maesteg,
Bridgend CF34 0BW

☎ 01656 732097

31 Nantymoel Hotel

Commercial St, Nantymoel, Bridgend CF32 7RB

☎ 01656 840384

32 Navigation Hotel

Duffryn Rd, Caerau, Maesteg, Bridgend CF34 0SS

☎ 01656 732141

33 The New Beethoven

81 Castle St, Maesteg, Bridgend CF34 9YL

☎ 01656 738484

Bar Food, Restaurant Menu, No Smoking Area

34 New Coytrahen Arms

115 Bethania St, Maesteg, Bridgend CF34 9PJ

☎ 01656 739714

Bar Food, Restaurant Menu, Accommodation,
No Smoking Area

35 The New House Inn

Thomas Crescent, North Cornelly,
Bridgend CF33 4HT

☎ 01656 749997

Real Ales, Bar Food, Restaurant Menu,
No Smoking Area

36 Nicholls Arms

Nicholls Rd, Coytrahen, Bridgend CF32 0EP

☎ 01656 724680

Real Ales, Bar Food, Restaurant Menu,
No Smoking Area

37 Oddfellows Arms

Bettws, Bridgend CF32 8TA

☎ 01656 725618

Real Ales

38 The Ogmore Junction

Blackmill Rd, Blackmill, Bridgend CF35 6DR

☎ 01656 840371

Real Ales, Bar Food, Restaurant Menu,
No Smoking Area

39 The Old House

Llangynwyd, Maesteg, Bridgend CF34 9SB

☎ 01656 733310

Real Ales, Bar Food, Restaurant Menu,
No Smoking Area

40 The Old Kings Head

15 Coychurch Rd, Pencoed, Bridgend CF35 5NH

☎ 01656 860203

41 Pant-Yr-Awel

Blackmill Rd, Lewistown, Bridgend CF32 7HU

☎ 01656 840257

Real Ales

42 The Pheasant

Heol Eglwys, Pen-Y-Fai, Bridgend CF31 4LY

☎ 01656 653614

Real Ales, Bar Food, Restaurant Menu

43 The Pied Piper

Kingsway, Bridgend Ind Estate, Bridgend CF31 3RY

☎ 01656 650260

Bar Food, Restaurant Menu

44 Prince of Wales

26 Prince Rd, Kenfig Hill, Bridgend CF33 6ED

☎ 01656 740468

45 Prince of Wales Inn

Ton Kenfig, Bridgend CF33 4PR

☎ 01656 740356

Real Ales, Bar Food, Restaurant Menu,
No Smoking Area

46 Prince of Wales Inn

Main Rd, Coychurch, Bridgend CF35 5HD

☎ 01656 860600

Real Ales, Bar Food, Restaurant Menu

47 The Railway Inn

Station Rd, Llangynwyd, Maesteg,
Bridgend CF34 9TF

☎ 01656 732188

48 The Ranch Steakhouse

Bridgend Rd, Maesteg, Bridgend CF34 0AX

☎ 01656 733178

Bar Food, Restaurant Menu, No Smoking Area

49 The Red Dragon

Litchard Hill, Bridgend CF31 1QJ

☎ 01656 654753

Real Ales, Bar Food, Restaurant Menu,
No Smoking Area

50 The Royal Hotel

Bridgend Rd, Pontycymer, Bridgend CF32 8EH

☎ 01656 870018

Real Ales, Bar Food, Restaurant Menu,
Accommodation

51 Royal Oak

Main Rd, Bryncethin, Bridgend CF32 9TG

☎ 01656 720083

Bar Food, Restaurant Menu

52 Royal Oak

Bethania St, Maesteg, Bridgend CF34 9ET

☎ 01656 810216

53 Royal Oak Inn

Station Rd, Kenfig Hill, Bridgend CF33 6EP

☎ 01656 740031

Real Ales

54 The Satellite Bar and Space Base

91 Hermon Rd, Maesteg, Bridgend CF34 0SY

☎ 01656 738957

Bar Food, Restaurant Menu, No Smoking Area

55 Six Bells
120 Heol West, Plas Coity, Bridgend CF35 6BH
☎ 01656 653192
Real Ales

56 The Squirrel Hotel
Alexandra Rd, Pontycymer, Bridgend CF32 8HA
☎ 01656 872361
Bar Food, Restaurant Menu, No Smoking Area

57 The Star Inn
Treoes, Bridgend CF35 5DL
☎ 01656 658458
Real Ales, Bar Food, Restaurant Menu,
No Smoking Area

58 Station Hotel
1 Caerau Rd, Maesteg, Bridgend CF34 0PB
☎ 01656 732074
Accommodation

59 The Swan Inn
128 Bridgend Rd, Aberkenfig, Bridgend CF32 9AE
☎ 01656 725612
Restaurant Menu

60 Three Horse Shoes
57 Cefn Rd, Cefn Cribbwr, Bridgend CF32 0BA
☎ 01656 740499
Real Ales

61 Three Horse Shoes
Lamb Row, South Cornelly, Bridgend CF33 4RL
☎ 01656 740037
Real Ales, Bar Food, Restaurant Menu,
No Smoking Area

62 The Two Brewers
Brackla Way, Brackla, Bridgend CF31 2AR
☎ 01656 661788
Real Ales, Bar Food, Restaurant Menu,
No Smoking Area

63 Tylers Arms
Llangynwyd, Maesteg, Bridgend CF34 0EH
☎ 01656 732317
Real Ales, Bar Food, Restaurant Menu

64 Ty-Risha Inn
Penycae Aberkenfig, Bridgend CF32 9SN
☎ 01656 725287
Bar Food, Restaurant Menu

65 The Walnut Tree Inn
110 Pisgah St, Kenfig Hill, Bridgend CF33 6DA
☎ 01656 740238

66 White Hart
42 Bridgend Rd, Garth, Maesteg,
Bridgend CF34 0NN
☎ 01656 738794

67 The White Horse Inn
Church Terrace, Coychurch, Bridgend CF35 5HF
☎ 01656 652583
Real Ales, Bar Food, Restaurant Menu,
No Smoking Area

68 Woodstock Inn
Station Rd, Kenfig Hill, Bridgend CF33 6EP
☎ 01656 741617
Real Ales, Accommodation

69 Wyndham Arms
Wyndham St, Ogmore Vale, Bridgend CF32 7EU
☎ 01656 840392
Real Ales, Bar Food, Restaurant Menu

70 Ye Olde Wine House
Pyle Road, Pyle, Bridgend CF33 6HR
☎ 01656 740135
Bar Food, Restaurant Menu

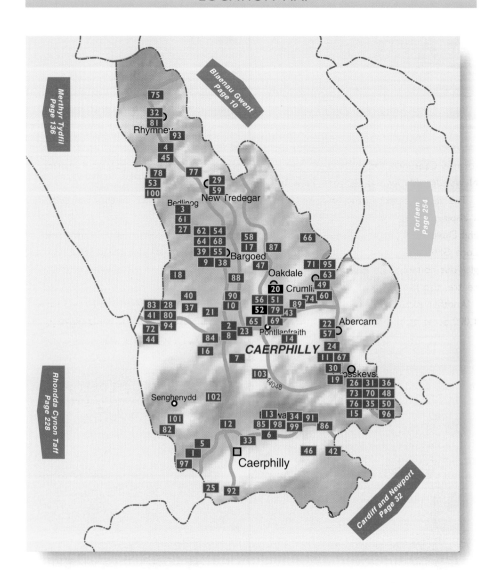

CAERPHILLY

CAERPHILLY • NEWBRIDGE • RHYMNEY

The county borough of Caerphilly was formed on April 1, 1996 by the merger of the Rhymney Valley district of Mid Glamorgan with the Islwyn borough of Gwent. Its main town is Caerphilly. Other towns in the county borough are Bedwas, Risca, Ystrad Mynach, Newbridge, Blackwood, Bargoed, New Tredegar and Rhymney.

The visitor centre in the town of Caerphilly has exhibitions on local history and culture, a display of Welsh crafts and a fine Welsh foods shop. Caerphilly Castle vies with Windsor and Dover in size and impressiveness, built primarily in the 13th century by the Norman Lord Gilbert de Clare. The region's beautiful Darran Valley is home to Parc Cwm Darran, a glorious country park that, along with an adventure playground and informative visitor centre, also has a six-acre coarse fishery.

Another natural showpiece can be found in Sirhowy Valley Country Park, covering some 1,000 acres of both woodland and farmland. The Park is the ideal place to enjoy walking,

Caerphilly Castle

cycling or riding along numerous dedicated trails. At the heart of the Country Park is Ynys Hywel Centre, a converted 17th-century farmhouse.

Near the town of Pontllanfraith lies Gelligroes Mill, a 17th-century water mill now restored to full working order. Cwncarn Forest Drive is a seven-mile stretch of high forest road that provides some of the most magnificent panoramic views of the South

Rhymney Viaduct

Wales countryside and, beyond, the Bristol Channel. Another attraction is the Mabinogion Sculpture Trail, depicting characters from the Celtic folklore tales of the Mabinogion. The Fourteen Locks Canal Centre just south of Risca has several walks which take in the locks, ponds, channels, tunnels and weirs, as well as the countryside in which the centre is sited.

Rhymney Valley

The village of Nelson is home to an open-air handball court dating back to the 1860s and still in use, as well as Llancaiach Fawr Manor, a handsome Elizabethan manor house which has been lovingly restored to the year 1645 and the time of the Civil War. Visitors to this living history museum can meet actors playing the parts of members of the Pritchard family and their servants, in authentic costumes, as they carry on with their daily lives.

1 Angel Inn

White Cross Lane, Penyrheol, Caerphilly,
Caerphilly CF83 2RL
☎ 02920 882952
Real Ales, Bar Food, No Smoking Area

2 The Angel Inn

Maesycwmmer, Caerphilly, Hengoed,
Caerphilly CF82 7PH
☎ 01443 814147
No Smoking Area

3 Bailey Arms Hotel

Bailey St, Deri, Bargoed, Caerphilly CF81 9HX
☎ 01443 830214
Real Ales, Bar Food, Restaurant Menu,
No Smoking Area

4 Blast Furnace Inn

Board St, Pontlottyn, Bargoed, Caerphilly CF81 9PP
☎ 01685 841305
Bar Food, Restaurant Menu, No Smoking Area

5 Bowls Inn

Bowls Terrace, Penrall, Caerphilly CF83 2RD
☎ 02920 882954
Bar Food, Restaurant Menu, No Smoking Area

6 Bridgend Inn

The Square, Bedwas, Caerphilly CF83 8DY
☎ 02920 864725
No Smoking Area

7 Bryn Meadows Golf & Country Hotel

Maesycwmer, Hengoed, Caerphilly CF82 7SN
☎ 01495 225590
Bar Food, Restaurant Menu, Accommodation,
No Smoking Area

8 Butchers Arms

Thomas St, Maesycwmmer, Hengoed,
Caerphilly CF82 7PH
☎ 01443 813402
Bar Food, Restaurant Menu, No Smoking Area

9 Capel Hotel

Park Place, Gilfach Fargoed, Caerphilly CF81 8LW
☎ 01443 830272
Real Ales, Bar Food, Accommodation,
No Smoking Area

10 The Castle Inn

Castle St, Fleur De Lys, Blackwood,
Caerphilly NP12 3UH
☎ 01443 830192
Real Ales, Bar Food, Restaurant Menu

11 The Castle Inn

Twyncarn Rd, Pontywaun, Newport,
Caerphilly NP11 7DU
☎ 01495 271232
Real Ales, Bar Food

12 The Cedar Tree Country Carvery and Lodge

Corbett Lane, Pwll-Y-Pant, Caerphilly CF83 3HX
☎ 02920 867049
Real Ales, Bar Food, Restaurant Menu,
No Smoking Area

13 Church House Inn

Church St, Bedwas, Caerphilly CF83 8AY
☎ 02920 885342
Real Ales, Bar Food, Restaurant Menu

14 Church Inn

Mynyddislwyn, Blackwood, Caerphilly NP12 2BG
☎ 01495 200262
Real Ales, Bar Food, Restaurant Menu,
No Smoking Area

15 Commercial Inn

Commercial St, Risca, Newport,
Caerphilly NP11 6BA
☎ 01633 612608
Real Ales

16 The Coopers Arms

Caerphilly Rd, Ystrad Mynach, Hengoed,
Caerphilly CF82 7EP
☎ 01443 814319

17 Countryman Inn

Bedwellty, Blackwood, Caerphilly NP12 0BJ
☎ 01443 821414
Real Ales, Bar Food, Restaurant Menu,
Accommodation, No Smoking Area

18 The Cross Inn

Heol Adan, Gelligaer, Hengoed, Caerphilly CF82 8FU
☎ 01443 879605
Real Ales, Bar Food, Restaurant Menu, No Smoking
Area

20 The Cross Oak

Penmaen, Blackwood, Gwent NP12 0DJ
☎ 01495 222264 ⊕ www.crossoak.com
Real Ales, Bar Food, Restaurant Menu,
No Smoking Area

The Cross Oak in Penmaen is a welcoming and
traditional inn with great food, drink and
hospitality.

Handsome and comfortable inside, there's also
a beautiful award winning mature garden to the

21 Crosskeys Hotel

Gelligaer Rd, Cefn Hengoed, Hengoed,
Caerphilly CF82 7HN
☎ 01443 813664

22 The Crown Inn

Danyrhiw Terrace, Abercarn, Newport,
Caerphilly NP11 4SP
☎ 01495 243059

rear of the pub – just the place to relax and enjoy
a quiet pint or meal on fine days.

Real ales are complemented by a good
selection of lagers, wines, cider, stout, spirits and
soft drinks – something to quench every thirst.

The menu and daily specials board offer guests
a good variety of tempting dishes including home-
made steak-and-ale pie, home-made lasagne verdi
and fresh fish and seafood dishes such as darne of
salmon and tiger prawns. The range of curries are
also well worth sampling.

- ☛ On the A4048 6 miles southwest of
  Pontypool
- 🍺 Bass Ruddles
- 🍴 Mon-Sat 12-2 & 6-9, Sun 12-2
- ♿ Some disabled access, garden
- 💳 All major cards
- 🏆 Enterprise Pub of the Year
- 🕐 12-3 & 6-11
- 🏛 Pontllanfraith 1 mile, Risca 8 miles, Caerphilly
  8 miles

19 The Cross Keys Hotel

High St, Cross Keys, Newport,
Caerphilly NP11 7BY
☎ 01495 270317
Real Ales, Bar Food

20 The Cross Oak

See panel above

23 Crown Pub

Bryn View, Pontllanfraith, Blackwood,
Caerphilly NP12 2HE
☎ 01495 223404
Real Ales, Bar Food

24 Cwmcarn Hotel

Newport Rd, Cwmcarn, Caerphilly NP11 7ND
☎ 01495 270643
Real Ales, Bar Food, Restaurant Menu,
No Smoking Area

25 Cwrt Rawlin Inn

Cwn Farm, Nantgarw, Caerphilly CF83 1NF

☎ 02920 868001

Restaurant Menu, No Smoking Area

26 The Darren

2 St Mary St, Risca, Newport,
Caerphilly NP11 6GU

☎ 01633 612414

Real Ales, Bar Food, Restaurant Menu

27 Darren Public House

New Rd, Deri, Bargoed, Caerphilly CF81 9GJ

☎ 01443 830257

28 Dynevor Arms

Commercial St, Nelson, Treharris,
Caerphilly CF46 6NF

☎ 01443 450295

Real Ales

29 Dynevor Arms Hotel

The Square, Tirphil, New Tredegar,
Caerphilly NP24 6ER

☎ 01443 834219

30 The Eagle Inn

High St, Cross Keys, Newport,
Caerphilly NP11 7FN

☎ 01495 272964

31 Exchange Inn

53 St Mary St, Risca, Newport,
Caerphilly NP11 6GQ

☎ 01633 612706

32 Farmers Arms

Brewery Row, Tredegar, Caerphilly NP22 5EZ

☎ 01685 840257

Bar Food, Restaurant Menu, No Smoking Area

33 Fishermans Rest Inn

Old Bedwas Rd, Caerphilly CF83 3BL

☎ 02920 863424

Bar Food, Restaurant Menu, No Smoking Area

34 Forge and Hammer Inn

White Hart Row, Machen, Caerphilly CF83 8QN

☎ 01633 440314

35 Forge Hammer Inn

Commercial St, Risca, Newport,
Caerphilly NP11 6EE

☎ 01633 613943

Bar Food, Restaurant Menu, Accommodation,
No Smoking Area

36 Fox and Hounds

Park Rd, Risca, Newport, Caerphilly NP11 6PW

☎ 01633 612937

Real Ales, Bar Food

37 The Fox and Hounds

Trosnant Crescent, Penybryn, Hengoed,
Caerphilly CF82 7FX

☎ 01443 816424

No Smoking Area

38 Griffin Inn

Hendreforgan, Gilfach Bargoed,
Caerphilly CF81 8LW

☎ 01443 672247

Real Ales

39 Hanbury Arms

Hanbury Rd, Bargoed, Caerphilly CF81 8QU

☎ 01443 821924

Bar Food, Restaurant Menu, No Smoking Area

40 Harp Inn

2 St Cattwgs Avenue, Gelligaer, Hengoed,
Caerphilly CF82 8FE

☎ 01443 830496

No Smoking Area

41 Hollybush Inn

High St, Nelson, Treharris, Caerphilly CF46 6HB

☎ 01443 450224

Bar Food

42 The Hollybush Inn and Restaurant

Lower Machen, Newport, Caerphilly NP10 8GB

☎ 01633 441326

Real Ales, Bar Food, Restaurant Menu,
No Smoking Area

43 Ivor Arms Public House

Newbridge Rd, Pontllanfraith, Blackwood,
Caerphilly NP12 2LD

☎ 01495 223131

Bar Food, Restaurant Menu, No Smoking Area

44 Lianfabon Inn

Treharris, Caerphilly CF46 6PG

☎ 01443 450264

Restaurant Menu, No Smoking Area

45 Lord Nelson Hotel

Heol Evan Wynne, Bargoed, Caerphilly CF81 9PQ

☎ 01685 841228

Real Ales, No Smoking Area

46 Maenllwyd Inn and Restaurant

Rudry, Caerphilly CF83 3EB

☎ 02920 882372

Real Ales, Bar Food, No Smoking Area

47 Maes Manor Hotel

Maesrudded Lane, Blackwood,
Caerphilly NP12 0AG

☎ 01495 220011

Bar Food, Restaurant Menu, Accommodation

48 The Manor

Thistle Way, Risca, Newport, Caerphilly NP11 6PL

☎ 01633 612723

No Smoking Area

49 Mason Arms

North Rd, Newbridge, Newport,
Caerphilly NP11 4AD

☎ 01495 249034

Real Ales, Bar Food

52 The Monkey Tree Hotel

Gordon Road, Blackwood, Gwent NP12 1DS

☎ 01495 230240

Restaurant Menu, Accommodation,
No Smoking Area

The Monkey Tree Hotel takes its name from the impressive and very beautiful tree to the front of the inn. A truly lovely inn family-run by Sue Brookes and her daughter Michelle, the inn began life as a farm built and owned by the famous Morgan family (Thomas Morgan was a colonel in the Civil War and uncle to Sir Captain Henry Morgan, once governor of Jamaica) and is set in its own grounds. The spacious and attractive restaurant is justly popular – booking required Friday and Saturday and for Sunday lunch. There's a carvery available Wednesday to Sunday at lunch and in the evening.

The upstairs accommodation boasts 16 comfortable rooms available on a bed-and-breakfast or bed, breakfast and dinner basis. The inn's Morgans Suite is the ideal place for family celebrations, with superb facilities and service.

☛ On the A4048, 8 miles south of Tredegar

🍴 12-3 & 6-9

🛏 16 en suite rooms

♫ Quiz Weds from 9, live music and disco Fri, karaoke and disco Sat & Sun

🅿 Parking, garden, children's play area, disabled access

💳 Not Amex

🕐 11.30-11 (Sun and Bank Holidays to 10.30)

🏛 Oakdale 2 miles, Tredegar 8 miles, Ebbw Vale 8 miles, Pontypool 12 miles

50 Masons Arms

Mill Terrace, Risca, Newport, Caerphilly NP11 6LH

☎ 01633 612951

51 The Masons Arms

Bridge St, Blackwood, Caerphilly NP12 1AX

☎ 01495 227979

Bar Food, Accommodation

52 The Monkey Tree Hotel

See panel opposite

53 Mount Pleasant Inn

Mount Pleasant Row, Pentwyn, Bargoed,
Caerphilly CF81 9NJ

☎ 01685 841307

54 Neuaddwen Inn

Bedwellty Rd, Aberbargoed, Bargoed,
Caerphilly CF81 9DN

☎ 01443 830352

55 New Duffryn Hotel

Commercial St, Aberbargoed, Bargoed,
Caerphilly CF81 9EW

☎ 01443 821271

No Smoking Area

56 New Foresters

110 High St, Blackwood, Caerphilly NP12 1AF

☎ 01495 223200

Restaurant Menu, Accommodation

57 The New Inn

1 Commercial Rd, Abercarn, Newport,
Caerphilly NP11 5AH

☎ 01495 243107

58 New Inn

Bedwellty, Blackwood,, Caerphilly NP12 0BD

☎ 01443 831625

Real Ales, Bar Food, Restaurant Menu,
No Smoking Area

59 New Tredegar Arms

James St, New Tredegar, Caerphilly NP24 6EN

☎ 01443 879665

60 Newbridge Hotel

High St, Newbridge, Newport, Caerphilly NP11 4FH

☎ 01495 246946

Bar Food

61 The Old Club

93 Bailey St, Deri, Bargoed, Caerphilly CF81 9HX

☎ 01443 830278

Real Ales

62 The Old Mill

Station Rd, Aberbargoed, Bargoed,
Caerphilly CF81 9AL

☎ 01443 831318

Bar Food, Restaurant Menu, No Smoking Area

63 Old Navigation

Hafodrynys Rd, Crumlin, Newport,
Caerphilly NP11 3PE

☎ 01495 248050

Bar Food, No Smoking Area

64 The Parc Hotel

Cardiff Rd, Bargoed, Caerphilly CF81 8SP

☎ 01443 837599

Bar Food, Restaurant Menu, Accommodation,
No Smoking Area

65 Penilwyn Manor

Pontllanfraith, Blackwood, Caerphilly NP12 2EQ

☎ 01495 223466

Bar Food, Restaurant Menu

66 Pentwyn Inn

Pentwyn Terrace, Pentwyn, Newport,
Caerphilly NP11 3JD

☎ 01495 217639

Real Ales, Bar Food

67 The Philanthropic Inn

Twyncarn Rd, Pontywaun, Newport,
Caerphilly NP11 7DU

☎ 01495 270448

68 Plasnewydd Hotel

Upper High St, Bargoed, Caerphilly CF81 8QY

☎ 01443 832272

69 Plough Inn

Pantydyn, Pontllanfraith, Blackwood,
Caerphilly NP12 2JJ

☎ 01495 229736

70 Prince of Wales

Dixon Place, Risca, Newport, Caerphilly NP11 6PY

☎ 01633 612780

Real Ales

71 Railway Hotel

Kendon Rd, Crumlin, Newport,
Caerphilly NP11 4PN

☎ 01495 243130

72 Railway Inn

Llanfabon Rd, Nelson, Treharris,
Caerphilly CF46 6PG

☎ 01443 453459

Bar Food, Restaurant Menu, No Smoking Area

73 Railway Tavern

1 Danygraig Rd, Risca, Caerphilly NP11 6DB

☎ 01633 615955

Real Ales, Bar Food, Restaurant Menu,
No Smoking Area

74 Red Lion Inn

Bryngwyn Rd, Newbridge, Caerphilly NP11 4GX

☎ 01495 243278

Real Ales

75 The Rhymney House

Rhymney Bridge, Rhymney, Tredegar,
Caerphilly NP22 5QG

☎ 01685 844040

Real Ales, Bar Food, Restaurant Menu,
Accommodation, No Smoking Area

76 Risca House Inn

Commercial St, Risca, Newport,
Caerphilly NP11 6AZ

☎ 01633 614918

77 The Rising Sun

Graig Rhymney, TirpHill, Caerphilly NP24 6LY

☎ 01443 839335

78 Rising Sun Inn

Station Terrace, Fochriw, Caerphilly CF81 9JN

☎ 01685 841435

Bar Food, Restaurant Menu, No Smoking Area

79 Rock & Fountain Inn

St David's Ave, Woodsfieldside, Caerphilly NP12 0PN

☎ 01495 223907

80 The Rowan Tree

Caerphilly Rd, Nelson, Treharris, Caerphilly CF46 6NH

☎ 01443 450265

Real Ales, Bar Food, No Smoking Area

81 The Royal Hotel

34 High St, Rhymney, Tredegar, Caerphilly NP22 5NB

☎ 01685 842888

82 The Royal Hotel

Harvard Rd, Abertridwr, Caerphilly CF83 4DP

☎ 02920 832025

83 The Royal Oak

Shingrig Rd, Nelson, Treharris, Caerphilly CF46 6DY

☎ 01443 451022

Real Ales, Restaurant Menu, No Smoking Area

84 The Royal Oak

Commercial St, Ystrad Mynach, Caerphilly CF82 7DY

☎ 01443 862345

Real Ales, Bar Food, Restaurant Menu,
No Smoking Area

85 Royal Oak Inn

Church St, Bedwas, Caerphilly CF83 8EA

☎ 02920 885237

Bar Food, Restaurant Menu, Accommodation,
No Smoking Area

86 Royal Oak Inn

Machen, Caerphilly CF83 8SN

☎ 01633 440394

Restaurant Menu, No Smoking Area

87 Sir Howy Arms Hotel

High St, Argoed, Blackwood, Caerphilly NP12 0HG

☎ 01495 223222

Bar Food, Restaurant Menu, Accommodation,
No Smoking Area

88 Sirhowy

61-63 High St, Blackwood, Caerphilly NP12 3SZ

☎ 01495 226374

Real Ales, Restaurant Menu, No Smoking Area

89 Three Horse Shoes Inn

High St, Pentwynmawr, Newbridge,
Caerphilly NP11 4HN

☎ 01495 243436

Real Ales, Bar Food, Restaurant Menu,
No Smoking Area

90 The Toby Jug Inn

Ivor St, Fleur De Lis, Blackwood, Caerphilly NP12 3RF

☎ 01443 879452

91 The Tradesmans Arms

45 Chatham, Machen, Caerphilly CF83 8SB

☎ 01633 440739

Bar Food

92 The Travellers Rest

Thornhill, Gelligaer, Caerphilly CF83 1LY

☎ 02920 859021

Real Ales, Bar Food, Restaurant Menu,
No Smoking Area

93 Tredegar Arms Hotel

Hill St, Rhymney, Tredegar, Caerphilly NP22 5JW

☎ 01685 841878

94 Tylers Arms

Heol Fawr, Nelson, Treharris, Caerphilly CF46 6NW

☎ 01443 450430

No Smoking Area

95 Viaduct Hotel

Crumlin Rd, Crumlin, Newport, Caerphilly NP11 3PF

☎ 01495 243186

Real Ales, Bar Food

96 Welsh Oak Inn

Rogerstone, Newport, Caerphilly NP10 9GG

☎ 01633 612446

Real Ales, No Smoking Area

97 White Cross Inn

Groeswen, Taffs Well, Cardiff, Caerphilly CF15 7UT

☎ 02920 851332

Real Ales, Bar Food, Restaurant Menu,
No Smoking Area

98 White Hart Inn

Church St, Bedwas, Caerphilly CF83 8EA

☎ 02920 885394

Real Ales, Bar Food, Restaurant Menu,
Accommodation, No Smoking Area

99 White Hart Inn

White Hart, Machen, Caerphilly CF83 8QQ

☎ 01633 441005

Real Ales, Bar Food, Restaurant Menu,
Accommodation, No Smoking Area

100 White Horse Inn

Davies Row, Pentwyn, Bargoed,
Caerphilly CF81 9NP

☎ 01685 841215

Restaurant Menu, No Smoking Area

101 The Windsor Hotel

Caerphilly Rd, Senghenydd, Caerphilly CF83 4FX

☎ 02920 830460

Real Ales

102 Wingfield Hotel

Wingfield Terrace, Llanbradach,
Caerphilly CF83 3NT

☎ 02920 884165

Real Ales, Bar Food, Restaurant Menu,
No Smoking Area

103 Ynysddu Hotel

Ynysddu, Newport, Caerphilly NP11 7JW

☎ 01495 200281

Real Ales, Bar Food, Restaurant Menu,
Accommodation

CARDIFF & NEWPORT

CARDIFF • NEWPORT • CARLEON

ardiff (Welsh: *Caerdydd*) is the capital and largest city of Wales. It is located in the traditional county of Glamorgan. A relatively small town until the early 19th century, it came to prominence quite suddenly as a result of the influx of industry into the region and the use of Cardiff as a major port for the transport of coal. Cardiff was made a city in 1905, and 50 years later was proclaimed capital of Wales.

Cardiff's port, known as Tiger Bay, was once one of the busiest ports in the world. After a long period of neglect, as 'Cardiff Bay' it is now being revived as a popular area for the arts, entertainment and nightlife. Much of the explosive growth has been due to the building of the Cardiff Barrage. The Welsh National Opera moved into the Wales Millennium Centre in the autumn of 2004.

As well as its justly famous Castle, Cardiff is home to the National Assembly for Wales, St David's Hall, the National Museum of Wales, and Cathays Park. Caroline Street is one of

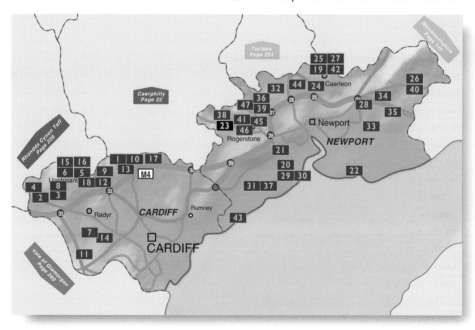

■ Cardiff and Newport Reference Number - Detailed Information

▨ Cardiff and Newport Reference Number - Summary Entry

Ceredigion Page 249 ▶ Adjacent area - refer to pages indicated

the third oldest streets in Cardiff and is a major link between two of its busiest streets. The city is also host to S A Brain, a brewery with premises in Cardiff since 1882. Famous Cardiffians have included Michael Aspel, Ryan Giggs, John Humphrys, Griff Rhys Jones, Shirley Bassey and Ivor Novello.

Newport (Welsh: *Casnewydd*) is the third largest city in Wales after

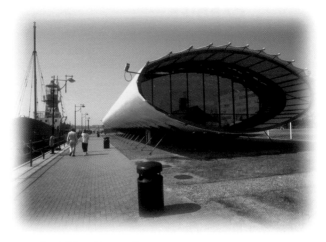

Cardiff Bay Visitor Centre

Cardiff and Swansea. Standing on the banks of the river Usk, it is the cultural capital of the traditional county of Monmouthshire, although an administrative county in its own right. The county borough of Newport was granted city status in 2002 to mark the Golden Jubilee. The full Welsh name for the city is *Casnewydd-ar-Wysg*, which literally means 'New Castle-on-Usk'. This refers to the 12th-century castle ruins near the city centre, which are 'new' compared to the Roman fortress at nearby Caerleon. The city's importance as a trading port in the middle ages was re-emphasized when a 15th-century ship, referred to locally as the Newport ship, was recently uncovered from the bank of the Usk within Newport during the construction of a new arts centre.

Newport is known for its many works of civic art, including the steel Wave on the banks of the Usk, and the mechanical clock in the city centre. It also has one of the few remaining working transporter bridges (the other British example being in Middlesbrough, Yorkshire).

Set in a beautiful 90-acre park, Tredegar House is one of the best examples of a 17th-century Charles II mansion in Britain. The earliest surviving part of the building dates back to the early 1500s. For over 500 years it was home to one of the greatest of Welsh families, the Morgans - later Lords Tredegar - until they left in 1951. The house was then used as a girl's school until it was bought by the council in 1974, giving rise to its present status as the grandest council house in Britain!

The river Usk at Newport has always proved an attractive place to make a home. Bronze Age fishermen settled around its fertile estuary and later the Celtic Silures built hill forts overlooking it. On the very edge of their empire, the Roman legions built a fortress at Caerleon to defend the river crossing. The Normans arrived in 1090 to build a castle and river crossing downstream. Around the settlement, the New Town grew to be become Newport, and was granted a charter by Hugh, Earl of Stafford in 1385. Newport was the focal point of a major Chartist uprising in 1839, where John Frost and 3,000 others marched on the Westgate Hotel. John Frost Square, in the centre of the city, is named in his honour.

CARDIFF

1 Best Western New House Country Hotel

Thornhill Rd, Thornhill, Cardiff CF14 9UA

☎ 02920 520280

Bar Food, Restaurant Menu, Accommodation, No Smoking Area

2 Caesars Arms

Cardiff Rd, Creigiau, Cardiff CF15 9NL

☎ 02920 890486

Real Ales, Bar Food, Restaurant Menu

3 Capital Serviced Apartments

28 Bronllwyn, Pentyrch, Cardiff CF15 9QL

☎ 02920 891414

Real Ales, Bar Food, Restaurant Menu, No Smoking Area

4 Creigiau Inn

Station Rd, Creigiau, Cardiff CF15 9NN

☎ 02920 890768

Real Ales, Bar Food, Restaurant Menu

5 Fagins Ale and Chop House

8 Cardiff Rd, Taffs Well, Cardiff CF15 7RE

☎ 02920 811800

Real Ales, Bar Food, Restaurant Menu, No Smoking Area

6 Gwaelod Y Garth Inn

Main Rd, Cardiff CF15 9HH

☎ 02920 810408

Real Ales, Bar Food, Restaurant Menu, Accommodation, No Smoking Area

7 The Jug and Bottle

125 Firs Avenue, Pentrabane, Cardiff CF5 3TL

☎ 02920 561275

Real Ales, Bar Food, Restaurant Menu

8 Lewis Arms

Heol Goch, Pentyrch, Cardiff CF15 9PN

☎ 02920 891641

Real Ales, Bar Food, Restaurant Menu, No Smoking Area

9 Lewis Arms

Mill Rd, Tongwynlais, Cardiff CF15 7JP

☎ 02920 810330

Real Ales, Bar Food, Accommodation, No Smoking Area

10 Manor Parc Country Hotel And Restaurant

Thornhill Rd, Thornhill, Cardiff CF14 9UA

☎ 02920 693723

Restaurant Menu, Accommodation, No Smoking Area

11 The Michaelston

105 Michaelston Rd, Cardiff CF5 4SY

☎ 02920 670006

Bar Food, Restaurant Menu, No Smoking Area

12 Old Ton Inn

Merthyr Rd, Tongwynlais, Cardiff CF15 7LF

☎ 02920 811865

No Smoking Area

13 Pentre Gwilym House

Thornhill Rd, Thornhill, Cardiff CF14 9UA

☎ 02920 613873

Bar Food, Restaurant Menu, No Smoking Area

14 Quarry House

St Fagans Rise, Llandaff, Cardiff CF5 3EZ

☎ 02920 565577

Bar Food, Restaurant Menu, No Smoking Area

15 The Swan Inn

68 Cardiff Rd, Glan Y Llyn, Cardiff CF15 7QE

☎ 02920 811600

Real Ales, Bar Food, Restaurant Menu, No Smoking Area

16 Taffs Well Inn

Cardiff Rd, Taffs Well, Cardiff CF15 7PR

☎ 02920 810324

Real Ales, Bar Food, Restaurant Menu,
No Smoking Area

17 The Ty Mawr

Graig Rd Lisvane, Thornhill, Cardiff CF14 0UF

☎ 02920 754456

Real Ales, Bar Food, Restaurant Menu,
No Smoking Area

18 Tynant Inn

Tynant Rd, Morganstown, Cardiff CF15 8LB

☎ 02920 843009

Real Ales, Bar Food, Restaurant Menu,
No Smoking Area

NEWPORT

19 The Angel Hotel

Goldcroft Common, Caerleon, Newport NP18 1NG

☎ 01633 420264

Real Ales, No Smoking Area

20 Church House Inn

Church Rd, St Brides,
Wentlooge, Newport NP10 8SN

☎ 01633 680807

Real Ales, Bar Food, Restaurant Menu,
Accommodation, No Smoking Area

21 The Duffryn

Duffryn, Newport NP10 8TE

☎ 01633 810922

Real Ales, No Smoking Area

22 The Farmers Arms

Goldcliff, Newport NP18 2AU

☎ 01633 272670

Real Ales, Bar Food, Restaurant Menu,
No Smoking Area

23 The Friendly Fox

See panel below

---

23 The Friendly Fox

Caerphilly Road, Rhiwderin, Bassaleg, Newport,
Gwent NP10 8RF

☎ 01633 894999

Real Ales, Bar Food, No Smoking Area

The Friendly Fox began life as a private house,
built in 1821. It opened as a pub in the mid-
1960s. Very attractive inside and out, the spacious
interior boasts a wealth of warm woods and is a
very pleasant mix of traditional and modern
features. Outside there's a beer garden – just the
place to enjoy a relaxing drink or meal on fine
days. Leaseholders Paul and Kim Wilde have been
here since December 2003, and offer a warm
welcome to all their guests.

Paul is a chef who has many years' experience
in the trade. He creates an outstanding array of
dishes for the menu and daily specials board,
including a choice of 13 different expertly-
prepared curries. Other specialities include
tempting stir-fries and chillis.

☛ On the A468 a short drive from the M4

🍺 Hancocks HB, rotating guest ale

🍴 Mon-Fri 12-2.30 & 5-8.30, Sat 12-8.30, Sun
12-4

🎵 Sun quiz from 8.30, Weds music quiz
from 9

🏕 Parking, garden

💳 All major cards

🕐 11.30-11 (Sun and Bank Holidays to 10.30)

Newport, Caerleon, Cwmbran, Rogerstone,
🏛 Caerphilly

24 ## The Gladiator

Pillmawr Rd, Malpas, Newport NP18 3QZ

☎ 01633 821353

Real Ales, Bar Food, No Smoking Area

25 ## Goldcroft Inn

Goldcroft Common, Newport NP18 1NG

☎ 01633 420504

Real Ales, Bar Food, Restaurant Menu

26 ## The Groes Wen Inn

Penhow, Caldicot, Newport NP26 3AD

☎ 01633 402001

Real Ales, Bar Food, Restaurant Menu

27 ## Hanbury Arms

Uskside, Caerleon, Newport NP18 1AA

☎ 01633 420361

Real Ales, Bar Food, No Smoking Area

28 ## The Hilton Hotel

Chepstow Rd, Langstone, Newport NP18 2LX

☎ 01633 413737

Bar Food, Restaurant Menu, Accommodation,
No Smoking Area

29 ## The Inn at the Elm Tree

St Brides, Wentlooge, Newport NP10 8SQ

☎ 01633 680225

Real Ales, Bar Food, Restaurant Menu,
Accommodation, No Smoking Area

30 ## Lighthouse Inn

Beach Rd, St Brides, Wentlooge,
Newport NP10 8SH

☎ 01633 680800

Bar Food, Restaurant Menu

31 ## Masons Arms

10 St Mellons Rd, Marshfield, Newport CF3 2TX

☎ 01633 680308

Real Ales, Bar Food, Restaurant Menu,
No Smoking Area

32 ## The Merry Miller

Monnow Way, Bettws, Newport NP20 7DB

☎ 01633 855965

33 ## The Milton Hotel

Milton Hill, Llanwern, Newport NP18 2DU

☎ 01633 412432

Real Ales

34 ## New Inn Hotel

Chepstow Rd, Langstone, Newport NP18 2JN

☎ 01633 412426

Bar Food, Restaurant Menu, Accommodation,
No Smoking Area

35 ## Old Barn Inn

Llanmartin, Newport NP18 2EB

☎ 01633 413382

Bar Food

36 ## The Olde Oak

Ruskin Avenue, Rogerstone, Newport NP10 0AA

☎ 01633 892883

Bar Food, Restaurant Menu

37 ## Port o' Call

140 Marshfield Rd, Marshfield, Newport CF3 2TU

☎ 01633 680171

Real Ales, Bar Food, Restaurant Menu,
No Smoking Area

38 ## Rhiwderin Inn

Caerphilly Rd, Rhiwderin, Newport NP10 8RX

☎ 01633 897722

Real Ales, Bar Food, Restaurant Menu,
No Smoking Area

39 ## The Rising Sun

Cefn Rd, Rogerstone, Newport NP10 9AQ

☎ 01633 895126

Real Ales, Bar Food, Restaurant Menu,
Accommodation, No Smoking Area

40 Rock And Fountain Inn

Penhow, Caldicot, Newport NP26 3AD

☎ 01633 400477

Real Ales, Bar Food, Restaurant Menu,
Accommodation, No Smoking Area

41 Ruperra House

Caerphilly Rd, Bassaleg, Newport NP10 8LJ

☎ 01633 893374

Real Ales, Bar Food

42 Ship Inn

New Rd, Caerleon, Newport NP18 1QF

☎ 01633 420087

Bar Food, Restaurant Menu, Accommodation,
No Smoking Area

43 Six Bells Hotel

Broad St, Common Peterstone Wentlooge,
Newport CF3 2TN

☎ 01633 682031

Real Ales, Bar Food, Restaurant Menu,
No Smoking Area

44 Three Horseshoes Inn

45 Pillmawr Rd, Newport NP20 6WG

☎ 01633 857510

Real Ales, Bar Food, Restaurant Menu,
No Smoking Area

45 The Three Salmons Inn

Western Valley Rd, Rogerstone,
Newport NP10 9DS

☎ 01633 660122

Real Ales, Bar Food

46 Tredegar Arms

4 Caerphilly Rd, Bassaleg, Newport NP10 8LE

☎ 01633 893247

Real Ales, Bar Food, Restaurant Menu

47 Tredegar Arms

Cefn Rd, Rogerstone, Newport NP10 9AS

☎ 01633 664999

Real Ales, Bar Food, Restaurant Menu,
No Smoking Area

CARMARTHENSHIRE

CARMARTHEN • LLANELLI • LLANDOVERY

armarthenshire is a county of contrasts, with a wealth of interesting sights and superb countryside to enchant all visitors. There are coastal strongholds at Laugharne and Kidwelly, abbey ruins at Talley and Whitland, and the famous rugby and industrial centre of Llanelli.

Covering some 1,000 square miles, the county also has beautiful clean beaches, seaside towns and villages, and rural idylls. A place of myths and legends, Carmarthenshire has remained essentially Welsh in most aspects.

11 Carmarthenshire Reference Number - Detailed Information

12 Carmarthenshire Reference Number - Summary Entry

Ceredigion
Page 249   Adjacent area - refer to pages indicated

The coastline, which is over 50 miles long, includes the award-winning Pembrey Country Park and beach, and Pendine, whose long stretch of sand has seen many land speed world records made and broken. Of the seaside villages, Laugharne is certainly the most well known, not least for being the place where Dylan Thomas lived for the last years of his short life. The village does not rely on its literary links, however, as it has one of the country's most handsome castles and offers wonderful views over the estuary of the River Taf.

Inland lies Carmarthen, the county town, whose origins lie back in the time of the Romans. The town is a centre for agriculture, while to the east is an area associated with the legends and mysteries of Merlin. Also in this part of Carmarthenshire is one of the country's most important projects – the National Botanic Garden of Wales. Dedicated to conservation, horticulture, science and education, and boasting the largest single-span glasshouse in the world, this is one of the country's newest gardens, while close by lies Aberglasney, one of the oldest: it was first mentioned in print in 1477.

Evidence of Roman occupation is most striking at the Dolaucothi Gold Mines, to the northwest of

Salmon Leap Waterfalls, Cenarth

Llandovery. At Cenarth, visitors can see salmon fishermen on the River Teifi using the traditional coracle, a tiny round boat whose origins are lost in the mists of time. A fascinating local museum tells the story of these distinctive little craft. Here too are the Salmon Leap Waterfalls.

Llanelli, southeast of Carmarthen, boasts the Millennium Coastal Park and Cycleway with its wetlands, gardens, woodlands, golf course and opportunities for sailing and watersports. East of Llanelli is the Wildfowl and Wetlands Trust bird sanctuary, a haven for wild plant and animal life with 200 acres of saltmarsh that is home to flocks of curlew, lapwing and redshank, which visitors can observe from secluded hides.

1 Abadam Arms

Porthyrhyd, Carmarthen,
Carmarthenshire SA32 8PL
☎ 01267 275278

2 Afon Duad Inn

Cwmduad, Carmarthen,
Carmarthenshire SA33 6XJ
☎ 01267 281357
Real Ales, Bar Food, Restaurant Menu,
Accommodation, No Smoking Area

3 The Albion Arms

Llansawel Rd, Llanybydder,
Carmarthenshire SA40 9RN
☎ 01570 480781
Real Ales, Restaurant Menu

4 Ammanford Hotel

31 Pontamman Rd, Pontamman, Ammanford,
Carmarthenshire SA18 2HX
☎ 01269 592598
Real Ales, Accommodation

5 The Angel Hotel

62 Rhosmaen St, Llandeilo,
Carmarthenshire SA19 6EN
☎ 01558 822765
Real Ales, Bar Food, Restaurant Menu,
Accommodation, No Smoking Area

6 Angel Inn

Salem, Llandeilo, Carmarthenshire SA19 7LY
☎ 01558 823394
Real Ales, Bar Food, Restaurant Menu,
No Smoking Area

7 Ashburnham Hotel

Ashburnham Rd, Pembrey, Burry Port,
Carmarthenshire SA16 0TH
☎ 01554 834455
Bar Food, Restaurant Menu, Accommodation,
No Smoking Area

8 The Baltic Inn

Ponthenry, Llanelli, Carmarthenshire SA15 5RE
☎ 01269 861409
Real Ales, Bar Food, Restaurant Menu,
Accommodation, No Smoking Area

9 The Beach Hotel

Pendine, Carmarthen,
Carmarthenshire SA33 4NY
☎ 01994 453469
Real Ales, Bar Food, Accommodation,
No Smoking Area

Set next to the Museum of Speed in Pendine, with views over the bay, The Beach Hotel is a convivial place offering genuine hospitality and friendly service.

Beer and Lager are served here, together with a choice of cider, stout, wines, spirits and soft drinks. The menu changes with the seasons, offering an excellent selection of dishes from Easter to the end of October.

The accommodation is available all year round, and includes a spacious family room that sleeps six. The inn makes a perfect base from which to explore the stunning coastline and the many other sights and attractions of the region.

- 🐾 Pendine is on the coast on the A4066, 13½ miles southwest of Carmarthen
- ❙❙ Easter to end October 12-2 & 6.30-8.30
- ⊨ 6 rooms with washing facilities
- 🅿 Parking, garden, disabled access
- 💳 All major cards
- ⏱ 11.30-11 (Sun and Bank Holidays to 10.30)
- 🏛 Laugharne 4 miles, St Clears 8 miles, Carmarthen 13½ miles

9 The Beach Hotel

See panel opposite

10 Bear Inn

Market Sq, Llandovery, Carmarthenshire SA20 0AB

☎ 01550 720728

Real Ales, Bar Food, Restaurant Menu

11 Belle View Inn

Llanllwni, Llanybydder, Carmarthenshire SA40 9SQ

☎ 01570 480495

Bar Food, Restaurant Menu, No Smoking Area

12 Bird In Hand

Trimsaran, Carmarthenshire SA17 4DG

☎ 01554 811261

Real Ales, Bar Food, Restaurant Menu

13 Bird In Hand

24 Carmarthen Rd, Fforest, Swansea,
Carmarthenshire SA4 0TU

☎ 01792 886001

Real Ales, Bar Food, Restaurant Menu,
No Smoking Area

14 Black Horse Inn

161 Iscoed Rd, Pontarddulais, Swansea,
Carmarthenshire SA4 0UN

☎ 01792 882239

Real Ales, Bar Food, Restaurant Menu,
No Smoking Area

15 The Black Horse Inn

Meinciau, Kidwelly, Carmarthenshire SA17 5LE

☎ 01269 860247

16 The Black Horse Inn

See panel below

17 Black Lion Hotel

See panel on page 42

18 Black Lion Hotel

Market Square, Llanybydder,
Carmarthenshire SA40 9UE

☎ 01570 480212

Real Ales, Bar Food, Restaurant Menu,
Accommodation, No Smoking Area

16 The Black Horse Inn

Pentrecwrt, Llandysul,
Carmarthenshire SA44 5AX

☎ 01559 362383

Bar Food, Restaurant Menu, No Smoking Area

Having recently undergone extensive and tasteful refurbishment, The Black Horse Inn presents an elegant and welcoming face to the world, and features a bright and pristine interior that's a happy marriage of modern and traditional, with comfortable and attractive seating, a large stonebuilt fireplace in the bar and an elegant feel in the newly created bistro. This charming and gracious part of the inn is painted in pale colours, pale woods and crisp linens. It seats 16 and boasts an across-the-board menu using the freshest local produce.

Tenants Chris, Lesley and their family have been here since October of 2004, offering genuine hospitality as well as excellent food and drink to all their guests.

This spacious inn is well-recommended locally and by the many return visitors who come to sample the delights of the menu and bar.

☛ On the A484 a few miles south of Llandysul

🍺 Double Dragon

🍴 Mon-Fri 4-9, Sat/Sun 12-9

⚒ Parking, disabled access, garden

🕐 Mon-Fri 4-11, Sat 12-11, Sun 12-10.30

🏛 Llandysul 5 miles, Capel Dewi 7 miles, New Quay 17 miles

17 Black Lion Hotel

St Clears, Pembrokeshire SA33 4AA
☎ 01994 231700

Real Ales, Bar Food, Restaurant Menu,
Accommodation, No Smoking Area

A family-run inn with a happy mix of traditional
and modern features, the Black Lion Hotel has
recently undergone a tasteful and conscientious
makeover to become a very handsome and
welcoming inn with food, drink and accommodation.

Food is served every day from 9 a.m. for a
hearty breakfast, until 2.30pm and again from

5.30pm to 8.30pm. There is a good choice of hot
and cold snacks and traditional favourites as well
as an all-day breakfast. At the moment Bed &
Breakfast is limited to 2 budget rooms with plans
to develop the large first floor area into 7 en-suite
bedrooms commencing in 2006.

As the hotel is just a few miles away from
Carmarthen, it makes an excellent base from
which to explore the many sights and attractions
of the region.

☛ Just off the A40 8½ miles southwest of
Carmarthen

🍺 London Pride, Evan Evans, draught Bass

🍴 9-2.30 and 5.30-8.30

🛏 Bed & Breakfast

🎵 Entertainment most weekends

🅿 Car park, disabled access and toilets

💳 All major cards

🕐 9.00am to midnight

🏛 Laugharne 2 miles, Pendine 5 miles,
Carmarthen 8½ miles

19 Black Lion Inn

Cwmffrwd, Abergwili, Carmarthen,
Carmarthenshire SA31 2NB
☎ 01267 231860
Bar Food, No Smoking Area

20 Black Lion Inn

Abergorlech, Carmarthen,
Carmarthenshire SA32 7SN
☎ 01558 685271
Real Ales, Bar Food, Restaurant Menu,
No Smoking Area

21 Black Lion Inn

Queens Square, Llangadog,
Carmarthenshire SA19 9EE
☎ 01550 777999

22 The Black Ox

High Street, Abergwili, Carmarthenshire SA31 2JB
☎ 01267 222458

Real Ales, Bar Food, Restaurant Menu,
No Smoking Area

☛ Off the A40, 1½ miles east of Carmarthen

🍺 2 rotating guest ales

🍴 Tues-Sat 12-2 & 6-9, Sun 12-2

🎵 Quiz third Sun of the month

🅿 Parking, disabled access

💳 All major cards

🕐 12-11 (Sun and Bank Holidays to 10.30)

🏛 Carmarthenshire County Museum, Merlin's
Hill Centre, Carmarthen 1½ miles

23 Blue Anchor

29 Pwll Rd, Llanelli, Carmarthenshire SA15 4BG
☎ 01554 741230

24 The Blue Bell Bar & Bistro

Market Square, Newcastle Emlyn,
Carmarthenshire SA38 9AA

☎ 01239 710132 ⊕ www.the-bluebell.com

Real Ales, Bar Food, Restaurant Menu, No
Smoking Area

Set in the heart of Newcastle Emlyn, the Blue Bell
Bar & Bistro dates back to the early 18th century.
From the outside it looks typically Georgian, with
a simple façade in white and blue, while inside it's
altogether more modern and pristine, with pale
woods and bright paintwork in the bar, and
exposed beamwork and quarry-tiled and parquet
flooring in the large restaurant area.

The restaurant seats 60, and has a menu that
changes daily and offers a range of outstanding
choices including fresh fish in season, one of the
many specialities here. There's also a conservatory
area and outdoor seating. Landlords

Chris and Dominique Davies have been here
since 2004, and offer all their guests a warm
welcome and genuine hospitality.

☞ On the A484 7 miles southeast of Cardigan

🍺 Speckled Hen and occasional guest ale

🍴 winter: Thurs/Fri/Sat 6-9; Sun 12-3; summer:
all day

🅿 Parking, disabled access, outdoor seating

💳 All major cards

🕐 11.30-3 & 6-11 (Sun and Bank Holidays to
10.30)

🏛 Henllyn 2 miles, Cenarth 3 miles, Drefach 4
miles, Carmarthen 14 miles

24 The Blue Bell Bar & Bistro

See panel above

25 The Bluebell Inn

Cynwyl Elfed, Elfed, Carmarthen,
Carmarthenshire SA33 6TL

☎ 01267 281780

Real Ales, Bar Food, Restaurant Menu,
No Smoking Area

26 The Boat House Hotel

1 Gosport St, Laugharne, Carmarthen,
Carmarthenshire SA33 4SY

☎ 01994 427263

Real Ales, Bar Food, Restaurant Menu,
Accommodation, No Smoking Area

27 The Bridgend Inn

Crugybar, Llanwrda, Carmarthenshire SA19 8UE

☎ 01558 650249

Real Ales, Bar Food, Restaurant Menu,
Accommodation, No Smoking Area

28 The Bristol Hotel

18-20 Station Rd, Burry Port,
Carmarthenshire SA16 0LR

☎ 01554 832450

Real Ales, Bar Food, Restaurant Menu,
Accommodation

29 Broadway Country House Hotel

Laugharne, Carmarthen,
Carmarthenshire SA33 4NU

☎ 01994 427969

Bar Food, Restaurant Menu, Accommodation,
No Smoking Area

33 The Bunch of Grapes

Newcastle Emlyn, Carmarthenshire SA38 9DU
☎ 01239 711185

Real Ales, Bar Food, Restaurant Menu, No Smoking Area

Located close to the castle in Newcastle Emlyn, The Bunch of Grapes is a real gem. Owned and run by Billy Brewer since 1987, this cheerful and attractive 16th-century coaching inn is cosy and rustic inside with open fires, a well-stocked bar and an excellent wine list. The pub is a regular entry in 'The Good Beer Guide' and was voted 'Camra Pub Of The Year 2004. It also has 'Cask Marque' accreditation and should not be missed by real ale enthusiasts.

The food is also excellent, with a range of home-cooked dishes to tempt every palate, including changing daily specials and plenty of choice for vegetarians.

Booking is advised for the traditional Sunday lunch and the evening non-smoking restaurant. The pub's lovely beer garden is also the setting for occasional barbecues.

☛ Newcastle Emlyn is on the A484 between Cardigan and Carmarthen

🍺 Rotating Guest Ales

♫ Occasional food-themed nights and live music every Thursday

♨ Parking, garden

🏛 Old Cilgwyn Gardens 1 mile, Henllan Railway 2 miles, Cenarth Falls and National Coracle Centre 2 miles, National Woollen Museum 4 miles

30 Browns Hotel

King St, Laugharne, Carmarthen, Carmarthenshire SA33 4RY
☎ 01994 427320
Real Ales, No Smoking Area

31 Brunant Arms

Caio, Llanwrda, Carmarthenshire SA19 8RD
☎ 01558 650483
Real Ales, Bar Food, Restaurant Menu

32 Bryn Fforest Inn

Pontnewydd, Trimsaran, Kidwelly, Carmarthenshire SA17 4LB
☎ 01554 810056
Real Ales, Bar Food, Accommodation, No Smoking Area

33 The Bunch of Grapes

See panel above

34 The Bush Inn

5 Maescanner Rd, Dafen, Llanelli, Carmarthenshire SA14 8LR
☎ 01554 749095

35 Butchers Arms

88 Lando Rd, Burry Port, Carmarthenshire SA16 0YB
☎ 01554 890473
Real Ales, Bar Food, No Smoking Area

36 Butchers Arms

Llanddarog, Carmarthen, Carmarthenshire SA32 8NS
☎ 01267 275330
Real Ales, Bar Food, Restaurant Menu, No Smoking Area

37 Carpenters Arms

Broadway, Laugharne,
Carmarthenshire SA33 4NS

☎ 01994 427435

Bar Food, Restaurant Menu, Accommodation,
No Smoking Area

- ☛ On the A4066 9 miles southwest of Carmarthen
- ▌ during opening hours
- ⊨ 4 en suite rooms
- ⚖ Parking, disabled access
- ⏱ summer: 12-11; winter: 4-11(Sun and Bank Holidays to 10.30)
- 🏛 St Clears ½ mile, Llansteffan 2 miles, Pendine 4½ miles

38 Castle Hotel

113 Rhosmaen St, Llandeilo,
Carmarthenshire SA19 6EN

☎ 01558 823446

Real Ales, Bar Food, Restaurant Menu,
No Smoking Area

39 Castle Hotel

Queens Square, Llangadog,
Carmarthenshire SA19 9BW

☎ 01550 777377

Real Ales, Bar Food, Restaurant Menu,
Accommodation, No Smoking Area

40 The Castle Inn

Bridge St, Llangennech, Llanelli,
Carmarthenshire SA14 8TW

☎ 01554 820112

41 The Castle Inn

The Square, Llansteffan, Carmarthen,
Carmarthenshire SA33 5JG

☎ 01267 241225

Real Ales, Bar Food, No Smoking Area

42 Caulfields Hotel

11 Station Rd, Burry Port,
Carmarthenshire SA16 0LR

☎ 01554 832288

Real Ales, Bar Food, Restaurant Menu,
Accommodation, No Smoking Area

43 Cennen Arms

Trapp, Llandeilo, Carmarthenshire SA19 6TP

☎ 01558 822330

Real Ales, Bar Food, Restaurant Menu,
No Smoking Area

44 Coasting Pilot Inn

Bridge St, Burry Port, Carmarthenshire SA16 0NR

☎ 01554 833520

Real Ales, Bar Food, Restaurant Menu,
No Smoking Area

45 College Inn

Derwydd Rd, Llandybie, Ammanford,
Carmarthenshire SA18 2LX

☎ 01269 851250

Real Ales, Bar Food, Restaurant Menu,
No Smoking Area

46 Colliers Arms

35 Cwmamman Rd, Garnant, Ammanford,
Carmarthenshire SA18 1NH

☎ 01269 826228

47 Colliers Arms

174 Saron Rd, Llandybie, Ammanford,
Carmarthenshire SA18 3LN

☎ 01269 592419

Bar Food, Restaurant Menu, No Smoking Area

48 Coopers Arms

Station Rd, Newcastle Emlyn,
Carmarthenshire SA38 9BX

☎ 01239 710323

Real Ales, Bar Food, Restaurant Menu,
No Smoking Area

49   Cornish Arms

Gors Road, Burry Port, Llanelli, Carmarthenshire
☎ 01554 833224

Real Ales, Bar Food, Restaurant Menu, No
Smoking Area

The Cornish Arms is a traditional village pub,
handsome and welcoming with a relaxed
ambience. This fine inn found off the A484
northwest of Llanelli is well worth seeking out.

Landlords Philip Martell and Keith Clarke offer
all their guests a warm welcome, and their
capable, friendly staff provide a high standard of
service and hospitality. Real ales are available,
together with a good selection of lagers, wine,
spirits, cider, stout and soft drinks.

The elegant restaurant features a menu and
daily specials boasting a range of home-cooked
dishes using the freshest ingredients, locally-
sourced wherever possible.

Outside there's an attractive beer garden.
Burry Port offers many attractions, not least the
lovely Marina and the motor racing circuit at
nearby Pembrey.

☛ Off the A484 3 miles northwest of Llanelli

🍺 Tetleys, Felinfoel, Double Dragon

🍴 Tues-Sun 12-3 & 6-9

🌳 Garden, patio

🕐 Tues-Sat 12-11, Sun and Bank Holidays to
10.30

🏛 Pembrey 1 mile, Llanelli 3 miles, Kidwelly 4
miles

51   The Cothi Bridge Hotel

Pontargothi, Nantgaredig, Carmarthen,
Carmarthenshire SA32 7NG
☎ 01267 290251
🌐 www.cothibridgehotel.co.uk

Bar Food, Restaurant Menu, Accommodation, No
Smoking Area

On the banks of the River Cothi in the Towy
Valley, The Cothi Bridge Hotel is a handsome and
spacious family-run hotel with great food, drink
and accommodation. Having undergone recent

refurbishment, the hotel's décor and furnishings
are tasteful and attractive. Comfortable and
welcoming throughout, the hotel has a relaxed
and friendly ambience.

Proprietor Sandie Jones and her family have
been here some 14 years. Sandie is an expert
cook who has built up a well-earned reputation
for the quality and tastiness of her cooking. As
well as lunchtime and evening meals, the hotel has
recently opened a coffee shop for morning coffees
and afternoon tea.

The hotel makes an excellent base from which
to explore sights and attractions such as
Aberglasney House and Gardens, The National
Botanical Gardens, Carmarthen and Llandeilo.

☛ On the A40 5 miles east of Carmarthen

🍴 12-2 & 6-9

🛏 10 en suite rooms

🌳 Parking, garden, patio, disabled access

💳 All major cards

🕐 12-11 (Sun and Bank Holidays to 10.30)

🏛 Carmarthen 5 miles, St Clears 6 miles,
Llandeilo 9 miles

49 Cornish Arms

See panel opposite

50 Corvus Inn

Station Rd, St Clears, Carmarthen,
Carmarthenshire SA33 4BG

☎ 01994 230965

Real Ales, Bar Food, Restaurant Menu,
No Smoking Area

51 The Cothi Bridge Hotel

See panel opposite

52 The Cottage Inn

Llandeilo, Carmarthenshire SA19 6SD

☎ 01558 822890

Real Ales, Bar Food, Restaurant Menu,
Accommodation, No Smoking Area

53 Croes Y Ceilog Inn

Llanwrda, Carmarthenshire SA19 8HD

☎ 01550 777320

54 The Cross Hands Hotel

Llandeilo Road, Cross Hands, Llanelli,
Carmarthenshire SA14 6NE

☎ 01269 845944

Real Ales, Bar Food, No Smoking Area

- ☛ Off J48 of the M4, 3 miles west of Llanelli
- 🍺 Double Dragon, Tetleys
- 🍴 12-9
- ♿ Parking, disabled access
- 💳 All major cards
- 🕐 12-11 (Sun and Bank Holidays to 10.30)
- 🏛 Llanelli 3 miles, Abergwili 12 miles, Kidwelly 15 miles, Carmarthen 17 miles

55 The Cross House Inn

Grist Square, Laugharne,
Carmarthenshire SA33 4SS

☎ 01994 427923

Real Ales, Bar Food, Restaurant Menu, No
Smoking Area

The Cross House Inn is a welcoming place with
many links to Dylan Thomas, in common with the
village itself. The accent's firmly on home cooking
here, with a menu full of home-made dishes using
the freshest locally-sourced produce including
Kiwi and Welsh specialities with the New Zealand
owner John welcoming you.

- ☛ 9 miles southwest of Carmarthen on the A4066
- 🍺 Bass plus occasional guest ale
- 🍴 12-3 & 6-9
- ♿ Parking, disabled access, baby changing facilities
- 💳 Not AMEX or Diner's
- 🕐 11.30-11 (Sun and Bank Holidays to 10.30)
- 🏛 St Clears ½ mile, Llansteffan 2 miles, Pendine 4 miles

56 The Cross Inn

Efailwen, Clynderwen, Carmarthenshire SA66 7XB

☎ 01994 419280

57 Cross Inn Hotel

Llanfihangel-Ar-Arth, Pencader,
Carmarthenshire SA39 9HX

☎ 01559 384838

Real Ales, Bar Food, Restaurant Menu,
No Smoking Area

58 Cross Keys Inn

78 Cwmamman Rd, Glanamman, Ammanford,
Carmarthenshire SA18 1DZ

☎ 01269 823926

59 Crosshands Hotel

Llanybydder, Carmarthenshire SA40 9TX

☎ 01570 480224

Bar Food, Accommodation, No Smoking Area

60 Cwmanne Tavern

Cwmanne, Lampeter SA48 8DR
☎ 01570 423861
⊕ www.cwmannetavern.co.uk

Real Ales, Bar Food, Restaurant Menu,
Accommodation, No Smoking Area

The Cwmanne Tavern is a spacious and comfortable inn just on the outskirts of Lampeter. Dating
back to 1712, this traditional coaching inn has a
tasteful and comfortable interior with black-and-
amber tiles, wooden pew-style seating and other

attractive features that add to the inn's warm and
welcoming ambience.

The real ales on tap are complemented by a
good selection of lagers, more than 20 bottled
continental beers, wines, spirits, cider, stout and
soft drinks. In the cosy restaurant, guests can
enjoy fine country cooking. The menu and daily
specials board offer a range of fresh beef, poultry,
fish and vegetarian dishes.

Accommodation is available for those who wish
to have a base from which to explore the many
sights and attractions of the region.

- ☛ On the A485 on the outskirts of Lampeter
- 🍺 3 rotating guest ales
- 🍴 Sat-Sun 12-2 & Tues-Sun 6-9
- 🛏 4 rooms, shared bathroom
- 🎵 Tues quiz, Sat live music
- ⚒ Parking, patio, disabled access
- 🕐 Mon-Fri 5-11, Sat 12-11, Sun and Bank
  Holidays 12-10.30
- 🏛 Capel Dewi 10 miles, Aberaeron 14 miles,
  New Quay 15 miles

60 Cwmanne Tavern

See panel above

61 Cwmdu Inn

Cwmdu, Llandeilo, Carmarthenshire SA19 7DY
☎ 01558 685088
Real Ales, Bar Food, No Smoking Area

62 Derlwyn Arms

118 Mountain Rd, Upper Brynamman, Ammanford,
Carmarthenshire SA18 1AN
☎ 01269 826380
Real Ales, No Smoking Area

63 The Drovers Arms

Main St, Ffarmers, Llanwrda,
Carmarthenshire SA19 8LJ
☎ 01558 650157
Bar Food, Restaurant Menu, No Smoking Area

64 Emlyn Arms Hotel

Bridge St, Newcastle Emlyn,
Carmarthenshire SA38 9DU
☎ 01239 710317
Bar Food, Restaurant Menu, Accommodation,
No Smoking Area

65 Engine Inn

New St, Burry Port, Carmarthenshire SA16 0RU
☎ 01554 833471

66 Farmers Arms

Glynmoch, Ammanford, Carmarthenshire SA18 2JQ
☎ 01269 823461

67 Farmers Arms

Graig, Burry Port, Carmarthenshire SA16 0DB
☎ 01554 834518
Bar Food, Restaurant Menu, No Smoking Area

68   Farmers Arms

62 Bridge St, Llangennech, Llanelli,
Carmarthenshire SA14 8TN

☎ 01554 820174

Real Ales

69   Farmers Arms

1 Norton Rd, Peny Groes, Llanelli,
Carmarthenshire SA14 7RT

☎ 01269 845696

Real Ales

70   The Farmers Arms

Llanfynydd, Carmarthen, Carmarthenshire SA32 7TG

☎ 01558 668291

Real Ales, Restaurant Menu, Accommodation

71   The Farmers Arms

Llanybri, Carmarthen, Carmarthenshire SA33 5HQ

☎ 01267 241846

Real Ales, Bar Food, Restaurant Menu,
No Smoking Area

72   The Farmers Arms

Llangyndeyrn, Kidwelly, Carmarthenshire SA17 5BN

☎ 01269 871022

Bar Food, Restaurant Menu, No Smoking Area

73   The Farmers Arms

Rhosmaen St, Llandeilo, Carmarthenshire SA19 6LW

☎ 01558 823783

Real Ales

74   The Farriers Arms

Cwmbach Rd, Llanelli, Carmarthenshire SA15 4PN

☎ 01554 774256

Real Ales, Bar Food, Restaurant Menu

75   The Fishermans Arms

3 Bridge St, Kidwelly, Carmarthenshire SA17 4UU

☎ 01554 891589

Real Ales

76   The Fishers Arms

See panel below

---

76   The Fishers Arms

Spring Gardens, Whitland, Carmarthenshire

☎ 01994 241329 🌐 www.fishersarms.co.uk

Bar Food, Restaurant Menu, Accommodation,
No Smoking Area

Dating back in parts to the 15th century, the
excellent Fishers Arms has bags of character and
a long pedigree of offering food, drink and a warm
welcome to weary travellers. Huge open fire,
exposed beamwork and cosy and comfortable
seating add to the pub's charm and relaxed
ambience. Owners Steve and Sharon have been
here since 2001. Steve looks after the beer and
front of house, while Sharon does the cooking.
The pub is shut on Mondays (except Bank Hols),
but the rest of the week guests can enjoy lunch
or dinner, with a range of dishes from fresh
sandwiches and hearty favourites such as sausage
and chips to steaks, chicken dishes, fish and
curries. On site, the inn also boasts a scenic
camping and caravan site complete with all
facilities. Handy for Oakwood Leisure Park and
Folly Farm as well as many other sights and
attractions of the region.

☛ Off the A40 6 miles from St Clears

🍺 Double Dragon, Best Bitter, Felinfoel

🍽 Tues-Sat 12-2.30 & 6.30-9, Sun 7-8.30

🎵 Occasional live music

🅿 Parking, garden, disabled access, camp and
caravan site

💳 All major cards

🕐 11.30-3 & 6.30-11 Tues-Thurs, 11.30-11 Fri
& Sat, 12-3 & 7-10.30 Sun, Closed Mon
(except Bank Holidays).

🏛 St Clears 6 miles, Laugharne 8 miles, Pendine
10 miles

77 The Forest Arms Hotel

Brechfa, Carmarthenshire SA32 7RA

☎ 01267 202339 🌐 www.forestarms.com

Real Ales, Bar Food, Restaurant Menu, Accommodation, No Smoking Area

Set in the beautiful Cothi valley and a favourite with walkers, fishermen and nature-lovers, The Forest Arms Hotel is a delightful, spacious and attractive country inn that boasts many of its original 17th-century features, including a huge stonebuilt open fire and exposed beamwork.

The menu offers a good choice of tempting dishes, and the real ales on tap are complemented by lagers, cider, stout, wines, spirits and soft drinks – something to quench every thirst.

Ideal as a base while fishing on the River Cothi (the inn has its own stretch of river that can be fished) and exploring the many sights and attractions – natural and man-made – dotted around the region, this fine inn is a comfortable and welcoming place to enjoy great food and drink and first-class accommodation.

🡒 Off the A485, 8 miles northwest of Llandeilo

🍺 Reverend James, Buckleys Best and rotating guest ales

🍴 12-2.30 & 6-9

🛏 4 en suite rooms

🅿 Parking, garden, disabled access

💳 All major cards

🕐 Mon-Fri 11-3 & 6-11, Sat 11-11, Sun 11-10.30

🏛 Pontarsais 3 miles, Llanarthney 5 miles, Llangathen 6 miles, Llandeilo 8 miles, Carmarthen 10 miles

---

77 The Forest Arms Hotel

See panel above

78 Fox and Hounds Inn

High St, Bancyfelin, Carmarthen, Carmarthenshire SA33 5ND

☎ 01267 211341

Real Ales, Bar Food, Restaurant Menu, Accommodation, No Smoking Area

79 Golden Grove Inn

Llanarthney, Carmarthen, Carmarthenshire SA32 8JU

☎ 01558 668551

Real Ales, Bar Food, Restaurant Menu, Accommodation, No Smoking Area

80 The Golden Grove Inn

16 High St, Llandybie, Ammanford, Carmarthenshire SA18 3HX

☎ 01269 850273

81 The Golden Lion Hotel

Penybanc, Ammanford SA18 3QP

☎ 01269 592280

Real Ales, Bar Food, Restaurant Menu, Accommodation, No Smoking Area

🡒 1½ miles from Ammanford off the A483

🍺 Courage Best, Brains

🍴 12-2.30

🛏 7 en suite rooms

🎵 Live music and karaoke Fri

🅿 Parking, garden, disabled access

💳 All major cards

🕐 12-11 (Sun and Bank Holidays to 10.30)

🏛 Ammanford 1½ miles, Pontarddulais 5 miles, Swansea 15 miles

82 The Green Bridge Inn

Pendine, Carmarthenshire SA33 4PL

☎ 01994 453550

Bar Food, Restaurant Menu, Accommodation, No Smoking Area

The Green Bridge Inn is a handsome and impressive establishment. Owned and family-run since 1994 by Hugh Owen and daughters Julie and Ann Marie, the inn boasts great food, drink and accommodation. Julie does the cooking, creating a range of tempting dishes using the freshest locally-sourced ingredients.

- ☛ Pendine is 13½ miles southwest of Carmarthen on the A4066; the inn is ¾ mile from the centre of Pendine towards Amroth

- ⅋ 12-2 & 6-9 when open

- ⊨ 3 en suite rooms.

- ♫ Occasional entertainment Sat night

- ⚒ Parking, disabled access, garden, camping and caravan site

- ⏱ summer: 12-11 (Sun and Bank Hols to 10.30); winter: Mon-Fri 7-11, Sat 12-11, Sun 7-10.30

- 🏛 Laugharne 3 miles, Amroth 5 miles, Whitland 6 miles, Carmarthen 13½ miles

84 Gwendraeth Arms

4 Gwendraeth Road, Tumble, Llanelli, Carmarthenshire SA14 6HS

☎ 01269 832818

Real Ales, Bar Food, Restaurant Menu, No Smoking Area

- ☛ J48 of the M4

- 🍺 Felinfoel, Tetleys

- ⅋ Fri-Sat 12-2 & 6-9.30, Sun 12-3

- ♫ Pool, darts

- ⚒ Parking, disabled access, garden, children's play area

- ⏱ Mon-Thurs 5-11, Fri-Sat 12-11, Sun and Bank Holidays 12-10.30

- 🏛 Millennium Coastal Park and Cycleway, Parc Howard Museum and Art Gallery, Stepney Wheel, Wildfowl and Wetlands Trust 3 miles

83 The Greyhound Inn

1 Fountain Rd, Llannon, Llanelli, Carmarthenshire SA14 6BE

☎ 01269 841410

Real Ales

85 Gwenilian Court Hotel

Kidwelly, Carmarthenshire SA17 4LW

☎ 01554 890453

Real Ales, Bar Food, Restaurant Menu, Accommodation, No Smoking Area

86 Gwenllian Court Hotel

Mynyddygarreg Rd, Mynyddygarreg, Kidwelly, Carmarthenshire SA17 4LW

☎ 01554 890217

Real Ales, Bar Food, Restaurant Menu, Accommodation, No Smoking Area

87 Half Moon Inn

281 Cwmammon Rd, Garnant, Ammanford, Carmarthenshire SA18 1LS

☎ 01269 825466

88 Halfway Hotel

33 Glyncoed Terrace, Llanelli, Carmarthenshire SA15 1EZ

☎ 01554 773571

Bar Food, Restaurant Menu, No Smoking Area

89 Halfway Inn

Pontantwn, Kidwelly, Carmarthenshire SA17 5HY

☎ 01269 860941

Real Ales, Bar Food, Restaurant Menu, Accommodation, No Smoking Area

90 The Halfway Inn

Nantgaredig, Carmarthen, Carmarthenshire SA32 7NL

☎ 01558 668337

Real Ales, Bar Food, Restaurant Menu, No Smoking Area

91 Hollybrook Tavern

Bronwydd, Carmarthen, Carmarthenshire SA33 6BE

☎ 01267 233521

Real Ales, Bar Food, No Smoking Area

92 Hope And Anchor
12 Stepney Rd, Burry Port,
Carmarthenshire SA16 0BH
☎ 01554 834144
Bar Food, Restaurant Menu

93 Hurst House Farm Ltd
East Marsh, Laugharne, Carmarthen,
Carmarthenshire SA33 4RS
☎ 01994 427417
Restaurant Menu, Accommodation,
No Smoking Area

94 The Incline Inn
61 Heol Y Pentre, Ponthenry, Llanelli,
Carmarthenshire SA15 5PY
☎ 01269 860573
Real Ales, Accommodation, No Smoking Area

95 The Iron Duke Hotel
Clynderwen, Carmarthenshire SA66 7NG
☎ 01437 563188

96 Ivy Bush
Emlyn Square, Newcastle Emlyn,
Carmarthenshire SA38 9BG
☎ 01239 710542
Real Ales, Bar Food

97 The Ivy Bush Inn
Church St, Llandybie, Ammanford,
Carmarthenshire SA18 3HZ
☎ 01269 850272
Real Ales, Accommodation

98 Joiners Arms
56-58 Llwynhendy Rd, Llanelli,
Carmarthenshire SA14 9HR
☎ 01554 754594
Real Ales, Bar Food, Restaurant Menu,
No Smoking Area

99 The Kings Arms
13 Maes Yr Eglwys, Llansaint, Kidwelly,
Carmarthenshire SA17 5JE
☎ 01267 267487
Bar Food, Restaurant Menu, No Smoking Area

100 Kings Arms Hotel
58 High St, Llandovery,
Carmarthenshire SA20 0DD
☎ 01550 721399
Real Ales, Bar Food, Accommodation,
No Smoking Area

101 Kings Head Inn
Waterloo Rd, Capel Hendre, Ammanford,
Carmarthenshire SA18 3SF
☎ 01269 842377
Real Ales, No Smoking Area

102 The Kings Head Inn
1 Market Square, Llandovery,
Carmarthenshire SA20 0AB
☎ 01550 720393
Real Ales, Bar Food, Restaurant Menu,
Accommodation, No Smoking Area

103 Lamb Inn
Llanboidy, Whitland, Carmarthenshire SA34 0EL
☎ 01994 448243
Real Ales, Bar Food, Accommodation,
No Smoking Area

104 Lamb Inn
Blaenwaun, Carmarthenshire SA34 0JD
☎ 01994 448440
Real Ales, Bar Food, No Smoking Area

105 The Lamb of Rhos Country Inn
Rhos, Llandysul, Carmarthenshire SA44 5EE
☎ 01559 370055
Real Ales, Bar Food, Restaurant Menu,
Accommodation, No Smoking Area

106 The Lewis Arms

Yspitty Road, Bynea, Llanelli,
Carmarthenshire SA14 9TD

☎ 01554 777795

Real Ales, Bar Food, Restaurant Menu,
No Smoking Area

- ☛ J47 of the M4 then the A484 between Swansea and Llanelli
- 🍺 Double Dragon, Budweiser on tap
- 🍴 12-9
- ♿ Parking, disabled access, garden
- 💳 All the major cards
- 🕐 12-11 (Sun to 10.30)
- 🏛 Gorseinon, Loughor, Llanelli, Swansea

107 Llwyndafydd Inn

Saron, Llandysul, Carmarthenshire SA44 5DR

☎ 01559 371048

Real Ales, Bar Food, Restaurant Menu,
No Smoking Area

108 Mansel Arms

Porthyrhyd, Carmarthen,
Carmarthenshire SA32 8BS

☎ 01267 275305

Real Ales, Bar Food, No Smoking Area

109 The Mansion House Hotel

Pant Yr Athro, Llanstephan, Carmarthen,
Carmarthenshire SA33 5AJ

☎ 01267 241515

Real Ales, Bar Food, Restaurant Menu,
Accommodation, No Smoking Area

110 Masons Arms

Alltwalis, Carmarthen, Carmarthenshire SA32 7EB

☎ 01559 384044

Real Ales, Bar Food

111 Mill At Glynhir

Glynhir Rd, Llandybie, Ammanford,
Carmarthenshire SA18 2TE

☎ 01269 850672

Real Ales, Restaurant Menu, Accommodation,
No Smoking Area

112 Neuadd Fawr Arms

Cilycwm, Llandovery, Carmarthenshire SA20 0ST

☎ 01550 721644

Bar Food, Restaurant Menu

113 Nevills Arms

21 Maescanner Rd, Dafen, Llanelli,
Carmarthenshire SA14 8LR

☎ 01554 774618

Real Ales, Bar Food, Restaurant Menu,
No Smoking Area

114 New Cross Inn

Dryslwyn, Carmarthen, Carmarthenshire SA32 8SD

☎ 01558 668276

Real Ales, Bar Food, Restaurant Menu,
No Smoking Area

115 New Lodge Inn

1 Heol-Y-Bryn, Pontyberem, Llanelli,
Carmarthenshire SA15 5AG

☎ 01269 870679

Real Ales, Bar Food, Restaurant Menu,
No Smoking Area

116 New Three Mariners Inn

Victoria St, Laugharne, Carmarthen,
Carmarthenshire SA33 4SE

☎ 01994 427426

Real Ales, Bar Food, Restaurant Menu

117 Norton Arms

43 Norton Rd, Peny Groes, Llanelli,
Carmarthenshire SA14 7RT

☎ 01269 845857

Real Ales

118 Old Bridge Inn

Bridge St, Llangennech, Llanelli,
Carmarthenshire SA14 8TW

☎ 01554 821301

Real Ales, Bar Food, Restaurant Menu,
No Smoking Area

119 Pantydderwen Tafarn

Old School Rd, Llangain, Carmarthen,
Carmarthenshire SA33 5AE

☎ 01267 241560

Real Ales, Bar Food, Restaurant Menu,
No Smoking Area

120 Pelican Inn

Sycamore St, Newcastle Emlyn,
Carmarthenshire SA38 9AP

☎ 01239 710606

Real Ales

121 Pemberton Arms

Colby Rd, Burry Port, Carmarthenshire SA16 0RH

☎ 01554 832129

Real Ales, Bar Food, Restaurant Menu

122 Pembrey Inn

30 Randell Square, Pembrey, Burry Port,
Carmarthenshire SA16 0UA

☎ 01554 834725

Real Ales, Bar Food, Restaurant Menu,
Accommodation, No Smoking Area

123 The Penybont Inn

Llanfynnyd, Carmarthen,
Carmarthenshire SA32 7TG

☎ 01558 668045

Bar Food, Restaurant Menu, Accommodation,
No Smoking Area

124 The Pen-y-Bont Inn

Llanglydwen, Nr Herron,
Carmarthenshire SA34 0XP

01994 419575

Real Ales, Bar Food, Restaurant Menu,
No Smoking Area

125 Phoenix Tavern

1 Penygroes Rd, Gorslas, Llanelli,
Carmarthenshire SA14 7LA

☎ 01269 844438

Real Ales, Bar Food, Restaurant Menu,
No Smoking Area

126 Picton House Country Club

Llanddowror, St Clears, Carmarthen,
Carmarthenshire SA33 4HJ

☎ 01994 230383

Bar Food, Restaurant Menu

127 Plas Parke Inn

Pentrecourt, Llandysul, Carmarthenshire SA44 5AX

☎ 01559 362684

Real Ales, Bar Food, Restaurant Menu,
No Smoking Area

128 The Plash Inn

Llanfallteg, Whitland, Carmarthenshire SA34 0UN

☎ 01437 563472

Real Ales, Bar Food, Restaurant Menu,
No Smoking Area

129 The Plough and Harrow

Henfwlch Rd, Carmarthen,
Carmarthenshire SA33 6AA

☎ 01267 221783

Bar Food, Restaurant Menu, No Smoking Area

130 The Plough and Harrow

56 Lady St, Kidwelly, Carmarthenshire SA17 4UD

☎ 01554 890250

Real Ales, Bar Food

131 The Plough & Harrow Inn

52 Betws Rd, Ammanford,
Carmarthenshire SA18 2HE

☎ 01269 596070

Real Ales

132 Plough Hotel

32 Stone St, Llandovery, Carmarthenshire SA20 0JP

☎ 01550 720576

Real Ales

133 Plough Hotel

Emlyn Square, Newcastle Emlyn,
Carmarthenshire SA38 9BG
☎ 01239 710994

134 Plough Inn

Felingwm, Carmarthen,
Carmarthenshire SA32 7PR
☎ 01267 290019
Bar Food, Restaurant Menu

135 Plough Inn

Rhosmaen, Llandeilo, Carmarthenshire SA19 6NP
☎ 01558 823431
Real Ales, Bar Food, Restaurant Menu,
Accommodation, No Smoking Area

136 The Plough Inn

Myddfai, Llandovery, Carmarthenshire SA20 0NZ
☎ 01550 720643
Real Ales, Bar Food, Restaurant Menu,
Accommodation

137 Portabello Inn Ltd

2 Stepney Rd, Burry Port,
Carmarthenshire SA16 0BH
☎ 01554 835371
Bar Food, No Smoking Area

138 Porth Hotel

Church St, Llandysul, Carmarthenshire SA44 4QS
☎ 01559 362202
Real Ales, Bar Food, Restaurant Menu,
Accommodation, No Smoking Area

139 Prince of Wales

Meinciau Rd, Mynyddygarreg, Kidwelly,
Carmarthenshire SA17 4RP
☎ 01554 890522
Real Ales, Bar Food, Restaurant Menu,
No Smoking Area

140 Prince of Wales

Porthyrhyd, Carmarthen,
Carmarthenshire SA32 8PL
☎ 01267 275711
Real Ales, Bar Food, Restaurant Menu

141 Queen Victoria Inn

21 Heol Y Meinciau, Pontyates, Llanelli,
Carmarthenshire SA15 5TR
☎ 01269 860416

142 Railway Hotel

Station Rd, Nantgaredig, Carmarthen,
Carmarthenshire SA33 4DF
☎ 01267 290211
Real Ales, Bar Food, No Smoking Area

143 The Ram Inn

Cwmann, Lampeter, Carmarthenshire SA48 8ES
☎ 01570 422556
Real Ales, Bar Food, Restaurant Menu,
No Smoking Area

144 Raven Inn

82 Cwmamman Rd, Garnant, Ammanford,
Carmarthenshire SA18 1ND
☎ 01269 823149
Real Ales, Bar Food, Restaurant Menu,
No Smoking Area

145 Red Cow Inn

Cwmfelin Rd, Bynea, Llanelli,
Carmarthenshire SA14 9LP
☎ 01554 773941

146 The Red Cow Inn

Llandeilo Rd, Llandybie, Ammanford,
Carmarthenshire SA18 3JA
☎ 01269 850384
No Smoking Area

147 Red Lion

2 Market Square, Llandovery,
Carmarthenshire SA20 0AA
☎ 01550 720813
Real Ales

148 The Red Lion

Llandeilo Rd, Llandybie, Ammanford,
Carmarthenshire SA18 3JA
☎ 01269 851202
Real Ales, Bar Food, Restaurant Menu,
No Smoking Area

151 The Red Lion Inn

24 Randell Square, Pembrey, Llanelli,
Carmarthenshire SA16 0UB

☎ 01554 832724

Real Ales, Bar Food, Restaurant Menu,
Accommodation, No Smoking Area

The Red Lion Inn was once, back in the 1600s,
the village magistrates' court and jailhouse. A real
gem, it is well worth seeking out. Recent
refurbishment has left the inn pristine and
comfortable inside and out. The range of real ales
is complemented by a good selection of lagers,

cider, stout, soft drinks, wines and spirits. The
menu offers a full range of everything from
sandwiches and snacks to home-made pies, steaks,
mixed grills, duck, seafood and vegetarian dishes.
For guests who'd like to use the inn as a touring
base there are three comfortable and cosy guest
bedrooms, while the region boasts many sights
and attractions including Pembrey Country Park
and Pembrey Saltmarsh, a local nature reserve and
Site of Special Scientific Interest.

☞ From J48 of the M4 take the A4138 to
Llanelli, then the A484 to Pembrey

🍺 Felinfoel, Double Dragon, Speckled Hen,
Spitfire, rotating guest ales

🍴 12-3 & 6-9

🛏 3 rooms

🎵 Quiz nights, bingo nights for charity

🅿 Parking, disabled access, garden/patio

🕐 12-3 & 6-11 (Sundays and Bank Holidays to
10.30)

🏛 Pembrey Country Park 1 mile, Millennium
Walkway, Motor Racing Circuit, Kidwelly
Castle 3 miles, Llanelli 4 miles

155 The Salutation Inn

Pontargothi, Carmarthenshire SA32 7NH
☎ 01267 290336

Real Ales, Bar Food, Restaurant Menu, No
Smoking Area

The Salutation Inn is a distinguished place dating
back to the 16th century. The wooden floors,
exposed beams, thick stone walls and other
original features attest to its long history of
offering sustenance and welcome to all visitors.

Mark Williams, his partner Aurwen and her
daughter Siân took over as tenants in 2004,

turning this fine inn round in that short time
thanks to the well-kept beer, excellent food and
warm hospitality. Guests choose from the menu
or specials board from a range of delicious dishes
expertly prepared – both Mark and Siân are chefs,
and use local produce wherever possible,
including fresh salmon from the River Cothi and
local game in season. Booking required on
Sundays.

Adjacent to the inn is a secure beer garden
with children's play area.

☞ Pontargothi is on the A40 between
Carmarthen and Llandeilo

🍺 3 real ales from the Felinfoel Brewery

🍴 summer: 11-9; winter: 12-2.30 & 6-9.30

🎵 Occasional – please ring for details

🅿 Parking, garden, children's play area, disabled
access

💳 Not Amex or Diners

🕐 11.30-11 (Sun and Bank Holidays to 10.30)

🏛 Llanarthney 3 miles, Carmarthen 6 miles,
Llandeilo 6 miles, Golden Grove 6 miles

149 The Red Lion

Church St, Llangadog, Carmarthenshire SA19 9AA

☎ 01550 777357

Real Ales, Bar Food, Restaurant Menu,
Accommodation, No Smoking Area

150 Red Lion Hotel

120 Iscoed Rd, Pontarddulais, Swansea,
Carmarthenshire SA4 0UN

☎ 01792 883989

151 The Red Lion Inn

See panel opposite

152 Red Lion Inn

Llandyfaelog, Kidwelly, Carmarthenshire SA17 5PR

☎ 01267 267530

Bar Food, Restaurant Menu, Accommodation,
No Smoking Area

153 Royal Oak Inn

Rhandirmwyn, Llandovery,
Carmarthenshire SA20 0NY

☎ 01550 760201

Bar Food, Restaurant Menu, Accommodation

154 Salt Rock Bar

11 Causeway St, Kidwelly,
Carmarthenshire SA17 4SU

☎ 01554 890777

Bar Food, Restaurant Menu, No Smoking Area

155 The Salutation Inn

See panel opposite

156 The Salutation Inn

See panel below

156 The Salutation Inn

33 New Road, Llandeilo,
Carmarthenshire SA19 6DF

☎ 01558 823325

Real Ales, Bar Food, Restaurant Menu,
No Smoking Area

Built in 1820, The Salutation Inn is a one-time
coaching inn that still boasts many original
features such as wood floors, real fires and
exposed stone walls adding to the inn's cosy and
traditional ambience. Owner David Hughes and
his conscientious staff offer a warm welcome and
excellent service to all their guests. David has
many plans for tasteful refurbishment, and during
the lifetime of this edition hopes to create a
conservatory restaurant to the rear and four en
suite guest bedrooms in the old coach house
adjacent to the pub.

In the mean time there's a good range of cask
conditioned real ales which are complemented by
a good selection of wines, lagers, cider, stout,
spirits and soft drinks.

☛ Just off the main A40 between Swansea and
Carmarthen

🍺 A selection of cask conditioned real ales

♫ Regular music nights

♿ Parking, disabled access

🕐 12noon - 11.30pm

🏛 Dinefwr Castle (in Llandeilo), Trapp 2½
miles, Golden Grove 3 miles, Llangathen 3
miles

157 Santa Clara

High St, St Clears, Carmarthen,
Carmarthenshire SA33 4EE

☎ 01994 231251

Real Ales, No Smoking Area

158 The Scotch Pine Inn

Mountain Rd, Betws, Ammanford,
Carmarthenshire SA18 2PL

☎ 01269 592569

Bar Food, Restaurant Menu

159 The Ship Aground Inn

123 Ashburnham Rd, Pembrey, Burry Port,
Carmarthenshire SA16 0TL

☎ 01554 832761

Bar Food, Restaurant Menu, No Smoking Area

160 Smiths Arms

Heol Y Foel, Foel Gastell, Llanelli,
Carmarthenshire SA14 7EL

☎ 01269 842213

Bar Food, Restaurant Menu, No Smoking Area

161 Smiths Arms

1 Pontardulais Rd, Llangennech, Llanelli,
Carmarthenshire SA14 8YE

☎ 01554 820305

Real Ales, Bar Food, Restaurant Menu,
No Smoking Area

162 The Smiths Arms

Llangynderyrn, Kidwelly,
Carmarthenshire SA17 5EN

☎ 01269 871554

Real Ales, Bar Food, Restaurant Menu,
No Smoking Area

163 The Smiths Arms

38 Gelli Rd, Llanelli, Carmarthenshire SA14 9AA

☎ 01554 772019

Real Ales, Bar Food, Restaurant Menu,
No Smoking Area

164 The Sporting Chance

See panel below

---

164 The Sporting Chance

Red Roses, Whitland, Carmarthenshire SA34 0PD

☎ 01834 831668

Real Ales, Bar Food, Restaurant Menu, No Smoking Area

The friendly and justly popular Sporting Chance is located opposite the ancient village church and chapel. This spacious and attractive inn is a welcome place to enjoy a relaxing drink or meal.

The inn serves morning coffee and afternoon tea as well as offering a full lunch and dinner menu. Known for its cuisine, the accent is firmly on quality here, with menus and specials board filled with tempting delights such as steaks, Welsh lamb, vegetarian tagliatelle, chicken au poivre, duck, lemon Sole, trout and more. There's also a children's menu and a choice of mouth-watering desserts including apple tart, bread-and-butter pudding and sticky toffee pudding.

All dishes are freshly prepared by the inn's chef using local produce wherever possible. Booking required Friday and Saturday evening and Sunday lunchtime.

☛ 13 miles west of Carmarthen on the B4328

🍺 Bass, Worthington and rotating guest ale

🍴 10-10

🅿 Parking, disabled access

💳 All major cards

🕐 11.30-11 (Sun and Bank Holidays to 10.30)

🏛 Pendine 5 miles, St Clears 4 miles, Narbeth 6 miles, Carmarthen 13 miles

165 Spring Well Inn

Pendine, Carmarthen, Carmarthenshire SA33 4PA

☎ 01994 453274

Real Ales, Bar Food, Restaurant Menu,
No Smoking Area

166 The Square &Compass

66 Heol Y Meinciau, Pontyates, Llanelli,
Carmarthenshire SA15 5RT

☎ 01269 861369

Bar Food, Restaurant Menu, No Smoking Area

167 Square & Compass Inn

Llandyfan, Llandybie, Ammanford,
Carmarthenshire SA18 2UD

☎ 01269 850402

Real Ales, Bar Food, Restaurant Menu,
No Smoking Area

168 The Stag

Five Rds, Llanelli, Carmarthenshire SA15 5YR

☎ 01269 860224

Real Ales, Bar Food, No Smoking Area

169 Stag And Pheasant

Llandeilo Rd, Carmel, Llanelli,
Carmarthenshire SA14 7SE

☎ 01269 832173

Real Ales, Bar Food, Restaurant Menu,
Accommodation, No Smoking Area

170 Station House Hotel

St Johns St, Whitland, Carmarthenshire SA34 0AP

☎ 01994 240556

Bar Food, No Smoking Area

171 The Sticks Hotel

Llansteffan, Carmarthen,
Carmarthenshire SA33 5JG

☎ 01267 241378

Real Ales, Bar Food, Restaurant Menu,
No Smoking Area

172 Stradey Arms

Llanelli, Carmarthenshire SA15 4ET

☎ 01554 757968

Real Ales, Bar Food, Restaurant Menu,
No Smoking Area

173 Taf Hotel

St Johns St, Whitland, Carmarthenshire SA34 0AP

☎ 01994 240356

Real Ales, Accommodation, No Smoking Area

174 Tafarn Beca

Trelech, Carmarthen, Carmarthenshire SA33 6RU

☎ 01994 484559

Real Ales, Bar Food

175 Tafarn Jem

Cwmann, Lampeter, Carmarthenshire SA48 8HF

☎ 01558 650633

Real Ales, Bar Food, Restaurant Menu,
No Smoking Area

176 Tafarn John Y Gwas

Drefach Felindre, Llandysul,
Carmarthenshire SA44 5XG

☎ 01559 370469

🌐 www.johnygwas.co.uk

**Real Ales, Bar Food, Restaurant Menu, No
Smoking Area**

☛ 12 miles north of Carmarthen on the A484

🍷 Three rotating guest ales

🍴 Weds-Sat 6-9

🅿 Parking

💳 All major cards

🕐 Mon 5-11, Tues-Fri 2-11, Sat 12-11, Sun 3-10.30

🏛 Llandysul 3 miles, Henllan 3 miles, Newcastle
Emlyn 4 miles, Cenarth Falls 10 miles

177 Tafarn Newydd Clynderwen

Clynderwen, Carmarthenshire SA66 7NE

☎ 01437 563969

Real Ales, Bar Food, Restaurant Menu,
Accommodation, No Smoking Area

181 Talardd Arms

Llanllwni, Pencader, Carmarthenshire SA39 9DX
☎ 01559 395633

Real Ales, Bar Food, Restaurant Menu, No Smoking Area

The Talardd Arms in Llanllwni is a very large and attractive traditional inn decorated and furnished to ensure guests' comfort. The ambience here is always friendly and welcoming. Owners Lysette and David ran a restaurant for four years before taking

over here in January of 2005. In a very short time they have built up a good following and are well-recommended locally thanks to the quality of the service, food and drink. David is an experienced chef who creates a tempting range of home-cooked food to order for the menu and daily specials. There's also a good selection of hot and cold bar meals. The inn plays host to occasional food-themed evenings – please ring for details.

☛ Found on the A485 southwest of Lampeter and east of Newcastle Emlyn, 12 miles north of Carmarthen

⊘ Tetleys, rotating guest ale

❙ 12-2 & 6-9

♫ Quiz night Thurs, occasional food-themed evenings

⚒ Parking, disabled access, garden

⚡ Not Amex or Diners

🕐 Easter-end Oct Tues-Sun 12-3 & 6-11; Nov-Easter Tues-Fri 6-11, Sat 12-11, Sun 12-3 & 6-10.30

🏛 Lampeter 9 miles, Newcastle Emlyn 12 miles, New Quay 15 miles, Carmarthen 12 miles

183 Telegraph Inn

Station Road, Llangadog, Carmarthenshire SA19 9LS
☎ 01550 777727

Real Ales, Bar Food, Accommodation, No Smoking Area

At the Telegraph Inn, a family-run Free House adjacent to the Heart of Wales Railway and dating back to the early 19th century, the food, drink and hospitality are second to none. Run by Keith and Heather Wrigley, the inn also offers self-catering accommodation available all year round. Keith does the cooking, creating an across-the-board menu of traditional favourites using locally-sourced produce. Booking required for Sunday

lunch. The menu includes specialities such as home-made lasagne, curry and chili con carne, faggots with mushy peas, steaks and mixed grills. The interior boasts exposed beamwork, while outside there's an attractive beer garden and children's play area. Heather has lived in the village for most of her life and is a good source of knowledge on the many sights and attractions of the region.

☛ On the A4069 five miles southwest of Llandovery

⊘ 2 rotating guest ales

❙ 12-2.30 per opening times; Tues-Sat 6.30-9

⊨ Self-catering flat sleeps 5

♫ Quiz last Sun of the month, occasional food-themed evenings

⚒ Parking, disabled access, garden, children's play area

🕐 Summer: 12-11 (Sun and Bank Holidays to 10.30); winter: Mon-Thurs 4.30-11, Fri 3-11, Sat 12-11, Sun 12-10.30

🏛 Talley 5 miles, Llandovery 5 miles, Llandeilo 8 miles

178 Tafarn Y Cwm

Cwm Trawsmawr, Carmarthen,
Carmarthenshire SA33 6NF

☎ 01267 231912

Real Ales, Bar Food, Restaurant Menu,
No Smoking Area

179 The Tafarn-Y-Garreg

Mynyddygarreg, Kidwelly,
Carmarthenshire SA17 4PY

☎ 01554 891366

Bar Food, Restaurant Menu, Accommodation,
No Smoking Area

180 Tafarn Y Sospan

8 Bassett Terrace, Llanelli,
Carmarthenshire SA15 4DY

☎ 01554 749249

Real Ales, Bar Food, Restaurant Menu,
No Smoking Area

181 Talardd Arms

See panel opposite

182 Talbot Inn

10 Pwll Rd, Llanelli, Carmarthenshire SA15 4AP

☎ 01554 773842

Real Ales, Bar Food, Restaurant Menu,
No Smoking Area

183 Telegraph Inn

See panel opposite

184 Temple Bar Inn

See panel below

185 Three Compasses

Crwbin, Kidwelly, Carmarthenshire SA17 5DR

☎ 01269 871030

Bar Food, Restaurant Menu, No Smoking Area

---

184 Temple Bar Inn

Carmel, Llanelli, Carmarthenshire SA14 7UF

☎ 01269 844535

🌐 www.templebarinn.co.uk

Bar Food, Restaurant Menu, No Smoking Area

The Temple Bar Inn is a spacious and attractive place run by Chris and Sue Powles. A good range of beers, lagers, cider, stout, wines, spirits and soft drinks – something to quench every thirst. This excellent inn serves up a good range of tasty dishes – everything from simple snacks to hearty daily specials – made using the freshest locally-sourced produce. Chris looks after the ales, while Sue does the cooking, whipping up expertly prepared and presented dishes for guests to savour.

The interior is cosy and welcoming, while outside guests can enjoy a relaxing drink or meal on fine days. The atmosphere is always friendly and informal, with Sue, Chris and their conscientious staff making sure all of their guests receive the best in service and hospitality.

🖝 Off the A476 (which is off the A48/J49 of the M4), northeast of Llanelli

🍴 12-2.30 & 6-9 (eves only in winter)

🎵 Occasional live music, quiz Mon from 9 p.m.

⚓ Parking, garden, disabled access

🕐 12-3 & 6-11 (Sun and Bank Holidays to 10.30)

🏛 Llanelli 17 miles, Gorslas 3 miles, Ammanford 8 miles

186 Three Horseshoes Inn

Cenarth, Newcastle Emlyn,
Carmarthenshire SA38 9JL
☎ 01239 710119
Real Ales, Restaurant Menu, No Smoking Area

187 Three Rivers Hotel and Spa

Ferryside, Carmarthenshire SA17 5TU
☎ 01267 267270
Bar Food, Restaurant Menu, Accommodation,
No Smoking Area

188 The Torbay Inn

27 Heol Cennen Ffairfach, Llandeilo,
Carmarthenshire SA19 6UL
☎ 01558 823140
Real Ales, Bar Food, Restaurant Menu,
No Smoking Area

189 Towy Bridge Inn

Rhandirmwyn, nr Llandovery,
Carmarthenshire SA20 0PE
☎ 01550 760370
Real Ales, Bar Food, Restaurant Menu

Cosy and compact, the Towy Bridge Inn is a
charming place to enjoy a drink or meal. A good
choice of home-cooked dishes are served
alongside the range of ales, and the décor and
atmosphere are simply delightful. Seating to the
front overlooks the beautiful surrounding
countryside and the river.

☛ Off the A483 north of Llandovery

🍺 2 rotating guest ales

🍴 12-3 & 6-9 (Easter-end Oct)

🅿 Parking, outdoor seating

🕐 Easter-end Oct: 12-3.30 & 6-11 (Sun and
Bank Holidays to 10.30); winter: evenings
only

🏛 Cilycwm 1½ miles, Llandovery 5 miles,
Llangadog 8 miles

190 Tregib Arms

39 Cwmgarw Road, Brynamman, Ammanford,
Carmarthenshire SA18 1BG
☎ 01269 823290

Bar Food, Restaurant Menu, Accommodation,
No Smoking Area

Here at the natural gateway to the Brecon
Beacons National Park, in the foothills of the Black
Mountains (the village's name means 'hill by the
River Amman'), the Tregib Arms is a pristine, warm
and welcoming inn with great food, drink and
accommodation. Husband-and-wife team Michael

and Edna Townend and their friendly staff offer all
their guests genuine hospitality and excellent
service. With real ales on tap together with lager,
cider, stout, wines, spirits and soft drinks there's
something to quench every thirst. Home-cooked
traditional Welsh fare is the order of the day here,
with tasty steaks among the many popular dishes
served. The accommodation is spacious and
attractively decorated, and the village makes a good
base from which to explore the range of natural
and man-made beauties throughout the region.

☛ 8½ miles southeast of Llandeilo on the
A4069

🍴 summer: see opening times; winter: Thurs/
Fri/Sat 6-9.30, Sun 12-2.30

🛏 3 rooms (2 en suite, 1 with private
bathroom)

🎵 Quiz Sun from 8.30 p.m.

🅿 Parking, garden, disabled access

💳 All major cards

🕐 Mon-Sat 6-11 p.m., Sun 12-3 & 7.00-10.30

🏛 Brecon Beacons National Park ½ mile,
Golden Grove 5 miles, Carreg Cennen
Castle 6 miles

190 Tregib Arms

See panel opposite

191 Waunwyllt Inn

Horeb Rd, Five Rds, Llanelli,
Carmarthenshire SA15 5AQ
☎ 01269 860209
Real Ales, Bar Food, Restaurant Menu,
No Smoking Area

192 The White Hall Hotel

High St, Llandovery, Carmarthenshire SA20 0PU
☎ 01550 721139
Real Ales, Bar Food, Restaurant Menu,
Accommodation, No Smoking Area

193 The White Hart

Cenarth, Newcastle Emlyn,
Carmarthenshire SA38 9JL
☎ 01239 710305
Real Ales, Bar Food, Restaurant Menu,
No Smoking Area

194 White Hart Inn

36 Carmarthen Rd, Llandeilo,
Carmarthenshire SA19 6RS
☎ 01558 823419
Real Ales, Bar Food, Restaurant Menu,
Accommodation, No Smoking Area

195 The White Hart Thatched Inn & Brewery

Llanddarog, Carmarthen,
Carmarthenshire SA32 8NT
☎ 01267 275395
Real Ales, Bar Food, Restaurant Menu,
No Smoking Area

196 White Horse Inn

Rhosmaen St, Llandeilo,
Carmarthenshire SA19 6EN
☎ 01558 822424
Real Ales

197 The White Lion Hotel

The Square, Ferryside,
Carmarthenshire SA17 5RW
☎ 01267 267214
Bar Food, Accommodation, No Smoking Area

198 The White Lion Inn

60 Pemberton Rd, Llanelli,
Carmarthenshire SA14 9BG
☎ 01554 757841
Real Ales

199 The White Lion Inn

Pwlltrap, St Clears, Carmarthen,
Carmarthenshire SA33 4AT
☎ 01994 230370
Real Ales, Bar Food, Restaurant Menu,
No Smoking Area

200 White Lion Inn

Causeway St, Kidwelly, Carmarthenshire SA17 4SU
☎ 01554 890313
Real Ales

201 The White Mill Inn

White Mill, Carmarthen,
Carmarthenshire SA32 7EN
☎ 01267 290239
Real Ales, Bar Food, Restaurant Menu,
Accommodation, No Smoking Area

202 Ye Olde Red Lion

5 Heol-Y-Plas, Llannon, Llanelli,
Carmarthenshire SA14 6AD
☎ 01269 841276
Bar Food, Restaurant Menu, No Smoking Area

203 Yr Hen Vic

82 New Rd, Llandeilo, Carmarthenshire SA19 6DF
☎ 01558 822596
Real Ales, Bar Food, Restaurant Menu,
No Smoking Area

CEREDIGION

ABERYSTWYTH • CARDIGAN • LAMPETER

The county of Ceredigion was once part of Dyfed (along with Pembrokeshire and Carmarthenshire); before that it was known as Cardiganshire or *Sir Aberteifi* in Welsh. It is a coastal county, bordered by Cardigan Bay to the west, Gwynedd to the north, Powys to the east, Carmarthenshire to the south, and Pembrokeshire to the southwest. The name Ceredigion means 'Land of Ceredig', who was a son of Cunedda, a Celtic chieftain who re-conquered much of Wales from the Irish around the 5th century AD.

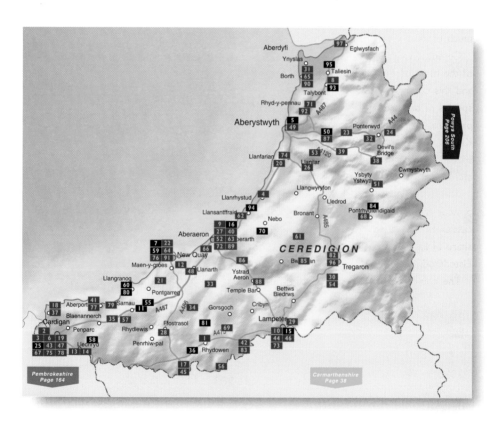

█1█ Ceredigion Reference Number - Detailed Information

12 Ceredigion Reference Number - Summary Entry

Ceredigion Page 249 ▶ Adjacent area - refer to pages indicated

The Cambrian Mountains cover much of the east of the county. In the south and west, the surface is less elevated. The highest point is Plynlimon at 2,486 feet, where five rivers have their source: the Severn, the Wye, the Dulas, the Llyfnant and the Rheidol, the last of which meets the Mynach in a 300-foot plunge at the Devil's Bridge chasm. The 50 miles of coastline has many sandy beaches. The chief river is the Teifi, which forms the border with Carmarthenshire and Pembrokeshire for much of its length.

Ceredigion's countryside features some of the most beautiful landscapes in Wales, and this county also attracts many rare species of bird, wildlife and plants. In particular it is home to the graceful Red Kite, and keen bird-watchers are well served by nature reserves around the Teifi and Dyfi estuaries and at Llangrannog, New Quay and Cors Caron.

Devil's Bridge Falls

The patron saint of Wales, St David, was born in Ceredigion and many famous Welsh princes are buried in the ruins of Strata Florida Abbey. Though not as well endowed with castles as the counties further north, both Aberystwyth and Cardigan castles saw their share of fighting, and Cardigan is credited with being the venue for the first recorded Eisteddfod, in 1176.

The county is justly famed for its coastline and the great sweep of Cardigan Bay. Many of the former fishing villages have now become genteel resorts. In the north of the county and close to the mouth of the River Dyfi is the great expanse of sand at Borth while, further south, the coastline gives way to cliffs and coves.

Other places of special interest include the Ceredigion Museum in Aberystwyth, the Vale of Rheidol Railway, the Welsh Gold Centre at Tregaron and the Llywernog Silver Lead Mine.

Coracle Fisherman

65

1 Alltyrodyn Arms

Rhydowen, Llandysul, Ceredigion SA44 4QB

☎ 01545 590319

Real Ales, Bar Food, Restaurant Menu,
No Smoking Area

2 Angel Hotel Ltd

36-40 St Marys St, Cardigan, Ceredigion SA43 1ET

☎ 01239 612561

Real Ales, Bar Food, Restaurant Menu,
Accommodation, No Smoking Area

3 Bell Hotel

4 Pendre, Cardigan, Ceredigion SA43 1JL

☎ 01239 612629

Real Ales, Bar Food, Restaurant Menu,
Accommodation, No Smoking Area

4 The Black Lion

Llanrhystud, Ceredigion SY23 5DG

☎ 01974 202338

Real Ales, Bar Food, Restaurant Menu,
Accommodation, No Smoking Area

5 The Black Lion

See panel below

6 The Black Lion Hotel

High St, Cardigan, Ceredigion SA43 1HJ

☎ 01239 612532

Real Ales, Bar Food, Restaurant Menu,
Accommodation, No Smoking Area

7 The Black Lion Hotel

See panel opposite

8 The Black Lion Hotel

The Square, Talybont, Ceredigion SY24 5ER

☎ 01970 832335

Real Ales, Bar Food, Restaurant Menu,
Accommodation, No Smoking Area

9 Black Lion Hotel

Alban Square, Aberaeron, Ceredigion SA46 0AJ

☎ 01545 571382

Real Ales, Bar Food, Restaurant Menu,
No Smoking Area

5 The Black Lion

Llanbadarn Fawr, Aberystwyth,
Ceredigion SY23 3RA

☎ 01970 623448

Real Ales, Bar Food

Dating back to the late 1700s, The Black Lion is spacious and welcoming. A wealth of traditional features such as the exposed ceiling beams and warm woods add to the inn's comfort and traditional ambience.

Tenant 'Dicky' Dickinson is ably assisted by his loyal staff – Mandy, Neil, Sugg, Charlene and Val – who offer all their guests great service and hospitality. A selection of real ales are complemented by a good choice of lagers, cider, stout, wines, spirits and soft drinks.

Varied dishes reflect the changing seasons and use the freshest locally-sourced ingredients. There's a separate no-smoking restaurant area within the inn's function room, open for diners only in the evenings.

Outside, there's a secure beer garden and children's play area.

☛ 1 mile east of Aberystwyth on the A44

🍺 Banks Bitter, Banks Original, Marstons Pedigree

🍴 Thurs-Sun 12-2 & Thurs-Sat 6-8

🎵 Quiz Fri night, occasional live music Sat night

🅿 Parking, garden, children's play area, disabled access

🕐 11.30-11 (Sun and Bank Holidays to 10.30)

🏛 Aberystwyth 1 mile, Borth 6 miles, Tre'r-ddol 10 miles, Devil's Bridge 10 miles

7 The Black Lion Hotel

Glanmor Terrace, New Quay,
Ceredigion SA45 9PT
☎ 01545 560209
⊞ www.blacklionnewquay.co.uk

Real Ales, Bar Food, Restaurant Menu,
Accommodation, No Smoking Area

Built in 1620, The Black Lion Hotel has a long and proud history of offering food, drink and shelter to weary travellers. This Free House is owned and personally run by Carol and Dave Bellamy, who have been in the licensing trade for more than 30

years. Their experience shows in the high standard of quality and service provided. Handsome and traditional throughout, there's also a superb garden overlooking the coastline where guests can enjoy a drink or meal on fine days. The separate no-smoking restaurant seats 30. Here guests choose from the menu or specials board for specialities that include home-made steak and ale pie, Cajun chicken and mushroom stroganoff. The Sunday lunch is justly popular. Booking required at weekends.

☛ On the A486 and off the main A487, 5 miles southwest of Aberaeron

🍺 Double Dragon, rotating guest ale

🍴 opening - 9.30 (Sun 9 p.m.)

🛏 6 en suite rooms, 2 with private bath

🎵 Live music Fri/Sat from 9.30 p.m.

⛁ Parking, garden

🚫 Not Amex

🕐 summer: 11.30-11; winter: Mon-Fri 5-11 (Sun and Bank Holidays to 10.30)

🏛 Llanina 1 mile, Cross Inn 2 miles, Aberaeron 5 miles, Aberarth 6 miles, Llanaeron 6 miles

---

10 Black Lion Royal Hotel

High St, Lampeter, Ceredigion SA48 7BG
☎ 01570 422172
Real Ales, Bar Food, Restaurant Menu,
Accommodation, No Smoking Area

11 The Brynhoffnant Inn

See panel on page 68

12 Cambrian Hotel

New Rd, New Quay, Ceredigion SA45 9SE
☎ 01545 560295
Real Ales, Bar Food, Restaurant Menu,
Accommodation, No Smoking Area

13 Carpenters Arms

Llechryd, Cardigan, Ceredigion SA43 2NT
☎ 01239 682692
Real Ales, Bar Food, Restaurant Menu,
Accommodation, No Smoking Area

14 Castell Malgwyn Hotel

Llechryd, Cardigan, Ceredigion SA43 2QA
☎ 01239 682382
Real Ales, Bar Food, Restaurant Menu,
Accommodation, No Smoking Area

15 The Castle Hotel

See panel on page 69

16 Castle Hotel

See panel on page 68

17 Cilgwyn Arms

Bridge St, Llandysul, Ceredigion SA44 4BA
☎ 01559 362506
Real Ales

18 Cliff Hotel

Gwbert-On-Sea, Cardigan, Ceredigion SA43 1PP
☎ 01239 613241
Real Ales, Bar Food, Restaurant Menu,
Accommodation, No Smoking Area

11   The Brynhoffnant Inn

Brynhoffnant, nr Llandysul, Ceredigion   SA44 6DU
☎ 01239 654961

Real Ales, Bar Food, Restaurant Menu, No Smoking Area

On the main coast road between Aberaeron and Cardigan, The Brynhoffnant Inn is a large and impressive inn dating back to 1860. Cosy and welcoming inside, it boasts low beamed ceilings, exposed stone walls and other traditional features. Justly popular with locals it is also a perfect place for visitors to the area to enjoy a relaxed drink or meal.

This Free House is owned by Colin and Fiona, who have been in the licensing trade for nearly 15 years. Fiona is the chef, creating a range of mouth-watering meals using locally-sourced produce including home-made beef lasagne, steak-and-kidney pie, chicken korma and nut roast.

Booking required at weekends. To the rear of the inn there's a secure garden and children's play area.

☞   On main A487, 10 miles northeast of Cardigan

🍺   Old Specked Hen, Buckleys Best, rotating guest ale

🍴   12-3 & 6-10

🎵   Occasional food-themed evenings

🅿   Parking, disabled access, garden

💳   Not Amex or Diners

🕐   12-11 (Sun and Bank Holidays to 10.30); Jan-Feb closed Mondays until 4 p.m.

🏛   Llangranog 2 miles, New Quay 8 miles, Cardigan 10 miles

16   Castle Hotel

Market Street, Aberaeron, Ceredigion   SA46 0AU
☎ 01545 570205

Real Ales, Bar Food, Restaurant Menu, Accommodation

Set within a short walk to the harbour and coast, the Castle Hotel is situated in the centre of Aberaeron. Run by David and Meinir since July of 2004, it's their first venture into the licensing trade and they're making quite a success of it. Attractive and welcoming, this large and spacious establishment boasts a wealth of warm woods in its décor and always has a friendly, relaxed ambience.

The restaurant is located upstairs and seats 60. The inn's talented and experienced chefs prepare a range of superb dishes including specialities such as steaks and fresh fish. Booking advised at all times.

The accommodation is comfortable and convenient for anyone wanting to explore this coastal region.

☞   On main A487, 5 miles north of New Quay

🍺   Hancocks HB, London Pride, rotating guest ale

🍴   Mon-Fri 12-9 throughout summer(occasionally during winter months)

🛏   6 en suite rooms

🎵   Occasional live entertainment

🅿   Parking, disabled access to the bar

💳   All the major cards

🕐   12-11 (Sun and Bank Holidays to 10.30) subject to changes

🏛   Aberarth 1 mile, Llannerch Aeron 3 miles, New Quay 5 miles

15 The Castle Hotel

High Street, Lampeter, Ceredigion SA48 7BG

☎ 01570 422554

Real Ales, Bar Food, Restaurant Menu, Accommodation, No Smoking Area

Relaxed and friendly, The Castle Hotel is a superb place in the heart of Lampeter. Owners John and Wendy Nicholas have over 15 years' experience in the trade, and it shows in the expert service and hospitality they and their staff offer. The food served includes home-made dishes, specialities such as sirloin steaks and a good selection of vegetarian dishes.

☛ Lampeter is at the crossroads of the A485, A482 and A475

🍺 Brains SA, Buckleys IPA and 2 rotating guest ales

🍴 Mon-Sat 11.30-2 & Mon-Fri 6.30-8.30

🛏 9 en suite rooms

🅿 Parking, some disabled access

💳 Not AMEX

🕐 11.30-11 (Sun and Bank Holidays to 10.30)

🏛 New Quay 14 miles, Cross Inn 12 miles, Capel Dewi 6 miles, Tregaron 8 miles

19 Commercial Hotel

50 Pendre, Cardigan, Ceredigion SA43 1JS

☎ 01239 612574

Real Ales

20 Conrah Country House Hotel

Chancery, Aberystwyth, Ceredigion SY23 4DF

☎ 01970 617941

Restaurant Menu, Accommodation, No Smoking Area

21 Crown Inn & Restaurant

Llwyndafydd, Llandysul, Ceredigion SA44 6BU

☎ 01545 560396

Real Ales, Bar Food, Restaurant Menu

22 Dolau Inn

Church St, New Quay, Ceredigion SA45 9NT

☎ 01545 560881

23 Druid Inn

Goginan, Aberystwyth, Ceredigion SY23 3NT

☎ 01970 880650

Real Ales, Bar Food, Restaurant Menu, Accommodation, No Smoking Area

24 Dyffryn Castell Hotel

Ponterwyd, Aberystwyth, Ceredigion SY23 3LB

☎ 01970 890237

Real Ales, Bar Food, Restaurant Menu, Accommodation, No Smoking Area

25 The Eagle Inn

See panel on page 70

26 The Falcon Inn

Llanilar, Aberystwyth, Ceredigion SY23 4PA

☎ 01974 241633

Real Ales, Bar Food, Restaurant Menu, No Smoking Area

27 Feathers Royal

Aberaeron, Ceredigion SA46 0AQ

☎ 01545 571740

Real Ales, Bar Food, Restaurant Menu, Accommodation, No Smoking Area

28 Ffostrasol Arms

Ffostrasol, Llandysul, Ceredigion SA44 4SY

☎ 01239 851348

Real Ales, Bar Food, Restaurant Menu, No Smoking Area

29 Fishers Arms

Cellan, Lampeter, Ceredigion SA48 8HU

☎ 01570 422895

Real Ales, Bar Food, Restaurant Menu, No Smoking Area

30 Foelallt Arms

Llanddewi Brefi, Tregaron, Ceredigion SY25 6RL

☎ 01974 298306

Real Ales, Bar Food, Restaurant Menu, Accommodation, No Smoking Area

31 Friendship Inn

High St, Borth, Ceredigion SY24 5JA

☎ 01970 871213

Real Ales, No Smoking Area

25 The Eagle Inn

Castle Street, Cardigan,
Carmarthenshire SA43 3AA

☎ 01239 612046

Real Ales, Bar Food, Restaurant Menu,
No Smoking Area

A Free House dating back to the late 1700s, The Eagle Inn in Cardigan is reached via the Cardigan Bridge from Cardigan Castle.

The inn boasts lots of character and charm, with a wealth of exposed beamwork and brasses adding to the traditional and cosy ambience.

Run by the Phillips family since 2002, the inn has a relaxed and friendly atmosphere all the time. The real ales on tap are complemented by a good range of wines, spirits, lagers, cider, stout and soft drinks.

The separate restaurant seats 30, with a menu of traditional favourites including home-made steak-and-kidney pie, beef curry, mixed grills, local salmon and more.

Roasts are added to the menu for Sunday lunch. Booking advised.

- ☛ 5 minutes' walk from the centre of Cardigan
- 🍺 Reverend James, Buckleys Best
- 🍴 12-9
- 🎵 Live entertainment Sat from 9 p.m.
- ♿ Parking, disabled access
- 🕐 11.30-11 (Sun to 10.30, Bank Holidays 11-Midnight)
- 🏛 Cardigan Heritage Centre next door, Gwbert-on-Sea 2½ miles, Mwnt 3½ miles

32 The George Borrow Hotel

Ponterwyd, Aberystwyth, Ceredigion SY23 3AD

☎ 01970 890230

Bar Food, Restaurant Menu, Accommodation,
No Smoking Area

33 Gilfach Inn

Mydroilyn, Lampeter, Ceredigion SA48 7QY

☎ 01545 580763

Bar Food, No Smoking Area

34 Glanyrafon Arms

Talgarreg, Llandysul, Ceredigion SA44 4ER

☎ 01545 590695

Real Ales, Bar Food, Accommodation,
No Smoking Area

35 Gogerddan Arms

Tanygroes, Cardigan, Ceredigion SA43 2HP

☎ 01239 810784

Real Ales, Bar Food, Restaurant Menu,
No Smoking Area

36 The Gwarcefel Arms

Prengwyn, Llandysul, Ceredigion SA44 4LU

☎ 01559 362720

Real Ales, Bar Food, Restaurant Menu,
No Smoking Area

- ☛ Adjacent to the A475 about 10 miles west of Lampeter
- 🍺 3 rotating guest ales
- 🍴 Mon-Sun 12-2.30 & Sun-Fri 6.30-9.30, Sat 6.30-10
- 🎵 Occasional live music
- ♿ Parking, disabled access
- 💳 Not AMEX
- 🕐 11.30-11 (Sun and Bank Holidays to 10.30)
- 🏛 Llandysul 5 miles, Capel Dewi 6 miles, Lampeter 10 miles, New Quay 15 miles

37 Gwbert Hotel

Cardigan, Ceredigion SA43 1PP

☎ 01239 612638

Real Ales, Bar Food, Restaurant Menu,
Accommodation, No Smoking Area

38 Hafod Arms Hotel

Devils Bridge, Aberystwyth, Ceredigion SY23 3JL

☎ 01970 890232

Real Ales, Bar Food, Restaurant Menu,
Accommodation, No Smoking Area

39 Halfway Inn

Devils Bridge Rd, Pisgah, Aberystwyth,
Ceredigion SY23 4NE

☎ 01970 880631

Real Ales, Bar Food, Restaurant Menu,
Accommodation, No Smoking Area

40 Harbour Master Hotel

Quay Parade, Aberaeron, Ceredigion SA46 0BT

☎ 01545 570755

Real Ales, Bar Food, Restaurant Menu,
Accommodation, No Smoking Area

41 Highcliffe Hotel & Restaurant

Aberporth, Cardigan, Ceredigion SA43 2DA

☎ 01239 810534

Bar Food, Restaurant Menu, Accommodation,
No Smoking Area

42 Highmead Arms Hotel

Llanwenog, Llanybydder, Ceredigion SA40 9SP

☎ 01570 480258

Bar Food, Restaurant Menu, No Smoking Area

43 Hope And Anchor

51 Pendre, Cardigan, Ceredigion SA43 1JS

☎ 01239 612337

Real Ales, Bar Food

44 Ivy Bush Inn

1 High St, Lampeter, Ceredigion SA48 7BA

☎ 01570 423058

Real Ales

45 Kings Arms Hotel

High St, Llandysul, Ceredigion SA44 4DL

☎ 01559 362265

Real Ales, Bar Food, Restaurant Menu,
Accommodation, No Smoking Area

46 Kings Head Inn

14 Bridge St, Lampeter, Ceredigion SA48 7HG

☎ 01570 422598

Real Ales, Bar Food, Restaurant Menu

47 Lamb Inn

4 Finchs Square, Cardigan, Ceredigion SA43 1BS

☎ 01239 613276

Accommodation

48 Llanina Hotel

Llanarth, Ceredigion SA47 0NP

☎ 01545 580732

Real Ales, Bar Food, Restaurant Menu,
Accommodation, No Smoking Area

49 Lletygwyn Hotel

Llanbadarn Fawr, Aberystwyth,
Ceredigion SY23 3SR

☎ 01970 623965

Restaurant Menu, Accommodation,
No Smoking Area

50 Maes Bangor Arms

See panel on page 72

51 Miners Arms

Pontrhydygroes, Pontrhydfendigaid, Ystrad Meurig,
Ceredigion SY25 6DN

☎ 01974 282238

Real Ales, Bar Food, Restaurant Menu,
No Smoking Area

52 Monachty Arms Hotel

7 Market St, Aberaeron, Ceredigion SA46 0AS

☎ 01545 570389

Real Ales, Bar Food, Restaurant Menu,
Accommodation, No Smoking Area

50　Maes Bangor Arms

Capel Bangor, Aberystwyth, Ceredigion SY23 3LT
☎ 01970 880923

Real Ales, Bar Food, Restaurant Menu, No Smoking Area

The Maes Bangor Arms is an impressive place dating back to the mid-1700s, with a wealth of traditional features such as the stonebuilt fireplace and exposed stonebuilt walls. Memorabilia adorns the walls, much of it donated by guests. Outside, there's a newly constructed beer garden – just the place to enjoy a relaxing drink or meal on fine days. Cosy and welcoming, the pub provides good food, drink and warm hospitality. Owners Neil and Sandra Lewis have been here since 2003, after having managed another public house in Aberystwyth for the previous three-and-a-half years. Their experience shows in the high standard of service and hospitality they offer all their guests. Neil does the cooking, creating an extensive menu of tempting dishes including specialities such as Welsh Black steaks. Booking is advised at weekends.

☛ Adjacent to the A44 a few miles east of Aberystwyth

🍺 1 from the Felinfoel Brewery and a rotating guest ale

🍴 summer: daily 12-9; winter: daily 12-2 & 6.30-9

🎵 Charity events throughout the year

🅿 Parking, disabled access, garden

🕐 summer: 12-11; winter: 12-3 & 6-11 (Sun and Bank Holidays to 10.30)

🏛 Aberystwyth, Borth Animalarium 5 miles, Ynyslas Sand Dunes and Visitor Centre 7 miles

55　The New Inn

Pentregat, Llandysul, Ceredigion SA44 5PT
☎ 01239 654285

Real Ales, Bar Food, Restaurant Menu, No Smoking Area

The New Inn is a spacious and welcoming Free House with two restaurants (both no smoking). Owners Ian and Tracey Gunn and their children have been here for several years now, having traded the hustle and bustle of London life for this scenic and tranquil part of Wales. Known near and far for the quality of the dishes served here, booking is advised at all times during the summer months, and for Saturday evening and Sunday lunchtime all year round. The Sunday lunchtime carvery is justly popular and sets a very high standard that other inns will find hard to match. Everything from the sandwiches to daily specials like lemon schnitzel, teriyaki chicken and peppered steak are cooked and prepared to perfection. Thursday lunchtime hosts an over-60s club. The décor includes low beams and other attractive traditional features; the seating is comfortable and the atmosphere always relaxed and friendly.

☛ 12 miles north of Cardigan on the A487

🍺 Worthington Cask, Double Dragon

🍴 12-2 & 6-9

🅿 Parking, disabled access

💳 All the major cards

🕐 12-2.30 & 6-11 (Sun and Bank Holidays to 10.30)

🏛 Llandysul 15 miles, Henllan 10 miles, Newcastle Emlyn 6 miles, Cenarth Falls 10 miles

53 New Cross Inn

New Cross, Aberystwyth, Ceredigion SY23 4LY

☎ 01974 261526

Bar Food, Restaurant Menu

54 New Inn

Llanddewi Brefi, Tregaron, Ceredigion SY25 6RS

☎ 01974 298452

Real Ales, Accommodation

55 The New Inn

See panel opposite

56 The Old Railway Inn

Maesycrugiau, Pencader, Ceredigion SA39 9LL

☎ 01559 395339

Bar Food, Restaurant Menu, Accommodation, No Smoking Area

57 Penbontbren Farm Hotel

Glynarthen, Llandysul, Ceredigion SA44 6PE

☎ 01239 810248

Real Ales, Bar Food, Restaurant Menu, Accommodation, No Smoking Area

58 Penllwyn Du Inn

Llandeodmore, Cardigan SA43 2LY

☎ 01239 682533

Real Ales, Bar Food, Restaurant Menu, No Smoking Area

🠶 Off the B4570 3½ miles from Cardigan

🍺 Brains, Buckley Best

🍽 Fri-Sun 12-2

🅿 Parking, disabled access, garden

🕐 summer: 12-11; winter: 3.30-11 (Sun and Bank Holidays to 10.30)

🏛 Cardigan 3½ miles, Gwbert-on-Sea 5 miles, Mwnt 6 miles, Felinwynt Rainforest and Butterfly Centre 10 miles

59 Penrhiwllan Inn

See panel below

60 The Pentre Arms

See panel on page 74

59 Penrhiwllan Inn

Llandysul Road, New Quay, Ceredigion SA45 9RF

☎ 01545 560471

🌐 www.therestaurantnewquay.com

Real Ales, Bar Food, Restaurant Menu, No Smoking Area

Set along the main road on the outskirts of New Quay, the Penrhiwllan Inn is a large and spacious inn with an enviable reputation for the quality of its food. The interior décor at this Free House is modern and elegant, with polished wood floors, seating in pale woods and delicate pastel

paintwork in the restaurant area, while the bar is altogether more traditional in feel, with exposed beam- and stonework and flagstone floors. The ever-changing menus feature tempting delights such as hot Mermaid salad (a warm salad with seared scallops, Welsh bacon and polenta), poached fillet of salmon, fruity tuna, locally-reared beef with apples and lamb with couscous and apricot sauce, all expertly cooked by the inn's accomplished chef. Booking required at weekends.

🠶 On the A486 on the edge of New Quay

🍺 Bass, Double Dragon

🍽 Tues-Sat 6.30-9.30; Sun 1-5

🎵 Live entertainment Fri from 8 p.m.

🅿 Parking, garden, disabled access

💳 Not Amex or Diners

🕐 12-11 (Sun and Bank Holidays to 10.30)

🏛 New Quay, Llanina 1 mile, Cross Inn 2 miles, Aberaeron 5 miles, Aberarth 6 miles, Llanaeron 6 miles

60 The Pentre Arms

Llangrannog, Ceredigion SA44 6SP
☎ 01239 654345

Real Ales, Bar Food, Restaurant Menu,
Accommodation, No Smoking Area

Built of local slate and stone and set right on the coast (it's the inn closest to the sea in all of Ceredigion), The Pentre Arms is owned and personally run by Mike Rutherford, a talented and experienced chef.

Here at this attractive and traditional inn,

guests choose off the menu or daily specials board from an excellent variety of dishes to suit all tastes. Specialities include fresh fish in season. Justly popular with locals and visitors alike, the inn has a warm and welcoming ambience. There is a non-smoking dining room.

The neighbouring cliffs and headlands of the picturesque resort of Llangrannog provide stunning views and exhilarating walks, and the inn boasts nine comfortable guest bedrooms for bed and breakfast, some overlooking the beach and sea, to use as a base while exploring the region.

- ☛ 12½ miles northeast of Cardigan on the B4334
- 🍺 Choice of Real Ales
- 🍽 12-2.00 & 6-9
- ⊨ 9 guest bedrooms
- 🅿 Parking, disabled access
- 💳 All major cards
- 🕐 12-11 (Sun to 10.30)
- 🏛 Aberporth 4 miles, Felinwynt 4 miles, Gwbert-on-Sea 8 miles, Cardigan 12½ miles

---

61 Penuwch Inn

Penuwch, Tregaron, Ceredigion SY25 6RA
☎ 01974 821318
Real Ales, Bar Food, Restaurant Menu,
No Smoking Area

62 Plas-Morfa Hotel

Llanon, Ceredigion SY23 5LX
☎ 01974 202415
Real Ales, Restaurant Menu, Accommodation,
No Smoking Area

63 Prince Of Wales

1 Queen St, Aberaeron, Ceredigion SA46 0BY
☎ 01545 570366
Bar Food, Restaurant Menu, No Smoking Area

64 Queens Hotel

Church St, New Quay, Ceredigion SA45 9NZ
☎ 01545 560650
Real Ales, Bar Food

65 The Railway Hotel

High St, Borth, Ceredigion SY24 5JE
☎ 01970 871348
Real Ales, Bar Food, Restaurant Menu,
No Smoking Area

66 Red Lion

Ffosyffin, Aberaeron, Ceredigion SA46 0HA
☎ 01545 570300
Bar Food, Restaurant Menu, No Smoking Area

67 Red Lion

Pwllhai, Cardigan, Ceredigion SA43 1DD
☎ 01239 612482
Real Ales, Bar Food, Restaurant Menu,
Accommodation, No Smoking Area

68 Red Lion Hotel

Pontrhydfendigaid, Ystrad Meurig,
Ceredigion SY25 6BH
☎ 01974 831232
Real Ales, Bar Food, Restaurant Menu,
Accommodation

69 Red Lion Inn

Cwrtnewydd, Llanybydder, Ceredigion SA40 9YN

☎ 01570 434302

Real Ales, Bar Food, Restaurant Menu,
Accommodation, No Smoking Area

70 Rhos Yr Hafod - The Cross Inn

See panel below

71 Rhydypennau Inn

Bow St, Ceredigion SY24 5AA

☎ 01970 828308

Real Ales, Bar Food, Restaurant Menu,
No Smoking Area

72 Royal Oak

North Rd, Aberaeron, Ceredigion SA46 0JG

☎ 01545 570233

Real Ales, Bar Food, No Smoking Area

73 The Royal Oak Hotel

High St, Lampeter, Ceredigion SA48 7BB

☎ 01570 423174

Real Ales, Bar Food, Restaurant Menu,
Accommodation, No Smoking Area

74 Royal Oak Inn

Llanfarian, Aberystwyth, Ceredigion SY23 4BS

☎ 01970 639403

Real Ales, Bar Food, Restaurant Menu,
Accommodation

75 The Schooner

21 High St, Cardigan, Ceredigion SA43 1JG

☎ 01239 613071

Bar Food, No Smoking Area

76 Seahorse Inn

Uplands Square, New Quay, Ceredigion SA45 9QH

☎ 01545 560736

Real Ales

70 Rhos Yr Hafod – The Cross Inn

Llanon, Ceredigion SY23 5NB

☎ 01974 272644

⊕ www.rhos-yr-hafod-inn.co.uk

Real Ales, Bar Food, No Smoking Area

Family-run by Robert and Julia Nicholls and their son Dai, who is an experienced professional chef, Rhos Yr Hafod is a spacious and handsome pub with a warm and friendly atmosphere. This Free House dates back to the early 1800s with later additions, and offers a high standard of food, drink and hospitality. It makes for a relaxed and very welcome place to stop for a break while exploring the coast and other attractions of the area. Creative dishes such as cashew nut paella and Stilton and vegetable crumble sit alongside traditional favourites like steak and kidney pudding and sausage and mash on the excellent menu. Dai uses local produce wherever possible and special diets and requests are happily catered for. Children welcome.

☛ The village of Cross Inn is on the B5477 about 4 miles west of the A487 and 12.5 miles north of New Quay

🍺 Boddingtons plus rotating guest ales

🍴 As per opening hours but no food Sun eves

🎵 Fortnightly quiz Sun, monthly live entertainment – ring for details

⚒ Parking, garden, disabled access

🕐 summer: Mon 6-11, Tues-Sat 12-2 & 6-11 (Sun and Bank Holidays to 10.30); winter: Tues-Sat 6-11 (Sun and Bank Holidays to 10.30)

🏛 Aberaeron 5 miles, New Quay 12.5 miles, Llanrhystud 5 miles

81 Tafarn Bach

Pontsian, Llandysul, Cardigan SA44 4TZ
☎ 01545 590269

Real Ales, Bar Food, Restaurant Menu, No Smoking Area

Tafarn Bach is an absolutely charming country inn dating back to the early 19th century but recently refurbished to create a happy mix of traditional and modern features.

Built into the side of a hill, areas of exposed rockface can be glimpsed behind and beside the

bar, adding to the rustic feel of this fine inn. Cosy and comfortable, the inn is run by husband-and-wife team Julia and Dorian Davies, who have been here since 2003.

Dorian looks after the well-kept ales while Julia does the cooking, creating a good selection of fresh dishes including specialities such as Welsh lamb chops.

The Sunday roasts are justly popular. Upstairs there's a large function suite, perfect for family gatherings and celebrations.

☛ Off the A475 exiting Lampeter

🍺 Brains Smooth

🍴 as opening hours

🎵 Occasional live music

♨ Parking, garden, patio, disabled access

🕐 Mon-Tues 5-11, Weds-Sat 12-11, Sun and Bank Holidays 12-10.30

🏛 Lampeter 5 miles, Llandysul 5 miles, Llanarth 12 miles

84 The Teifi Inn

Ffair Rhos, Ystrad Meurig, Ceredigion SY25 6BP
☎ 01974 831608

Real Ales, Bar Food, Restaurant Menu

The Teifi Inn dates back to the 12th century, and was once used as a watering hole for passing monks. Set in the pretty hamlet of Ffair Rhos, this distinctive Free House is run by Jacky – known by everyone as Blodwen – who has been here since June of 2004. Spacious and attractive, this traditional inn has a large stonebuilt open fire, exposed beamwork and a fascinating collection of

ceramic tankards adorning the ceiling. Real ales are complemented by a good selection of other thirst-quenchers including lagers, cider, stout, wines, spirits, soft drinks and hot beverages.

Guests choose off the menu and daily specials board from a good variety of hot and cold dishes, prepared with the freshest local iingredients. Booking advised at all times.

☛ Just off the B4343 and not far off the B4340, about 12 miles southeast of Aberystwyth

🍺 Reverend James and a rotating guest ale

🍴 Thurs, Fri & Sat evening 6.30-9, Sun lunch 12-2

🎵 Live entertainment third Sat of the month

♨ Parking

🚫 Not Amex

🕐 6-11 Mon, Wed - Sat, 12 -3 Sat & Sun (Bank Holidays to 10.30)

🏛 Devil's Bridge 8 miles, Tregaron 8 miles, Aberystwyth 12 miles, Strata Florida Monastry 1 mile, Fishing permits supplied for Teifi Pools ½mile.

77 Ship Hotel

West St, Aberporth, Cardigan,
Ceredigion SA43 2DB
☎ 01239 810822
Real Ales, Bar Food

78 Ship Inn

1 Pendre, Cardigan, Ceredigion SA43 1JL
☎ 01239 614840
Real Ales, Bar Food

79 Ship Inn

Tresaith, Cardigan, Ceredigion SA43 2JL
☎ 01239 810380
Real Ales, Bar Food, Restaurant Menu,
Accommodation

80 The Ship Inn

Llangrannog, Ceredigion SA44 6SL
☎ 01239 654423
Real Ales, Bar Food, Restaurant Menu, No
Smoking Area

Set by the water's edge and against an impressive
backdrop of hills, The Ship Inn is a large and
pristine pub built of local slate and stone. With
lots of old-world character and charm, the inn
makes a welcoming place to enjoy a relaxed drink
and dishes from the comprehensive menu
including fresh fish, steaks and tempting vegetarian
meals.

🖝 9½ miles northwest of Cardigan on the
B4334

🍺 Rotating guest ales

🍴 12-2.30 & 6-9

🎵 Occasional live entertainment – please ring
for details

🅿 Parking, disabled access

🚫 Not AMEX

🕐 11.30-11 (Sun and Bank Holidays to 10.30)

🏛 Aberporth 3 miles, Aberaeron 14 miles,
Cardigan 9½ miles

81 Tafarn Bach

See panel opposite

82 Talbot Hotel

The Square, Tregaron, Ceredigion SY25 6JL
☎ 01974 298208
Real Ales, Bar Food, Restaurant Menu,
Accommodation, No Smoking Area

83 Tanygraig Inn

Llanybydder, Ceredigion SA40 9XS
☎ 01570 480542
Real Ales

84 The Teifi Inn

See panel opposite

85 Three Horse Shoe Inn

Llangeitho, Tregaron, Ceredigion SY25 6TW
☎ 01974 821244
Real Ales, Bar Food, Restaurant Menu,
Accommodation, No Smoking Area

86 Tyglyn Hotel And Holiday Estate

Ciliau Aeron, Lampeter, Ceredigion SA48 8DD
☎ 01570 470625
Real Ales, Bar Food, Restaurant Menu,
Accommodation, No Smoking Area

87 Tynllidiart Arms

Capel Bangor, Aberystwyth, Ceredigion SY23 3LR
☎ 01970 880248
Real Ales, Bar Food, Restaurant Menu,
No Smoking Area

88 Vale Of Aeron Inn

Ystrad Aeron, Felinfach, Lampeter,
Ceredigion SA48 8AE
☎ 01570 470385
Real Ales, Bar Food, Restaurant Menu

89 Victoria Hotel

Victoria St, Aberaeron, Ceredigion SA46 0DA
☎ 01545 571838
Real Ales, Bar Food, Accommodation,
No Smoking Area

90 The Victoria Inn

High St, Borth, Ceredigion SY24 5HZ

☎ 01970 871417

Real Ales, Bar Food, Restaurant Menu, Accommodation, No Smoking Area

91 Wellington Inn

Wellington Place, New Quay,
Ceredigion SA45 9NR

☎ 01545 560245

Real Ales, Bar Food, Restaurant Menu, Accommodation

92 Welsh Black

Bow St, Ceredigion SY24 5AT

☎ 01970 828361

Real Ales, Bar Food, Restaurant Menu, Accommodation, No Smoking Area

93 White Lion Hotel

Talybont, Aberystwyth SY24 5ER

☎ 01970 832245

🌐 www.whitelionhoteldyfed.co.uk

Real Ales, Bar Food, Restaurant Menu, Accommodation, No Smoking Area

Dating back to the early 1800s, the White Lion Hotel offers real ales, good food and comfortable accommodation. Tenants Maureen and John are a friendly and hospitable couple who offer all their guests a warm welcome. Maureen does the cooking, creating a good variety of dishes, from sandwiches to steaks and other hearty favourites. Booking advised at all times.

☛ Talybont is on the A487, 7 miles N of Aberystwyth

🍺 Bass Mild, Banks Bitter and a rotating guest ale

🍴 12-3 & 6-10

🛏 4 en suite rooms

🎵 Evening of Welsh poetry, music and more once a month, Fri – ring for details

💳 All major cards

🕐 11.30-11 (Sun and Bank Holidays to 10.30)

🏛 Aberystwyth 7 miles, Machynlleth 11 miles

94 White Swan Inn

See panel opposite

95 The Wildfowler

Tre'r-ddol, Machynlleth, Powys SY20 8PN

☎ 01970 832000

🌐 www.thewildfowler.co.uk

Real Ales, Bar Food, No Smoking Area

The Wildfowler is a spacious and welcoming pub with traditional features such as exposed beamwork and brickwork that add to the pub's warmth and relaxed ambience. Tenants Chris and Michelle have been here since May of 2003, and have built up an enviable reputation for hospitality and the pub's cuisine. Chris, a professional chef, has been in catering for 18 years. Steaks are his speciality, and all meats are sourced locally.

☛ On main A487 south of Machynlleth

🍺 Greene King IPA plus rotating guest ale

🍴 Tues-Sun 12-2 & 6-9

🚗 Off-road car park, disabled access, garden

🕐 11.30-2.30 & 5-11; Sat 11.30-11 (Sun and Bank Holidays to 10.30). Closed Mon in winter

🏛 Coast 3 miles, Machynlleth 4 miles, Aberystwyth 8 miles

96 Y Llew-Coch

Tregaron, Ceredigion SY25 6HH

☎ 01974 298266

Real Ales, Bar Food, Accommodation

97 Ynyshir Hall Country House Hotel

Eglwysfach, Machynlleth, Ceredigion SY20 8TA

☎ 01654 781209

Restaurant Menu, Accommodation, No Smoking Area

94 White Swan Inn

Llanon, Ceredigion SY23 5HY

☎ 01974 202721

Real Ales, Bar Food, Restaurant Menu, No Smoking Area

The White Swan Inn is a friendly Free House run by local couple Arwyn and Helen Williams, who have been here for seven years and have made the pub a haven of hospitality.

Pristine and spacious, the inn is located in the coastal village of Llanon, well worth seeking out

for its convivial atmosphere. Real ale and a good selection of lagers, ciders, stout, wines, spirits and soft drinks quench every thirst, while the menu and specials board offer up a range of freshly prepared dishes.

To the rear of the premises, the restaurant is no-smoking an seats 60 in great comfort. Booking advised at all times in the summer months, and is essential all year round for the superb Sunday lunch. Children welcome.

☛ Llanon is on the coast, 5 miles north of Aberaeron just off the A487

🍺 Worthington Cask

🍴 Opening time-9.30

🎵 Pool table, darts

🅿 Parking, garden, disabled access

💳 All major cards

🕐 summer: 11.30-11 (Sun and Bank Holidays to 10.30); winter: 11.30-3 & 6-11 (Sun and Bank Holidays to 10.30)

🏛 Aberaeron 5 miles, New Quay 7 miles, Llanrhystud 5 miles

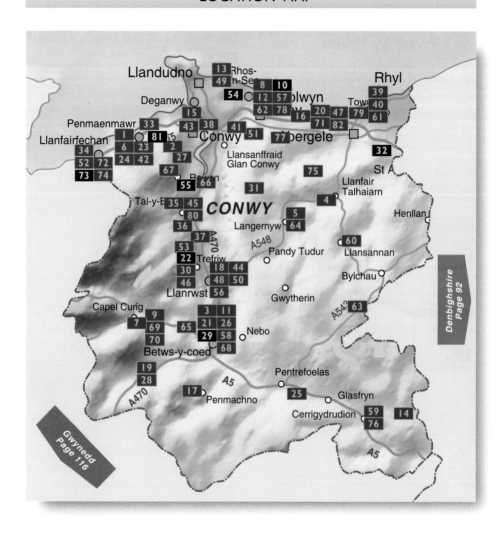

CONWY

LLANDUDNO • ABERGALE • BETWS-Y-COED

The north Wales county of Conwy contains the settlements of Llandudno, Betws-y-Coed, Conwy, Colwyn and Colwyn Bay, and has a total population of about 100,000. The River Conwy rises in Snowdonia and flows through Betws-y-Coed en route to the Irish Sea by Conwy Castle. The borough straddles the traditional area of Caernarfonshire and Denbighshire.

The coast of North Wales is a perennially popular stretch of British coastline that draws visitors in their thousands to its holiday resorts. This very traditional region, where Welsh is often still spoken on a daily basis, has many treasures, both man-made and natural, to discover. The coastline was once strewn with small fishing villages; with the coming of the railway, these villages expanded to accommodate visitors from the industrial towns of Lancashire. Not only were boarding houses and hotels built for the society visitors coming to take the sea air, but amusements and entertainment became regular features. Llandudno, always considered a 'cut above', retains much of its Victorian and Edwardian charm, while Colwyn Bay is a genteel place with many fine 19th-century buildings and an attractive promenade. It is also home to the Welsh Mountain Zoo, a conservation centre for rare and endangered species. At Abergele, five miles east of Colwyn Bay, the natural caverns of Cefn-Yr-Ogo offer magnificent views of the surrounding coastline.

At Llanfairfechan, seven miles northeast of Bangor, there's a long stretch of sandy beach amid stunning scenery, and a nature reserve at Traeth Lafan.

It was also here along the coast that Edward I built his Iron Ring of castles. While many are in ruins, Conwy Castle, now a World Heritage Site, is not only massive but was built in such a position that the surrounding land provides suitable protection from attack.

This county is also proud to be the setting for Bodnant Gardens (National Trust), laid out

by the second Lord Aberconway in 1875. The rhododendrons, camellias and magnolias are truly magnificent, while the summer herbaceous borders, roses and water lilies provide colour that continues into the autumn. Bodnant also boasts fountains, a laburnum arch, a lily terrace and a stepped pergola.

Conwy Castle

81

1 The Alexandra Hotel
High St, Penmaenmawr, Conwy LL34 6NF
☎ 01492 622484
Real Ales

2 Berthlwyd Hall
Llechwedd, Conwy LL32 8DQ
☎ 01492 592409
Bar Food, Accommodation, No Smoking Area

3 Best Western Waterloo Hotel
Betws-Y-Coed, Conwy LL24 0AR
☎ 01690 710411
Real Ales, Bar Food, Restaurant Menu,
Accommodation, No Smoking Area

4 Black Lion Hotel
Llanfairtalhaiarn, Abergele, Conwy LL22 8RY
☎ 01745 720205
Real Ales, Bar Food, Restaurant Menu,
No Smoking Area

5 The Bridge Inn
Llangernyw, Abergele, Conwy LL22 8PP
☎ 01745 860672
Bar Food, Restaurant Menu, No Smoking Area

6 Bron Eryri Hotel
Bangor Rd, Penmaenmawr, Conwy LL34 6AF
☎ 01492 623978
Real Ales

7 Bryn Tyrch Hotel
Capel Curig, Betws-Y-Coed, Conwy LL24 0EL
☎ 01690 720223
Real Ales, Bar Food, Restaurant Menu,
Accommodation, No Smoking Area

8 Cayley Arms
69 Rhos Promenade, Rhos On Sea, Colwyn Bay,
Conwy LL28 4EN
☎ 01492 546622
Real Ales, Bar Food, Restaurant Menu,
No Smoking Area

10 Conwy Vale Hotel

Llanrwst Road, Glan Conwy LL28 5SS
☎ 01492 580218

Real Ales, Bar Food, Restaurant Menu,
No Smoking Area

Pleasant and welcoming inside and out, The
Conwy Vale has a spacious bar well-stocked with
ales, wines, spirits and soft drinks and a good
menu and daily specials of tempting meals and
snacks. Specialities include chicken goujons in
sweet and sour sauce, and breaded chicken fillet.
The snacks include a good selection of tasty filled

baguettes. The handsome restaurant is intimate
and cosy – booking required Saturday evening and
Sunday lunchtime. There's also a second-floor
extra dining area known as The View Room for
the outstanding vista it offers over the River
Conwy towards Conwy Castle.

This very attractive inn is staffed by friendly
locals who make every effort to ensure that
guests enjoy the best of Welsh hospitality.
Children welcome.

☛ South off main A55, on the A470 toward
Betws-y-Coed

🍺 2 rotating guest ales

🍴 12-2.30 (to 3 p.m. summer) & Thurs-Sat 6-9

🎵 Mon quiz from 9.30 p.m.; snooker room;
occasional live entertainment

🚗 Car park, garden, children's play area, access
for people with disabilities

🚫 No smoking in restaurant

🕐 11.30-11 (Sun and Bank Holidays to 10.30)

🏛 Llandudno 2 miles, Bodnant Gardens 2 miles,
Colwyn Bay 4 miles

9 Cobdens Hotel

Capel Curig, Betws-Y-Coed, Conwy LL24 0EE

☎ 01690 720243

Real Ales, Restaurant Menu, Accommodation, No Smoking Area

10 Conwy Vale Hotel

See panel opposite

11 Cross Keys Hotel

Hollyhead Rd, Betws-Y-Coed, Conwy LL24 0BN

☎ 01690 710334

Bar Food, Restaurant Menu, Accommodation, No Smoking Area

12 The Cross Keys Inn

Llanrwst Rd, Glan Conwy, Colwyn Bay, Conwy LL28 5SS

☎ 01492 580292

Real Ales

13 Crosskeys Inn

Pendre Rd, Penrhynside, Llandudno, Conwy LL30 3DW

☎ 01492 546415

Real Ales, Bar Food

14 Crown Inn

Llanfihangel, Glyn Myfyr, Corwen, Conwy LL21 9UL

☎ 01490 420209

Real Ales, Bar Food

15 Deganwy Castle Hotel

Station Rd, Deganwy, Conwy LL31 9DA

☎ 01492 583555

Real Ales, Bar Food, Restaurant Menu, Accommodation, No Smoking Area

16 Dulas Arms

Abergele Rd, Llanddulas, Abergele, Conwy LL22 8HP

☎ 01492 515747

Real Ales, Bar Food, Accommodation, No Smoking Area

17 The Eagles

Penmachno, Betws-Y-Coed, Conwy LL24 0UG

☎ 01690 760177

Real Ales, Accommodation, No Smoking Area

18 Eagles Hotel

Ancaster Square, Llanrwst, Conwy LL26 0LG

☎ 01492 640454

Real Ales, Bar Food, Restaurant Menu, Accommodation, No Smoking Area

19 Elens Castle Hotel

Dolwyddelan, Conwy LL25 0EJ

☎ 01690 750207

Bar Food, Restaurant Menu, Accommodation, No Smoking Area

20 Fair View Inn

Abergele Rd, Llanddulas, Abergele, Conwy LL22 8HH

☎ 01492 515780

Real Ales, Bar Food, Restaurant Menu, No Smoking Area

21 Fairhaven Hotel

Holyhead Rd, Betws-Y-Coed, Conwy LL24 0AY

☎ 01690 710307

Restaurant Menu, Accommodation, No Smoking Area

22 Fairy Falls Hotel

See panel on page 84

23 Fairy Glen Inn

Conwy Old Rd, Penmaenmawr, Conwy LL34 6SP

☎ 01492 623107

Real Ales, Bar Food, Restaurant Menu, Accommodation, No Smoking Area

24 Gay Pennant Hall

Beach Rd, Penmaenmawr, Conwy LL34 6AY

☎ 01492 622878

Real Ales, Bar Food, Restaurant Menu, Accommodation, No Smoking Area

25 The Giler Arms Hotel

Rhydlydan Pentrefoelas, Betws-Y-Coed, Conwy LL24 0LL

☎ 01690 770612

Real Ales, Bar Food, Accommodation, No Smoking Area

22 Fairy Falls Hotel

Conwy Road, Trefriw LL27 0JH

☎ 01492 640250

Real Ales, Bar Food, Restaurant Menu,
Accommodation, No Smoking Area

Fairy Falls Hotel is a welcoming traditional inn
occupying a tranquil location in the lovely village
of Trefriw, and takes its name from the local
attraction reached via a footpath from Trefriw
Woollen Mill (in operation since the 1830s) and
the setting of a Roman spa and still offering
visitors a chance to take the waters. Dating back
in parts to the 1710, the inn offers quality food,

drink and accommodation. Real ales and a good
range of lagers, cider, stout, wines, spirits and soft
drinks are complemented by an excellent menu
and daily specials using locally-sourced ingredients.
Lunchtime and evening meals are served from
12.30 to 2.30 and 6 to 9. Booking advised for
Friday and Saturday evenings. Carvery lunch every
Sunday 12 to 3pm. Guests can enjoy their drink
or meal in the bar, restaurant or outside where
tables skirt the riverside.

☞ On B5106 north of Betws-y-Coed and
south of Conwy

🍺 Brains SA, Flowers IPA plus occasional guest
ale

🍴 12-2.30 & 6-9 (up to 9.30 in peak season)

🛏 6 en suite rooms (3 on ground floor)

⚒ Car park, riverside seating, function room

💳 All major cards

♜ Welsh Tourist Board 2 stars

🕐 12-11 (Sun to 10.30)

🏛 Betws-y-Coed 5 miles, Swallow Falls 6 miles,
Conwy Falls 6 miles, Ty Hill 8 miles, Bethesda
9 miles, Bangor 14 miles

29 The Gwydyr Hotel

Betws-y-Coed, North Wales LL24 0AB

☎ 01690 710777 🌐 www.gwydyrhotel.co.uk

Bar Food, Restaurant Menu, Accommodation, No
Smoking Area

Set amid lush and lovely scenery, The Gwydyr
Hotel is ideal as a base for exploring Snowdonia
and the many sights and attractions of the region.

The accommodation is nothing short of
superb, with everything from traditional doubles

and singles to family rooms. The drawing room is
the place to relax and enjoy the afternoon cream
teas, while the lounge bar serves a varied
selection of wines, beers, spirits and soft drinks.
The hotel's extensive menu serves up breakfast,
lunch and dinner to suit all tastes.

One of the many perks of staying at this fine
hotel is the fishing available: special fly-fishing,
spinning and bait fishing holidays for salmon or sea
trout can be arranged by the day, week or season
along miles of the Rivers Conwy and Lledr.

☞ In the centre of Betws-y-Coed on the A5

🍴 12-9

🛏 19 en suite rooms

⚒ Car park, disabled access

💳 Not Amex or Diners

♜ 2 Stars Welsh Tourist Board

🕐 12-11 (Sun and Bank Holidays to 10.30)

🏛 Conwy Falls, fishing on the Rivers Conwy
and Lledr, Gwydyr Forest Park

26 Glan Aber Hotel

Holyhead Rd, Betws-Y-Coed, Conwy LL24 0AB

☎ 01690 710325

Real Ales, Bar Food, Restaurant Menu, Accommodation, No Smoking Area

27 The Groes Inn

Tyn Y Groes, Conwy LL32 8TN

☎ 01492 650545

Real Ales, Bar Food, Restaurant Menu, Accommodation, No Smoking Area

28 The Gwydyr Hotel

Dolwyddelan, Conwy LL25 0EJ

☎ 01690 750209

Real Ales, Bar Food, Restaurant Menu, Accommodation, No Smoking Area

29 The Gwydyr Hotel

See panel opposite

30 Hafod Country House

Conwy Rd, Trefriw, Conwy LL27 0RQ

☎ 01492 640029

Restaurant Menu, Accommodation, No Smoking Area

31 Holland Arms

Trofarth, Abergele, Conwy LL22 8BG

☎ 01492 650777

Real Ales, Restaurant Menu

32 The Kinmel Arms

See panel below

32 The Kinmel Arms

St George, near Abergele, North Wales LL22 9BP

☎ 01745 832207

⊕ www.thekinmelarms.co.uk

Real Ales, Restaurant Menu, Accommodation, No Smoking Area

The Kinmel Arms is a superb place where the best of traditional features are matched happily with modern comforts, earning it its ranking as one of the best and most popular eateries in North Wales.

This 17th-century listed building oozes style and quality, and owners Lynn and Tim Watson

have engaged four superb chefs who are talented and innovative, creating a range of superb dishes with an accent on the freshest and healthiest ingredients. The restaurant is beautiful – polished wood floors, marble table-tops and modern wicker seating – and the menu is complimented by an excellent wine list. The Kinmel Arms also boasts four contemporary and elegant king-size guest suites.

- 🡆 1 mile south of the A547, close to J24a off the A55
- 🍺 Good selection of changing guest ales
- 🍽 Tues-Sat 12-2 & 7-9.30; Sun 12-4; Bank Hols 12-2 & 6.30-9.30
- 🛏 4 en suite rooms
- 🎵 Gourmet evenings – ring for details
- 🅿 Parking, disabled access, garden
- 💳 All major cards
- 🏅 AA, Good Food Guide, CAMRA Good Pub Guide, 150 Best True Taste of Wales Restaurants, Best Dining Pub in Wales (Les Routiers 2003)
- 🕐 Tues-Sat 12-3 & 7-11; Sun 12-5.30; Bank Hols 12-3 & 6.30-11
- 🏛 Abergele 2 miles, Bodelwyddan 2 miles, Colwyn Bay 6 miles

33 The Legend Inn
Ysgubor Wen Rd, Dwygyfychi, Penmaenmawr,
Conwy LL34 6PS
☎ 01492 623231
Bar Food, Restaurant Menu, No Smoking Area

34 Llanfair Arms
Mill Rd, Llanfairfechan, Conwy LL33 0TT
☎ 01248 680521
Real Ales, Bar Food

35 The Lodge Hotel
Tal Y Bont, Conwy LL32 8YX
☎ 01492 660766
Real Ales, Restaurant Menu, Accommodation,
No Smoking Area

36 The Lord Newborough
Conway Rd, Dolgarrog, Conwy LL32 8JX
☎ 01492 660549
Restaurant Menu, No Smoking Area

37 Maenan Abbey Hotel
Maenan, Llanrwst, Conwy LL26 0UL
☎ 01492 660247
Real Ales, Bar Food, Restaurant Menu,
Accommodation, No Smoking Area

38 Maggie Murphys
Pentywyn Rd, Deganwy, Conwy LL31 9TH
☎ 01492 583695
Bar Food, Restaurant Menu

39 Main St Nightclub
Towyn Rd, Towyn, Abergele, Conwy LL22 9EN
☎ 01745 344334
Real Ales, Restaurant Menu

40 The Morton Arms
Sandbank Rd, Towyn, Abergele, Conwy LL22 9LB
☎ 01745 330211
Restaurant Menu, Accommodation,
No Smoking Area

41 Mountain View Hotel
Mochdre, Colwyn Bay, Conwy LL28 5AT
☎ 01492 544724
Real Ales, Bar Food, Restaurant Menu,
No Smoking Area

42 Mountain View Hotel
Pant Yr Afon, Penmaenmawr, Conwy LL34 6AA
☎ 01492 623446
Real Ales, Bar Food, Restaurant Menu,
Accommodation, No Smoking Area

43 The Mulberry
Conwy Marina, Morfa Drive, Conwy LL32 8EP
☎ 01492 583350
Real Ales, Bar Food, Restaurant Menu,
No Smoking Area

44 New Inn
Denbigh St, Llanrwst, Conwy LL26 0LL
☎ 01492 640476
Real Ales

45 The Old Bull Inn
Llanbedr-Y-Cennin, Conwy LL32 8JB
☎ 01492 660508
Real Ales, Bar Food, No Smoking Area

46 The Old Ship
Trefriw, Conwy LL27 0JH
☎ 01492 640013
Real Ales, Bar Food, No Smoking Area

47 Park Hotel
9 Marine Rd, Pensarn, Abergele, Conwy LL22 7PR
☎ 01745 832149
Real Ales, Bar Food, Restaurant Menu,
Accommodation

48 Pen Y Bryn Hotel
Ancaster Square, Llanrwst, Conwy LL26 0LH
☎ 01492 640678
Real Ales

49 Penrhyn Old Hall

Penrhyn Old Rd, Penrhyn Bay, Llandudno,
Conwy LL30 3EE

☎ 01492 549888

Real Ales, Bar Food, Restaurant Menu,
No Smoking Area

50 Pen-Y-Bont Inn

Bridge St, Llanrwst, Conwy LL26 0NE

☎ 01492 640202

Real Ales, Bar Food, No Smoking Area

51 Pen-Y-Bryn

Pen Y Bryn Rd, Upper Colwyn Bay, Colwyn Bay,
Conwy LL29 6DD

☎ 01492 533360

Real Ales, Bar Food, Restaurant Menu,
No Smoking Area

52 Penybryn Hotel

Penybryn Rd, Llanfairfechan, Conwy LL33 0TU

☎ 01248 680017

Real Ales, Bar Food, Restaurant Menu,
Accommodation, No Smoking Area

53 Princes Arms Hotel

Trefriw, Conwy LL27 0JP

☎ 01492 640592

Restaurant Menu, Accommodation

54 The Queens Head & Storehouse Cottage

See panel below

55 The Red Lion

See panel on page 88

---

54 The Queen's Head & Storehouse Cottage

Glanwydden, Nr Llandudno, Conwy LL31 9JP

☎ 01492 546570

🌐 www.queensheadglanwydden.co.uk

Real Ales, Bar Food, Accommodation,
No Smoking Area

One of the finest and best-known inns in Wales,
The Queen's Head in Glanwydden offers excellent
food, wine and a warm welcome to all guests.
Professional chefs expertly prepare and present an
impressive range of delicious dishes, earning the
inn a place in guides such as AA's *Britain's Best*

Country Pubs for Food Lovers and the Michelin guide
to *Eating Out in Pubs.* The bar boasts a relaxed
atmosphere and roaring log fire – just the place to
enjoy a pre-dinner drink. Accommodation is
available at Storehouse Cottage, recently featured
at length in *Real Homes* magazine. This romantic and
cosy traditional country cottage sleeps two; it has
been lovingly restored to offer the best in comfort
while losing none of its original charm.

🠒 Just 5 minutes from the A55 south of
Llandudno

🍺 Tetleys, Burton and rotating guest ale

🍴 12-2 & 6-9; Sun 12-9

🛏 Storehouse Cottage: 1 single and 1 double
room en suite

♿ Car park, garden, level access for people with
disabilities

💳 All the major cards

⭐ 5 stars (catering); 4 diamonds (B&B)

🕐 Mon-Sat 11.30-3 & 6-11 (Sundays 11.30-
10.30)

🏛 Conwy Castle 2 miles, Railway Museum at
Betws-y-Coed 2 miles, Colwyn Bay 6 miles,
Llandudno 4 miles

55 The Red Lion

Tyn Y Groes, Conwy LL32 8TJ
☎ 01492 650245
Real Ales, Bar Food, Accommodation

Built during the 1800s, The Red Lion began life as a farmhouse before becoming a licensed premises in the 1840s. Set in a picturesque village surrounded by lovely countryside, the inn boasts a warm and welcoming atmosphere. The restaurant is spacious and attractive, with a menu featuring everything from light snacks to meat, chicken, fish, seafood and vegetarian dishes, together with changing daily specials. On Sunday,

traditional roasts are added to the main menu. Owners Peredur and Sue Morris are both cooks, creating a range of locally-sourced dishes including hearty specialities such as steaks and mixed grills made with gammon, steak, chop, burger, black pudding, sausage, mushroom, onion rings, tomatoes and fried egg. The inn also makes an excellent touring base, with one spacious family room available.

☞ South of Conwy on the B5106

🍺 Lee's Bitter and rotating guest ale

🍴 12-7; Sun 12-7 as opening times permit (see below)

🛏 1 en suite family room

♪ Live music Fri-Sat; bingo every other Thurs

🚗 Car park, garden

🕐 Winter Mon-Tues 4.30-11; Weds-Fri 12.00-3 & 4.30-11; Sat 12.00-11 (Sun and Bank Holidays to 10.30) Summer: Mon-Tues 4.30-11; Weds-Sat 12.00-11 (Sun and Bank Holidays to 10.30)

🏛 Bangor 12 miles, Conwy 2 miles, Llandudno 5 miles

56 Red Lion Hotel

12 Denbigh St, Llanrwst, Conwy LL26 0LL
☎ 01492 640496

57 Rhos Fynach

Rhos Promenade, Rhos On Sea, Colwyn Bay, Conwy LL28 4NG
☎ 01492 548185
Real Ales, Bar Food, Restaurant Menu, No Smoking Area

58 Royal Oak Hotel

Holyhead Rd, Betws-Y-Coed, Conwy LL24 0AY
☎ 01690 710219
Real Ales, Bar Food, Restaurant Menu, Accommodation, No Smoking Area

59 Saracens Head

Cerrigydrudion, Corwen, Conwy LL21 9SY
☎ 01490 420327
Real Ales, Bar Food, Restaurant Menu, Accommodation, No Smoking Area

60 Saracens Head Hotel

Llansannan, Denbigh, Conwy LL16 5HH
☎ 01745 870212
Real Ales, Restaurant Menu, Accommodation, No Smoking Area

61 The Seagull Inn

Towyn Rd, Towyn, Abergele, Conwy LL22 9EN
☎ 01745 361937
Bar Food, Restaurant Menu, No Smoking Area

62 The Ship

Llandudno Rd, Rhos On Sea, Colwyn Bay,
Conwy LL28 4TR

☎ 01492 540198

Real Ales, Bar Food, Restaurant Menu,
No Smoking Area

63 The Sportsmans Arms

Bylchau, Denbigh, Conwy LL16 5SW

☎ 01745 550214

Real Ales, Bar Food

64 Stag Hotel

Llangernyw, Abergele, Conwy LL22 8PP

☎ 01745 860213

Real Ales, Bar Food, Restaurant Menu,
No Smoking Area

65 Swallow Falls Hotel

Betwy-Y-Coed, Betws-Y-Coed, Conwy LL24 0DW

☎ 01690 710796

Real Ales, Bar Food, Restaurant Menu,
Accommodation, No Smoking Area

66 Tal-Y-Cafn Hotel

Tal-Y-Cafn, Colwyn Bay, Conwy LL28 5RR

☎ 01492 650203

Real Ales, Restaurant Menu, Accommodation,
No Smoking Area

67 Ty Gwyn Hotel

Rowen, Conwy LL32 8YU

☎ 01492 650232

Real Ales, Bar Food, Restaurant Menu,
Accommodation, No Smoking Area

68 Ty Gwyn Hotel And Restaurant

Betws-Y-Coed, Conwy LL24 0SG

☎ 01690 710383

Real Ales, Bar Food, Restaurant Menu,
Accommodation, No Smoking Area

69 Tyn-Y-Coed Hotel

Capel Curig, Betws-Y-Coed, Conwy LL24 0EE

☎ 01690 720331

Real Ales, Bar Food, Accommodation,
No Smoking Area

70 Tyn-Y-Coed Hotel

Betws-Y-Coed, Conwy LL24 0EE

☎ 01690 720330

Real Ales, Bar Food, Restaurant Menu,
Accommodation, No Smoking Area

71 The Valentine Inn

Mill St, Llanddulas, Abergele, Conwy LL22 8ES

☎ 01492 518189

Real Ales, Bar Food

72 Victoria Inn

Penmaenmawr Rd, Llanfairfechan, Conwy LL33 0PB

☎ 01248 680169

Real Ales

73 The Village Inn

See panel on page 90

74 Virginia Inn

Mill Rd, Llanfairfechan, Conwy LL33 0TS

☎ 01248 680584

Real Ales

75 Wheatsheaf Inn

Betws-Yn-Rhos, Abergele, Conwy LL22 8AW

☎ 01492 680218

Real Ales, Bar Food, Restaurant Menu,
Accommodation, No Smoking Area

76 The White Lion Hotel

Cerrigydrudion, Corwen, Conwy LL21 9SW

☎ 01490 420202

Real Ales, Bar Food, Restaurant Menu,
Accommodation, No Smoking Area

73 The Village Inn

Penmaenmawr Road, Llanfairfechan,
Conwy LL33 0NU

☎ 01248 680620

Real Ales, Bar Food, Restaurant Menu,
Accommodation, No Smoking Area

Known as the coastal gateway to Snowdonia
National Park, Llanfairfechan is an ideal holiday
centre and base from which to explore the
seaside, glorious countryside and nearby Aber
Falls, and The Village Inn offers accommodation
together with great food and drink to all guests.
The inn boasts a restaurant and separate bistro,

which takes its name, 'Three Streams', from the
local attraction set within the Llanfairfechan hills.
Local produce, meats and seafood are used to
create a range of delicious dishes such as prime
Welsh Black beef steaks, guinea fowl, roast sea
bass, venison and a good choice of vegetarian
dishes. The dessert selection is equally impressive,
so make sure you leave enough room! This
charming Victorian inn has four very comfortable
and welcoming guest bedrooms, with two more
to become available during the lifetime of this
edition.

☛ One minute off A55 between Conwy and
Bangor

🍺 Tetleys, Abbot and rotating guest ale

🍴 Tues-Sat 12-2 & 5.30-8.30; Sun 12-4 (to 5 in
summer)

🛏 4 bedrooms

⛲ Car park, garden, disabled access

💳 Not Amex

🕐 12-23.00hrs (Sun and Bank Holidays to
10.30; closed Mon lunch in winter)

🏛 Snowdonia National Park 2 miles, Conwy 6
miles

81 Y Dwygyfylchi

Conwy Old Road, Penmaenmawr LL34 6SP

☎ 01492 623395

Real Ales, Bar Food, Accommodation,
No Smoking Area

Known locally as Bedol, Y Dwygyfylchi began life
as a coaching inn and is set on the old drovers'
road. The name means 'the meeting of two
valleys', and this friendly and welcoming place is a
cosy retreat for today's busy travellers.

The menu is very good, with an extensive

range of hot and cold dishes made with locally-
sourced produce and served at llunch and dinner.
The Sunday lunches and mixed grill dish are very
popular.

This handsome, traditional inn also boasts an
en suite guest bedroom – and at just a few miles
or so from the coast, makes an excellent touring
base within easy reach of many of the sights and
attractions of the region.

☛ 1 mile off the main A55 coastal road

🍺 Burtonwood Bitter and rotating guest ale

🍴 12-2 & 6-9 Tues-Sun and Bank Holidays

🛏 1 en suite room

🎵 Tues quiz from 9 p.m., live music twice-
monthly Saturday eves

⛲ Garden, access for people with disabilities

💳 All the major cards

🕐 Summer: 11.30-11 (Sun and Bank Holidays
to 10.30) Winter: Mon-Fri 6-11, Sat 11.30-11
(Sun and Bank Holidays to 10.30)

🏛 Conwy 3 miles, Llandudno 5 miles,
Llanfairfechan 2 miles

77 The White Lion Inn

Llanelian, Colwyn Bay, Conwy LL29 8YA

☎ 01492 515807

Real Ales, Bar Food, Restaurant Menu,
No Smoking Area

78 Whitehall Hotel

Cayley Promenade, Rhos On Sea, Colwyn Bay,
Conwy LL28 4EP

☎ 01492 547296

Bar Food, Restaurant Menu, Accommodation,
No Smoking Area

79 Windjammers Wine Bar

Towyn Rd, Belgrano, Abergele, Conwy LL22 9AD

☎ 01745 832341

Bar Food

80 Y Bedol Inn

Conway Rd, Tal-Y-Bont, Conwy LL32 8QF

☎ 01492 660501

Real Ales, Bar Food, Restaurant Menu,
No Smoking Area

81 Y Dwygyfylchi

See panel opposite

82 The Yacht

1 Marine Rd, Pensarn, Abergele, Conwy LL22 7PR

☎ 01745 824052

Bar Food

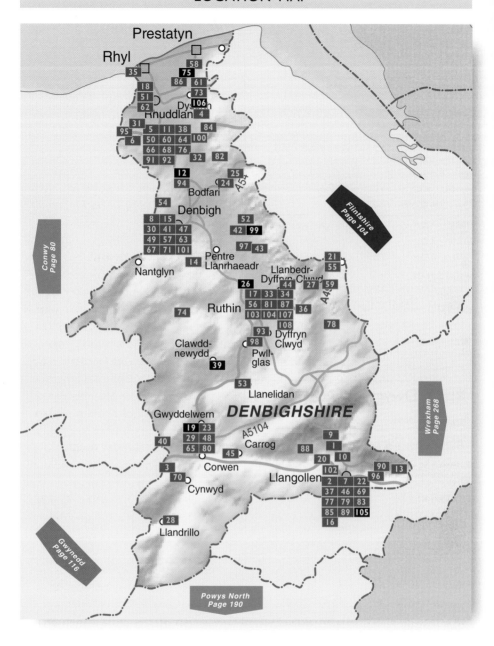

Prestatyn

Rhyl

58
35
75
86 61
18
51 73
62 Dy 106 n
Rhuddlan 4
31
95 5 11 38 84
6 50 60 64 100
66 68 76
91 92 32 82
12
94
Bodfari

54
Denbigh
8 15
30 41 47
49 57 63
67 71 101
52
42 99
97 43

Pentre
14 Llanrhaeadr
Nantglyn

Llanbedr-
Dyffryn-Clwyd
26 44 27 59
17 33 34
56 81 87
74 103 104 107 36
Ruthin
108
78
93 Dyffryn
98 Clwyd
Clawdd-
newydd Pwll-
39 glas

53
Llanelidan

DENBIGHSHIRE

Gwyddelwern
19 23 A5104
29 48 Carrog 9
40 1
65 80 88
45 20 10
3 102 90 13
70 Corwen 96
Cynwyd Llangollen
2 7 22
37 46 69
77 79 83
28 85 89 105
Llandrillo 16

Conwy Page 80

Flintshire Page 104

Wrexham Page 268

Gwynedd Page 116

Powys North Page 190

■ Denbighshire Reference Number - Detailed Information

▨ Denbighshire Reference Number - Summary Entry

Ceredigion Page 249 ▸ Adjacent area - refer to pages indicated

DENBIGHSHIRE
DENBIGH • RUTHIN • PRESTATYN

Denbighshire (Welsh: *Sir Ddinbych*) in northern Wales has always been one of the 13 traditional counties of Wales, though its current administrative boundaries differ substantially from its traditional ones. The current Denbighshire was created in 1996.

Forming part of the North Wales Borderlands, Denbighshire plays host to the broad, gentle sweep of the Vale of Clwyd with historic towns such as Ruthin, St Asaph and Denbigh. Recorded as a small border town in the 11th century, Denbigh, whose Welsh name *Dinbych* means 'little fort', grew to become a residence for Welsh princes and a leading centre of Welsh power. With buildings dating from the 1500s onwards, most of the centre is now a conservation area. A large stretch of the Town Walls still exists and can be walked today, while the ruins of the Castle are still an impressive sight, crowning the top of a steep hill above the town. At Dyserth, eight miles north of Denbigh, Bodrhyddan Hall was the 17th-century manor house of the Conwy family. Here visitors can see panels in what is

Ruthin Castle

known as the White Drawing Room that came from the chapel of the Spanish Armada that foundered off the coast of Anglesey. The Gardens here are of interest, too, the main feature being a box-edged Victorian parterre designed by William Andrews Nesfield, father of William Eden Nesfield who went on to design the Royal Botanic Gardens at Kew.

On the banks of the River Alun, at the southern end of the Clwydian Range, Llanarmon-yn Iâl is capital of the Iâl region and occupies a very attractive and scenic position. Bodelwyddan, some seven miles northwest of Denbigh, is home to the eye-catching Marble Church and Bodelwyddan Castle, a Victorian country house and estate, and the Welsh home of the National Portrait Gallery.

This area has many sites of historic significance. Prestatyn, to the east, lies at one end of Offa's Dyke. Built more as a line of demarcation than as a fortification, the dyke runs from the coast southwards to Chepstow. Still substantially marking the border, many sections of this ancient earthwork are visible and can be seen from the waymarked footpath that runs along its length. To the extreme southeast of the county, Llangollen is a busy and picturesque town that draws visitors from all over the world, who come not only to enjoy Llangollen's beautiful riverside position but for the annual International Musical Eisteddfod, held here since 1947.

1 Abbey Grange Hotel

Horseshoe Pass Rd, Llangollen,
Denbighshire LL20 8DD

☎ 01978 860753

Real Ales, Bar Food, Restaurant Menu,
Accommodation, No Smoking Area

2 Bensons Hotel

11 Bridge St, Llangollen, Denbighshire LL20 8PF

☎ 01978 860952

Real Ales, Bar Food, Restaurant Menu,
Accommodation

3 Blue Lion Hotel

Main St, Cynwyd, Corwen, Denbighshire LL21 0LE

☎ 01490 412106

Real Ales, Bar Food, Restaurant Menu

4 The Blue Lion Inn and Restaurant

Cwm Dyserth, Rhyl, Denbighshire LL18 5SG

☎ 01745 570733

Real Ales, Bar Food, Restaurant Menu,
Accommodation, No Smoking Area

5 Bod Erw Hotel

The Roe, St Asaph, Denbighshire LL17 0LA

☎ 01745 584638

Real Ales, Bar Food, Restaurant Menu,
Accommodation, No Smoking Area

6 Bodelwyddan Castle Hotel

Bodelwyddan, Denbighshire, Denbighshire LL18 5YA

☎ 01745 585088

Restaurant Menu, Accommodation,
No Smoking Area

7 Bridge End Hotel

Mill St, Llangollen, Denbighshire LL20 8RY

☎ 01978 860634

Real Ales, Bar Food, Restaurant Menu,
Accommodation

8 Britannia Inn

Love Lane, Denbigh, Denbighshire LL16 3LU

☎ 01745 813180

9 Britannia Inn

Horseshoe Pass, Llangollen,
Denbighshire LL20 8DW

☎ 01978 860144

Bar Food, Restaurant Menu, Accommodation,
No Smoking Area

10 Bryn Derwen Hotel

Abbey Rd, Llangollen, Denbighshire LL20 8EF

☎ 01978 860583

Bar Food, Restaurant Menu, Accommodation,
No Smoking Area

11 Bryn Dinas Hotel

Chester St, St Asaph, Denbighshire LL17 0RE

☎ 01745 582128

Real Ales, Bar Food

12 Bryn Glas Hotel

St Asaph Road, Trefnant, Denbigh LL16 5UD

☎ 01745 730868 Fax: 01745 730590

⊕ www.brynglashotel.co.uk

☛ Adjacent to the main A525 in Trefnant, 2 miles off the main A55 coastal road

🍺 1 rotating guest ale

🍴 12-2 & 6.30-8.30 Sunday-Saturday

🛏 4 en suite rooms (all wheelchair friendly)

♿ Car park; level access for people with disabilities

💳 All the major cards

🕐 12-2 & 5-11 (Sun and Bank Holidays to 10.30)

13 Bryn Howel Hotel

Llangollen, Denbighshire LL20 7UW

☎ 01978 860331

Bar Food, Restaurant Menu, Accommodation,
No Smoking Area

14 Bryn Morfydd Hotel

Llanrhaeadr, Llanynys, Denbighshire LL16 4NP

☎ 01745 890280

Bar Food, Restaurant Menu, Accommodation,
No Smoking Area

15 Bull Hotel

Hall Square, Denbigh, Denbighshire LL16 3NU
☎ 01745 812582
Real Ales, Bar Food, Restaurant Menu,
Accommodation, No Smoking Area

16 The Bull Inn

Castle St, Llangollen, Denbighshire LL20 8NY
☎ 01978 860220
Real Ales, Bar Food, Restaurant Menu,
No Smoking Area

17 Castle Hotel

Ruthin, Denbighshire LL15 1AA
☎ 01824 702479
Real Ales, Bar Food, Restaurant Menu,
Accommodation, No Smoking Area

18 Castle Inn

Castle St, Rhuddlan, Rhyl, Denbighshire LL18 5AE
☎ 01745 590391
Real Ales

19 Central Hotel & Tudor Restaurant

See panel below

20 Chain Bridge Hotel

Berwyn, Llangollen, Denbighshire LL20 8BS
☎ 01978 860215
Bar Food, Restaurant Menu, Accommodation,
No Smoking Area

21 Colomendy Arms

Gwernymynydd Rd, Cadole, Mold,
Denbighshire CH7 5LL
☎ 01352 810217
Real Ales

22 The Corn Mill

Dee Lane, Llangollen, Denbighshire LL20 8PN
☎ 01978 869555
Real Ales, Bar Food, Restaurant Menu,
No Smoking Area

---

19 Central Hotel & Tudor Restaurant

The Square, Corwen, Denbighshire LL21 0DE
☎ 01490 412462
Restaurant Menu, Accommodation,
No Smoking Area

Dating back to the mid-1700s, Central Hotel &
Tudor Restaurant was once known as The
Feathers
Temperance
Hotel. These
days, temper-
ance is a thing of
the past: a range
of local ales and
other thirst-
quenchers are
served to
residents and
diners alike.
Owned and run
by Barbara and
Keiran, this
friendly and

tastefully decorated small hotel offers all guests a
warm welcome in picturesque surroundings. The
handsome Tudor Restaurant seats 48 and offers
an extensive range of dishes. Steaks are just one
of the many specialities of the house. The
premises also incorporates a café open daily,
serving everything from cakes and scones to main
meals such as home-made pies. Children welcome.
Pets by arrangement.

☛ The hotel is located in the heart of Corwen,
10 miles west of Llangollen on the A5

🍺 Local brews

🍴 Winter: Fri-Sat 7-10 Summer: Thurs-Sat 7-10
& Sun lunchtime. Café: Winter: 8-5 Summer
8-7

🛏 7 en suite rooms

🅿 Car park

💳 All the major cards

🚫 No smoking in restaurant, Licensed for
residents and diners only

🏛 Llangollen 10 miles, Glyn Ceiriog 5 miles,
Chirk 15 miles

23 Crown Inn
Bridge St, Corwen, Denbighshire LL21 0AH
☎ 01490 413188
Real Ales, Bar Food

24 The Dinorben Arms Inn
Bodfari, Denbigh, Denbighshire LL16 4DA
☎ 01745 710309
Real Ales, Bar Food, Restaurant Menu,
No Smoking Area

25 Downing Arms
Mold Rd, Bodfari, Denbigh,
Denbighshire LL16 4DW
☎ 01745 710265
Real Ales, Bar Food, Restaurant Menu,
No Smoking Area

26 The Drovers Arms
See panel below

27 Druid Inn
Ruthin Rd, Llanferres, Mold, Denbighshire CH7 5SN
☎ 01352 810225
Real Ales, Bar Food, Restaurant Menu,
Accommodation, No Smoking Area

28 Dudley Arms Hotel
High St, Llandrillo, Corwen, Denbighshire LL21 0TL
☎ 01490 440223
Real Ales, Bar Food, Restaurant Menu,
Accommodation, No Smoking Area

29 Eagles Hotel
The Square, Corwen, Denbighshire LL21 0DG
☎ 01490 413280
Real Ales

30 The Eagles Inn
Back Row, Denbigh, Denbighshire LL16 3TE
☎ 01745 813203
Real Ales, Bar Food, Restaurant Menu,
Accommodation

26 The Drovers Arms
Rhewl, nr Ruthin, Denbighshire LL15 2UD
☎ 01824 703163 ⊕ www.ukpubzone.com
Real Ales, Bar Food, Restaurant Menu,
No Smoking Area

Set against a backdrop of rolling hills in the village of Rhewl, close to Ruthin town centre, The Drovers Arms is a spacious and welcoming inn. Dating back to the 17th century, the interior is very appealing, with exposed beams, open fires and other traditional features. Run by Allen Given and Amanda Nancarrow, this Free House always has a friendly and relaxed atmosphere. Amanda does the cooking, creating a range of hearty and delicious dishes. Originally from Cornwall, her specialities include home-made Cornish pasties (available Saturday lunchtime), as well as home-made chips, chicken Americana and much more. The banks of the River Clwydog and the surrounding countryside provide very pleasant walks, and walkers are welcome to use the large car park and facilities.

- 🚩 Adjacent to the A525, 1½ miles from Ruthin
- 🍺 London Pride, Youngers
- 🍴 12-2 & 6-9
- 🎵 Bank Hol 'bash' with pig roasts, live bands
- 🅿 Parking, garden, children's play area, disabled access
- 💳 Not Amex
- 🏆 Denbighshire Pub of the Year 2004 (Denbighshire Free Press)
- 🕐 Mon-Fri 12-3 & 6-11, Sat 12-11, Sun and Bank Holidays 12-10.30
- 🏛 Ruthin 1½ miles, Denbigh 5 miles, Mold 8 miles

31 Faenol Fawr Manor Hotel

The Village, Bodelwyddan, Denbighshire LL18 5UN
☎ 01745 591691
Bar Food, Restaurant Menu, Accommodation,
No Smoking Area

32 The Farmers Arms

Waen, Nr St Asaph, Denbighshire LL17 0DY
☎ 01745 582190
Real Ales, Bar Food, Restaurant Menu,
No Smoking Area

33 The Farmers Arms

Mwrog St, Ruthin, Denbighshire LL15 1LB
☎ 01824 707290
Real Ales, Bar Food, Restaurant Menu,
Accommodation

34 Feathers Inn

52 Well St, Ruthin, Denbighshire LL15 1AW
☎ 01824 703295
Real Ales

35 The Ferry Hotel

Foryd Rd, Kinmel Bay, Rhyl, Denbighshire LL18 5AR
☎ 01745 353910

36 The Forge

Mold Rd, Llanbedr Dyffryn Clwyd, Ruthin,
Denbighshire LL15 1YF
☎ 01824 702761
Restaurant Menu, No Smoking Area

37 Gales of Llangollen

18 Bridge St, Llangollen, Denbighshire LL20 8PF
☎ 01978 860089
Bar Food, Restaurant Menu, Accommodation,
No Smoking Area

38 The Gamekeeper

Lower St, St Asaph, Denbighshire LL17 0SG
☎ 01745 583514
Real Ales, Bar Food, Restaurant Menu,
No Smoking Area

39 The Glan Llyn Inn

Clawddnewydd, Ruthin LL15 2NA
☎ 01824 750754

Real Ales, Bar Food, Restaurant Menu, No
Smoking Area

The Glan Llyn Inn is a spacious and tasteful inn
with a good mix of traditional and modern
features and overlooks the village pond. Owner
Nigel has over six years' experience in the trade
and has been here at this welcoming Free House
since 2003.

Real ales, together with a good selection of
lagers, wines, spirits and soft drinks, can be
accompanied by the good variety of bar snacks
available at lunch and in the evenings, along with
daily specials.

In the conservatory restaurant, which seats 50,
the excellent menu offers a wealth of tempting,
meat, fish and vegetarian dishes. The Sunday roasts
are well worth the journey. Booking advised
Friday and Saturday evenings. Flat access into
premises for people with disabilities. Children
welcome.

☛ Clawddnewydd is found on the B5105
between Ruthin and Cerrigydrudion

🍺 Banks Best and 2 rotating guest ales

🍴 Tues-Sat 12-2 & 6-9; Sun 12-8

♫ Occasional – please ring for details

⚓ Car park, outdoor seating overlooking the
village pond

💳 Not Amex or Diners

🚫 No smoking in restaurant

🕐 11.30-11 (Sun and Bank Holidays to 10.30)

🏛 Ruthin 5 miles, Denbigh 10 miles

39 **The Glan Llyn Inn**

See panel on page 97

40 **The Goat Inn**

Maerdy, Corwen, Denbighshire LL21 0NR

☎ 01490 460536

Real Ales, Bar Food, Restaurant Menu,
Accommodation, No Smoking Area

41 **The Golden Lion**

1 Back Row, Denbigh, Denbighshire LL16 3TE

☎ 01745 812227

42 **Golden Lion Inn**

Llandyrnog, Denbigh, Denbighshire LL16 4HG

☎ 01824 790373

Real Ales, Bar Food, Restaurant Menu,
No Smoking Area

43 **The Golden Lion Inn**

Llangynhafal, Denbigh, Denbighshire LL16 4LN

☎ 01824 790451

Real Ales, Bar Food, Restaurant Menu,
No Smoking Area

44 **Griffin Inn**

Ruthin, Denbighshire LL15 1UP

☎ 01824 702792

Real Ales, Bar Food, Restaurant Menu,
Accommodation, No Smoking Area

45 **The Grouse Inn**

Carrog, Corwen, Denbighshire LL21 9AT

☎ 01490 430272

Real Ales, Bar Food, Restaurant Menu

46 **The Hand Hotel**

Bridge St, Llangollen, Denbighshire LL20 8PL

☎ 01978 860303

Real Ales, Bar Food, Restaurant Menu,
Accommodation, No Smoking Area

47 **The Hand Inn**

Henllan St, Denbigh, Denbighshire LL16 3PF

☎ 01745 814286

Real Ales, Bar Food

48 **Harp Hotel**

The Square, Corwen, Denbighshire LL21 0DE

☎ 01490 412967

Real Ales

49 **Hope and Anchor Inn**

94 Vale St, Denbigh, Denbighshire LL16 3BW

☎ 01745 815115

Real Ales, Accommodation, No Smoking Area

50 **The Kentigern Arms**

High St, St Asaph, Denbighshire LL17 0RG

☎ 01745 584157

Real Ales, Bar Food

51 **Kings Head**

High St, Rhuddlan, Rhyl, Denbighshire LL18 2TU

☎ 01745 590345

Real Ales, Bar Food, Restaurant Menu

52 **The Kinmel Arms Tavern**

Llandyrnog, Denbigh, Denbighshire LL16 4HN

☎ 01824 790291

Real Ales, Bar Food, Restaurant Menu,
No Smoking Area

53 **Leyland Arms**

Llanelidan, Ruthin, Denbighshire LL15 2PT

☎ 01824 750502

Real Ales, Bar Food, Restaurant Menu,
Accommodation, No Smoking Area

54 **Llindir Inn**

Llindir St, Henllan, Denbigh, Denbighshire LL16 5BH

☎ 01745 812640

Real Ales, Bar Food, Restaurant Menu,
No Smoking Area

55 **Loggerheads Inn**

Ruthin Rd, Gwernymynydd, Mold,
Denbighshire CH7 5LH

☎ 01352 810337

Real Ales, Bar Food, Restaurant Menu

56 Manorhaus Hotel

Well St, Ruthin, Denbighshire LL15 1AH

☎ 01824 704830

Restaurant Menu, Accommodation,
No Smoking Area

57 The Masons Arms

Rhyl Rd, Denbigh, Denbighshire LL16 3DT

☎ 01745 812463

58 Miners Arm

23 Ffordd Talargoch, Meliden, Prestatyn,
Denbighshire LL19 8LA

☎ 01745 852005

Real Ales, Bar Food, Restaurant Menu,
No Smoking Area

59 Miners Arms

Village Rd, Maeshafn, Mold, Denbighshire CH7 5LR

☎ 01352 810464

Real Ales, Bar Food

60 New Inn

Lower Denbigh Rd, St Asaph,
Denbighshire LL17 0EF

☎ 01745 582588

Real Ales, Accommodation

61 The New Inn

Waterfall Rd, Dyserth, Rhyl, Denbighshire LL18 6ET

☎ 01745 570482

Real Ales, Bar Food, Restaurant Menu,
No Smoking Area

62 New Inn Hotel

High St, Rhuddlan, Rhyl, Denbighshire LL18 2TY

☎ 01745 591305

Real Ales, Bar Food, Restaurant Menu,
Accommodation, No Smoking Area

63 The Old Vaults

40-42 High St, Denbigh, Denbighshire LL16 3RY

☎ 01745 815142

Real Ales

64 Oriel House Hotel

Upper Denbigh Rd, St Asaph,
Denbighshire LL17 0LW

☎ 01745 582716

Bar Food, Restaurant Menu, Accommodation,
No Smoking Area

65 Owain Glyndwr Hotel

The Square, Corwen, Denbighshire LL21 0DL

☎ 01490 412115

Bar Food, Restaurant Menu, No Smoking Area

66 Plas Elwy Hotel

The Roe, St Asaph, Denbighshire LL17 0LT

☎ 01745 582089

Restaurant Menu, Accommodation,
No Smoking Area

67 The Plough Inn

Bridge St, Denbigh, Denbighshire LL16 3TF

☎ 01745 812961

Real Ales, Bar Food, Restaurant Menu,
No Smoking Area

68 The Plough Inn

The Roe, St Asaph, Denbighshire LL17 0LU

☎ 01745 585080

Real Ales, Bar Food, Restaurant Menu,
No Smoking Area

69 The Ponsonby Arms

Mill St, Llangollen, Denbighshire LL20 8RY

☎ 01978 861119

Real Ales, Bar Food, No Smoking Area

70 Prince of Wales Inn

Cynwyd, Corwen, Denbighshire LL21 0LD

☎ 01490 412450

71 The Railway

2 Ruthin Rd, Denbigh, Denbighshire LL16 3EL

☎ 01745 812376

Real Ales

72 Red Lion Hotel

Llansannan, Denbigh, Denbighshire LL16 5HG

☎ 01745 870256

Real Ales, Bar Food, No Smoking Area

73 Red Lion Hotel

Waterfall Rd, Dyserth, Rhyl, Denbighshire LL18 6ET

☎ 01745 570404

74 Red Lion Hotel

Ruthin, Denbighshire LL15 2DN

☎ 01824 710664

Real Ales, Bar Food, Restaurant Menu, Accommodation, No Smoking Area

75 Red Lion Inn

See panel below

76 Red Lion Inn

Gemig St, St Asaph, Denbighshire LL17 0RY

☎ 01745 584475

Real Ales, Bar Food

77 River Lodge

Mill St, Llangollen, Denbighshire LL20 8RY

☎ 01978 869019

Accommodation

78 Rose & Crown

Graianrhyd, Mold, Denbighshire CH7 4QW

☎ 01824 780727

Real Ales, Bar Food, No Smoking Area

79 The Royal Hotel

Bridge St, Llangollen, Denbighshire LL20 8PG

☎ 01978 860202

Bar Food, Restaurant Menu, Accommodation, No Smoking Area

80 Royal Oak

London Rd, Corwen, Denbighshire LL21 0DR

☎ 01490 412372

---

75 Red Lion

4 Ffordd Talargoch, Meliden, Prestatyn LL19 8LA

☎ 01745 852565

⊕ www.redlionmeliden.co.uk

Real Ales, Bar Food, Restaurant Menu, Accommodation, No Smoking Area

The Red Lion in Meliden dates back about 400 years and is located next to the village church of St Meliden, which is mentioned in the Domesday Book.

This handsome premises boasts a welcoming and relaxed ambience. A large and interesting collection of ceramic mugs hang from one part of the beamed ceiling, and the décor and furnishings are comfortable and traditional throughout. Outside there's a large and lush garden with mature trees and landscaped areas – perfect for enjoying a refreshing drink or meal on fine days.

The outstanding food served at lunch and dinner includes home-made specialities such as cod Mornay, lamb Henry and Hunter's chicken. The accommodation comprises two attractive and very comfortable guest bedrooms available all year round.

☛ 12½ miles east of Colwyn Bay on the A547

🍺 Bass, Boddingtons plus a rotating guest ale

🍴 12-2 and Mon-Sat 6-9

🛏 2 en suite rooms

🅿 Car park, disabled access, garden

💳 Not Amex

🕐 11.30-11 (Sun and Bank Holidays to 10.30)

🏛 Craig Fawr nature reserve, Rhyl 8 miles, Prestatyn 12 miles

81 Ruthin Castle

Ruthin, Denbighshire LL15 2NU

☎ 01824 702664

Bar Food, Restaurant Menu, Accommodation, No Smoking Area

82 Salisbury Arms

Tremeirchion, St Asaph, Denbighshire LL17 0UN

☎ 01745 710262

Real Ales, Bar Food, Restaurant Menu, No Smoking Area

83 Smithfield Hotel

Llangollen, Denbighshire LL20 8NF

☎ 01978 860107

Real Ales, Bar Food, Restaurant Menu, No Smoking Area

84 Smithy Arms

Holywell Rd, Rhuallt, St Asaph, Denbighshire LL17 0TR

☎ 01745 582298

Bar Food, Restaurant Menu, No Smoking Area

85 Star Inn

Queen St, Llangollen, Denbighshire LL20 8LA

☎ 01978 861644

86 Star Inn

75 Ffordd Talargoch, Meliden, Prestatyn, Denbighshire LL19 8NR

☎ 01745 852134

Real Ales

87 The Star Inn

55 Clwyd St, Ruthin, Denbighshire LL15 1HH

☎ 01824 703614

88 Sun Inn

Rhewl, Llangollen, Denbighshire LL20 7YT

☎ 01978 861043

Real Ales, Bar Food

89 The Sun Inn

Regent St, Llangollen, Denbighshire LL20 8HN

☎ 01978 860233

Real Ales, No Smoking Area

90 Sun Trevor

Sun Bank, Llangollen, Denbighshire LL20 8EG

☎ 01978 860651

Real Ales, Bar Food, Restaurant Menu, No Smoking Area

91 The Swan Inn

The Roe, St Asaph, Denbighshire LL17 0LT

☎ 01745 582284

Real Ales

92 Talardy Hotel

The Roe, St Asaph, Denbighshire LL17 0HY

☎ 01745 584957

Real Ales, Bar Food, Restaurant Menu, Accommodation, No Smoking Area

93 Three Pigeons Inn

Graigfechan, Ruthin, Denbighshire LL15 2EH

☎ 01824 703178

Real Ales, Bar Food, Restaurant Menu, Accommodation, No Smoking Area

94 The Trefnant Inn

Trefnant, Denbighshire, Denbighshire LL16 5UG

☎ 01745 730636

Real Ales, Bar Food, Restaurant Menu, No Smoking Area

95 Ty Fry Inn

Bodelwyddan, Rhyl, Denbighshire LL18 5TE

☎ 01745 582209

96 Tyn Y Wern Hotel

Holyhead Rd, Llangollen, Denbighshire LL20 7PH

☎ 01978 860252

Restaurant Menu, Accommodation, No Smoking Area

97 The White Horse

Hendrerwydd, Denbigh, Denbighshire LL16 4LL

☎ 01824 790218

Restaurant Menu

98 The White Horse

Llanfair Dyffryn Clwyd, Ruthin, Denbighshire LL15 2RU

☎ 01824 707496

Real Ales, Bar Food, Restaurant Menu

99 The White Horse – Y Ceffyl Gwyn

Llandyrnog, Nr Denbigh LL16 4HG
☎ 01824 790582

Real Ales, Bar Food, Restaurant Menu

Here in the very picturesque village of Llandyrnog, The White Horse (Y Ceffyl Gwyn) is a truly charming inn owned and run by Hilary, her partner Merfyn and her sister Alex.

Alex is the chef, and the inn is renowned for its food. The menu changes every four months with the seasons and boasts a range of tempting starters, main courses and traditional favourites such as mussels in cream sauce, grilled goat's cheese, sirloin steak with black pudding and Stilton, and slow-roasted lamb shoulder with leek mash, together with a good choice of vegetarian dishes and daily specials; there is also a full children's menu.

The inn has two restaurant areas seating a total of 58. Booking is required every evening and Sunday lunchtime.

- 🠒 3 miles east of Denbigh on the B5429
- 🍺 2 rotating guest ales
- 🍴 12-2 & 6-9 Tues-Sun and Bank Holidays
- ♿ Car park, access for people with disabilities
- 💳 Not Amex or Diners
- 🕐 12-2 & 6-11 (Sun and Bank Holidays to 10.30)
- 🏛 Denbigh 3 miles, Colwyn Bay 12 miles, Chester 20 miles

105 Wynnstay Arms Hotel

Llangollen LL20 8PF
☎ 01978 860710
🌐 www.wynnstay-arms.co.uk

Real Ales, Bar Food, Restaurant Menu, Accommodation, No Smoking Area

Wynnstay Arms Hotel is a handsome and welcoming inn dating back to the early 1600s. A Free House run by the Hallam family for over 30 years, this friendly inn offers first-class food, drink and accommodation. Head chef Tom creates an impressive range of dishes using the freshest ingredients. Snacks such as burgers, salads, omelettes, sausages and lasagne (served Monday to Saturday midday

to 6 p.m.) are complemented by an extensive evening menu of meals including steaks, lamb, salmon and vegetarian options, together with changing daily specials. The comfortable accommodation comprises a choice of bedrooms in the inn or three newly-created bunkrooms within the old stables yard. Children welcome. Inn has access for people with disabilities.

- 🠒 The inn is in the centre of Llangollen a few minutes' walk from the railway station
- 🍺 Abbot, Burton, guest ale, CAMRA listed
- 🍴 12-9
- 🛏 4 en suite rooms (B&B or room-only), 3 bunkrooms sleeping 5/6
- 🎵 Monthly folk club, occasional live music
- ♿ Car park, terraced seating area to rear
- 💳 Not Amex or Diners
- 🚭 No smoking in restaurant
- 🕐 11.30-11 (Sun and Bank Holidays to 10.30)
- 🏛 Llangollen, Plas Newydd 1 mile, Wrexham 10 miles, Oswestry 10 miles, Snowdonia National Park 20 miles, Valle Crucis Abbey 2 miles, Pontcysyllte Aquaduct 4 miles.

99 The White Horse

See panel opposite

---

100 White House Hotel

Holywell Rd, Rhuallt, Denbighshire LL17 0AW

☎ 01745 582155

Real Ales, Bar Food, Restaurant Menu, Accommodation, No Smoking Area

---

101 White Lion

Back Row, Denbigh, Denbighshire LL16 3TE

☎ 01745 812155

Restaurant Menu

---

102 Wild Pheasant Hotel

Berwyn Rd, Llangollen, Denbighshire LL20 8AD

☎ 01978 860629

Bar Food, Restaurant Menu, Accommodation, No Smoking Area

---

103 The Wine Vaults

2 Castle St, Ruthin, Denbighshire LL15 1DP

☎ 01824 702067

Real Ales

---

104 Wynnstay Arms

Well St, Ruthin, Denbighshire LL15 1AN

☎ 01824 703147

Real Ales, Bar Food, Accommodation

---

105 Wynnstay Arms Hotel

See panel opposite

---

106 Y-Bodunig

See panel below

---

107 Ye Olde Anchor Inn

2 Rhos St, Ruthin, Denbighshire LL15 1DY

☎ 01824 702813

Real Ales, Bar Food, Restaurant Menu, Accommodation, No Smoking Area

---

108 Ye Olde Cross Keys

Llanfwrog, Ruthin, Denbighshire LL15 2AD

☎ 01824 705281

Real Ales, Restaurant Menu, No Smoking Area

---

106 Y-Bodunig

High Street, Dyserth, Denbighshire LL18 6AA

☎ 01745 570333

Real Ales, Bar Food, Restaurant Menu

Y-Bodunig is a handsome traditional stonebuilt inn located on the main street in Dyserth. The interior is all wood and brass, with a roaring real fire adding to the cosy and welcoming atmosphere. The inn dates back to the early 1800s, and the name, translated into English, means 'The Lonely Man' or 'The Lonely Place' – a reference to the region's tranquillity and

peacefulness. Home-cooking is the hallmark of this fine inn. There are traditional bar snacks (breakfasts also available – please ring for details) and take-away facilities. In the evening the menu is much more extensive, with a range of traditional meals. The restaurant seats 20, while outside there's a small beer garden with terraced seating. Children welcome up to 9 p.m., and later if dining.

🍺 2¾ miles from Prestatyn on the A5151

🍺 M & B Mild, Greene King IPA, rotating guest ale

🍴 Mon-Sat 6-9; Sun 12-3

🎵 Karaoke or live music Fri from 9; sing-along Sat from 9

🅿️ Car park, beer garden, access for people with disabilities

🚫 No smoking in dining area

🕐 Summer: 11.30-11 (Sun and Bank Holidays to 10.30) Winter (Jan-May): Mon-Thurs 4-11; Fri-Sat 12-11; Sun 11-10.30

🏛 Dyserth Waterfall 2 miles, Prestatyn 2¾ miles

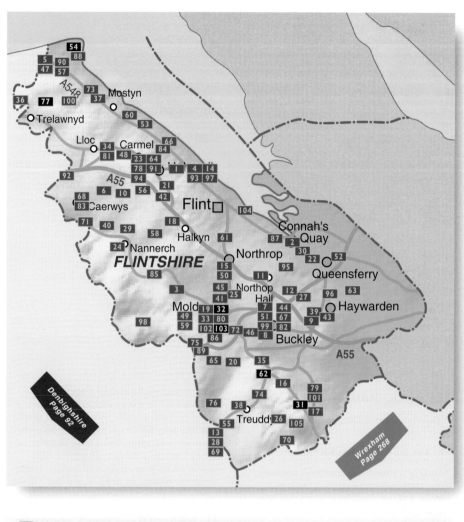

FLINTSHIRE

MOLD • HOLYWELL • FLINT

Flintshire (Welsh: *Sir y Fflint*) is a county in northern Wales. Places in Flintshire include Buckley, Flint, Hawarden, Holywell, Mold. It borders, in England, Merseyside (across the River Dee) and Cheshire, and, in Wales, Wrexham and Denbighshire.

The current administrative Flintshire came into existence in 1996. Flintshire is also a traditional county of Wales. The historic county does not have the boundaries of modern administrative Flintshire, in particular it has a large exclave called Maelor Saesneg.

The smooth brown slopes of the Clwydian Range ascend from the broad and fertile plains of the Vale of Clwyd, and Moel Famau ('the Mother of Mountains'), at some 1,820 feet high, is the range's highest peak. It is well worth the climb to the summit, as not only are there the remains of a Jubilee Tower, started in 1810 to commemorate George III's Gold Jubilee (though since blown down in a storm), but the panoramic views are breathtaking. There is a Country Park surrounding the mountain peak.

Mold is the small county town of Flintshire, boasts Bailey Hill among its attractions, the site of a Norman motte and bailey fortification built at this strategic point overlooking the River Alyn. Four miles west of Mold is Loggerheads Country Park, situated on the edge of

Moel Famau

the Clwydian Range. Classified as an Area of Outstanding Natural Beauty, this large park has various trails that start near the late-18th-century mill building that once used water from the River Alyn to drive a water wheel and two sets of stones to grind corn from local farms.

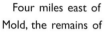
Clwydian Mountains

Four miles east of Mold, the remains of Ewloe Castle are hidden in a steeply wooded glen. Just to the north lies Wepre Country Park. The village of Hawarden, close to the English border, boasts the one-time home of William Gladstone, while the village of Halkyn lies close to the long ridge of the Halkyn Mountains, which rise to some 964 feet at their highest point and are scarred by the remains of ancient lead mines and quarries, some of which date back to Roman times.

In Holywell there is one of the Seven Wonders of Wales, namely St Winefride's Well, once a place of pilgrimage. Linking Holywell with the ruins of Basingwerk Abbey is the Greenfield Valley Heritage Park, 70 acres of pleasant woodland and lakeside walks.

1 ## Abbots Arms

Penymaes Rd, Holywell, Flintshire CH8 7BD

☎ 01352 710347

2 ## Albion Hotel

Church Rd, Connahs Quay, Deeside,
Flintshire CH5 4AD

☎ 01244 813370

Real Ales, Accommodation

3 ## Antelope

Rhydymwyn, Mold, Flintshire CH7 5HE

☎ 01352 741247

Real Ales, Bar Food, Restaurant Menu,
Accommodation, No Smoking Area

4 ## Bagilt Arms

High St, Bagillt, Flint, Flintshire CH6 6ED

☎ 01352 763995

5 ## Beachcomber Inn

Shore Rd, Gronant, Prestatyn, Flintshire LL19 9SS

☎ 01745 853188

Real Ales, Bar Food, Restaurant Menu,
No Smoking Area

6 ## Black Lion Inn

Babell, Holywell, Flintshire CH8 8PZ

☎ 01352 720239

Real Ales, Bar Food, Restaurant Menu,
No Smoking Area

7 ## The Black Lion

Mold Rd, Buckley, Flintshire CH7 2JA

☎ 01244 550308

8 ## The Blue Anchor Inn

Buckley, Mold, Flintshire CH7 2NH

☎ 01244 550585

9 ## Blue Bell Inn

Hawarden, Deeside, Flintshire CH5 3DH

☎ 01244 534885

Real Ales, Bar Food, No Smoking Area

10 ## The Bluebell Inn

Rhosesmor Rd, Halkin, Holywell,
Flintshire CH8 8OL

☎ 01352 780309

Real Ales, Bar Food, Restaurant Menu

11 ## Boars Head Inn

Village Rd, Northop Hall, Mold, Flintshire CH7 6HS

☎ 01244 815995

12 ## The Boars Head

Hollywell Rd, Ewloe, Deeside, Flintshire CH5 3BS

☎ 01244 531065

Real Ales, Bar Food

13 ## Bodidris Hall Hotel

Bodidris Estate, Llandegla, Wrexham,
Flintshire LL11 3AL

☎ 01978 790434

Bar Food, Restaurant Menu, Accommodation,
No Smoking Area

14 ## Boot Hotel

High St, Bagillt, Flint, Flintshire CH6 6HE

☎ 01352 713390

Real Ales, Bar Food

15 ## Boot Inn

High St, Northop, Mold, Flintshire CH7 6BQ

☎ 01352 840247

Real Ales, Bar Food, Restaurant Menu,
No Smoking Area

16 ## Bridge Inn

Wrexham Rd, Pontblyddyn, Mold,
Flintshire CH7 4HN

☎ 01352 770087

Real Ales, Bar Food, Restaurant Menu,
No Smoking Area

17 ## The Bridge Inn

Hawarden Rd, Caergwrle, Wrexham,
Flintshire LL12 9DT

☎ 01978 760977

Real Ales, Bar Food, Restaurant Menu,
No Smoking Area

18 Britannia Inn

Pentre Rd, Halkyn, Holywell, Flintshire CH8 8BS

☎ 01352 780272

Real Ales, Restaurant Menu, No Smoking Area

19 Bryn Awel Hotel

Denbigh Rd, Mold, Flintshire CH7 1BL

☎ 01352 758622

Bar Food, Restaurant Menu, Accommodation,
No Smoking Area

20 The Butchers Arms

Village Rd, Mold, Flintshire CH7 4EW

☎ 01352 752514

Real Ales, No Smoking Area

21 Calcot Arms

Halkyn Rd, Holywell, Flintshire CH8 7SJ

☎ 01352 711079

Bar Food

22 The Clwyd

28 Chester Rd, West Shotton, Deeside,
Flintshire CH5 1BY

☎ 01244 813304

23 Cross Foxes

Brynford St, Holywell, Flintshire CH8 7RD

☎ 01352 712391

24 Cross Foxes

Village Rd, Nannerch, Mold, Flintshire CH7 5RD

☎ 01352 741293

Real Ales, Bar Food, Restaurant Menu,
No Smoking Area

25 Cross Keys

Main Rd, Sychdyn, Mold, Flintshire CH7 6EA

☎ 01352 753582

Real Ales, Bar Food, Restaurant Menu,
No Smoking Area

26 Cross Keys

Llanfynydd, Wrexham, Flintshire LL11 5HH

☎ 01978 760333

Real Ales, Bar Food, Restaurant Menu,
No Smoking Area

27 Crown & Liver Inn

Ewloe, Deeside, Flintshire CH5 3DN

☎ 01244 531182

Real Ales, Bar Food, No Smoking Area

28 The Crown Hotel

Ruthin Rd, Llandegla, Wrexham, Flintshire LL11 3AD

☎ 01978 790228

Real Ales, Bar Food, Restaurant Menu,
No Smoking Area

29 Crown Inn

Lixwm, Holywell, Flintshire CH8 8NQ

☎ 01352 781112

Real Ales, Bar Food, Restaurant Menu,
No Smoking Area

30 Customs House

High St, Connahs Quay, Deeside,
Flintshire CH5 4DF

☎ 01244 812166

31 The Derby Arms

Derby Road, Caergwrle, Flintshire LL12 9AB

☎ 01978 760733

Bar Food

☛ A541 off main A483 signposted Mold; the
inn can be found off the main road in Derby
Road

❙ Cold bar snacks only

♫ Piano for anyone wishing to play

♿ Access for people with disabilities; function
room for 100

🕐 Mon-Thu 4-11; Fri 3-11; Sat 11-11; Sun 12-3,
7-10.30

🏛 Caergwrle Castle 1 mile, Wrexham 4 miles,
Hawarden Castle 5 miles, Loggerheads
Country Park 6 miles

32 The Dolphin Inn

High Street, Mold, Flintshire CH7 1BH
☎ 01352 705011/705015
Fax: 01352 705012
🌐 www.dolphininn.biz
e-mail: thedolphininn@aol.com

Restaurant Menu, Accommodation,
No Smoking Area

Dating back to the 1870s, The Dolphin Inn is a
Grade II listed building that was once part of the
town courthouse. Situated just a few hundred
metres from the centre of Mold, the inn has
tempting bar meals and main courses which guests
choose from the menu or specials board, and
upstairs accommodation available all year round. A
hearty breakfast is included in the tariff.

☛ Off the A54, 5 miles south of Flint

🍴 Mon-Thurs 12-2.30 & 6-9, Fri 12-2.30, Sat
12-4, Sun 12-3

🛏 6 rooms, tea/coffee making facilities

🎵 Weekly entertainment pub quiz, disco/
karaoke

🅿 Parking, beer garden, patio.

🕐 12-11 (Sun and Bank Holidays to 10.30)

🏛 Loggerheads Country Park & Countryside
Centre, Ewloe 4 miles, Flint 5 miles,
Hawarden 5 miles, Holywell 8 miles

33 Drovers Arms

Denbigh Rd, Mold, Flintshire CH7 1BP
☎ 01352 753824
Real Ales, Bar Food

34 Druid Inn

The Village, Gorsedd, Holywell, Flintshire CH8 8QZ
☎ 01352 710944
Real Ales, Bar Food, Restaurant Menu

35 Druid Inn

Pontblyddyn, Mold, Flintshire CH7 4HG
☎ 01352 770292
Real Ales, Bar Food, Restaurant Menu,
No Smoking Area

36 Eagle And Child Inn

Gwaenysgor, Rhyl, Flintshire LL18 6EP
☎ 01745 856391
Real Ales, Bar Food, Restaurant Menu,
No Smoking Area

37 The Farmers Arms

Main Rd, Ffynnongroyw, Holywell,
Flintshire CH8 9SW
☎ 01745 560359
Real Ales

38 The Farmers Arms

Ffordd Y Llan, Treuddyn, Mold, Flintshire CH7 4LN
☎ 01352 770975
Real Ales, Bar Food

39 Fox & Grapes Hotel

6 The Highway, Hawarden, Deeside,
Flintshire CH5 3DH
☎ 01244 532565
Real Ales, Bar Food, Restaurant Menu,
Accommodation, No Smoking Area

40 Fox Inn

The Village, Ysceifiog, Holywell, Flintshire CH8 8NJ
☎ 01352 720241
Real Ales, Bar Food, Restaurant Menu

41 Glasfryn

Raikes Lane, Sychdyn, Mold, Flintshire CH7 6LR
☎ 01352 750500
Real Ales, Bar Food, Restaurant Menu,
No Smoking Area

42 Glen Yr Afon Inn

Milwr, Holywell, Flintshire CH8 8HE
☎ 01352 710052
Real Ales, Restaurant Menu, Accommodation,
No Smoking Area

43 Glynne Arms

Harden, Deeside, Flintshire CH5 3NS
☎ 01244 520323
Real Ales, Bar Food

44 The Glynne Arms

Fore St, Buckley, Mold, Flintshire CH7 3DU
☎ 01244 550610
Real Ales

45 Griffin

41 High St, Mold, Flintshire CH7 6RO
☎ 01352 750697
Real Ales, Bar Food

46 The Griffin Inn

102 Mold Rd, Mynydd Isa, Mold, Flintshire CH7 6TF
☎ 01352 752019
Bar Food

47 The Gronant Inn

Llanasa Rd, Prestatyn, Flintshire LL19 9TG
☎ 01745 853725
Real Ales, Bar Food, Restaurant Menu,
No Smoking Area

48 Halfway House

Allt-Y-Golch, Carmel, Holywell, Flintshire CH8 8QT
☎ 01352 710289
Real Ales, Bar Food, Restaurant Menu

49 Hand Inn

Church Lane, Gwernaffield, Mold,
Flintshire CH7 5DT
☎ 01352 740581
Real Ales, Bar Food

50 Highfield Hall Hotel

Northop, Mold, Flintshire CH7 6AX
☎ 01352 840221
Bar Food, Restaurant Menu, Accommodation,
No Smoking Area

51 Hope & Anchor The

Ewloe Place, Buckley, Mold, Flintshire CH7 3NL
☎ 01244 550607
Real Ales

52 Hotel Leprechaun

Welsh Rd, Garden City, Deeside,
Flintshire CH5 2HX
☎ 01244 812575
Real Ales, Bar Food, Restaurant Menu,
Accommodation, No Smoking Area

54 Lighthouse Inn

Station Road, Talacre, North Wales CH8 9RD
☎ 01745 856237

Real Ales, Bar Food, Restaurant Menu

The Lighthouse Inn has built up an enviable reputation for quality and great food and drink. Newly redecorated to incorporate the best of traditional features alongside modern comforts, the interior is welcoming and always boasts a relaxed and convivial ambience.

With a good selection of draught ales, three bitters, five lagers together with cider, stout, wines, spirits and soft drinks, there is something to please every palate. In the newly refurbished restaurant, the menu offers a great deal of choice including home-made dishes and fish specialities.

Outside there's a lovely garden complete with children's play area – just the place to enjoy a drink or meal on fine days.

Owner Cheryl Doyle and her capable, friendly staff offer all their guests the very best in hospitality and service.

☞ Off the coastal A548 road near Holywell

🍴 9.30-8.30 (summer); 11.00-6.00 (winter)

♫ Ring for details

⛱ Car park, garden, children's play area, BBQ, disabled access

💳 All major cards

🕐 summer: 11.30-11.00, winter:(January and February only) 4.00-11.00

🏛 Nearest beach 2 minutes walk other beaches nearby, Prestatyn 4 miles, Rhyl 8 miles

53 Kinsale Hall & Country Club

Llanerch-y-mor, Holywell, Flintshire CH8 9DT

☎ 01745 560001

Real Ales, Bar Food, Restaurant Menu, Accommodation, No Smoking Area

54 Lighthouse Inn

See panel opposite

55 Liver Inn

Ffordd Corwen, Rhydtalog, Mold, Flintshire CH7 4LF

☎ 01824 780244

Real Ales, Bar Food, No Smoking Area

56 Llyn Y Mawn Inn

Brynford Hill, Brynford, Holywell, Flintshire CH8 8AD

☎ 01352 714367

Real Ales, Bar Food, Restaurant Menu, Accommodation, No Smoking Area

57 Lodge Inn

Coast Rd, Gwespyr, Holywell, Flintshire CH8 9JN

☎ 01745 857135

Real Ales, Restaurant Menu, No Smoking Area

58 Miners Arms

Rhes-y-cae, Holywell, Flintshire CH8 8JG

☎ 01352 781636

Real Ales

59 The Miners Arms

Church Lane, Gwernaffield, Mold, Flintshire CH7 5DT

☎ 01352 740803

60 Mostyn Lodge Hotel

Coast Rd, Mostyn, Holywell, Flintshire CH8 9HF

☎ 01745 561197

Real Ales, Bar Food, Restaurant Menu

62 The New Inn

Corwen Road, Pontblyddyn, Mold, Flintshire CH7 4HR

☎ 01352 771459

⊕ http://hompages.tesco.net/sandra.hunt1

Real Ales, Bar Food, Restaurant Menu, No Smoking Area

The New Inn offers home-cooked food, great drink and genuine hospitality to all guests. Owners Sandra and Dave Hunt are friendly and welcoming hosts. This large and handsome inn dates back to the late 1700s and is tastefully decorated.

Justly renowned for its food, guests choose from the menu or specials board from a range of specialities created by chef Sandra, and including a chicken and bacon dish in Stilton sauce. The Sunday roast dinners are a real must. Upstairs there's a no-smoking restaurant that seats 30, while downstairs the dining area seats 26. The inn also serves real ales together with a good selection of lagers, wines, spirits and soft drinks. Children welcome.

☛ South of Mold on the A541 to Pontblyddyn, then right onto the A5104 (Corwen Road)

🍺 Reverend James plus 2 rotating guest ales

🍴 Mon-Thurs 12-8.30; Fri-Sat 12-9.30; Sun 12-7.15

♫ Tues folk singing from 9 p.m.

⛭ Car park, access for people with disabilities, garden, children's play area

💳 Not Amex or Diners

🕐 11.30-11 (Sun and Bank Holidays to 10.30)

🏛 Corwen 10 miles, Mold 5 miles, Ruthin 8 miles, Wrexham 20 miles

61 Mountain Park

Northop Rd, Flint Mountain, Flint,
Flintshire CH6 5QG
☎ 01352 736000
Real Ales, Bar Food, Restaurant Menu,
Accommodation, No Smoking Area

62 The New Inn

See panel on page 111

63 The New Inn

Deeside, Flintshire CH5 2PT
☎ 01244 535852

64 Old Wine Vaults

Cross St, Holywell, Flintshire CH8 7LP
☎ 01352 714801
Real Ales

65 Owain Glyndwr Inn

Glyndwr Rd, Gwernymynydd, Mold,
Flintshire CH7 5LP
☎ 01352 752913
Real Ales

66 The Packet House

Mostyn Rd, Greenfield, Holywell, Flintshire CH8 7EJ
☎ 01352 714774

67 The Parrot Inn

Drury Lane, Buckley, Mold, Flintshire CH7 3DX
☎ 01244 550477

68 Piccadilly Inn

Mold, Flintshire CH7 5AW
☎ 01352 720284

69 The Plough Inn

Ruthin Rd, Llandegla, Wrexham, Flintshire LL11 3AB
☎ 01978 790672

70 The Poachers Cottage

High St, Ffrith, Wrexham, Flintshire LL11 5LH
☎ 01978 756465
Real Ales

71 Pwll Gwyn

Denbigh Rd, Afonwen, Mold, Flintshire CH7 5UB
☎ 01352 720227
Real Ales, Bar Food, Restaurant Menu,
Accommodation, No Smoking Area

72 Queens Head

Chester Rd, Mold, Flintshire CH7 1UQ
☎ 01352 753667
Restaurant Menu, No Smoking Area

73 Railway Inn

Main Rd, Ffynnongroyw, Holywell,
Flintshire CH8 9SN
☎ 01745 560447

74 The Railway Inn

Corwen Rd, Pontybodmin, Mold,
Flintshire CH7 4TG
☎ 01352 771255
Real Ales

75 Rainbow Inn

Ruthin Rd, Gwernymynydd, Mold,
Flintshire CH7 5LG
☎ 01352 752575

76 The Raven Inn

Chapel St, Llanarmon yn Lal, Mold,
Flintshire CH7 4OE
☎ 01824 780787
Real Ales, Bar Food

77 Red Lion Country Inn

See panel opposite

78 Red Lion Hotel

28 High St, Holywell, Flintshire CH8 7LH
☎ 01352 710097

79 Red Lion Hotel

Hawarden Rd, Hope, Wrexham,
Flintshire LL12 9NG
☎ 01978 760508
Real Ales, Bar Food, Restaurant Menu,
No Smoking Area

77 Red Lion Country Inn

Llanasa, Nr Holywell, Flintshire CH8 9NE
☎ 01745 854291

Real Ales, Bar Food, Restaurant Menu,
Accommodation, No Smoking Area

The Red Lion Country Inn is handsome and
welcoming, a spacious inn boasting traditional
features such as the massive stonebuilt fireplace,
adding to the cosy ambience.

Very much a family-run inn, owners Mary and
John, who have been here since 1999, are ably
assisted by their son, licensee Ian and his partner
Joanne, daughter Jane and her husband Gareth

(Gareth is in charge of the cellar and beer) and
daughter Victoria and her husband Haydn. Ian,
Jane and Victoria are all chefs, and create an
extensive menu of delicious bar meals and main
courses using the freshest ingredients. Booking
required at weekends.

☛ Llanasa can be reached by taking the A55
and then the A5151 and turning right at
Trelawnyd

🍺 Websters, Courage Directors

‖ Mon-Thurs 12-2.30 & 5.30-9.30; all day Fri-
Sun

🛏 5 en suite rooms

♫ Live entertainment first Fri of the month

🅿 Car park, courtesy bus for people living or
staying nearby, access for people with
disabilities

⊘ Not Amex or Diners

🏵 Welsh Tourist Board 3 stars (accommodation)

🕐 11.30-11 (Sun and Bank Holidays to 10.30)

🏛 Prestatyn 4 miles, Bodryddan Hall 4 miles,
Rhyl 6 miles

80 The Red Lion

Wrexham St, Mold, Flintshire CH7 1ET
☎ 01352 758739
Real Ales

81 Rock Inn

St Asaph Rd, Lloc, Holywell, Flintshire CH8 8RD
☎ 01352 710049
Real Ales, Bar Food, Restaurant Menu,
No Smoking Area

82 Rose & Thistle

60 Spon Green, Buckley, Mold, Flintshire CH7 3BH
☎ 01244 540112
Real Ales, No Smoking Area

83 Royal Oak

Water St, Caerwys, Mold, Flintshire CH7 5AT
☎ 01352 720269

84 Royal Oak

Greenfield Rd, Holywell, Flintshire CH8 7QB
☎ 01352 714463
Bar Food, Restaurant Menu, No Smoking Area

85 Royal Oak Inn

Denbigh Rd, Hendre, Mold, Flintshire CH7 5QE
☎ 01352 741466
Real Ales

86 Ruthin Castle

75 New St, Mold, Flintshire CH7 1NY
☎ 01352 752748
Real Ales

87 Sir Gerwain & The Green Knight

Golftyn Lawe, Connahs Quay, Deeside,
Flintshire CH5 4BH
☎ 01244 812623
Real Ales, Bar Food

88 Smugglers Inn

Station Rd, Talacre, Flintshire CH8 9RD

☎ 01745 852070

Real Ales, Bar Food, Restaurant Menu,
No Smoking Area

89 Swan Inn

Swan Lane, Gwernymynyd, Flintshire CH7 4AT

☎ 01352 752537

Real Ales, Bar Food, No Smoking Area

90 Talacre Arms

Gwespyr Hill, Gwespyr, Holywell, Flintshire CH8 9JS

☎ 01745 855898

Real Ales

91 Talacre Arms

New Rd, Holywell, Flintshire CH8 7LS

☎ 01352 710357

Accommodation

92 Travellers Inn

Mold, Flintshire CH7 5BL

☎ 01352 720251

Real Ales, Bar Food, Restaurant Menu,
Accommodation, No Smoking Area

93 Upper Ship Inn

Sandy Lane, Bagillt, Flint, Flintshire CH6 6EQ

☎ 01352 732189

94 The Victoria Inn

Baggauit, Flint, Flintshire CH6 6JB

☎ 01352 714251

Real Ales

95 The Wepre Inn

Wepre Lane, Deeside, Flintshire CH5 4JU

☎ 01244 818123

Bar Food, Restaurant Menu, No Smoking Area

103 Y Pentan

3 New Street, Mold, Flintshire CH7 1NY

☎ 01352 758884

Real Ales, Bar Food, Restaurant Menu

Occupying a corner position in the heart of Mold,
Y Pentan is a large and welcoming inn that is
handsome and traditional inside and out. The
interior boasts a wealth of wood – the floors, bar,
seating and ceilings are all warm wood tones,
while the unusual décor in the bar/music room
includes electric guitars adorning the walls.

A full history of the inn and how it came to
have its present name (it was known as The Cross
Keys until 1981) is proudly displayed for all to see.
The menu includes home-cooked ham, Cajun
chicken and steak pie, baguettes, steaks and more,
along with a good range of daily specials. Children
welcome.

☛ The inn is located in the centre of Mold, 10
miles west of Chester on the A55/A494

🍺 Rotating guest ale

🍴 Mon-Sat 10.30-3

🎵 Thurs jam sessions from 8.30 p.m., Fri-Sat
disco from 8 p.m., Sun karaoke from 8 p.m.,
occasional live bands

♿ Access for people with disabilities, nearby
car parks

💳 All the major cards

🕐 11.30-11 (Sun and Bank Holidays to 10.30)

🏛 Chester 10 miles, Ruthin 10 miles, Prestatyn
20 miles

96 The White Bear Inn

Mancot Lane, Mancot, Deeside, Flintshire CH5 2AH

☎ 01244 539077

Real Ales, Bar Food

97 White Horse Inn

High St, Bagillt, Flintshire CH6 6AP

☎ 01352 733283

Real Ales, Bar Food, Restaurant Menu

98 White Horse Inn

The Square, Cilorin, Flintshire CH7 5NN

☎ 01352 740142

Real Ales, Bar Food

99 The White Lion

Mold Rd, Buckley, Mold, Flintshire CH7 2NH

☎ 01244 548502

Real Ales, Restaurant Menu, No Smoking Area

100 White Lion Inn

Glan-yr-afon, Holywell, Flintshire CH8 9BQ

☎ 01745 560280

Real Ales

101 White Lion Inn

Hawarden Rd, Hope, Wrexham,
Flintshire LL12 9NF

☎ 01978 760572

Real Ales

102 Y Delyn Wine Bar

3 King St, Mold, Flintshire CH7 1LA

☎ 01352 759642

Real Ales

103 Y Pentan

See panel opposite

104 Yacht Inn

291 Chester Rd, Oakenholt, Flint,
Flintshire CH6 5SE

☎ 01352 733288

Real Ales, Bar Food

105 Ye Olde Talbot Inn

Cymau Rd, Cymau, Wrexham, Flintshire LL11 5LB

☎ 01978 761410

Real Ales

■ Gwynedd Reference Number - Detailed Information

▢ Gwynedd Reference Number - Summary Entry

Ceredigion
Page 249   Adjacent area - refer to pages indicated

GWYNEDD

CAERNARFON • PWLLHELI • FFESTINIOG

The county of Gwynedd, named after the old Kingdom of Gwynedd, was created in 1974 as one of the eight new administrative counties of Wales. Although one of the biggest in terms of geographical area, it was also one of the most sparsely populated. A large proportion of the population being Welsh-speaking, it became once again a centre of nationalism, with Plaid Cymru gaining a toehold which helped the party on to greater success.

In the latest round of local government reorganisation, on April 1, 1996, it was reconstituted to cover a different area, losing Anglesey, which became a county in its own right, and Aberconwy to the new Conwy county borough.

As the new Gwynedd covers most of the traditional counties of Caernarfonshire (less the part in the borough of Conwy) and Merionethshire, the reconstituted county was originally named Caernarfonshire and Merionethshire. As one of its first actions, the Council renamed the county Gwynedd on April 2 1996.

Caernarfon and Bangor lie at opposite ends of the Menai Strait, the channel of water that separates mainland Wales from the Isle of Anglesey.

A cathedral and university city, Bangor has a wide variety of architectural styles that serve as a reminder of the city's long history. A monastic community was founded here as early as AD 525.

To the west of the town and overlooking Beaumaris on the Isle of Anglesey lies Penrhyn Castle (National Trust), a dramatic structure begun by Thomas Hopper in 1820. The gouged rock of the Penrhyn Slate Quarries, some five miles southeast of Bangor, forms a huge hillside amphitheatre.

The Lleyn Peninsula forms the great curve of Caernarfon Bay – over 100 miles of its shoreline have been designated an Area of Outstanding Natural Beauty. During the Middle Ages, Bardsey Island, lying off the western tip of the peninsula, was a place of pilgrimage.

Moelwyn Bach, Snowdonia

Caernarfon Castle, as much as royal residence as a fortress, was the place where Edward I created the first Prince of Wales when he crowned his own son. Centuries later, in 1969, it was in the grounds of this splendid castle that Queen Elizabeth invested the same title on her eldest son, Prince Charles.

Harlech Castle

Of the three National Parks in Wales, Snowdonia, at 840 square miles, is the largest and certainly the most dramatic scenically. Embracing a number of mountain and hill ranges, Snowdonia extends southwards into the heart of Wales and incorporates stretches of the coastline and Cader Idris. There are several routes to the summit, the least arduous being the Snowdon Mountain Railway that runs from Llanberis.

Portmeirion

The southern region of Snowdonia National Park is dominated by two natural features: to the east there is Bala Lake (or Llyn Tegid) and to the southwest is Cader Idris. Bala is a Site of Special Scientific Interest, with many walks and also a narrow-gauge railway that runs along the eastern bank. To the south of Dolgellau, the chief market town of southern Snowdonia, lies Cader Idris, at 2,927 feet dominating the surrounding coast and countryside.

Edward I's Iron Ring of Fortresses stretched down as far as Harlech Castle, now a World Heritage Site.

1 Abbeyfield Hotel

Talybont, Bethesda, Bangor, Gwynedd LL57 3UR

☎ 01248 352219

Real Ales, Bar Food, Restaurant Menu,
Accommodation, No Smoking Area

2 The Aber Falls Tavern

Aber Rd, Abergwyngregyn, Llanfairfechan,
Gwynedd LL33 0LD

☎ 01248 680579

Real Ales, Bar Food, Restaurant Menu,
Accommodation, No Smoking Area

3 Ael-Y-Bryn Hotel

Dyffryn Ardudwy, Gwynedd LL44 2BE

☎ 01341 242701

Real Ales, Bar Food, Restaurant Menu,
Accommodation, No Smoking Area

4 Alexandra Hotel

North Rd, Caernarfon, Gwynedd LL55 1BA

☎ 01286 672871

Real Ales

5 Anglesey Arms Hotel

Slate Quay, Caernarfon, Gwynedd LL55 1SG

☎ 01286 672158

Real Ales, Bar Food, Accommodation

6 Arbour Hotel

Marine Parade, Barmouth, Gwynedd LL42 1NE

☎ 01341 280459

Bar Food, Restaurant Menu, Accommodation,
No Smoking Area

7 The Arthur Hotel

6 Marine Parade, Tywyn, Gwynedd LL36 0DE

☎ 01654 712146

Restaurant Menu, Accommodation,
No Smoking Area

8 The Australia Public House

31 High St, Porthmadog, Gwynedd LL49 9LR

☎ 01766 510930

Real Ales, Bar Food, No Smoking Area

9 The Bae Abermaw

Panorama Rd, Barmouth, Gwynedd LL42 1DQ

☎ 01341 280550

Restaurant Menu, Accommodation,
No Smoking Area

10 Bala Lake Hotel

Llangower, Bala, Gwynedd LL23 7BT

☎ 01678 521585

Bar Food, Restaurant Menu, Accommodation,
No Smoking Area

11 Bar Llewelyn

Caernarfon, Gwynedd LL55 1RF

☎ 01286 674333

Bar Food, Restaurant Menu, No Smoking Area

12 Barmouth Hotel

Church St, Barmouth, Gwynedd LL42 1EG

☎ 01341 280400

13 Bedol Y

Bethel, Caernarfon, Gwynedd LL55 1AX

☎ 01248 670155

Real Ales, Bar Food, No Smoking Area

14 Black Boy Inn

Northgate St, Caernarfon, Gwynedd LL55 1RW

☎ 01286 673604

Real Ales, Bar Food, Restaurant Menu,
Accommodation, No Smoking Area

15 Bodfor Hotel

Aberdovey, Gwynedd LL35 0EA

☎ 01654 767475

Accommodation, No Smoking Area

16 Braich Goch Inn

See panel on page 120

17 Brigands Inn

Mallwyd, Machynlleth, Gwynedd SY20 9HJ

☎ 01650 531208

Real Ales, Bar Food, Restaurant Menu,
Accommodation, No Smoking Area

16 Braich Goch Bunkhouse & Inn

Corris, Machynlleth, Powys SY20 9RD

☎ 01654 761229 ⊕ www.braichgoch.co.uk

Real Ales, Accommodation, No Smoking Area

☛ Adjacent to the A487 at Corris

🍺 Rotating guest ales

⊨ 6 rooms (4 en suite)

⚒ Outdoor activity centre

🏵 Welsh Tourist Board 3 stars

🕓 Thurs-Sat and Bank Holidays 6-11

🏛 King Arthur's Labyrinth, Corris Craft Centre, Dolgellau 6 miles

18 The Britannia Inn

New St, Aberdovey, Gwynedd LL35 0EG

☎ 01654 767426

Real Ales, Bar Food, Restaurant Menu, No Smoking Area

19 Bron Eifion Country House Hotel

Criccieth, Gwynedd LL52 0SA

☎ 01766 522385

Real Ales, Bar Food, Restaurant Menu, Accommodation, No Smoking Area

20 Brondanw Arms

Llanfrothen, Penrhyndeudraeth, Gwynedd LL48 6AQ

☎ 01766 770555

Real Ales, Bar Food, Restaurant Menu, No Smoking Area

23 Bryn Hir Arms

High Street, Criccieth, Gwynedd LL52 0BT

☎ 01766 522493

Restaurant Menu, No Smoking Area

Set just a short stroll from Criccieth Castle and the seafront, Bryn Hir Arms is a traditional stonebuilt inn dating back to 1631, when it was built as a farmhouse.

Cosy and comfortable, the inn retains many attractive original features such as the exposed beamwork. The bar stocks a good selection of draught keg ales including Tetleys, Caffreys, Guinness and Greenalls Mild, together with a good range of lagers, wines, spirits and soft drinks.

Tasty snacks and meals from the menu and specials board are served in the bar, the intimate bistro and in the large rear garden, with a good choice of home-cooked dishes using locally-sourced ingredients.

The inn also boasts a separate games room with its own bar. Children welcome.

☛ The inn is on Criccieth's main street (A497)

🍺 12-2.30 & 6-9.30

⚒ Car park, garden, games room, disabled access

All major cards

 11.30-11 (Sun and Bank Holidays to 10.30)

🕓 Porthmadog 4 miles, Portmeirion 6 miles, Blaenau Ffestiniog 10 miles

🏛

21 Bryn Arms

Gellilydan, Blaenau Ffestiniog,
Gwynedd LL41 4EN

☎ 01766 590379

Real Ales, Bar Food, Restaurant Menu,
No Smoking Area

22 Bryn Eglwys Country House Hotel

Bryn Eglwys, Beddgelert, Caernarfon,
Gwynedd LL55 4NB

☎ 01766 510260

Restaurant Menu, Accommodation,
No Smoking Area

23 Bryn Hir Arms

See panel opposite

24 Bryn Mor Hotel

Caernarfon, Gwynedd LL54 5TW

☎ 01286 830314

Restaurant Menu, Accommodation,
No Smoking Area

25 Bryncynan Inn

Morfa Nefyn, Pwllheli, Gwynedd LL53 6AA

☎ 01758 720879

Real Ales, Bar Food, Restaurant Menu,
Accommodation, No Smoking Area

26 The Bull Inn

69 High St, Bethesda, Bangor, Gwynedd LL57 3AR

☎ 01248 600438

Real Ales

27 Cadwgan Hotel

Llwyn Cadwgan, Dyffryn Ardudwy,
Gwynedd LL44 2HA

☎ 01341 247240

Real Ales, Bar Food, Restaurant Menu,
Accommodation, No Smoking Area

28 Caeau Capel Hotel

Rhodfar Mor Nefyn, Pwllheli, Gwynedd LL53 6EB

☎ 01758 720240

Real Ales, Restaurant Menu, Accommodation,
No Smoking Area

29 Castle Hotel

Castle Square, Caernarfon, Gwynedd LL55 2NF

☎ 01286 677970

30 Castle Hotel

Castle Sq, Harlech, Gwynedd LL46 2YH

☎ 01766 780529

Real Ales, Bar Food, Restaurant Menu,
Accommodation, No Smoking Area

31 The Castle Inn

1 Parciau Terrace, Criccieth, Gwynedd LL52 0RW

☎ 01766 523515

Real Ales, Bar Food

32 Celtic Royal Hotel

Bangor St, Caernarfon, Gwynedd LL55 1AY

☎ 01286 674477

Bar Food, Restaurant Menu, Accommodation,
No Smoking Area

33 Cliffs Inn

Beach Rd, Morfa Nefyn, Pwllheli,
Gwynedd LL53 6BY

☎ 01758 720356

Real Ales, Bar Food, Restaurant Menu,
Accommodation, No Smoking Area

34 Clifton House Hotel

Smithfield Square, Dolgellau, Gwynedd LL40 1ES

☎ 01341 422554

Restaurant Menu, Accommodation,
No Smoking Area

35 Coach Inn

Clynnog Fawr, Caernarfon, Gwynedd LL54 5PB

☎ 01286 660212

Real Ales, Bar Food, Restaurant Menu,
Accommodation, No Smoking Area

36 Commercial Hotel

Commercial Square, Blaenau Ffestiniog,
Gwynedd LL41 3HP

☎ 01766 830296

Real Ales

37 Corbett Arms Hotel

Corbett Square, Tywyn, Gwynedd LL36 9DG

☎ 01654 710264

Bar Food, Restaurant Menu, Accommodation, No Smoking Area

38 Cross Foxes Hotel

Trawsfynydd, Blaenau Ffestiniog, Gwynedd LL41 4SE

☎ 01766 540204

Real Ales, Bar Food, Accommodation

39 The Crown

Church St, Barmouth, Gwynedd LL42 1EW

☎ 01341 280326

Real Ales

40 Crown Hotel

37-39 High St, Pwllheli, Gwynedd LL53 5RT

☎ 01758 612664

Restaurant Menu, Accommodation, No Smoking Area

41 The Crown Inn

See panel below

42 Cwellyn Arms

Rhydd Ddu, Caernarfon, Gwynedd LL54 6TL

☎ 01766 890321

Real Ales, Bar Food, Restaurant Menu, Accommodation, No Smoking Area

43 Deucoch Hotel

Sarn Bach, Abersoch, Pwllheli, Gwynedd LL53 7LD

☎ 01758 712680

Real Ales, Bar Food, Restaurant Menu, Accommodation, No Smoking Area

44 Dol Peris Hotel

High St, Llanberis, Caernarfon, Gwynedd LL55 4HA

☎ 01286 870350

Restaurant Menu, Accommodation, No Smoking Area

---

41 The Crown – Y Goran

15/19 High Street, Caernarfon LL55 1RH

☎ 01286 675969

Bar Food, Restaurant Menu, No Smoking Area

Dating back to 1610 and recently refurbished so that it is now open-plan and much more airy and spacious, Y Goran (The Crown) is set in the heart of Caernarfon overlooking the castle. The interior is comfortable and welcoming, with a happy mix of modern and traditional features.

Everything from breakfasts to late dinners are available here, where owner Pam, a qualified chef, blends the freshest ingredients to create a range of tempting dishes and snacks. Sandwiches, steaks, haddock, lamb – all the traditional and hearty favourites are here. Pam's husband Paul looks after the bar, stocking a good selection of draught keg bitters, lagers, cider and stout, together with wines, spirits and soft drinks.

Although there is no accommodation here, Pam and Paul are happy to advise on local B&Bs. Children welcome.

☞ In centre of Caernarfon, overlooking the Castle.

🍴 10-9

♫ Tues folk singing from 9 p.m.

💳 All the major cards

🕐 10-11 (Sun and Bank Holidays to 10.30)

🏛 Llanberis 8 miles, Snowdonia National Park 7 miles

45 The Dolbrodmaeth Riverside Hotel

Dinas Mawddwy, Machynlleth, Gwynedd SY20 9LP

☎ 01650 531333

Real Ales, Bar Food, Restaurant Menu

46 Douglas Arms Hotel

High St, Bethesda, Bangor, Gwynedd LL57 3NU

☎ 01248 600219

Real Ales, No Smoking Area

47 Dovey Inn

8 Sea View Terrace, Aberdovey, Gwynedd LL35 0EF

☎ 01654 767332

Real Ales, Bar Food, Accommodation,
No Smoking Area

48 Dyffryn Country Inn

Dyffryn Ardudwy, Gwynedd LL44 2HD

☎ 01341 247498

Real Ales, Bar Food, Restaurant Menu,
No Smoking Area

49 The Eagles Hotel

Tithebarn St, Caernarfon, Gwynedd LL55 2RF

☎ 01286 674517

50 The Fairbourne Hotel

Beach Rd, Fairbourne, Gwynedd LL38 2HQ

☎ 01341 250203

Real Ales, Bar Food, Restaurant Menu,
Accommodation, No Smoking Area

51 The Feathers Inn

Llanystumdwy, Criccieth, Gwynedd LL52 0SH

☎ 01766 523276

Real Ales

52 Ffestiniog Railway & Spooners Bar

Harbour Station, Porthmadog, Gwynedd LL49 9NF

☎ 01766 512340

53 Fronoleu Hall

Llanaber, Barmouth, Gwynedd LL42 1YT

☎ 01341 280491

Restaurant Menu, Accommodation,
No Smoking Area

54 Garddfon Inn

Beach Rd, Y Felinheli, Gwynedd LL56 4RQ

☎ 01248 670359

Real Ales, Bar Food, Restaurant Menu,
No Smoking Area

55 Garthangharad Hotel

Llwyngwril, Gwynedd LL37 2UZ

☎ 01341 250484

Real Ales, Bar Food, Accommodation,
No Smoking Area

56 George III Hotel

Penmaenpool, Dolgellau, Gwynedd LL40 1YD

☎ 01341 422525

Real Ales, Bar Food, Restaurant Menu,
Accommodation, No Smoking Area

57 The George Inn

35-37 Carneddi Rd, Bethesda, Bangor,
Gwynedd LL57 3SE

☎ 01248 600015

Real Ales

58 George IV Hotel

High St, Criccieth, Gwynedd LL52 0BS

☎ 01766 522168

Real Ales, Bar Food, Restaurant Menu,
Accommodation, No Smoking Area

59 Glyntwrog Inn

Llanrug, Caernarfon, Gwynedd LL55 4AN

☎ 01286 671191

Real Ales, Bar Food, Restaurant Menu,
No Smoking Area

60 Glyn-Y-Coed Hotel

Portmadoc Rd, Criccieth, Gwynedd LL52 0HP

☎ 01766 522870

Real Ales, Bar Food, Restaurant Menu,
Accommodation, No Smoking Area

61 Glyn-Y-Weddw Arms

Llanbedrog, Abersoch, Pwllheli, Gwynedd LL53 7TH

☎ 01758 740212

Real Ales, Bar Food, Restaurant Menu,
No Smoking Area

62 The Goat Hotel

41 Stryd Fawr, Bala, Gwynedd LL23 7AF

☎ 01678 521189

Real Ales, Bar Food, Accommodation,
No Smoking Area

63 Goat Hotel

Station Rd, Pen-Y-Groes, Caernarfon,
Gwynedd LL54 6NW

☎ 01286 880241

Real Ales, No Smoking Area

64 Gors Bach Inn

Llanddeiniolen, Caernarfon, Gwynedd LL55 3AD

☎ 01248 670221

Restaurant Menu, No Smoking Area

65 Grapes Hotel

Maentwrog, Blaenau Ffestiniog,
Gwynedd LL41 4HN

☎ 01766 590365

Real Ales, Bar Food, Restaurant Menu,
Accommodation, No Smoking Area

66 Griffin Inn

Penrhyndeudraeth, Gwynedd LL48 6LW

☎ 01766 771706

Bar Food

67 Guarrymans Arms

Pen-Y-Groes, Caernarfon, Gwynedd LL54 6SG

☎ 01286 880418

Real Ales

68 Gwernan Lake Hotel

Islawdref, Dolgellau, Gwynedd LL40 1TL

☎ 01341 422488

Real Ales, Bar Food, Restaurant Menu,
Accommodation, No Smoking Area

69 Gwesty Minffordd Hotel

Tal-Y-Llyn, Tywyn, Gwynedd LL36 9AJ

☎ 01654 761665

Real Ales, Bar Food, Restaurant Menu,
Accommodation, No Smoking Area

70 Gwynedd Hotel and Restaurant

High St, Llanberis, Caernarfon, Gwynedd LL55 4SU

☎ 01286 870203

Real Ales, Bar Food, Restaurant Menu,
Accommodation, No Smoking Area

71 Halfway House

Bontddu, Dolgellau, Gwynedd LL40 2UE

☎ 01341 430635

Real Ales, Bar Food, Restaurant Menu,
No Smoking Area

72 Halfway House

Bangor Rd, Y Felinheli, Gwynedd LL56 4JQ

☎ 01248 670992

Real Ales, Bar Food, Restaurant Menu,
Accommodation, No Smoking Area

73 Halfway Inn

Hyfrydle Rd, Pen-Y-Groes, Caernarfon,
Gwynedd LL54 6HG

☎ 01286 880433

74 The Harbour Hotel

Lonengan, Abersoch, Pwllheli, Gwynedd LL53 7HR

☎ 01758 712406

Accommodation, No Smoking Area

75 Harp Inn

Llandwrog, Caernarfon, Gwynedd LL54 5SY

☎ 01286 831071

Real Ales, Bar Food, Restaurant Menu,
Accommodation, No Smoking Area

76 The Harp Inn

South Penrallt, Caernarfon, Gwynedd LL55 1NS

☎ 01286 676715

Bar Food, No Smoking Area

77 The Heights Hotel

74 High Street, Llanberis, Gwynedd LL55 4HB

☎ 01286 871179

⊕ www.heightshotel.co.uk

Real Ales, Restaurant Menu, Accommodation, No Smoking Area

Set in Snowdonia, The Heights Hotel offers good food, drink and comfortable accommodation. Captivating views and a range of activities make this an ideal base for exploring the region. Guests can choose from the bar menu or enjoy an evening meal in the Dizzy Heights Bistro, where the cuisine is modern and innovative.

☞ On the A4086, 9 miles southeast of Caernarfon

🍺 3 rotating guest ales

🍴 summer: 12-3 & 6-9; winter: Sat-Sun 12-2, Weds-Sun 6-9

🛏 8 en suite rooms plus 3 bunkhouses sleeping 8 each

♫ Live music Fri from 8 p.m.

⚘ Parking, some disabled access, garden

💳 All the major cards

🕐 summer: Mon-Sat 12-11, Sun 12-10.30; closed Mon-Thurs until 3 p.m. in winter

🏛 Snowdon Mountain Railway, Padarn Country Park, Welsh Slate Museum, Caernarfon 9 miles

78 Hendre Mynach Hall

Llanaber Rd, Barmouth, Gwynedd LL42 1YH

☎ 01341 280549

79 The Hole In The Wall Inn

Hole In The Wall St, Caernarfon, Gwynedd LL55 1RF

☎ 01286 672145

Bar Food

80 Hotel Plas Dinorwic

Fford Siabod, Y Felinheli, Gwynedd LL56 4XA

☎ 01248 670559

Bar Food, Accommodation, No Smoking Area

81 The Kings Head

High St, Bethesda, Bangor, Gwynedd LL57 3AN

☎ 01248 600753

82 Kings Head Hotel

Glanypwll, Blaenau Ffestiniog, Gwynedd LL41 3PD

☎ 01766 830219

Real Ales

83 Lake View Hotel and Restaurant

Tan Y Pant, Llanberis, Caernarfon, Gwynedd LL55 4EL

☎ 01286 870422

Restaurant Menu, Accommodation, No Smoking Area

84 The Last Inn

See panel on page 126

85 Lion Hotel

Y Maes, Criccieth, Gwynedd LL52 0AA

☎ 01766 522460

Real Ales, Bar Food, Restaurant Menu, No Smoking Area

86 Lion Hotel

High St, Harlech, Gwynedd LL46 2SG

☎ 01766 780731

Real Ales, Bar Food, Accommodation

87 Lion Hotel

Tudweiliog, Pwllheli, Gwynedd LL53 8ND

☎ 01758 770244

Real Ales, Bar Food, Restaurant Menu, Accommodation, No Smoking Area

88 The Lion Hotel

High St, Barmouth, Gwynedd LL42 1DS

☎ 01341 280324

Real Ales, Restaurant Menu, Accommodation, No Smoking Area

89 Llanfair Arms

Groeslon, Caernarfon, Gwynedd LL54 7DE

☎ 01286 830743

Real Ales, No Smoking Area

84 The Last Inn

Church Street, Barmouth LL42 1EL
☎ 01344 280530
Real Ales, Bar Food, Restaurant Menu,
Accommodation

Set just a few hundred yards from the seafront in
Barmouth, The Last Inn is a spacious and very
handsome inn dating back in parts to the late
1400s. The interior is very cosy and intimate, with
traditional features and a warm and relaxed
ambience throughout.

Tempting meals are served every day at lunch
and dinner – booking required at weekends and
Bank Holidays. Traditional favourites are complemented by imaginative choices from the menu or
daily specials board.

There is no accommodation on site, but the
owners also play host to a charming holiday home
close by, which sleeps eight and is available all year
round, making a perfect base from which to
explore not just the attractions of the seaside and
Barmouth itself, but the surrounding region.

☞ Barmouth is on the A496 south of Harlech

🍺 Marstons Pedigree

🍴 12-3 & 6.30-9

🛏 Holiday home available (sleeps 8)

🎵 Weds quiz (winter) from 9; Irish music twice
yearly (March and Oct – ring for details)

💳 Not Amex

🕐 11.30-11 (Sun and Bank Holidays to 10.30)

🏛 Dolgellau 8 miles, Harlech 10 miles, Shell
Island 8 miles

90 Llangollen Vaults

31 High St, Bethesda, Bangor, Gwynedd LL57 3AN
☎ 01248 600491
Real Ales, Bar Food

91 Madryn Arms

Chwilog, Pwllheli, Gwynedd LL53 6SH
☎ 01766 810250
Bar Food, Restaurant Menu

92 The Manod

High St, Blaenau Ffestiniog, Gwynedd LL41 4DB
☎ 01766 830346
Real Ales

93 The Marine Hotel

See panel opposite

94 Marwyn Hotel

21 Marine Parade, Barmouth, Gwynedd LL42 1NA
☎ 01341 280185
Restaurant Menu, Accommodation

95 Miner's Arms

Llechwedd Slate Caverns, Blaenau Ffestiniog,
Gwynedd LL41 3NB
☎ 01766 830306
Bar Food, No Smoking Area

96 Min-Y-Mor Hotel

Marine Promenade, Barmouth, Gwynedd LL42 1HW
☎ 01341 280555
Real Ales, Restaurant Menu, Accommodation,
No Smoking Area

97 The Mitre Hotel

Mitre Square, Pwllheli, Gwynedd LL53 5HE
☎ 01758 614201
Real Ales, Bar Food, No Smoking Area

98 Mynydd Ednyfed Country House Hotel

Caernarfon Rd, Criccieth, Gwynedd LL52 0PH
☎ 01766 523269
Restaurant Menu, Accommodation,
No Smoking Area

93 The Marine Hotel

Castle Street, Criccieth, Gwynedd LL52 0EA

☎ 01766 522946

Real Ales, Restaurant Menu, Accommodation, No Smoking Area

Occupying an enviably lovely location in Criccieth, an unspoilt seaside resort on the fringes of Snowdonia National Park, Marine Hotel offers superb food, drink and accommodation. The hotel, set opposite Criccieth Castle, began life as a private residence for a Lancashire mill owner, and was built in the late 19th century. It became a hotel in the early 1900s. The real ales served in the cosy, friendly bar are complemented by a good selection of draught keg ales, lagers, cider and stout, wines, spirits and soft drinks. The restaurant menu and specials board offer up a range of tempting evening meals prepared using the freshest ingredients. Most of the guest bedrooms are on the first floor, and some include private seating areas where guests can enjoy fine views of the castle and seafront.

☛ Opposite Criccieth Castle – follow signs for the Castle from the centre of Criccieth (on the A497)

🍺 Rotating guest ales

🍴 6.30-7.30

🛏 15 en suite rooms

🅿 Adjacent off-road parking, disabled access

💳 All major cards

🏆 Welsh Tourist Board 2 stars

🕐 11.30-11 (Sun and Bank Holidays to 10.30)

🏛 Seafront, Criccieth Castle, Porthmadog 4 miles, Portmeirion 6 miles, Blaenau Ffestiniog 10 miles

99 Nanhoron Arms Hotel

Ffordd Dewi Sant Nefyn, Pwllheli, Gwynedd LL53 6EA

☎ 01758 720203

Real Ales, Bar Food, Restaurant Menu, Accommodation, No Smoking Area

100 Newborough Arms

Bontnewydd, Caernarfon, Gwynedd LL55 2UG

☎ 01286 673126

Real Ales, Bar Food, Restaurant Menu, No Smoking Area

101 Oakeley Arms Hotel

Tan-Y-Bwlch, Cae Clyd Manod, Blaenau Ffestiniog, Gwynedd LL41 3YU

☎ 01766 590277

Real Ales, Bar Food, Restaurant Menu, Accommodation, No Smoking Area

102 Padarn Lake Hotel

High St, Llanberis, Caernarfon, Gwynedd LL55 4SU

☎ 01286 870260

Real Ales, Bar Food, Restaurant Menu, Accommodation, No Smoking Area

103 Palace Vaults

22 Palace St, Caernarfon, Gwynedd LL55 1RR

☎ 01286 672093

Bar Food, Restaurant Menu, No Smoking Area

104 Pale Hall Hotel

Pale Estate, Llandderfel, Bala, Gwynedd LL23 7PS

☎ 01678 530285

Bar Food, Restaurant Menu, Accommodation, No Smoking Area

105 Pen Y Bont Hotel

Tal-Y-Llyn, Tywyn, Gwynedd LL36 9AJ

☎ 01654 782285

Real Ales, Bar Food, Restaurant Menu, No Smoking Area

106 Penbont Inn

Llanrug, Caernarfon, Gwynedd LL55 4AY

☎ 01286 674473

Real Ales, Bar Food, No Smoking Area

107 Pengwern Arms Hotel

Church Square, Llan Ffestiniog, Blaenau Ffestiniog, Gwynedd LL41 4PB

☎ 01766 762210

Real Ales, Bar Food, Restaurant Menu, Accommodation, No Smoking Area

108 Penhelig Arms Hotel

27-29 Terrace Rd, Aberdovey, Gwynedd LL35 0LT

☎ 01654 767215

Real Ales, Bar Food, Restaurant Menu, Accommodation, No Smoking Area

109 Peniarth Arms

Bryncrug, Tywyn, Gwynedd LL36 9PH

☎ 01654 711505

Real Ales, Bar Food, Restaurant Menu, Accommodation, No Smoking Area

110 Penmaenuchaf Hall Hotel

Penmaenpool, Dolgellau, Gwynedd LL40 1YB

☎ 01341 422129

Bar Food, Restaurant Menu, Accommodation, No Smoking Area

111 Penrhyn Arms

Sarn, Pwllheli, Gwynedd LL53 8DU

☎ 01758 730218

Accommodation, No Smoking Area

112 Pen-Y-Bont Hotel

Sarn, Pwllheli, Gwynedd LL53 8DT

☎ 01758 730478

Real Ales, Bar Food, Restaurant Menu, No Smoking Area

113 Pen-Y-Gwryd Hotel

Nant Gwynant, Caernarfon, Gwynedd LL55 4NT

☎ 01286 870211

Real Ales, Bar Food, Restaurant Menu, Accommodation, No Smoking Area

114 Plas Bodegroes Restaurant

Plas Bodegroes Efailnewydd, Pwllheli, Gwynedd LL53 5TH

☎ 01758 612363

Accommodation, No Smoking Area

115 Plas Coch Hotel

52 High St, Bala, Gwynedd LL23 7AB

☎ 01678 520309

Bar Food, Accommodation, No Smoking Area

116 Plas Dolmelynllyn Hall

Ganllwyd, Dolgellau, Gwynedd LL40 2HP

☎ 01341 440273

Restaurant Menu, Accommodation, No Smoking Area

118 The Prince Llewelyn Hotel

Smith Street, Beddgelert, Gwynedd LL55 4UY

☎ 01766 890242

🌐 www.princellewelyn.fsnet.co.uk

Restaurant Menu, Accommodation, No Smoking Area

The handsome Prince Llewelyn Hotel is a peaceful home from home with excellent accommodation, home-cooked food and a range of real ales and good wines. Beddgelert makes a charming base from which to explore the many sights and attractions of the region. The guest bedrooms are comfortable and attractive.

☞ The inn is in the heart of Beddgelert, at the junction of the A4085 and A498

🍺 Robinsons Unicorn and rotating guest ale

🍴 12-2 & 6-8.30

🛏 12 rooms (9 en suite)

💳 All the major cards

🕐 Mon-Thurs 11.30-2.30 & 6-11 (Sun and Bank Holidays to 10.30); Fri-Sat 11.30-11

🏛 Mount Snowdon, the coast 6 miles, Porthmadog 7 miles, Portmeirion 9 miles, Caernarfon 12 miles

117 Porth Tocyn Hotel

Bwlchtocyn, Abersoch, Pwllheli, Gwynedd LL53 7BU

☎ 01758 713303

Restaurant Menu, Accommodation,
No Smoking Area

118 The Prince Llewelyn

See panel opposite

119 Prince of Wales

42 High St, Llanberis, Caernarfon, Gwynedd LL55 4EU

☎ 01286 870708

Real Ales

120 Prince of Wales Hotel

High St, Criccieth, Gwynedd LL52 0HB

☎ 01766 522556

Real Ales, Bar Food, No Smoking Area

121 Prince of Wales Hotel

Bangor St, Caernarfon, Gwynedd LL55 1AR

☎ 01286 673367

Real Ales, Bar Food, Restaurant Menu,
Accommodation

122 Quality Hotel Snowdonia

Llanberis, Caernarfon, Gwynedd LL55 4TY

☎ 01286 870253

Real Ales, Bar Food, Restaurant Menu,
Accommodation, No Smoking Area

123 Queens Hotel

Morfa Rd, Harlech, Gwynedd LL46 2UF

☎ 01766 780480

Real Ales, Bar Food, Accommodation,
No Smoking Area

124 The Queens Hotel

1 High St, Blaenau Ffestiniog, Gwynedd LL41 3ES

☎ 01766 830055

Real Ales, Bar Food, Accommodation,
No Smoking Area

125 The Queens Hotel

Station Rd, Porthmadog, Gwynedd LL49 9HT

☎ 01766 512583

Real Ales, Bar Food, No Smoking Area

126 Railway Inn

Main St, Abergynolwyn, Tywyn, Gwynedd LL36 9YW

☎ 01654 782279

Real Ales, Bar Food, Restaurant Menu,
Accommodation, No Smoking Area

127 Red Lion Hotel

Dinas Mawddwy, Machynlleth, Gwynedd SY20 9JA

☎ 01650 531247

Real Ales, Bar Food, Restaurant Menu,
Accommodation, No Smoking Area

128 Rhiw Goch Inn

Bron Aber Trawsfftnydd, Blaenau Ffestiniog,
Gwynedd LL41 4UY

☎ 01766 540374

Real Ales, Bar Food, Restaurant Menu,
No Smoking Area

129 The Rivals Inn

Llanaelhaiarn, Caernarfon, Gwynedd LL54 5AG

☎ 01758 750669

Real Ales, Bar Food, Restaurant Menu,
No Smoking Area

130 Riverside Hotel - 16th Century Coaching Inn

Pennal, Nr Machynlleth, Powys SY20 9DW

☎ 01654 791285

**Real Ales, Restaurant Menu, Accommodation,
No Smoking Area**

☛ Pennal is on the A493 west of Machynlleth

🍺 Rotating guest ales

🍴 12-2.30 & 6-9.30

🛏 7 en suite rooms

🅿 Car park, garden, disabled access

💳 All major cards

🕐 11.00-3 & 6-11 (Sun and Bank Holidays to 10.30)

🏛 Machynlleth 4 , coast 2, Aberdyfi 4, Tywyn 7

131 The Riverside Hotel

Abersoch, Pwllheli, Gwynedd LL53 7HW

☎ 01758 712419

Bar Food, Restaurant Menu, Accommodation

132 Royal Goat Hotel

Beddgelert, Caernarfon, Gwynedd LL55 4YE

☎ 01766 890224

Bar Food, Restaurant Menu, Accommodation,
No Smoking Area

133 The Royal Madoc Arms Hotel

Market Square, Tremadog, Porthmadog,
Gwynedd LL49 9RB

☎ 01766 512021

Real Ales, Bar Food, Restaurant Menu,
Accommodation, No Smoking Area

134 Royal Oak

Ffordd Llanllechid, Bethesda, Bangor,
Gwynedd LL57 3EE

☎ 01248 602167

135 Royal Ship Hotel

Queens Square, Dolgellau, Gwynedd LL40 1AR

☎ 01341 422209

Real Ales, Bar Food, Restaurant Menu,
Accommodation, No Smoking Area

136 Rum Hole Tavern

Ffordd Newydd, Harlech, Gwynedd LL46 2UB

☎ 01766 780477

Bar Food, Restaurant Menu, Accommodation,
No Smoking Area

137 The Ship and Castle

53 High St, Porthmadog, Gwynedd LL49 9LR

☎ 01766 512217

Real Ales, Bar Food

138 Ship and Castle Hotel

9-11 Bangor St, Caernarfon, Gwynedd LL55 1AT

☎ 01286 672303

Bar Food, Accommodation

139 The Ship Hotel

34-36 Y Stryd Fawr, Bala, Gwynedd LL23 7AG

☎ 01678 520414

Bar Food, Restaurant Menu, Accommodation

140 Ship Hotel

Aberdaron Gwynned, Pwllheli, Gwynedd LL53 8BE

☎ 01758 760204

Real Ales, Bar Food, Restaurant Menu,
Accommodation, No Smoking Area

141 Ship Inn

Lon Gerddi Edern, Pwllheli, Gwynedd LL53 8YP

☎ 01758 720559

Restaurant Menu, Accommodation,
No Smoking Area

142 Ship Inn

Pwllheli, Gwynedd LL53 7PE

☎ 01758 740270

Real Ales, Bar Food, Restaurant Menu,
No Smoking Area

143 The Snowdon Inn

Llanberis Rd, Cwm Y Glo, Caernarfon,
Gwynedd LL55 4EE

☎ 01286 870289

Real Ales, Bar Food, Restaurant Menu,
Accommodation

144 Snowdonia Parc Brew Pub

See panel opposite

145 The Sportsman Hotel

High St, Nefyn, Pwllheli, Gwynedd LL53 6HD

☎ 01758 720205

Real Ales

146 Springfield Hotel

Beach Rd, Fairbourne, Gwynedd LL38 2PX

☎ 01341 250414

Real Ales, Bar Food, Restaurant Menu,
Accommodation, No Smoking Area

144 Snowdonia Parc Brew Pub

Waunfawr, Nr Caernarfon, Gwynedd LL55 4AQ
☎ 01286 650218/409
⊕ www.snowdonia-parc.co.uk

Real Ales, Bar Food, Restaurant Menu,
No Smoking Area

Originally a stationmaster's house and dating back to Victorian times, Snowdonia Parc Brew Pub is set in its own extensive grounds including a stretch of the River Gwyrfai. The pub is famous for its own ales, made with the finest malts and hops and clear Snowdonia water.

The restaurant serves an extensive menu much of which is genuinely home-cooked. Everything from soups and sandwiches to filled Yorkshire puddings, pies and casseroles is here, made with traditionally-reared meats. The puddings – apple pie, jam roly poly, bread-and-butter pudding and more – are well worth leaving room for!

This superb inn also boasts a small but charming caravan and camping site, so guests who come to enjoy the food and drink can stay to use the inn as a touring base. Families with dogs are welcome.

☞ Waunfawr is on the A4085 4 miles S of Caernarfon

🍺 Microbrewery on site

🍴 11am-8.15pm all day

⊨ Camping and caravan site

💳 All the major cards

🕐 11am-11pm (Sun 10.30pm and Bank Holidays to 11.30pm)

🏛 Welsh Highland Railway (adjacent), Snowdonia, Caernarfon to Beddgelert & Portmadoc (2006)

147 St Davids Hotel

Harlech, Gwynedd LL46 2PT
☎ 01766 780366
Real Ales, Bar Food, Restaurant Menu, Accommodation, No Smoking Area

148 St Tudwals Inn

High St, Abersoch, Pwllheli, Gwynedd LL53 7DS
☎ 01758 712539
Bar Food, Restaurant Menu, Accommodation, No Smoking Area

149 The Stables Hotel

Llanwnda, Caernarfon, Gwynedd LL54 5SD
☎ 01286 830711
Real Ales, Bar Food, Restaurant Menu, Accommodation, No Smoking Area

150 The Stag Inn

Bridge St, Dolgellau, Gwynedd, LL40 1AU
☎ 01341 422533
e-mail: jostocks9717@hotmail.com

Real Ales, Bar Food, Restaurant Menu

☞ In the heart of Dolgellau on the A470

🍺 Burtonwood Bitter plus changing guest ale

🍴 bar snacks 12-11 (Sun and Bank Holidays to 10.30)

🎵 Quiz night alternate Tues from 8.30, karaoke on request, pool room

🅿 Parking, garden, petting zoo, some disabled access

🕐 12-11 (Sun and Bank Holidays to 10.30)

🏛 Coed y Brenin Forest Park 4 miles, Tal-y-llyn 5½ miles, Barmouth 6 miles

151 The Sun Inn

Llanengan, Abersoch, Pwllheli, Gwynedd LL53 7LG
☎ 01758 712660
Real Ales, Bar Food, Restaurant Menu

152 Tafarn Dwynant

Ceinws, Machynlleth, Gwynedd SY20 9HA
☎ 01654 761660
Real Ales, Bar Food, Restaurant Menu

153 Tafarn Glanaber

Beach Rd, Morfa-Bychan, Porthmadog,
Gwynedd LL49 9YA
☎ 01766 514917
Real Ales, Bar Food, Restaurant Menu,
No Smoking Area

154 Tafarn Y Porth

5-9 Eastgate St, Caernarfon, Gwynedd LL55 1AG
☎ 01286 662920
Real Ales, Bar Food, Restaurant Menu,
No Smoking Area

155 Tafarn Yr Eryrod

See panel below

156 Tal-Y-Don Hotel

High St, Barmouth, Gwynedd LL42 1DL
☎ 01341 280508
Real Ales, Bar Food, Accommodation

157 Tanronnen Inn

Beddgelert, Caernarfon, Gwynedd LL55 4YB
☎ 01766 890347
Real Ales, Bar Food, Restaurant Menu,
Accommodation, No Smoking Area

158 Torrent Walk Hotel

Smithfield St, Dolgellau, Gwynedd LL40 1AA
☎ 01341 422858
Real Ales, Bar Food, Accommodation,
No Smoking Area

155 Tafarn Yr Eryrod

Llanuwchllyn, Nr Bala, Gwynedd LL23 7UB
☎ 01678 540278

**Real Ales, Bar Food, Restaurant Menu,
No Smoking Area**

A wonderful old stone building that began life as a farmhouse, hidden from the main Dolgellau to Bala road and older than the village church, Tafarn Yr Eryrod (The Eagles Inn) is traditional and welcoming, with low beamed ceilings and an inglenook fireplace, spacious and airy rooms and a warm ambience. Flowers from the gloriously colourful beer garden adorn the tables.

This friendly inn is family-run by Eleri Pugh, with assistance from her sons Gareth, Elgan and Owain, and husband Meirion, who tends the garden and superb blooms. Eleri is also the chef, creating excellent meals (booking required at weekends); the changing menu boasts traditional favourites lamb, beef, local produce and fresh fish.

- 🚩 5 miles southwest of Bala on the A494
- 🍺 1 rotating guest ale
- 🍴 12-2.30 & 6-9.30
- ♿ Car park, ramp into and within premises for people with disabilities, beer garden
- 💳 All the major cards
- 🕐 31st Oct-25thMarch every night 6-11 but closed Mon, Tues , Wed lunchtime, Summer: 11.30-11 (Sun and Bank Holidays to 10.30)
- 🏛 Bala 5 miles, Portmeirion 15 miles

160 The Tredegar Arms

10 College Green, Tywyn, Gwynedd LL36 9BS

☎ 01654 710368

Real Ales, Bar Food

Pristine and welcoming, Tredegar Arms is set in the heart of the charming village of Tywyn, close to attractions such as the Talyllyn Railway, Bird Rock (where cormorants still nest) and Castel-y-Bere, scene of Prince Llewelyn's last stand against England's Edward I. The pub boasts a handsome and attractive interior with comfortable seating

and, covering part of the ceiling, an outstanding mural painted in the mid-19th century by an impoverished French artist as a way to pay for his lodgings and featuring the faces of four local people. Real ales are complemented by hearty food at lunch and dinner, with a varied menu of traditional favourites. Owner Toni Southam has been here for 12 years, and is a friendly host as well as the chef. Together with her husband Neil and their proficient staff, they offer all their guests a warm and genuine welcome and real hospitality.

☞ On A493 in heart of Tywyn

🍺 Worthington Cask Regular plus 2 rotating guest ales

🍴 12-2 & 6.30-8.30

🎵 Sun and Thurs from 8 p.m.

🪑 Garden, disabled access

💳 All major cards

🕐 11.30-11 (Sun and Bank Holidays to 10.30)

🏛 Talyllyn Railway 1 mile, Aberdyfi 3½ miles, Dolgellau 15 miles

159 Tower Hotel

High St, Pwllheli, Gwynedd LL53 5RR

☎ 01758 612865

Real Ales, Accommodation

160 The Tredegar Arms

See panel above

161 Trefeddian Hotel

Aberdyfi, Aberdovey, Gwynedd LL35 0SB

☎ 01654 767213

Bar Food, Restaurant Menu, Accommodation, No Smoking Area

162 Tu Hwnt Ir Afon In

Rhydyclafdy, Pwllheli, Gwynedd LL53 7YH

☎ 01758 740235

Real Ales, Bar Food, Restaurant Menu, No Smoking Area

163 Twthill Vaults

Caernarfon, Gwynedd LL55 1PB

☎ 01286 673279

164 Ty Cloc Restaurant

Gallt-Y-Glyn, Llanberis, Gwynedd LL55 4EL

☎ 01286 870370

Restaurant Menu, Accommodation, No Smoking Area

165 Ty Coch Inn

Porthdinllaen, Morfa Nefyn, Gwynedd LL53 6DB

☎ 01758 720498

Bar Food, Restaurant Menu, Accommodation, No Smoking Area

166 Tyddyn Llwyn Hotel

Morfa Bychan Rd, Porthmadog, Gwynedd LL49 9UR

☎ 01766 513903

Real Ales, Bar Food, Restaurant Menu, Accommodation, No Smoking Area

167 Ty-Mawr Hotel

Llanbedr, Gwynedd LL45 2NH

☎ 01341 241440

Real Ales, Bar Food, Restaurant Menu, Accommodation, No Smoking Area

168 Tyn Y Groes Hotel

Ganllwyd, Dolgellau, Gwynedd LL40 2HN

☎ 01341 440275

Real Ales, Bar Food, Restaurant Menu,
Accommodation, No Smoking Area

169 Tynycornel Hotel

Tal-Y-Llyn, Tywyn, Gwynedd LL36 9AJ

☎ 01654 782282

Bar Food, Restaurant Menu, Accommodation,
No Smoking Area

170 Tyr Graig Castle Hotel

Llanaber Rd, Barmouth, Gwynedd LL42 1YN

☎ 01341 280470

171 Unicorn Inn

Smithfield Square, Dolgellau, Gwynedd LL40 1ES

☎ 01341 422742

Real Ales, Bar Food, Restaurant Menu

172 Vaynol Arms

Pentir, Bethesda, Bangor, Gwynedd LL57 4EA

☎ 01248 362896

Real Ales, Bar Food, Restaurant Menu,
Accommodation, No Smoking Area

173 Vaynol Arms

Abersoch, Pwllheli, Gwynedd LL53 7AP

☎ 01758 712776

Real Ales, Bar Food

174 The Victoria Hotel

Snowdon Street, Pen-y-Groes, Gwynedd LL54 6NG

☎ 01286 880087

Bar Food, Restaurant Menu

☛ Just off the main A487 close to the junction
with the B4418.

🍴 12-9 (from Easter 2005)

🅿 Adjacent off-road car park, disabled access

🚫 No smoking in restaurant or bedrooms

🕐 11.30-11 (Sun and Bank Holidays to 10.30)

🏛 Caernarfon 3 miles, Llanberis 5 miles,
Snowdon 4 miles

175 Victoria Hotel

High St, Bethesda, Bangor, Gwynedd LL57 3AN

☎ 01248 600481

Real Ales

176 Victoria Hotel

Embankment Rd, South Beach, Pwllheli,
Gwynedd LL53 5AA

☎ 01758 612834

Real Ales, Bar Food, Accommodation,
No Smoking Area

177 Victoria Hotel

Bangor St, Y Felinheli, Gwynedd LL56 4PZ

☎ 01248 670456

Real Ales, No Smoking Area

178 Victoria Inn

Llanbedr, Gwynedd LL45 2LD

☎ 01341 241213

Real Ales, Bar Food, Restaurant Menu,
Accommodation, No Smoking Area

179 The Wayside Pub and
Restaurant

Llanaber, Barmouth, Gwynedd LL42 1RR

☎ 01341 280200

Real Ales, Bar Food, Restaurant Menu,
No Smoking Area

180 White Lion Royal Hotel

61 High St, Bala, Gwynedd LL23 7AE

☎ 01678 520314

Real Ales, Bar Food, Restaurant Menu,
Accommodation, No Smoking Area

181 Whitehall

Corbett Square, Tywyn, Gwynedd LL36 9DF

☎ 01654 710212

Real Ales, Bar Food, Restaurant Menu,
No Smoking Area

182 Whitehall Hotel

Gaol St, Pwllheli, Gwynedd LL53 5RG

☎ 01758 614188

187 Ye Olde Bull's Head

78 High Street, Bala, Gwynedd LL23 7AD
☎ 01678 520438
Real Ales, Bar Food, Accommodation

Large, handsome and offering the best in traditional comforts, Ye Olde Bull's Head (Yr Hen Ben Tarw) offers great food, drink and accommodation. Set in the centre of popular and lovely Bala, this former coaching inn dates back to 1692.

Real fires, exposed beamwork and other traditional features add to the cosiness and relaxed ambience of the inn, while the guest bedrooms are tastefully decorated and comfortably furnished. Specialities of the menu and specials board include the mouthwatering mixed grill and steak dishes.

Owner Ellie Gumbley does all the cooking, and is quite a talented cook. Her husband Dave looks after the well-kept ales and front of house, and together with their staff offer all their guests a warm welcome and a high standard of service and quality.

Children welcome.

☛ In the centre of Bala on the A494

🍺 Abbot and rotating guest ale

🍴 12-3 & Sun-Fri 6-9

🛏 4 rooms

🅿 Parking, some disabled access

🕐 11.30-11 (Sun and Bank Holidays to 10.30)

🏛 Bala Lake, Bala Railway

---

183 Woodlands Hall Hotel

Edern, Pwllheli, Gwynedd LL53 6JB
☎ 01758 720425
Real Ales, Bar Food, Restaurant Menu, Accommodation, No Smoking Area

184 Wynnes Arms

Manod Rd, Blaenau Ffestiniog, Gwynedd LL41 4AR
☎ 01766 830401

185 Y Goron Fach

Hole In The Wall St, Caernarfon,
Gwynedd LL55 1RF
☎ 01286 673338
Real Ales, Bar Food, No Smoking Area

186 Y Meirion

High St, Blaenau Ffestiniog, Gwynedd LL41 3AE
☎ 01766 830761
Real Ales, Bar Food, Restaurant Menu,
No Smoking Area

187 Ye Olde Bulls Head

See panel above

188 Ysgethin Inn

Barmouth, Talybont, Gwynedd LL43 2AN
☎ 01341 247578
Real Ales, Bar Food, Restaurant Menu,
No Smoking Area

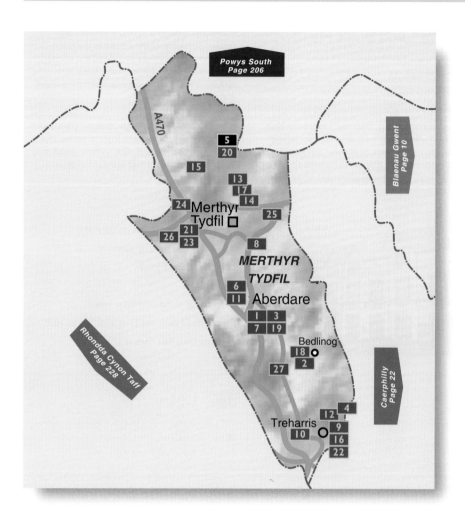

■ Merthyr Tydfil Reference Number - Detailed Information

12 Merthyr Tydfil Reference Number - Summary Entry

Ceredigion
Page 249   Adjacent area - refer to pages indicated

MERTHYR TYDFIL

MERTHYR TYDFIL • TREHARRIS • BEDLINOG

Merthyr Tydfil (in Welsh *Merthyr Tudful*) is a town and county borough in south Wales, with a population of about 55,000. A small village until the time of the Industrial Revolution, its reserves of iron ore, coal, limestone and water made it an ideal site for ironworks. By 1851 it was the largest town in Wales, with a population of 46,000. The current borough boundaries date back to 1974, when the former county borough of Merthyr Tydfil expanded slightly to cover Vaynor in Glamorgan and Bedlinog in Brecon. The district became a county borough again on April 1, 1996.

The main road in this area of Wales, the A645, acts as a dividing line: to the south are the historic valleys once dominated by coal mining and the iron and steel industries, while to the north lie the unspoilt southern uplands of the Brecon Beacons National Park. This rigidly observed divide is explained by its geology,

Cyfarthfa Castle

as the coal-bearing rocks of the valleys end here and give way to the limestone and old red sandstone rocks of the Brecon Beacons. The close proximity of the two different types of rocks also explains the nature and growth of industry in this particular area of South Wales, as the iron-smelting process required not just coal but also limestone. The iron ore was locally available, too. These ingredients all came together in the most productive way at Merthyr Tydfil, and this former iron and steel capital of the world was once the largest town in Wales.

Described as 'the most impressive monument of the Industrial Iron Age in Southern Wales', Cyfarthfa Castle is a grand mansion situated in beautiful and well-laid-out parkland. Today the mansion is home to a Museum and Art Gallery which not only covers the social and industrial history of the area but also has an extensive collection of fine and decorative art.

From Pontsticill, three miles north of Merthyr Tydfil, the Brecon Mountain Railway travels a short yet very scenic route up to Pontsticill Reservoir.

1 The Angel Inn

Bridge St, Troedyrhiw, Merthyr Tydfil CF48 4DX
☎ 01443 693726
Real Ales, No Smoking Area

2 The Bedlinog Inn

High St, Bedlinog, Treharris, Merthyr Tydfil CF46 6TG
☎ 01443 710222

3 Belle Vue Hotel

21-22 Bridge St, Troedyrhiw,
Merthyr Tydfil CF48 4DT
☎ 01443 690318
Real Ales

4 Bontnewydd Hotel

High St, Trelewis, Treharris, Merthyr Tydfil CF46 6AB
☎ 01443 410309

5 The Butchers Arms

See panel below

6 The Colliers Arms Bar And Restaurant

69 Nightingale St, Abercanaid,
Merthyr Tydfil CF48 1EJ
☎ 01443 690376
Bar Food, Restaurant Menu, No Smoking Area

7 Dynevor Arms

Ash Rd, Troedyrhiw, Merthyr Tydfil CF48 4HH
☎ 01443 690604

8 Farmers Arms

Mountain Hare, Abercanaid,
Merthyr Tydfil CF47 0LH
☎ 01685 722131

9 Glantaff Inn

Cardiff Rd, Quakers Yard, Treharris,
Merthyr Tydfil CF46 5AH
☎ 01443 410822
Real Ales, Bar Food, Restaurant Menu,
No Smoking Area

5 The Butchers Arms

Pontsticill, Mid-Glamorgan, Powys CF48 2UE
☎ 01685 723544

Real Ales, Restaurant Menu, No Smoking Area

The Butchers Arms in Pontsticill, just a few miles from Merthyr Tydfil, is a spotless and cosy hidden gem with a traditional old-fashioned décor including comfortable upholstered seating in the bar and lounge. Outside there's a small patio area where guests can enjoy a relaxing drink or meal on fine days. Licensees Edward and Sandra have been here since late 2004; it's their first venture into the licensing trade and they've made the most of this opportunity to create a successful and welcoming pub. From the grounds of the pub you are treated to the most amazing views over the Fechan Valley and down to the River Taf. Tasty snacks are on hand during opening hours, with a range of sandwiches, rolls and hot and cold savouries. Dishes on the menu include a hearty and delicious gammon steak, fish, home-made pies and steaks, with an accent on hearty and genuine home cooking.

🖝 3 miles north of Merthyr Tydfil off the A465 and B4554

🍺 Brains Smooth, rotating guest ale

🍴 12-2.30 & 7-9

♫ Thurs quiz night

🅿 Parking, patio

🕐 summer: 11.30-11; winter: 5-11 p.m. (Sun and Bank Holidays to 10.30)

🏛 Brecon Mountain Railway, Merthyr Tydfil 3 miles

10 Great Western Hotel

Edwardsville, Treharris, Merthyr Tydfil CF46 5NR

☎ 01443 410528

Bar Food, Restaurant Menu, No Smoking Area

11 Llwyn-Yr-Eos Inn

Canal Bank, Abercanaid,
Merthyr Tydfil CF48 1AJ

☎ 01443 690269

12 Navigation Hotel

Fox St, Treharris, Merthyr Tydfil CF46 5HE

☎ 01443 410329

Restaurant Menu, No Smoking Area

13 Pant Cad Ifor Inn

Ifor Pant Rd, Pant, Merthyr Tydfil CF48 2DD

☎ 01685 723688

Real Ales, Bar Food, Restaurant Menu,
No Smoking Area

14 Pantyscallog Inn

Pantyscallog Terrace, Pant,
Merthyr Tydfil CF48 2BT

☎ 01685 384153

15 Pontsarn Inn

Pontsarn Lane, Merthyr Tydfil CF48 2TS

☎ 01685 374786

Real Ales, Bar Food, Restaurant Menu,
Accommodation, No Smoking Area

16 Quakers Yard Inn

1 Dan-Y-Twyn, Quakers Yard, Treharris,
Merthyr Tydfil CF46 5AN

☎ 01443 412902

17 Quarrymans Arms

18 Francis Terrace, Pant,
Merthyr Tydfil CF48 2DA

☎ 01685 374733

Real Ales, No Smoking Area

18 The Railway Inn

High St, Bedlinog, Treharris, Merthyr Tydfil CF46 6RP

☎ 01443 710439

19 Railway Inn

56 Bridge St, Troedyrhiw, Merthyr Tydfil CF48 4JU

☎ 01443 690305

Real Ales, Bar Food, Restaurant Menu,
No Smoking Area

20 Red Cow Inn

Merthyr Tydfil, Merthyr Tydfil CF48 2UN

☎ 01685 384828

Real Ales, Bar Food

21 Red Lion Inn

82 Heolgerrig Rd, Heolgerrig,
Merthyr Tydfil CF48 1SB

☎ 01685 379101

22 The Royal Hotel

Thornwood Place, Treharris,
Merthyr Tydfil CF46 5AB

☎ 01443 412198

23 Six Bells

Heolgerrig Rd, Merthyr Tydfil CF48 1RP

☎ 01685 722016

24 Station Hotel

Station Rd, Cefn Coed, Merthyr Tydfil CF48 2NB

☎ 01685 376914

Real Ales, Bar Food

25 Tredegar Arms Hotel

66 High St, Dowlais Top, Merthyr Tydfil CF48 3PW

☎ 01685 377467

Bar Food, Restaurant Menu, Accommodation,
No Smoking Area

26 Twyn Carmel Inn

Twyn Carmel, Abercanaid, Merthyr Tydfil CF48 1PP

☎ 01685 370200

Bar Food, Restaurant Menu, No Smoking Area

27 Windsor Hotel

Windsor Place, Merthyr Vale,
Merthyr Tydfil CF48 4SB

☎ 01443 690360

No Smoking Area

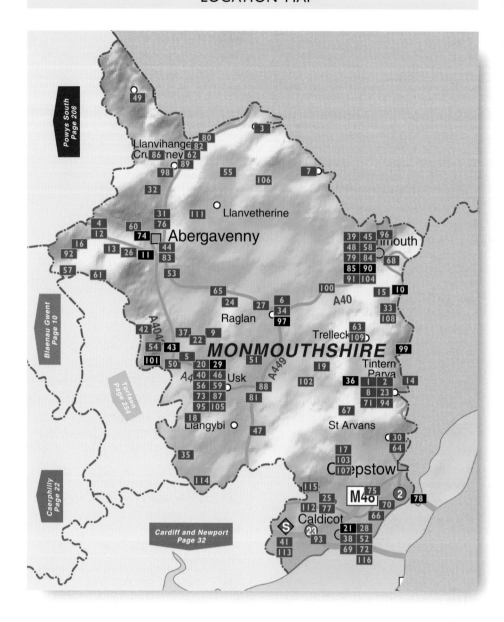

MONMOUTHSHIRE

MONMOUTH • ABERGAVENNY • USK

Monmouthshire (Welsh: Sir Fynwy) covers the eastern half of the traditional county - namely the following towns: Abergavenny, Caldicot, Chepstow, Monmouth and Usk. The area has the following borders: East - District of Forest of Dean, Gloucestershire; southwest - City of Newport; west - County Borough of Torfaen; northwest- Powys; northeast – Herefordshire.

Monmouth is a prosperous and charming old market town grew up at the confluence of three rivers – the Wye, Monnow and Trothy – all of which are noted for their fishing. The River Wye is crossed by a five-arched bridge built in 1617, while the Monnow boasts the most impressive of the town's bridges. Monnow Bridge is one of Monmouth's real gems; its sturdy fortified gatehouse, dating from the 13th century, is the only one of its kind in Britain. Long before the bridge came Monmouth Castle, first built in 1068 and rebuilt by John of Gaunt in the 1300s. It was the birthplace of Henry V in 1387. Today the castle houses both the Castle Museum and Regimental Museum. The King's Garden is a recreation of a small medieval courtyard garden planted with herbs that would have been common in the 14th century.

The Kymin (National Trust) is a hill overlooking the River Wye, practically on the English border, from where spectacular views across the picturesque landscape can be seen. Tintern Abbey is another attraction of the borough, beside the River Wye. Set in the village of Tintern Parva, nestling among the wooded slopes of the valley and designated an Area of Outstanding Natural Beauty. Chepstow is of course famous for its racecourse offering both Flat and National Hunt racing, lying within the grounds of historic Piercefield Park and Piercefield Picturesque Walk, which follows the River Wye cliff up to the Eagle's Nest. Chepstow is also one end of Offa's Dye, the 8th-century defensive ditch and bank built by the King of Mercia and the starting-point for the long-distance Wye Valley and

Gloucestershire Way walks.

Abergavenny Castle boasts a restored keep and hunting lodge, home to a museum where exhibits from prehistoric times to the present day detail the history of the town and surrounding area. Abergavenny is also one of the most accessible gateways to the Brecon Beacons National Park.

Tintern Abbey

1 The Abbey Hotel (Tintern) Ltd

Tintern, Chepstow, Monmouthshire NP16 6SF

☎ 01291 689777

Real Ales, Bar Food, Restaurant Menu, Accommodation, No Smoking Area

2 Anchor Inn

Tintern, Chepstow, Monmouthshire NP16 6TE

☎ 01291 689207

Real Ales, Bar Food, Restaurant Menu, Accommodation, No Smoking Area

3 Angel Inn

Grosmont, Abergavenny, Monmouthshire NP7 8EP

☎ 01981 240646

Real Ales, Bar Food, Restaurant Menu

4 Beaufort Arms

Main Rd, Gilwern, Abergavenny, Monmouthshire NP7 0AR

☎ 01873 832235

Real Ales, Bar Food

5 The Beaufort Arms

Monkswood, Usk, Monmouthshire NP15 1QA

☎ 01495 785215

Real Ales, Bar Food

6 The Beaufort Arms

High St, Raglan Village, Usk, Monmouthshire NP15 2DY

☎ 01291 690412

Real Ales, Bar Food, Restaurant Menu, Accommodation, No Smoking Area

7 The Bell At Skenfrith

Skenfrith, Monmouthshire NP7 8UH

☎ 01600 750235

Real Ales, Restaurant Menu, Accommodation

8 Best Western Royal George Hotel

Tintern, Chepstow, Monmouthshire NP16 6SF

☎ 01291 689205

Real Ales, Bar Food, Restaurant Menu, Accommodation, No Smoking Area

9 Black Bear Inn

Bettws Newydd, Usk, Monmouthshire NP15 1JN

☎ 01873 880701

Real Ales, Bar Food, Restaurant Menu, Accommodation, No Smoking Area

10 The Boat Inn

Lone Lane, Penallt, Monmouthshire NP25 4AJ

☎ 01600 712615

Real Ales, Bar Food

☛ Off the A466 2 miles south of Monmouth

🍴 12-2 & 6-9

♫ Regular music nights

⛰ Garden, riverside location, disabled access

💳 All major cards

🏅 Best Real Ales winner Monmouthshire 2003

🕐 11.30-11 (Sun and Bank Holidays to 10.30)

🏛 Monmouth 2 miles, Tintern Abbey 5 miles, Chepstow 10 miles

11 The Bridge Inn

See panel opposite

12 Bridgend Inn

49 Main Rd, Gilwern, Abergavenny, Monmouthshire NP7 0AU

☎ 01873 830939

Real Ales, Bar Food, No Smoking Area

13 Bridgend Inn

Church Lane, Govilon, Abergavenny, Monmouthshire NP7 9RP

☎ 01873 830177

Real Ales, Bar Food

14 The Brockweir Country Inn

Brockweir, Chepstow, Monmouthshire NP16 7NG

☎ 01291 689548

Real Ales, Bar Food, Accommodation

11 The Bridge Inn

Merthyr Road, Llanfoist, Abergavenny,
Monmouthshire NP7 9LH

☎ 01873 853045

Real Ales, Bar Food, Restaurant Menu, No
Smoking Area

The Bridge Inn is an unpretentious and welcoming traditional pub with a fine range of food and drink. There's a vast choice of delicious things to eat – everything from breakfast (from 9.00a.m.) and a range of hearty snacks such as steak and ale pie, faggots and peas, home-made rabbit pie and

other traditional favourites can be sampled here. Landlady Sally is also the chef, and her expertise in the kitchen shows in every dish.

The interior is warm and welcoming, while there's also an attractive beer garden set on the riverside – the perfect place to enjoy a relaxing drink or meal on fine days.

Well-kept ales are offered alongside a good range of lagers, cider, stout, wines, spirits and soft drinks.

☛ 1 mile from Abergavenny off the A40/A4042/ A465

🍺 London Pride, Speckled Hen, Brains Smooth

🍴 Breakfast Mon-Sat 9-11am, Lunch Mon-Sat 12-2pm, Evening Wed-Sat 7-8.30pm, Traditional Sun Lunch 12-2.15pm

🎵 Quiz nights

🅿 Parking, disabled access, garden

💳 All major cards

🕐 11-11 (Tuesday 11-9, Sunday 12-7)

🏛 Abergavenny 1 mile, Blaenavon 4 miles, Usk 6 miles, Monmouth 12 miles

15 Bush Inn

Penallt, Monmouth, Monmouthshire NP25 4SE

☎ 01600 772765

Real Ales, Bar Food, Restaurant Menu,
Accommodation, No Smoking Area

16 The Cambrian

Clydach, Abergavenny, Monmouthshire NP7 0LY

☎ 01873 830759

Accommodation

17 The Carpenters Arms

Shirenewton, Chepstow,
Monmouthshire NP16 6BU

☎ 01291 641231

Real Ales, Bar Food, Restaurant Menu

18 The Carpenters Arms

Coedypaen, Pontypool, Monmouthshire NP4 0TH

☎ 01291 672621

Bar Food, Restaurant Menu

19 Carpenters Arms

Llanishen, Chepstow, Monmouthshire NP16 6QH

☎ 01600 860812

Real Ales, Bar Food, Restaurant Menu,
No Smoking Area

20 The Castle Hotel

7 Twyn Square, Usk, Monmouthshire NP15 1BH

☎ 01291 673037

Bar Food, Restaurant Menu, Accommodation,
No Smoking Area

21 The Castle Inn

See panel on page 144

22 Chainbridge Inn

Kemeys Commander, Usk,
Monmouthshire NP15 1PP

☎ 01873 880243

Real Ales, Bar Food, Restaurant Menu,
Accommodation, No Smoking Area

21 The Castle Inn

64 Church Road, Caldicot NP26 4HW
☎ 01291 420509
Real Ales, Bar Food, No Smoking Area

The Castle Inn is a handsome 17th-century stonebuilt inn that presents a charming and cheerful exterior to the world. Inside, the atmosphere is warm and welcoming. After careful and sensitive restoration, the inn is a happy marriage of traditional and modern comforts.

Taking its name from Caldicot Castle, just a few yards away, the inn serves a range of cask ales complemented by a good variety of lagers, cider, stout, wines, spirits and soft drinks to quench the thirst.

All-day light bites are served, together with separate lunch and dinner menus offering a selection of tempting traditional dishes made with the freshest locally-sourced produce.

Outside, there's a lovely garden, patio area and children's playground to enjoy on fine days.

☞ From J23 of the M4, follow the signs for Caldicot Castle. The village is 15 miles south of Monmouth on the B4245

🍺 3 rotating guest ales

🍴 Mon-Sat 12-3 & 5.30-9.30, Sun 12-6

♫ Quiz Sun night from 8.30 p.m.

⚓ Parking, garden, patio, children's play area

💳 All major cards

🕐 12-11 (Sun and Bank Holidays to 10.30)

🏛 Caldicot Castle, Caerwent 1 mile, Chepstow 5 miles, Raglan 12 miles

---

23 The Cherry Tree Inn

Raglan Rd, Tintern, Chepstow,
Monmouthshire NP16 6TH
☎ 01291 689292
Real Ales, Bar Food, Restaurant Menu,
Accommodation, No Smoking Area

24 The Clytha Arms

Clytha, Abergavenny, Monmouthshire NP7 9BW
☎ 01873 840206
Real Ales, Bar Food, Restaurant Menu,
Accommodation, No Smoking Area

25 Coach and Horses Inn

Caerwent, Caldicot, Monmouthshire NP26 5AX
☎ 01291 420352
Real Ales, Bar Food, Restaurant Menu,
Accommodation, No Smoking Area

26 Cordell Country Inn

Blaenavon Rd, Govilon, Abergavenny,
Monmouthshire NP7 9NY
☎ 01873 830436
Real Ales, Bar Food, Restaurant Menu,
No Smoking Area

27 The Cripple Creek Inn

Old Abergavenny Rd, Raglan, Usk,
Monmouthshire NP15 2AA
☎ 01291 690256
Real Ales, Restaurant Menu, No Smoking Area

28 The Cross Inn

1 Newport Rd, Caldicot,
Monmouthshire NP26 4BG
☎ 01291 420692
Real Ales

29 The Cross Keys Inn

See panel opposite

29 The Cross Keys Inn

Bridge St, Usk, Monmouthshire NP15 1BG
☎ 01291 672535
🌐 www.crosskeysinn.barbox.net

Real Ales, Bar Food, Restaurant Menu,
Accommodation, No Smoking Area

The Cross Keys Inn is a distinctive place with a long and enviable history of offering food, drink and a warm welcome to weary travellers. Dating back to 1368, this classic establishment has many original features that add to the inn's cosy and traditional ambience. Owner Geraldine Griffiths has been here some 12 years, and this experience shows in the genuine hospitality and warm welcome she offers all her guests. Everything on

the menu and specials board is home-prepared. Specialities include steak and ale pie, salmon Gigi and other hearty traditional favourites. Booking advised at weekends. Usk has many wonderful sights and attractions, and also makes a good base from which to explore the region – the accommodation at this fine inn is available on a B&B basis.

☞ Off the A449 11½ miles southwest of Monmouth 8 miles from M4 corridor.

🍺 Tomas Watkin Whoosh, Bass Real Ales!

🍴 Mon-Thurs 12-2 & 7-9, Fri 12-2 & 7-9.30, Sat 12-2.30 & 7-9.30, Sun 12-2.30

🛏 4 en suite rooms

🎵 Occasional charity nights – please ring for details

🅿 Off-road car park, some disabled access, patio, garden

💳 All major cards

🏆 Champions Usk in Bloom, Real Fire Pub of the Year

🕐 Mon-Sat 11.30-3 & 6.30-11, Sun 12-3.30

🏛 River Usk, Usk Castle, Museum of Rural Life, Golf Clubs & Fishing

30 Crosskeys Hotel

Coleford Rd, Tutshill, Chepstow,
Monmouthshire NP16 7BN
☎ 01291 624977

Real Ales, Bar Food, Restaurant Menu,
Accommodation

31 Crown and Sceptre Inn

Hereford Rd, Mardy, Abergavenny,
Monmouthshire NP7 6HU
☎ 01873 852295

32 The Crown at Pantygelli

Old Hereford Rd, Pantygelli, Abergavenny,
Monmouthshire NP7 7HR
☎ 01873 853314

Real Ales, Bar Food, Restaurant Menu,
No Smoking Area

33 The Crown at Whitebrook

Whitebrook, Monmouth,
Monmouthshire NP25 4TX
☎ 01600 860254

Restaurant Menu, Accommodation,
No Smoking Area

34 The Crown Inn

Usk Rd, Raglan, Usk, Monmouthshire NP15 2EB
☎ 01291 690232

Real Ales, Bar Food

35 Farmers Arms

Llandegveth, Newport, Monmouthshire NP18 1HX
☎ 01633 450244

Real Ales, Bar Food, Restaurant Menu

36 The Fountain Inn

Trellech Grange, Tintern, Chepstow NP16 6QW
☎ 01291 689303
🌐 www.fountaininn-tintern.com

Real Ales, Bar Food, Restaurant Menu,
Accommodation, No Smoking Area

The Fountain Inn is an excellent Free House well
worth seeking out. for the high standard of food,
drink and accommodation. Licensees Tim and Tina
Heselton who are also the chef's create a wide
and varied menu using the freshest locally-
sourced ingredients, with steaks, lamb cutlets, stir-
fries, fresh fish board and more.

- ☞ West off the B4293, south off the A40 and
  east off the A449
- 🍺 3 rotating guest ales, including one from the
  Wye Valley Brewery
- 🍴 12-2.30 & 7-9.15
- 🛏 3 en suite rooms
- 🎵 Beer festival in July 05
- 🅿 Parking, disabled access, garden
- 💳 All the major cards
- 🕐 Tues-Sat 12-3 & 6.30-11 (Sun and Bank
  Holidays to 10.30)
- 🏛 Tintern 1½ miles, Chepstow 7 miles, Usk 12
  miles

37 The Foxhunter

Nantyderry, Abergavenny, Monmouthshire NP7 9DN
☎ 01873 881101
Real Ales, Bar Food, Restaurant Menu

38 The Galleon

180a Newport Rd, Caldicot,
Monmouthshire NP26 4AA
☎ 01291 430438

39 The Gatehouse Public House And Restaurant

Old Monnow Bridge, Monmouth,
Monmouthshire NP25 3EG
☎ 01600 713890
Real Ales, Bar Food, Restaurant Menu,
No Smoking Area

40 Glen-Yr-Afon House Hotel

Pontypool Rd, Llanbadoc, Usk,
Monmouthshire NP15 1SY
☎ 01291 672302
Real Ales, Bar Food, Accommodation,
No Smoking Area

41 The Golden Lion

The Square, Magor, Caldicot,
Monmouthshire NP26 3HY
☎ 01633 880312
Real Ales, Bar Food

42 The Goose And Cuckoo

Upper Lanover, Abergavenny,
Monmouthshire NP7 9ER
☎ 01873 880277
Bar Food, Restaurant Menu

43 The Goytre Arms

See panel opposite

44 Great Western Hotel

24 Station Rd, Abergavenny,
Monmouthshire NP7 5HS
☎ 01873 859125
Real Ales, Bar Food, Restaurant Menu,
Accommodation, No Smoking Area

45 Green Dragon Inn

St Thomas Square, Monmouth,
Monmouthshire NP25 5ES
☎ 01600 712561
Real Ales, Bar Food, Restaurant Menu

46 The Greyhound Inn

1 Chepstow Rd, Usk, Monmouthshire NP15 1BL
☎ 01291 672074
Real Ales

47 The Greyhound Inn

Llantrissent, Usk, Monmouthshire NP15 1LE
☎ 01291 672505
Real Ales, Bar Food, Accommodation, No Smoking
Area

43 The Goytre Arms

Penperlleni, Monmouthshire NP4 0AH

☎ 01873 880376

Real Ales, Bar Food, Restaurant Menu, No Smoking Area

Surrounded by great walking country, The Goytre Arms is a friendly, family-run pub managed by mother-and-daughter team Norma and Tracey, ably assisted by Norma's brother David. Here since 2001, they have made the pub a haven of comfort and relaxation, serving up great ales, food and hospitality.

The inn started life in the late 1700s as three cottages, later becoming an ale shop, a carpenter's and a blacksmith's.

The well-cared for public rooms have a simple, traditional appeal. The changing menu makes the best use of the freshest seasonal ingredients.

Booking is required at weekends. Some dishes are traditional pub classics, while others have a more contemporary ring, with plenty of choice for meat-eaters and vegetarians alike.

☛ Penperlleni is adjacent to the A4042 midway between Abergavenny and Pontypool

🍺 Brains SA, Bass Cask and rotating guest ales

🍴 12-2.30 & 6-9.30

⚒ Parking, some disabled access, garden, patio

💳 All major cards

🕐 12-3 & 6-11 (Sun and Bank Holidays to 10.30)

🏛 Pontypool 5 miles, Abergavenny 6 miles, Blaenavon 7 miles

48 The Griffin Inn

1 Whitecross St, Monmouth, Monmouthshire NP25 3BY

☎ 01600 712541

Real Ales

49 Half Moon Hotel

Llanthony, Abergavenny, Monmouthshire NP7 7NN

☎ 01873 890611

Real Ales, Bar Food, Restaurant Menu, Accommodation, No Smoking Area

50 Halfway House

Berthon Rd, Little Mill, Pontypool, Monmouthshire NP4 0HL

☎ 01495 785252

Real Ales

51 The Hall Inn

Gwehelog, Usk, Monmouthshire NP15 1RB

☎ 01291 672381

Real Ales, Bar Food, Restaurant Menu, Accommodation

52 The Haywain

Sandy Lane, Caldicot, Monmouthshire NP26 4NE

☎ 01291 435151

Bar Food, No Smoking Area

53 Horse And Jockey Inn

Old Raglan Rd, Hardwick, Abergavenny, Monmouthshire NP7 9AA

☎ 01873 854220

Real Ales, Bar Food, Restaurant Menu

54 Horseshoe Inn

Mamhilad, Pontypool, Monmouthshire NP4 8QZ

☎ 01873 880542

Real Ales, Bar Food, Restaurant Menu, Accommodation, No Smoking Area

55 Hunters Moon Inn

Llangattock, Lingoed, Abergavenny, Monmouthshire NP7 8RR

☎ 01873 821499

Real Ales, Bar Food, Restaurant Menu, Accommodation, No Smoking Area

56 The Inn Between
53 Bridge St, Usk, Monmouthshire NP15 1BQ
☎ 01291 672838
Bar Food

57 The Jolly Colliers
Waenllapria, Llanelly Hill, Abergavenny,
Monmouthshire NP7 0PW
☎ 01873 830408
Real Ales, Bar Food

58 The Kings Head
Agincourt Square, Monmouth,
Monmouthshire NP25 3BT
☎ 01600 713417
Real Ales, Bar Food, Restaurant Menu,
Accommodation, No Smoking Area

59 Kings Head Hotel
18 Old Market St, Usk, Monmouthshire NP15 1AL
☎ 01291 672963
Real Ales, Bar Food, Restaurant Menu,
Accommodation, No Smoking Area

60 Lamb and Flag Hotel
Brecon Rd, Llanwenarth, Abergavenny,
Monmouthshire NP7 7EW
☎ 01873 857611
Bar Food

61 Lamb and Fox
Pwlldu, Pontypool, Monmouthshire NP4 9SS
☎ 01495 790196
Real Ales, Bar Food, Restaurant Menu

62 Lancaster Arms
Old Hereford Rd, Pandy, Abergavenny,
Monmouthshire NP7 8DW
☎ 01873 890699
Bar Food, Restaurant Menu

63 The Lion Inn
Trelleck, Monmouth, Monmouthshire NP25 4PA
☎ 01600 860322
Real Ales, Bar Food, Restaurant Menu,
Accommodation, No Smoking Area

64 Live And Let Live Inn
Coleford Rd, Tutshill, Chepstow,
Monmouthshire NP16 7BN
☎ 01291 624782
Real Ales, Bar Food

65 Llansantffraed Court Hotel
Llanvihangel, Gobion, Abergavenny,
Monmouthshire NP7 9BA
☎ 01873 840678
Real Ales, Bar Food, Restaurant Menu,
Accommodation, No Smoking Area

66 Marriott St Pierre Hotel and Country Club
St Pierre Park, Hayesgate, Chepstow,
Monmouthshire NP16 6YA
☎ 01291 625261
Bar Food, Restaurant Menu, Accommodation,
No Smoking Area

67 Masons Arms
Devauden, Chepstow,
Monmouthshire NP16 6PE
☎ 01291 650315
Real Ales

68 Mayhill Hotel
Mayhill Ind Est, Monmouth,
Monmouthshire NP25 3LX
☎ 01600 712765
Real Ales, Accommodation, No Smoking Area

69 The Measure Inn
63-65 Newport Rd, Caldicot,
Monmouthshire NP26 4BR
☎ 01291 424808
Real Ales, Bar Food, No Smoking Area

70 Millers Arms
Mathern, Chepstow, Monmouthshire NP16 6JD
☎ 01291 622133
Real Ales, Bar Food, Restaurant Menu,
Accommodation, No Smoking Area

71 The Moon and Sixpence

Tintern, Chepstow, Monmouthshire NP16 6SG
☎ 01291 689284
Bar Food, Restaurant Menu

72 Mr Chaplins

16 Sandy Lane, Caldicot, Monmouthshire NP26 4NA
☎ 01291 425087

73 Nags Head Inn

6 Twyn Square, Usk, Monmouthshire NP15 1BH
☎ 01291 672820
Real Ales, Bar Food, Restaurant Menu

74 Navigation Inn

See panel below

75 The New Inn

Pwllmeyric, Chepstow, Monmouthshire NP16 6LF
☎ 01291 622670
Real Ales, Bar Food, Restaurant Menu,
No Smoking Area

76 The New Inn

Hereford Rd, Mardy, Abergavenny,
Monmouthshire NP7 6LE
☎ 01873 853512
Real Ales

77 Northgate Inn

Caerwent, Caldicot, Monmouthshire NP26 5NZ
☎ 01291 425292
Real Ales, Bar Food, Restaurant Menu,
No Smoking Area

78 The Old Ferry Inn

See panel on page 150

79 The Old Nags Head

Granville St, Monmouth,
Monmouthshire NP25 3DR
☎ 01600 713782
Real Ales, Bar Food, No Smoking Area

---

74 The Navigation Inn

51 Main Road, Gilwern, near Abergavenny,
Monmouthshire NP7 5UH
☎ 01873 832015

Real Ales, Bar Food

The Navigation Inn is well worth seeking out. Tucked away in the village of Gilwern, this large and spacious inn serves up real ales alongside a good range of lagers, cider, stout, wines, spirits and soft drinks.

Straightforward, simple traditional favourites – burgers, cod, lasagne – make up the bar menu, while the restaurant features more hearty and home-cooked dishes such as steaks, gammon and chicken using the freshest local ingredients.

Simon and Karen Dewey have been here only a short time, but their enthusiasm and commitment shows in their determination to breathe new life into this venerable inn. Cosy and comfortable throughout, with a very relaxed and welcoming ambience, this fine inn goes from strength to strength.

- 4 miles from Abergavenny off the A465
- Brains SA plus rotating guest ale
- summer: 12-9.30; winter: 12-6
- Karaoke Sat night, live music monthly, pool table, darts
- Parking, garden
- 11.30-11 (Sun and Bank Holidays to 10.30)
- Brecon-to-Newport Canal, Abergavenny Castle and museums 4 miles, Blaenavon (Big Pit Mine, Ironworks, Pontypool & Blaenavon Railway) 6 miles, Monmouth 12 miles

78 The Old Ferry Inn

Beachley, Chepstow, Monmouthshire NP16 7HH

☎ 01291 622474

⊕ www.theoldferryinn.co.uk

Real Ales, Bar Food, Restaurant Menu, Accommodation, No Smoking Area

Views over the Severn are just one of the many attractive features of the excellent Old Ferry Inn tucked beneath the Severn Bridge in Beachley. Set in England but with a Welsh postcode, this spacious and attractive inn offers the best of both worlds. Alongside the real ale on tap there's a

very good selection of lagers, ciders, stout, wines, spirits and soft drinks. Everything from snacks such as soups and baguetts to fresh fish dishes, beef, steak, chicken and more listed on the specials board which changes regularly to offer the freshest in local produce, all home-prepared and attractively presented. Owners Murray and Linda Hunt have been here since 2002, bringing real enthusiasm to their roles as hosts and offering all their guests a warm welcome and a high standard of service and quality.

☞ Off the A48 2 miles from Chepstow, under the Severn Bridge at Beachley

🍺 Freeminer/Guest

🍴 Tues-Sat 12-2.30, Tues-Thurs 7-9, Fri-Sat 7-9.30, Sun 12-7

🛏 12 rooms (awaiting grading)

🎵 Occasional entertainment

🅿 Large car park, disabled spaces and some disabled access

💳 All major cards

🕐 Tues-Sat 12-3 & 6.30-11, Sun 12-8

🏛 River Severn, Chepstow 2 miles

80 The Old Pandy Inn

Hereford Rd, Pandy, Abergavenny, Monmouthshire NP7 8DR

☎ 01873 890208

Real Ales, Bar Food, Restaurant Menu, Accommodation, No Smoking Area

81 The Olway Inn Hotel

Llangeview, Usk, Monmouthshire NP15 1EN

☎ 01291 672047

Real Ales, Bar Food, Restaurant Menu

82 Park Hotel

Pandy, Abergavenny, Monmouthshire NP7 8DS

☎ 01873 890271

Real Ales, Bar Food, Restaurant Menu, Accommodation, No Smoking Area

83 Plas Derwen

Monmouth Rd, Abergavenny, Monmouthshire NP7 9SP

☎ 01873 853144

Real Ales, Bar Food, Restaurant Menu, No Smoking Area

84 The Punch House Hotel

4 Agincourt Square, Monmouth, Monmouthshire NP25 3BT

☎ 01600 713855

Real Ales, Bar Food, Restaurant Menu, Accommodation, No Smoking Area

85 The Queens Head

See panel opposite

85 The Queens Head

St James Street, Monmouth,
Monmouthshire NP25 3DL
☎ 01600 712767

Real Ales, Bar Food, Restaurant Menu,
Accommodation, No Smoking Area

The Queens Head occupies a listed 17th-century building in the heart of Monmouth. It has been a coaching inn since it was first constructed. Monmouth's only true music pub, the inn holds regular music nights featuring different musical styles and performers.

The traditional atmosphere is heightened by a number of original features such as the exposed beamwork, slate floors and open fires.

Owner Manse Phillips is also a qualified chef, preparing a range of tempting snacks and meals for the menu and specials board, which change regularly to make the most of the freshest seasonal produce.

The accommodation at this fine inn comprises two doubles, two twins and one triple room, available all year round.

☛ Off the main street in Monmouth, which can be reached via the A40 or A466

🍺 3 rotating guest ales

🍴 12-3 & 6-9

🛏 5 en suite rooms

🎵 Jazz music Weds, jazz/blues Thurs, Irish music every other Tues and every Sunday evening

💳 All major cards

🕐 11.30-11 (Sun and Bank Holidays to 10.30)

🏛 Monmouth Castle, Nelson Museum, The Kymin

86 Queens Head Inn

Cwmyoy, Abergavenny, Monmouthshire NP7 7NE
☎ 01873 890241
Real Ales, Bar Food

87 R+R Restaurant

7-9 Bridge St, Usk, Monmouthshire NP15 1BQ
☎ 01291 672459
Bar Food, Restaurant Menu

88 The Rat Trap Hotel

Chepstow Rd, Llangeview, Usk,
Monmouthshire NP15 1EY
☎ 01291 673288
Bar Food, Restaurant Menu, Accommodation,
No Smoking Area

89 Rising Sun

Pandy, Abergavenny, Monmouthshire NP7 8DL
☎ 01873 890254
Real Ales, Bar Food

90 The Riverside Hotel

See panel on page 152

91 Robin Hood Inn

126 Monnow St, Monmouth,
Monmouthshire NP25 3ED
☎ 01600 713240
Real Ales, Bar Food, Restaurant Menu,
No Smoking Area

92 Rock & Fountain Hotel

Clydach, Abergavenny, Monmouthshire NP7 0LL
☎ 01873 830393
Real Ales, Bar Food, Restaurant Menu,
Accommodation, No Smoking Area

93 The Roggiett Hotel

8 Station Rd, Rogiet, Caldicot,
Monmouthshire NP26 3UE
☎ 01291 420259
Bar Food, Restaurant Menu, Accommodation

90 The Riverside Hotel

Cinderhill Street, Monmouth,
Monmouthshire NP25 5EY
☎ 01600 715577
⊕ www.riversidehotelmonmouth.co.uk

Real Ales, Bar Food, Restaurant Menu,
Accommodation, No Smoking Area

Reached over a bridge near the centre of Monmouth, The Riverside Hotel is a charming place to enjoy a drink, meal or very good accommodation. Handy for all the sights and attractions of the region, this distinguished hotel is run by Gareth Collins, who has, in a short time and ably assisted by his father, created a haven of relaxation in understated and tasteful surroundings. In the elegant restaurant the chef serves up only the freshest and finest steaks, fish, home-cooked pies, curries, pasta and more. The accommodation consists of singles, double and twins, all en suite, two with disabled access. Part of the Minotel franchise, guests can expect a high standard of quality and service throughout this fine hotel.

☞ In the centre of Monmouth, which can be reached via the A40 or A466

🍺 Bass Cask

🍴 12-2.30 & 6-9.30

🛏 17 en suite rooms

🅿 Car park, patio, disabled access

💳 All major cards

🕐 9-11 (Sun and Bank Holidays to 10.30)

🏛 Monmouth Castle, Nelson Museum, The Kymin

---

94 Rose & Crown

Monmouth Rd, Tintern, Monmouthshire NP16 6SE
☎ 01291 689254
Real Ales, Bar Food, Restaurant Menu,
Accommodation, No Smoking Area

95 Royal Hotel

26 New Market St, Usk, Monmouthshire NP15 1AT
☎ 01291 672931
Real Ales, Bar Food, Restaurant Menu

96 The Royal Oak

Hereford Rd, Monmouth,
Monmouthshire NP25 3GA
☎ 01600 772505
Real Ales, Bar Food, Restaurant Menu

97 The Ship Inn

See panel opposite

98 Skirrid Mountain Inn

Llanvihangel, Crucorney, Abergavenny,
Monmouthshire NP7 8DH
☎ 01873 890258
Real Ales, Bar Food, Restaurant Menu,
No Smoking Area

99 The Sloop Inn

See panel opposite

100 Somerset Arms

Dingestow, Monmouth, Monmouthshire NP25 4BP
☎ 01600 740632
Real Ales, Bar Food, Restaurant Menu,
No Smoking Area

101 The Star Inn

See panel on page 154

97 The Ship Inn

8 High Street, Raglan, near Usk, Gwent NP15 2DY

☎ 01291 690635 Fax: 01291 691462

e-mail: jane@roper0203.fsnet.co.uk

Real Ales, Bar Food

An honest village pub that serves the entire community, The Ship Inn is a pristine example of the best in traditional village inns: warm and welcoming, with great food and drink.

The interior boasts original features such as the huge open fireplace and exposed ceiling

beamwork, adding to the cosy atmosphere. Beers from local breweries including Wye Valley, Brains and Brecon Brewery sit happily alongside a good range of lagers, ciders, stout, wines, spirits and soft drinks.

The food is simply superb, with tasty home-cooked specials with real taste, including hearty traditional favourites such as liver and onions and cheese-and-potato pie, all cooked to perfection.

Owner Jane Roper has surrounded herself with excellent staff who offer all their guests the very best in service and hospitality. Children welcome.

☛ 6½ miles southwest of Monmouth off the A40

🍺 local brews

🍴 12-3 & 6-9

🪑 Patio seating, disabled access via alleyway

💳 All major cards

🕐 11.30-11 (Sun 12 noon to 10.30)

🏛 Raglan Castle, Clytha Castle, Monmouth

99 The Sloop Inn

Llandogo, Monmouthshire NP25 4TW

☎ 01594 530291

🌐 www.thesloopinn.co.uk

Real Ales, Bar Food, Restaurant Menu, Accommodation, No Smoking Area

The Sloop Inn is a distinguished inn in the capable hands of Peter Morse – he and his wife are new to the licensing trade, and bring a wealth of enthusiasm to their labour of love: to improve this famous local pub and make it once again the envy

of all those around it. To aid them in this ambition they have a very talented chef who prepares a range of delicious dishes at lunch and dinner.

The interior includes a very attractive and comfortable lounge area and an elegant restaurant. Outside there's a patio area and beer garden for enjoying a pint or meal on fine days.

The accommodation is cosy and tastefully furnished and decorated – one of the guest bedrooms boasts a handsome and supremely comfortable four-poster bed.

☛ 2 miles north of Tintern Parva off the A466

🍺 Doombar and three changing guest ales

🍴 Tues-Sat 12-2.30 & 6-9.30, Sun 12-2.30

🛏 4 en suite rooms

🎵 Quiz night – please ring for details

🪑 Parking, garden, patio, disabled access

💳 All major cards

🕐 12-3 & 6-11 (Sundays to 10.30)

🏛 Tintern Abbey, Monmouth 7½ miles, Chepstow 8 miles

101 The Star Inn

Mamhilad, Monmouthshire NP4 0JF

☎ 01495 785319

Real Ales, Bar Food, Restaurant Menu, No Smoking Area

The roaring log fire and other traditional features mark the 18th-century Star Inn as a true country pub in all the best ways. A warm and friendly welcome can be found here, together with a good range of ales and simple, hearty food. The Sunday lunch is a particularly treat, with large portions of tempting meats, veg and puddings. The menu also

boasts a good range of traditional favourites, all using the freshest locally-sourced ingredients and home-prepared to order. Large and spacious while retaining an intimate and relaxed atmosphere, this proper village inn is well worth seeking out while exploring the region, as it's the perfect place to unwind over a good drink or meal and amid very pleasant surroundings.

☞ The village of Mamhilad is just off the A4042 about 4 miles north of Pontypool

🍺 HB, Bass Cask plus 2 rotating guest ales

🍴 Tues-Sat 12-2 & 6-9, Sun 12-2

🎵 Quiz every other Sun, beer and cider festival every August Bank Hol

⚒ Parking, garden, children's play area, disabled access

💳 All major cards

🏅 Cask Marque winner 2003; Taste of Wales winner 2002

🕐 Mon 6-11, Tues-Thurs 12-2.30 & 6-11, Fri-Sat 12-11 (Sun and Bank Holidays to 10.30)

🏛 Brecon-to-Newport Canal 50 yards, Pontypool 4 miles, Blaenavon 4 miles

102 The Star Inn

Llanfihangel-Tor-Y-Mynydd, Llansoy, Usk, Monmouthshire NP15 1DT

☎ 01291 650256

Real Ales, Bar Food, Restaurant Menu, No Smoking Area

103 The Tan House Inn

Shire Newton, Chepstow, Monmouthshire NP16 6AQ

☎ 01291 641644

Bar Food

104 The Three Horseshoes

21 Drybridge St, Monmouth, Monmouthshire NP25 5AD

☎ 01600 712802

Real Ales, Bar Food, No Smoking Area

105 Three Salmons Hotel

Bridge St, Usk, Monmouthshire NP15 1RY

☎ 01291 672133

Real Ales, Bar Food, Restaurant Menu, Accommodation, No Smoking Area

106 The Three Salmons Inn

Cross Ash, Abergavenny, Monmouthshire NP7 8PB

☎ 01873 821297

Real Ales, Bar Food, Restaurant Menu

107 Tredegar Arms

The Square, Shirenewton, Chepstow, Monmouthshire NP16 6RQ

☎ 01291 641274

Real Ales, Bar Food, Restaurant Menu, Accommodation, No Smoking Area

108 The Trekkers

The Narth, Monmouth, Monmouthshire NP25 4QG

☎ 01600 860367

Real Ales, Bar Food, Restaurant Menu,
No Smoking Area

109 The Village Green Restaurant

Chepstow Rd, Trelleck, Monmouth,
Monmouthshire NP25 4PA

☎ 01600 860119

Real Ales, Bar Food

110 Wain-Y-Clare Inn

Usk Rd, Cwmoody, Pontypool,
Monmouthshire NP4 0JA

☎ 01495 785216

Real Ales, Bar Food, Restaurant Menu

111 Walnut Tree Inn

Llandewi, Skirrid, Abergavenny,
Monmouthshire NP7 8AW

☎ 01873 852797

Restaurant Menu, No Smoking Area

112 Wentwood Inn

Five Lanes, Caerwent, Caldicot,
Monmouthshire NP26 5PE

☎ 01291 430835

Real Ales, Bar Food, Accommodation,
No Smoking Area

113 The Wheatsheaf Inn

Magor, Caldicot, Monmouthshire NP26 3HN

☎ 01633 880608

Real Ales, Bar Food, Restaurant Menu,
Accommodation, No Smoking Area

114 The Wheatsheaf Inn

Llanhennock, Newport, Monmouthshire NP18 1LT

☎ 01633 420468

Real Ales, Bar Food, Restaurant Menu

115 Woodland Restaurant & Bar

Llanvair Discoed, Chepstow,
Monmouthshire NP16 6LX

☎ 01633 400313

Real Ales, Bar Food, Restaurant Menu,
No Smoking Area

116 Ye Olde Tippling Philosopher

108 Chepstow Rd, Caldicot,
Monmouthshire NP26 4JA

☎ 01291 420337

Real Ales, Bar Food, Restaurant Menu,
Accommodation, No Smoking Area

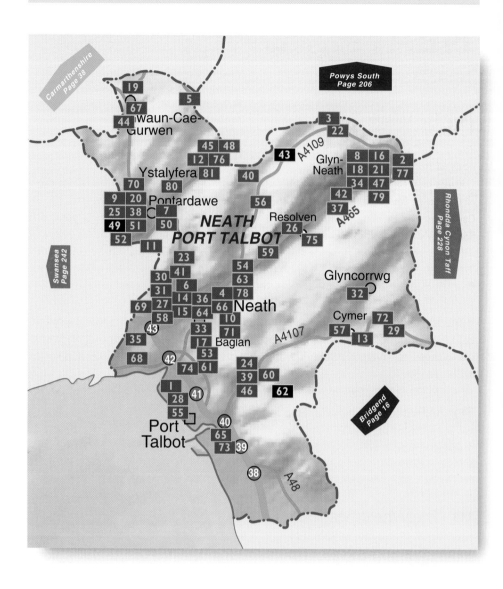

NEATH PORT TALBOT

NEATH • PORT TALBOT • PONTARDAWE

Neath Port Talbot (Welsh: *Castell-nedd Port Talbot*) is a county borough in Glamorgan, South Wales. The borough borders Bridgend and Rhondda Cynon Taf to the east, Powys and Carmarthenshire to the north, and Swansea to the west. Its main towns, as the name of the authority suggests, are Neath and Port Talbot.

It was created on 1 April 1996 from the former districts of Neath, Port Talbot and part of Lliw Valley. Settlements in the district include Aberdulais, Briton Ferry, Bryncoch, Cadoxton, Crynant, Cymmer, Glyn Neath, Gwaun Cae Gurwen, Margam, Neath, Pontardawe, Pontrhydyfen, Port Talbot, Resolven, Seven Sisters, Skewen and Ystalyfera.

Named for the Talbot family, who developed the town's docks in the 19th century, Port Talbot saw significant expansion again in the 20th century when a new deep-water harbour was opened by the Queen in 1970. Today the town is home to the solar centre of Baglan Bay Energy Park, explaining the history of the area.

The town of Neath has its origins in Roman times, and remains of Roman *Nidum* can still be seen close to the ruins of Neath Abbey, founded by Richard de Granville on land seized from the Welsh in 1130. It was also de Granville who built Neath Castle in the mid-12th century.

Aberdulais Falls (National Trust) have been harnessed for a number of industries over the years; its Turbine House provides access to a unique fish pass.

To the north, west and south of the village of Cynonville lies the Afan Forest Park, a large area of woodland where there are trails for cycling, walking and pony-trekking. The Park's Countryside Centre has an exhibition exploring the landscape and history of the Afan Valley.

Neath Abbey

Margam Country Park covers some 800 acres and boasts a classical 18th-century orangery, a restored Japanese garden from the 1920s, waymarked trails, a deer park, birds of prey centre and the Margam Stones Museum, where visitors can see a collection of early Christian memorials dating from Roman times through to the 10th and 11th centuries.

1 The Amazon

Parry Rd, Port Talbot, Neath Port Talbot SA12 7TR

☎ 01639 884099

Bar Food, Restaurant Menu, No Smoking Area

2 The Angel Inn

Pontneathvaughan Rd, Glynneath, Neath,
Neath Port Talbot SA11 5NR

☎ 01639 722013

Real Ales, Bar Food, Restaurant Menu,
No Smoking Area

3 The Ashgrove Inn

Onllwyn Rd, Coelbren, Neath,
Neath Port Talbot SA10 9NW

☎ 01639 701155

Real Ales

4 The Bear Inn

Bear House, Pen-y-Dre, Neath,
Neath Port Talbot SA11 3HD

☎ 01639 620885

Bar Food, Restaurant Menu

5 Boblen

24 Bryn Rd, Cwmllynfell, Neath Port Talbot SA9 2FJ

☎ 01639 830236

Bar Food, Restaurant Menu, No Smoking Area

6 Bryncoch Inn

Tyn Yr Heol Rd, Bryncoch, Neath,
Neath Port Talbot SA10 7EB

☎ 01639 634921

Real Ales, Bar Food, Restaurant Menu,
No Smoking Area

7 The Butchers Arms

Alltwen Hill, Pontardawe,
Neath Port Talbot SA8 3BP

☎ 01792 863100

Real Ales, Bar Food, Restaurant Menu,
No Smoking Area

8 The Butchers Arms

Merthyr Rd, Pontwalby, Neath,
Neath Port Talbot SA11 5LR

☎ 01639 722155

9 Castle Hotel

High St, Pontardawe, Swansea,
Neath Port Talbot SA8 4HU

☎ 01792 865491

10 Cimla Hotel

Cimla Rd, Neath, Neath Port Talbot SA11 3UG

☎ 01639 769621

Bar Food

11 Colliers Arms

154 Swansea Rd, Pontardawe, Swansea,
Neath Port Talbot SA8 4BU

☎ 01792 864847

Real Ales

12 The Corner House

70 Commercial St, Ystalyfera, Swansea,
Neath Port Talbot SA9 2HS

☎ 01639 849420

Real Ales, Bar Food, Restaurant Menu,
No Smoking Area

13 Croeserw Hotel

63 South Avenue Cymmer, Port Talbot,
Neath Port Talbot SA13 3RA

☎ 01639 851611

14 The Cross Keys Hotel

Old Rd, Skewen, Neath,
Neath Port Talbot SA10 6AR

☎ 01792 815244

Real Ales, Bar Food, Accommodation,
No Smoking Area

15 The Crown

216 New Rd, Skewen, Neath,
Neath Port Talbot SA10 6EW

☎ 01792 411270

Real Ales

16 Crown Inn

21 Gelliceibryn, Glynneath, Neath,
Neath Port Talbot SA11 5ED

☎ 01639 720719

Real Ales

17 The Crown Inn

244 Neath Rd, Briton Ferry, Neath,
Neath Port Talbot SA11 2AX

☎ 01639 813427

Real Ales, Bar Food, Restaurant Menu,
No Smoking Area

18 The Crown Inn

High St, Glynneath, Neath,
Neath Port Talbot SA11 5BR

☎ 01639 720463

Real Ales

19 The Crown Inn

27 Park St, Lower Brynamman, Ammanford,
Neath Port Talbot SA18 1TF

☎ 01269 825510

Real Ales

20 Dillwyn Arms

1 Herbert St The Cross, Pontardawe, Swansea,
Neath Port Talbot SA8 4EB

☎ 01792 863310

Bar Food, Restaurant Menu, Accommodation,
No Smoking Area

21 Dinas Rock Hotel

Glynneath, Neath, Neath Port Talbot SA11 5AP

☎ 01639 722816

Real Ales

22 The Dyffryn

58 Main Rd, Dyffryn Cellwen, Neath,
Neath Port Talbot SA10 9LA

☎ 01639 700577

Real Ales

23 Dyffryn Arms

Neath Rd, Bryncoch, Neath,
Neath Port Talbot SA10 7YF

☎ 01639 636184

Real Ales

24 Dylons

Old Market Square, Tyr Owen Row, Cwmavon,
Port Talbot, Neath Port Talbot SA12 9BE

☎ 01639 882882

Bar Food, Restaurant Menu

25 Dynevor Arms

James St, Pontardawe, Neath Port Talbot SA8 4LR

☎ 01792 863750

Accommodation, No Smoking Area

26 Farmers Arms

Glynneath Rd, Resolven, Neath,
Neath Port Talbot SA11 4DW

☎ 01639 710264

Real Ales, Bar Food

27 Farmers Arms

42 Burrows Rd, Skewen, Neath,
Neath Port Talbot SA10 6AB

☎ 01792 816326

Real Ales, Bar Food, Restaurant Menu,
No Smoking Area

28 Four Winds Hotel

Princess Margaret Way, Port Talbot,
Neath Port Talbot SA12 6QW

☎ 01639 884548

Real Ales, Bar Food, Restaurant Menu

29 The Gelli

Commercial St ,Abergwynfi, Port Talbot,
Neath Port Talbot SA13 3YL

☎ 01639 851627

Bar Food, Restaurant Menu, No Smoking Area

30 Glyn Clydach

Longford Road, Dyffryn, Neath,
Neath Port Talbot SA10 7AJ

☎ 01792 813701

Real Ales, Bar Food, Restaurant Menu,
Accommodation, No Smoking Area

31 Glyn Clydach Coach House

Longford Rd, Bryncoch, Neath,
Neath Port Talbot SA10 7AJ

☎ 01792 816307

Real Ales, Bar Food, Restaurant Menu,
Accommodation, No Smoking Area

32 Glyncorrwg Hall

33-35 Cymmer Rd, Glyncorrwg, Port Talbot,
Neath Port Talbot SA13 3AB

☎ 01639 852499

Bar Food, Restaurant Menu, No Smoking Area

33 The Grandison Hotel

175 Pant Yr Heol, Briton Ferry, Neath,
Neath Port Talbot SA11 2HB

☎ 01639 769726

Real Ales, Bar Food, Restaurant Menu,
No Smoking Area

34 Halfway House Hotel

Aberdare Rd, Glynneath, Neath,
Neath Port Talbot SA11 5HY

☎ 01639 720364

Real Ales, No Smoking Area

35 Holiday Inn Express

Neath Rd Llandarcy, Neath,
Neath Port Talbot SA10 6JQ

☎ 01792 818700

Real Ales, Accommodation, No Smoking Area

36 Hope and Anchor

New Rd, Neath, Neath Port Talbot SA10 7NG

☎ 01792 324731

Bar Food

37 Horgan Ltd

High St, Cwmgwrach, Neath,
Neath Port Talbot SA11 5TA

☎ 01639 722725

Real Ales

38 Ivy Bush Hotel

103 High St, Pontardawe, Swansea,
Neath Port Talbot SA8 4JN

☎ 01792 862370

39 Jersey Arms

Jersey Terrace, Cwmavon, Port Talbot,
Neath Port Talbot SA12 9AS

☎ 01639 898283

40 The Kingfisher

Crynant, Neath, Neath Port Talbot SA10 8PP

☎ 01639 750040

Bar Food, No Smoking Area

41 The Lamb and Flag

Main Rd, Bryncoch, Neath,
Neath Port Talbot SA10 7TW

☎ 01639 642922

Real Ales, Bar Food, Restaurant Menu,
No Smoking Area

42 Lamb and Flag Hotel

Wellfield Place, Glynneath, Neath,
Neath Port Talbot SA11 5EP

☎ 01639 720227

Real Ales, Bar Food, Restaurant Menu,
Accommodation, No Smoking Area

43 Merlins & Call of the Wild

44/46 Commercial Street, Ystradgynlais,
Swansea SA9 1JH

☎ 01639 700388

⊕ www.backpackerwales.com

Bar Food, Accommodation

☛ 16 miles north of Swansea on A4067

🍴 Café open 9am-3pm Mon-Fri, 9am-1pm Sat
Pub at weekends

🛏 Merlins: Budget dormitory accommodation

🕐 Open all day everyday by arrangement

🏛 Adventure activities booked through Merlins
with Call of the Wild, Dan-yr-Ogof Caves 4
miles, Brecon 19½ miles, Gower Coast 25
miles

44 Mount Pleasant Inn

29 Graig Rd, Gwaun Cae Gurwen, Ammanford,
Neath Port Talbot SA18 1EH

☎ 01269 824942

45 The New Swan

50 Gurnos Rd, Ystalyfera, Swansea,
Neath Port Talbot SA9 2HY

☎ 01639 843002

46 The Oakwood

Church Square, Cwmavon, Port Talbot,
Neath Port Talbot SA12 9AP

☎ 01639 896271

No Smoking Area

47 The Oddfellows Arms

68 High St, Glynneath, Neath,
Neath Port Talbot SA11 5AW

☎ 01639 722384

Real Ales, Accommodation, No Smoking Area

48 The Old Swan Inn

58 Gurnos Rd, Ystalyfera, Swansea,
Neath Port Talbot SA9 2HY

☎ 01639 842315

Bar Food, Restaurant Menu

49 The Other Place

See panel below

50 Pen-Yr-Allt Inn

Alltwen Hill, Alltwen, Swansea,
Neath Port Talbot SA8 3BP

☎ 01792 863320

Bar Food, Restaurant Menu, Accommodation

51 Pink Geranium Village Hotel

31-33 Herbert St P, Pontardawe, Swansea,
Neath Port Talbot SA8 4EB

☎ 01792 862255

Real Ales, Bar Food, Accommodation

52 Pontardawe Inn

Herbert St, Pontardawe, Swansea,
Neath Port Talbot SA8 4ED

☎ 01792 830791

Real Ales, Bar Food, Restaurant Menu,
No Smoking Area

49 The Other Place

Ywisderw Road, Pontardawe, Swansea SA8 4EG

☎ 01792 862999

Real Ales, Bar Food, Restaurant Menu,
No Smoking Area

A friendly face greets every visitor to The Other Place, a large and traditional pub upholding the long and fine tradition of Welsh hospitality and service.

Set on the A474, at the gateway to the Black Mountains, the pub makes an excellent place to stop and enjoy a relaxed drink or meal while exploring the many sights and attractions of the region. Real ales are complemented by a full range of lagers, cider, stout, wines, spirits and soft drinks – something to quench every thirst.

Simple and simply delicious hearty meals are served here – baked potatoes, fish and chips, pies and other traditional favourites, cooked to order.

Landlord Andrew Davies is well on his way to realising his ambition of making this Pontardawe's best pub.

- ☛ 8 miles northeast of Swansea on the A474
- 🍺 Tetleys and Worthington Cream Flow
- 🍴 Tues-Sun 12-3 & Tues-Sat 6-9
- 🎵 Quiz night Mon, occasional live music – please ring for details
- ♿ Disabled access
- 🕐 11-11 (Sun and Bank Holidays to 10.30)
- 🏛 Ystalfera 3 miles, Ammanford 10 miles, Swansea 8 miles

53 Puddlers Arms

2 Shelone Rd, Briton Ferry, Neath,
Neath Port Talbot SA11 2PS

☎ 01639 812265

Real Ales

54 Railway Tavern

Dulais Fach Rd, Tonna, Neath,
Neath Port Talbot SA10 8EP

☎ 01639 637025

Real Ales

55 The Red Dragon

Moorland Rd, Port Talbot,
Neath Port Talbot SA12 6JZ

☎ 01639 898229

56 Red Lion Hotel

Main Rd Crynant, Neath,
Neath Port Talbot SA10 8RD

☎ 01639 750357

57 Refreshment Rooms

The Old Station, Cymmer, Port Talbot,
Neath Port Talbot SA13 3HY

☎ 01639 850901

Real Ales, Bar Food, Restaurant Menu,
No Smoking Area

58 Rock and Fountain

20 Burrows Rd, Skewen, Neath,
Neath Port Talbot SA10 6AB

☎ 01792 812068

Bar Food

59 Rock and Fountain Inn

Aberdulais, Neath, Neath Port Talbot SA10 8HN

☎ 01639 642681

Real Ales, Bar Food, Restaurant Menu,
No Smoking Area

60 Rolling Mill

Salem Rd, Cwmavon, Port Talbot,
Neath Port Talbot SA12 9EW

☎ 01639 896347

Bar Food, Restaurant Menu, No Smoking Area

61 Rose and Crown Inn

21 Bethel St, Briton Ferry, Neath,
Neath Port Talbot SA11 2EZ

☎ 01639 821700

Real Ales

62 The Royal Oak

Maesteg Road, Bryn, Port Talbot,
Neath Port Talbot SA13 2RW

☎ 01639 896712

Real Ales, Bar Food

☛ Off the A4107 at J40 of the M4

🍺 Brains SA, rotating guest ale

🍴 Thurs-Sun 12-2.30, Thurs-Sat 6-9

🅿 Parking, garden

🕐 Mon-Weds 2.30-4.30 7 7-11, Thurs-Sat 12-11 (Sun and Bank Holidays to 10.30)

🏛 Maesteg 2 miles, Tondu 8 miles, Port Talbot 6 miles, Neath 10 miles

63 Royal Oak Inn

Henfaes Rd Tonna, Neath,
Neath Port Talbot SA11 3EZ

☎ 01639 643512

Real Ales, No Smoking Area

64 Smiths Arms

New Rd, Neath Abbey, Neath,
Neath Port Talbot SA10 7DG

☎ 01639 643180

Real Ales, Bar Food, Restaurant Menu,
No Smoking Area

65 Somerset Arms

Commercial Rd, Taibach, Port Talbot,
Neath Port Talbot SA13 1LP

☎ 01639 875051

Bar Food, Restaurant Menu, No Smoking Area

66 Star Inn

83 Penydre, Neath, Neath Port Talbot SA11 3HF

☎ 01639 637745

67 TJS Tavern

50 Heol Y Gors, Cwmgors, Ammanford,
Neath Port Talbot SA18 1PT
☎ 01269 825553
Real Ales, Restaurant Menu, Accommodation,
No Smoking Area

68 The Tower
(Swansea Bay)

Ashleigh Terrace, Jersey Marine, Neath,
Neath Port Talbot SA10 6JL
☎ 01792 814155
Accommodation, No Smoking Area

69 The Travellers Well

Dynevor Place, Skewen, Neath,
Neath Port Talbot SA10 6RG
☎ 01792 812002
Real Ales

70 Travellers Well

Commercial Rd, Rhydyfro, Swansea,
Neath Port Talbot SA8 4SS
☎ 01792 862893

71 The Tudor Inn

Cae Rhys Ddu Rd, Cimla, Neath,
Neath Port Talbot SA11 1JA
☎ 01639 642769
Bar Food, Restaurant Menu, No Smoking Area

72 Tunnel Hotel

Heol-Y-Nant Blaengwynfi, Port Talbot,
Neath Port Talbot SA13 3UB
☎ 01639 852275
No Smoking Area

73 Twelve Knights Hotel

Margam Rd, Margam, Port Talbot,
Neath Port Talbot SA13 2DB
☎ 01639 882381
Real Ales, Bar Food, Restaurant Menu,
Accommodation, No Smoking Area

74 Tyn-Y-Twr Tavern

St Illtyds Drive, Baglan, Port Talbot,
Neath Port Talbot SA12 8AU
☎ 01639 812887
Bar Food, No Smoking Area

75 The Vaughan Arms

Glynneath, Neath, Neath Port Talbot SA11 4NA
☎ 01639 710212

76 Wern Fawr Inn

47 Wern Rd, Ystalyfera, Swansea,
Neath Port Talbot SA9 2LX
☎ 01639 843625
Real Ales

77 The White Horse Inn

High St, Pontneathvaughan, Neath,
Neath Port Talbot SA11 5NP
☎ 01639 721219
Real Ales, Bar Food, Restaurant Menu,
Accommodation, No Smoking Area

78 Whittington Arms

Park St Tonna, Neath, Neath Port Talbot SA11 3JF
☎ 01639 643229
Real Ales, Bar Food, Restaurant Menu,
No Smoking Area

79 The Woolpack

68 High St, Glynneath, Neath,
Neath Port Talbot SA11 5DA
☎ 01639 720289
Real Ales

80 Ynysmeudwy Arms

168 Ynysmeudwy Rd, Pontardawe, Swansea,
Neath Port Talbot SA8 4QJ
☎ 01792 869542
Bar Food

81 Ystradgynlais Arms

Cyfing Rd, Ystalyfera, Swansea,
Neath Port Talbot SA9 2BS
☎ 01639 842301

PEMBROKESHIRE

FISHGUARD • HAVERFORDWEST • PEMBROKE

Pembrokeshire (Welsh: *Sir Benfro*) shares a border with Carmarthenshire and its close neighbour to the north is Ceredigion (Cardiganshire). The county, founded in 1282 by order of Edward I of England, has long been split between its anglicised south, known as Little England beyond Wales, and Welsh north.

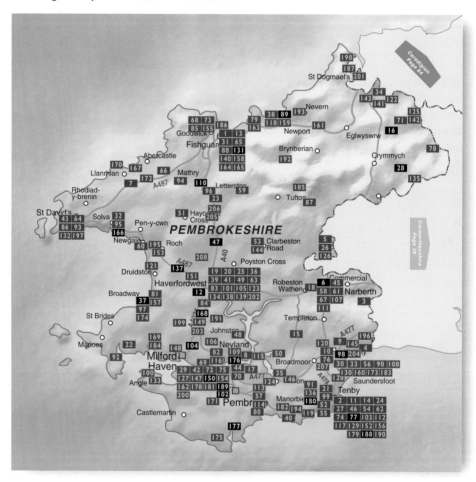

11 Pembrokeshire Reference Number - Detailed Information

12 Pembrokeshire Reference Number - Summary Entry

Ceredigion
Page 249
Adjacent area - refer to pages indicated

Home to Britain's only coastal national park – the Pembrokeshire Coast National Park – is a leading European holiday destination that attracts visitors who come to enjoy the spectacular grandeur and tranquil beauty of the countryside and take in some of the 186-mile coastal cliff-top path. The coastal region offers wonderful walking and glorious views and is a paradise for bird-watchers. Incorporating one of the most fantastic stretches of natural beauty in Europe, the Pembrokeshire Coast National Park begins (or ends) on the south-facing shoreline near Tenby. Running right around the ruggedly beautiful southwestern tip of Wales, around St Brides Bay and up along the north-facing coast almost to Cardigan, the Park also includes quiet fishing villages, the huge cliffs at Castlemartin, sweeping golden beaches and small, often busy harbours. Although not strictly on the coast, the labyrinthine Cleddau river system also lies within the Park's boundaries, and here there are delightful little villages such as Cresswell and Carew as well as the superb sheltered harbour of Milford Haven. Offshore there are various islands including Grassholm, Ramsey, Skokholm and Skomer, which have changed little since they were named by Viking invaders. Many are now bird and wildlife sanctuaries of international importance. Grassholm is home to thousands of gannets, Skokholm has Manx shearwaters, and Skomer has shearwaters and puffins. Ramsey harbours such species as choughs and the red-legged crow, and it is also the resting place of many Welsh saints. However, one island, Caldey, has for over 1,500 years been the home of a religious community that continues today to live a quiet and austere life.

At the highest point of the Preseli Hills, at Foel Cwmcerwyn (1,759 feet), the views stretch as far as Snowdonia to the north and the Gower Peninsula to the south. Littered with prehistoric sites, in the foothills is the Gwaun Valley, at the heart of which Gerddi Gardens offer an abundant display of miniature plants, dwarf conifers and alpines in attractive landscaped surroundings through which runs a fast-flowing stream.

The huge headland at Strumble Head, with its lighthouse warning ships off the cliffs on

the approach to Fishguard harbour, offers some spectacular coastal scenery as well as an outlook over the great sweep of Cardigan Bay.

Home to the last invasion of Britons, the country's smallest city, and numerous prehistoric remains, Pembrokeshire is also home to the corgi.

Porthclais Harbour, Fishguard

1   Abergwaun Hotel

Market Square, Fishguard,
Pembrokeshire SA65 9HA
☎ 01348 872077
Real Ales, Bar Food, Restaurant Menu

2   Albany Hotel

22-23 The Norton, Tenby,
Pembrokeshire SA70 8AB
☎ 01834 842698
Real Ales, Bar Food, Restaurant Menu,
Accommodation, No Smoking Area

3   The Alpha Inn

Alpha House, Tavernspite, Whitland,
Pembrokeshire SA34 0NL
☎ 01834 831484
Real Ales, Bar Food, Restaurant Menu,
No Smoking Area

4   Amroth Arms

Amroth, Narberth, Pembrokeshire SA67 8NG
☎ 01834 812480
Real Ales, Bar Food, Restaurant Menu,
No Smoking Area

5   Angel Inn

Llandissilio, Clynderwen, Pembrokeshire SA66 7TG
☎ 01437 563428
Real Ales

6   The Angel Inn

See panel below

7   Artramont Arms

Croesgoch, Haverfordwest,
Pembrokeshire SA62 5JP
☎ 01348 831309
Real Ales, Bar Food, Restaurant Menu,
No Smoking Area

---

6   The Angel Inn

43 High Street, Narberth,
Pembrokeshire SA67 7AS
☎ 01834 860579

Real Ales, Bar Food, Restaurant Menu,
Accommodation, No Smoking Area

Pristine and welcoming, The Angel is a fine inn offering great food and drink daily, as well as en suite bed-and-breakfast accommodation. Dating back to the early 1800s, with later additions, the inn is located in the heart of Narberth – an ideal place to use as a base while exploring the region. Tenants Sandy and Eddie Mutch and their conscientious, friendly staff offer a warm welcome and a high standard of service to all their guests. Sandy is the cook, whipping up a good variety of hot and cold dishes in the bar and restaurant. Guests choose off the menu or specials board from dishes such as home-made lasagne, wedge of lamb and home-made burgers. Wherever possible, the produce used to create these dishes is sourced locally.

☛ On the A478, 9½ miles east of Haverfordwest

🍺 Rev James, Buckleys Best

🍴 12-2.30 & 6-9

🛏 8 rooms

⚒ Parking, disabled access, garden

💳 Not Amex or Diners

🕐 12-3 & 6-11 (Sun and Bank Holidays to 10.30)

🏛 Canaston Bridge 2½ miles, The Rhos 6 miles, Llys-y-fran 8 miles, Scolton 8 miles, Haverfordwest 9½ miles

8 The Bar

Neyland Yacht Haven, Brunel Quay, Neyland,
Milford Haven, Pembrokeshire SA73 1PY

☎ 01646 602550

Bar Food, Restaurant Menu, No Smoking Area

9 Bayview Hotel

Pleasant Valley Stepaside, Saundersfoot, Narberth,
Pembrokeshire SA67 8LR

☎ 01834 813417

Real Ales, Bar Food, Restaurant Menu,
Accommodation, No Smoking Area

10 Begelly Arms Hotel

New Rd Begelly, Begelly, Kilgetty,
Pembrokeshire SA68 0YF

☎ 01834 813285

Real Ales, Bar Food, Restaurant Menu,
Accommodation, No Smoking Area

11 Belgrave Hotel

Esplanade, Tenby, Pembrokeshire SA70 7DU

☎ 01834 842377

12 The Bellevue

See panel below

13 Bennetts Navy Tavern

20 High St, Fishguard, Pembrokeshire SA65 9AR

☎ 01348 875554

Bar Food, Restaurant Menu, No Smoking Area

14 The Blue Dolphin Hotel And Restaurant

St Mary St, Tenby, Pembrokeshire SA70 7HW

☎ 01834 842590

Real Ales, Bar Food, Restaurant Menu,
Accommodation, No Smoking Area

---

12 The Bellevue

Portfield, Haverfordwest,
Pembrokeshire SA61 1BS

☎ 01437 762128

Real Ales, Bar Food, Restaurant Menu,
No Smoking Area

Delicious lunchtime snacks and breakfasts available. Senior citizen lunch specials, grills and traditional home cooked food. Steaks, grills and home cooked Beef & Ale pie with Felinfoel Double Dragon ale which is brewed in Llanelli are just a few selections from the evening menu. Add to this some excellent ales with a genuine Welsh warm welcome and great hospitality (croeso cymraeg) and you have a winning recipe for success. Owners Jill and John David assisted by manager Gareth Bennett together have a wealth of experience which makes this fine place a 'destination pub' for its food and ales.

The décor and furnishings are traditional and very comfortable and attractive, while the clientele is a happy mix of locals and visitors alike, drawn to the pub's relaxed atmosphere and high standard of service and quality. Bellevue has ample parking and a pleasant enclosed Beer Garden. Ideal for all age groups.

☛ On the outskirts of Portfield, 1 mile from Haverfordwest off the A40

🍺 Abbot Ale, Worthington Cask, rotating guest ale

🍴 12-2, 6-8.30

🎵 Pool, darts

♿ Parking, disabled access, garden

🕐 11-11 Mon-Sat, Sunday 12-10.30

🏛 Haverfordwest 1 mile, Little Haven 5 miles, Milford Haven 10 miles

15 Boars Head Inn

Templeton, Narberth, Pembrokeshire SA67 8SD
☎ 01834 860286
Real Ales, Bar Food, No Smoking Area

16 The Boncath Inn

See panel below

17 Brewery Inn

Cosheston, Pembroke Dock,
Pembrokeshire SA72 4UD
☎ 01646 686678
Real Ales, Bar Food, Restaurant Menu,
Accommodation

18 The Bridge Inn

Coxlake, Narberth, Pembrokeshire SA67 8EJ
☎ 01834 860541
Real Ales, Bar Food, Restaurant Menu,
No Smoking Area

19 Bridgend Hotel

Bridgend Square, Haverfordwest,
Pembrokeshire SA61 2ND
☎ 01437 767863
Bar Food

20 The Bristol Trader

Quay St, Haverfordwest, Pembrokeshire SA61 1BE
☎ 01437 762122
Real Ales, Bar Food, Restaurant Menu,
No Smoking Area

21 The Broadmead Hotel

Heywood Lane, Tenby, Pembrokeshire SA70 8DA
☎ 01834 842641
Restaurant Menu, Accommodation,
No Smoking Area

22 The Brook Inn

Brookside, St Ishmaels, Haverfordwest,
Pembrokeshire SA62 3TE
☎ 01646 636277
Bar Food, Restaurant Menu, No Smoking Area

---

16 The Boncath Inn

Boncath, Pembrokeshire SA37 0JN
☎ 01239 841241
Real Ales, Bar Food

Located just five miles from Cardigan, The Boncath Inn is a fine example of a welcoming rural Welsh Inn, traditional and spotlessly kept. Real ales are licensee Marcus' passion: he has a cellar filled with a range of beers. The Inn also provides a good selection of lagers, cider, stout, wines, spirits and soft drinks. The food is just as impressive, all home-cooked and hearty. Specialities include the delicious

steak and ale pie. Marcus and his partner Hedydd have been here since 2003, and have the enthusiasm, dedication and zeal to make this Inn a must for visitors to the Cardigan area.

The only hostelry in the village, it provides a particularly convivial meeting place for the local communities and is also a popular stopping-off place for motorists in need of a break in their journey. Several Guest houses are within walking distance.

☛ On the B4332, 1 mile east from the jnc. with A478 (Cardigan to Tenby) in dir. Cenarth

🍺 Worthington Cask plus 4 rotating guest ales

🍴 Mon-Sat 12-2 & 6-9, Sun 12.30-2.30

🎵 Quiz Sun

⚒ Parking, garden, patio, disabled access

💳 All major cards

🕐 Mon-Sat 11-11, Sun and Bank Holidays 12-10.30

🏛 Bro-Meigan Gardens 2 miles, Cenarth 5 miles, Newcastle Emlyn 6 miles, Pembrokeshire National Park 3 miles, Newport Pembs 8 miles, Cigerran Castle 3 miles, Cardigan 5 miles

23 Brynawelon Country Hotel

Letterston, Haverfordwest,
Pembrokeshire SA62 5UD

☎ 01348 840307

Real Ales, Bar Food, Restaurant Menu,
Accommodation, No Smoking Area

24 Buccaneer Inn

St Julians St, Tenby, Pembrokeshire SA70 7AS

☎ 01834 842273

Real Ales, Bar Food

25 Bull Inn

108 Prendergast, Haverfordwest,
Pembrokeshire SA61 2PP

☎ 01437 762047

Real Ales, Bar Food

26 The Bush Inn

Llandissilio, Clynderwen, Pembrokeshire SA66 7TS

☎ 01437 563040

Real Ales, Bar Food, Restaurant Menu,
Accommodation, No Smoking Area

27 The Bush Inn

St George St, Tenby, Pembrokeshire SA70 7JB

☎ 01834 843498

Real Ales

28 Butchers Arms

See adjacent panel

29 Caledonia Inn

High St, Pembroke Dock,
Pembrokeshire SA72 6PA

☎ 01646 684615

Real Ales

30 Cambrian Hotel

Cambrian Terrace, Saundersfoot,
Pembrokeshire SA69 9ER

☎ 01834 812448

Real Ales, Bar Food, Restaurant Menu,
Accommodation, No Smoking Area

28 Butchers Arms

Tegryn, Llanryrnach, Pembrokeshire SA35 0BL

☎ 01239 698680 ⊕ www.tegryn.co.uk

Real Ales, Bar Food, Restaurant Menu,
No Smoking Area

Dating back to 1826, the Butchers Arms in Tegryn is a venerable place with excellent food and drink. Warm Welsh hospitality is the order of the day here, as owners Tim and Kerrie and their friendly staff make sure every guest receives the very best service. The menu offers a good selection of traditional favourites using locally-sourced produce wherever possible.

☛ South of Cardigan off the A478

🍺 Rotating guest ale

🍴 lunch when open (see below) & to 9.30 eves

♫ Occasional entertainment

♪ Parking, disabled access

🍴 Tues-Sun and Bank Hol 12-3 & 6-9; winter:
🕐 Tues-Fri 6-9 & Sat/Sun 12-3 & 6-9

🏛 Cilgerran 2 miles, Llanfair-Nant-Gwyn 4 miles, Cardigan 6 miles

31 Cambrian Inn

Hamilton St, Fishguard, Pembrokeshire SA65 9HL

☎ 01348 873848

32 Cambrian Inn

6 Main St, Solva, Haverfordwest,
Pembrokeshire SA62 6UU

☎ 01437 721210

Real Ales, Bar Food, Restaurant Menu,
No Smoking Area

33 Captains Table

The Harbour, Saundersfoot,
Pembrokeshire SA69 9HE

☎ 01834 812435

Real Ales, Bar Food, Restaurant Menu,
No Smoking Area

34 Cardiff Arms
High St, Cilgerran, Cardigan,
Pembrokeshire SA43 2SQ
☎ 01239 614600
Real Ales, Bar Food, No Smoking Area

35 Carew Inn
Carew, Tenby, Pembrokeshire SA70 8SL
☎ 01646 651267
Real Ales, Bar Food, Restaurant Menu,
No Smoking Area

36 Carmarthen Arms
31 Cartlett, Haverfordwest,
Pembrokeshire SA61 2LH
☎ 01437 763461
Real Ales

37 The Castle
See panel below

38 Castle Hotel
Bridge St, Newport, Pembrokeshire SA42 0TB
☎ 01239 820742
Real Ales, Bar Food, Restaurant Menu,
Accommodation, No Smoking Area

39 The Castle Hotel
Castle Square, Haverfordwest,
Pembrokeshire SA61 2AA
☎ 01437 769322
Bar Food, Restaurant Menu, Accommodation,
No Smoking Area

40 Castle Inn
Manorbier, Tenby, Pembrokeshire SA70 7TE
☎ 01834 871268
Bar Food, Restaurant Menu, No Smoking Area

37 The Castle

Little Haven, Haverfordwest,
Pembrokeshire SA62 3UG
☎ 01437 781445
🌐 www.castlelittlehaven.co.uk

Real Ales, Bar Food, Restaurant Menu,
Accommodation, No Smoking Area

Built as an inn back in 1871, The Castle is a
charming and welcoming place set in the
picturesque village of Little Haven. A happy
marriage of traditional and modern, the interior
boasts spacious bars and a cosy dining area.

Proprietors Malcolm and Mary Whitewright
have been here since 2001, and take justified
pride in the quality of service and hospitality they
offer all their guests. Their chef, Fred, is a talented
and creative cook who prepares a range of dishes
for the menu and daily specials, using the freshest
locally-sourced ingredients. Specialities include
Pembrokeshire organic beef, pork and lamb
dishes, together with locally-caught fish and local
Pant Mawr Farmhouse Cheeses.

The two comfortable and attractively furnished
guest bedrooms are available all year round.

- On the coast off the A487 via Haverfordwest
- Brains and 3 rotating guest ales
- 12-2 & 6-8.30
- 2 en suite rooms
- Parking, disabled access, outdoor seating
- Not Amex
- 12-2.30 & 6-11 (Sun and Bank Holidays to 10.30), all day from end June-early Sept
- Coast, Haverfordwest 5 miles, Milford Haven 5 miles

41 Charlie Sports Bar

1-2 Dark St, Haverfordwest,
Pembrokeshire SA61 2DS

☎ 01437 760718

Accommodation

42 The Charlton Hotel

20 Bush St, Pembroke Dock,
Pembrokeshire SA72 6AX

☎ 01646 680033

Real Ales

43 City Inn

New St, St Davids, Haverfordwest,
Pembrokeshire SA62 6SU

☎ 01437 720829

Real Ales, Bar Food, Accommodation

44 Cleddau Bridge Hotel

Essex Rd, Pembroke Dock,
Pembrokeshire SA72 6EG

☎ 01646 685961

Bar Food, Restaurant Menu, No Smoking Area

45 Coach & Horses

Narberth, Pembrokeshire SA67 7AR

☎ 01834 861320

Real Ales, Bar Food

46 Coach and Horses

Upper Frog St, Tenby, Pembrokeshire SA70 7JD

☎ 01834 842704

Real Ales, Bar Food

47 The Corner Piece

See panel below

---

47 The Corner Piece Inn

Rudbaxton, Haverfordwest,
Pembrokeshire SA52 5PG

☎ 01437 741460

Real Ales, Bar Food, Restaurant Menu,
No Smoking Area

The Corner Piece Inn is a cosy and comfortable place to enjoy some great food, drink and hospitality. Run by Paula and Michael Davies – Paula does the cooking while Michael makes sure his ales are among the finest in Pembrokeshire – this convivial inn is a welcome haven for travellers

taking the ferry and exploring the Gwaun Valley. This traditional old coaching inn boasts many original features, including some resident ghosts. The menu offers a fabulous choice of dishes – everything from jacket potatoes to smoked mackerel, home-made pies, mixed grills and fresh beef and fish dishes. The dining area is more like a private home than a public space – intimate and charming, with subdued lighting and homely features like the brickbuilt fireplace and pictures adorning the walls. Children welcome.

☛ Rudbaxton is 2 miles north of Haverfordwest off the A40

🍺 Double Dragon and Worthington Cask

🍴 12-2.30 & 6-9.30 (Sunday lunch 12-2.30)

⛏ Parking, garden, children's play area, disabled access

💳 All the major cards

🕐 11-3 & 5-11 (Sun and Bank Holidays to 10.30)

🏛 Haverfordwest 2 miles, Scolton 3 miles, Llys-y-fran 6 miles

48 The Cottage Inn

Llangwm, Haverfordwest,
Pembrokeshire SA62 4HH

☎ 01437 891494

Real Ales, Bar Food, Restaurant Menu

49 The County Hotel

Salutation Square, Haverfordwest,
Pembrokeshire SA61 2NB

☎ 01437 762144

Restaurant Menu, Accommodation,
No Smoking Area

50 Cresselly Arms

Cresswell Quay, Cresswell,
Pembrokeshire SA68 0TE

☎ 01646 651210

Real Ales, Bar Food

51 Cross Inn

Haycastle Cross, Haverfordwest,
Pembrokeshire SA62 5PR

☎ 01348 840216

Real Ales, Bar Food, No Smoking Area

52 The Cross Inn

Penally, Tenby, Pembrokeshire SA70 7PU

☎ 01834 844665

Bar Food, Restaurant Menu

53 The Cross Inn

Clarbeston Rd, Pembrokeshire SA63 4UL

☎ 01437 731506

Real Ales, Bar Food, Restaurant Menu,
No Smoking Area

54 The Crown Inn

Lower Frog St, Tenby, Pembrokeshire SA70 7HU

☎ 01834 842796

Real Ales, Bar Food, Restaurant Menu

55 The Crown Inn

Penally, Tenby, Pembrokeshire SA70 7PT

☎ 01834 844030

Real Ales, Bar Food, Restaurant Menu

56 Cwmwennol Country House Hotel

Swallow Tree Woods, Saundersfoot,
Pembrokeshire SA69 9DE

☎ 01834 813430

Bar Food, Restaurant Menu, Accommodation,
No Smoking Area

57 Dial Inn

The Ridgeway, Lamphey, Pembroke,
Pembrokeshire SA71 5NU

☎ 01646 672426

Real Ales, Restaurant Menu, Accommodation,
No Smoking Area

58 Dragon Inn

Water St, Narberth, Pembrokeshire SA67 7AT

☎ 01834 861667

Real Ales, Bar Food, No Smoking Area

59 Drovers Arms

Puncheston, Haverfordwest,
Pembrokeshire SA62 5RJ

☎ 01348 881469

Bar Food, Restaurant Menu, No Smoking Area

60 Duke of Edinburgh Inn

Newgale, Haverfordwest, Pembrokeshire SA62 6AS

☎ 01437 720586

Real Ales, Bar Food, No Smoking Area

61 The Eagle Inn

Water St, Narberth, Pembrokeshire SA67 7AT

☎ 01834 860769

Real Ales, Bar Food, Restaurant Menu,
Accommodation, No Smoking Area

62 Evergreen Inn

The Green, Tenby, Pembrokeshire SA70 8EY

☎ 01834 843364

Real Ales

63 Farmers Arms

Holloway, Haverfordwest,
Pembrokeshire SA61 2JL

☎ 01437 762432

Real Ales

64 Farmers Arms

Goat St, St Davids, Haverfordwest,
Pembrokeshire SA62 6RF

☎ 01437 720328

Real Ales, Bar Food, Restaurant Menu,
Accommodation, No Smoking Area

65 The Farmers Arms

Market Square, Fishguard,
Pembrokeshire SA65 9HA

☎ 01348 874655

Real Ales

66 The Farmers Arms

Mathry, Haverfordwest,
Pembrokeshire SA62 5HB

☎ 01348 831284

Real Ales, Bar Food, No Smoking Area

67 The Farmers Arms

1 Northfield Rd, Narberth,
Pembrokeshire SA67 7AA

☎ 01834 860372

Real Ales, No Smoking Area

68 Ferry Boat Inn & Restaurant

Wren Rd, Goodwick, Nr Fishguard,
Pembrokeshire SA64 0AA

☎ 01348 874747

Real Ales, Restaurant Menu, Accommodation,
No Smoking Area

69 Ferry House Inn

Hazelbeach, Neyland, Milford Haven, Pembrokeshire
SA73 1EG

☎ 01646 600270

Real Ales, Bar Food, Restaurant Menu,
Accommodation, No Smoking Area

70 The Ferry Inn

Pembroke Ferry, Pembroke Dock,
Pembrokeshire SA72 6UD

☎ 01646 682947

Real Ales, Bar Food, No Smoking Area

71 Ffynone Arms

Newchapel, Boncath, Pembrokeshire SA37 0EH

☎ 01239 841800

Real Ales, Bar Food, Restaurant Menu

72 The First and Last

London Rd, Pembroke Dock,
Pembrokeshire SA72 6TX

☎ 01646 682687

Real Ales, Bar Food, No Smoking Area

73 Fishguard Bay Hotel

Quay Rd, Goodwick, Pembrokeshire SA64 0BT

☎ 01348 873571

Bar Food, Restaurant Menu, Accommodation,
No Smoking Area

74 Five Arches Tavern

St Georges St, Tenby, Pembrokeshire SA70 7JB

☎ 01834 842513

Real Ales, Bar Food

75 The Flying Boat

6 Queen St, Pembroke Dock,
Pembrokeshire SA72 6JL

☎ 01646 682810

Real Ales, Accommodation, No Smoking Area

76 The Fountain Head Inn

Pentlepoir, Saundersfoot,
Pembrokeshire SA69 9BH

☎ 01834 812483

Real Ales, Bar Food, Restaurant Menu,
Accommodation, No Smoking Area

77 Fourcroft Hotel

See panel on page 174

78 Fox And Hounds

Cwmcych, Newcastle Emlyn,
Pembrokeshire SA38 9RR

☎ 01239 698308

Real Ales

77 Fourcroft Hotel

North Beach, Tenby, Pembrokeshire SA70 8AP

☎ 01834 842886

🌐 www.fourcroft-hotel.co.uk

Real Ales, Bar Food, Restaurant Menu,
Accommodation, No Smoking Area

The Fourcroft Hotel is a gracious and elegant
establishment set on the cliffs above Tenby's North
Beach. Most of the comfortable guest bedrooms
overlook the bay. In the convivial Hollywood Bar,
you can relax with a drink and the restaurant
boasts a superb range of delicious options. Leisure
facilities include the pool, fitness suite, sauna and
games room.

- ☛ On the A478
- 🍺 Brains
- 🍴 12-2.30 & 7-9
- 🛏 40 en suite rooms
- 🅿 Parking, garden
- 💳 All the major cards
- 🏅 3 Stars Wales Tourist Board, RAC and AA
- 🕐 12-11 (Sun and Bank Holidays to 10.30)
- 🏛 Tenby, Saundersfoot 2½ miles, Caldey Island 2½ miles, Stepaside 4 miles, Amroth 4½ miles

79 Freemasons Arms Hotel

Dinas Cross, Newport, Pembrokeshire SA42 0UW

☎ 01348 811243

Real Ales, Bar Food, Restaurant Menu,
Accommodation, No Smoking Area

80 Freshwater Inn

Jason Rd, Freshwater East, Pembroke,
Pembrokeshire SA71 5LE

☎ 01646 672828

Real Ales, Bar Food, Restaurant Menu,
No Smoking Area

81 Galleon Inn

35-35A Enfield Rd, Broad Haven, Haverfordwest,
Pembrokeshire SA62 3JW

☎ 01437 781467

Real Ales, Bar Food, Restaurant Menu,
No Smoking Area

82 Gate Inn

Dwrbach, Fishguard, Pembrokeshire SA65 9QY

☎ 01348 873739

Bar Food, Restaurant Menu, No Smoking Area

83 The Georges Restaurant and Cafe Bar

24 Market St, Haverfordwest,
Pembrokeshire SA61 1NH

☎ 01437 766683

Real Ales, Bar Food, Restaurant Menu,
No Smoking Area

84 The Glen

Merlins Hill, Haverfordwest,
Pembrokeshire SA61 1XA

☎ 01437 760070

Real Ales, Bar Food, Restaurant Menu,
No Smoking Area

85 Glendower Hotel

Glendower Square, Goodwick,
Pembrokeshire SA64 0DH

☎ 01348 872873

Real Ales, Bar Food, Restaurant Menu,
Accommodation, No Smoking Area

86 Glenydd Guest House

51 Nun St, St Davids, Haverfordwest,
Pembrokeshire SA62 6NU

☎ 01437 720576

Bar Food, Restaurant Menu, No Smoking Area

87 The Globe Inn

Maenclochog, Clynderwen,
Pembrokeshire SA66 7LE

☎ 01437 532269

Real Ales, Bar Food

88 The Globe Inn

28-30 Main St, Fishguard,
Pembrokeshire SA65 9HJ

☎ 01348 872500

Real Ales, Bar Food, No Smoking Area

89 Golden Lion Inn

See panel opposite

89 Golden Lion Country Inn

East Street, Newport, Pembrokeshire SA42 0SY

☎ 01239 820321

🌐 www.Goldenlionpembs.co.uk

Real Ales, Restaurant Menu, Accommodation, No Smoking Area

The Golden Lion Country Inn is a hotel first and foremost, offering excellent accommodation and genuine hospitality to all guests. Owners Kristina and Daron Paish have been here since 2001, and bring a lot of enthusiasm to their high standard of service and quality. The inn is traditional, warm and welcoming, with cosy features such as

beamed ceilings and a wealth of wood panelling. The bar stocks a good range of beverages – everything from real ales to soft drinks – while all the food is home-cooked, including pies, curries, an excellent choice of steak and fish dishes and daily specials. Meals can be enjoyed throughout the bar or in the no-smoking restaurant. The accommodation is superb, with 17 handsome and very comfortable en suite guest bedrooms. Some rooms are adapted for disabled access.

☛ Newport is on the A487 6 miles east of Fishguard

🍺 OSB, guest ale

🍴 12-2 & 6-9.30

🛏 14 en suite rooms, self-contained cottage with 3 bedrooms

♫ Thurs quiz night, live music monthly, pool table, darts

🅿 Car park, garden, some disabled access

💳 All major cards

🕐 11.30-11 (Sun and Bank Holidays to 10.30)

🏛 Golf, watersports, fishing, walking, birdwatching, Fishguard 6 miles, Cardigan 6 miles

90 The Gower Hotel

Milford Terrace, Saundersfoot, Pembrokeshire SA69 9EL

☎ 01834 813452

Real Ales, Bar Food, Restaurant Menu, Accommodation, No Smoking Area

91 Greenhills Country Hotel

High St, St Florence, Tenby, Pembrokeshire SA70 8LW

☎ 01834 871291

Real Ales, Bar Food, Restaurant Menu, Accommodation, No Smoking Area

92 The Griffin Inn

Dale, Haverfordwest, Pembrokeshire SA62 3RB

☎ 01646 636227

Real Ales, Bar Food, Restaurant Menu

93 The Grove

High St St, St Davids, Haverfordwest, Pembrokeshire SA62 6SB

☎ 01437 720341

Real Ales, Bar Food, Restaurant Menu, Accommodation, No Smoking Area

94 Gwesty Bach

Castle Morris, Haverfordwest, Pembrokeshire SA62 5ER

☎ 01348 840668

95 The Harbour Inn

31-33 Main St, Solva, Haverfordwest, Pembrokeshire SA62 6UT

☎ 01437 720013

Real Ales, Bar Food, No Smoking Area

98 The Hean Castle Inn

High Street, Saundersfoot,
Pembrokeshire SA69 9AL

☎ 01834 812311

Bar Food, Restaurant Menu, No Smoking Area

The Hean Castle Inn resembles just that – the tall, pink-stone exterior has features of a medieval palace. Inside, the décor is traditional and comfortable.

This family-run pub is convivial and friendly, and is run by the Lloyd family, who have nearly 15 years' experience – experience that shows in the quality of the food, drink and hospitality on offer.

Tasteful and cosy, the restaurant boasts many traditional features such as the exposed beamwork and has an intimate, elegant ambience. The menu offers a good selection of expertly prepared dishes made using the freshest ingredients, locally-sourced wherever possible.

The beers here include Boddingtons among a very good range of favourites including lagers, cider, stout, wines, spirits and soft drinks.

☛ 2½ miles north of Tenby on the B4316

🍴 April-Sept as for opening hours

♫ Disco Fri & Sat night 9-11

🪑 Patio

🕐 12-11 (Sun and Bank Holidays to 10.30)

🏛 Coast, Tenby 2½ miles, Stepaside 1½ miles, Amroth 3 miles

102 Highgate Inn Hotel

Hundleton, Pembroke, Pembrokeshire SA71 5RD
☎ 01646 685904

Real Ales, Restaurant Menu, Accommodation, No Smoking Area

Tucked away on the B4319 just west of Pembroke, the Highgate Inn Hotel offers excellent food, drink and accommodation amid delightful scenery and not far from the coast.

This award-winning hotel has a good selection of real ales together with wines, spirits, soft

drinks, lagers, cider and stout – something to quench every thirst, while the elegant restaurant provides delicious freshly prepared food at lunch and dinner. In the spacious lounge, bar snacks and afternoon cream teas are served. Outside there's a lovely garden.

The accommodation was recently refurbished and provides attractive and comfortable rooms, and the hotel makes an ideal base for exploring the many sights and attractions of the region.

☛ On the B4319, 2 miles west of Pembroke

🍺 Brains, Worthington Cask

🍴 summer: all day; winter: 12-2.30 & 6.30-9.30

🛏 5 en suite rooms

♫ Live music at weekends

🪑 Parking, disabled access, garden

💳 All major cards

🕐 12-11 (Sun and Bank Holidays to 10.30)

🏛 Coast 4 miles, Pembroke 2 miles, Pembroke Dock 4 miles

96 Harp Inn

31 Haverfordwest Rd, Letterston, Haverfordwest,
Pembrokeshire SA62 5UA

☎ 01348 840061

Real Ales, Bar Food, Restaurant Menu,
No Smoking Area

97 Haven Fort Hotel

Settlands Hill Little Haven, Haverfordwest,
Pembrokeshire SA62 3LA

☎ 01437 781401

Real Ales, Bar Food, Restaurant Menu,
Accommodation, No Smoking Area

98 The Hean Castle Inn

See panel opposite

99 Heywood Mount Hotel And Spa Leisure Suite

Heywood Lane, Tenby, Pembrokeshire SA70 8DA

☎ 01834 842087

Bar Food, Restaurant Menu, Accommodation,
No Smoking Area

100 The Hibernia Inn

60 Angle Village, Angle, Pembroke,
Pembrokeshire SA71 5AT

☎ 01646 641517

Real Ales, Bar Food, Restaurant Menu,
No Smoking Area

101 The Hideaway Cellar Bar

25-27 Hill St, Haverfordwest,
Pembrokeshire SA61 1QH

☎ 01437 764302

102 Highgate Inn Hotel

See panel opposite

103 Hope And Anchor Inn

St Julian St, Tenby, Pembrokeshire SA70 7AX

☎ 01834 842131

Real Ales, Bar Food, No Smoking Area

104 The Horse & Jockey

See panel below

104 The Horse & Jockey

Neyland Road, Steyton, Milford Haven,
Pembrokeshire SA73 1AP

☎ 01646 692166

🌐 www.thehorseandjockey.co.uk

Real Ales, Bar Food, Restaurant Menu,
No Smoking Area

The spacious and handsome Horse & Jockey is a welcoming pub tucked away in the attractive village of Steyton.

Home-made soups, freshly baked pies and a range of home-cooked traditional favourites are on the menu here, with the freshest locally-sourced ingredients used to create a range of tasty options.

A good wine list complements the range of real ale, lagers, cider, stout (the brewery has awarded the inn for having the best-kept Guinness in Pembrokeshire by the brewery), spirits and soft drinks available.

At present the guest bedrooms are being refurbished, but should be available within the lifetime of this edition for anyone wishing to explore this scenic part of Pembrokeshire.

- On the A4076 5 miles north of Pembroke
- Rotating guest ale
- Tues 6-9, Weds-Sat 12-2 & 6-9, Sun 12-3
- Parking, disabled access, garden, patio
- All major cards
- 11.30-11 (Sun and Bank Holidays to 10.30)
- Neyland 1 mile, Pembroke Dock 3 miles, Pembroke 5 miles, Milford Haven 7 miles

105 Hotel Mariners

Mariners Square, Haverfordwest,
Pembrokeshire SA61 2DU

☎ 01437 763353

Real Ales, Bar Food, Restaurant Menu,
Accommodation, No Smoking Area

106 The Huntsman Inn

3 West St, Rosemarket, Milford Haven,
Pembrokeshire SA73 1JH

☎ 01646 600514

Real Ales, Bar Food, Restaurant Menu,
No Smoking Area

107 Ivy Bush Inn

5 High St, Narberth, Pembrokeshire SA67 7AR

☎ 01834 860679

Real Ales, Bar Food, Restaurant Menu,
Accommodation, No Smoking Area

108 The Jalna Hotel

Stammers Rd, Saundersfoot,
Pembrokeshire SA69 9HH

☎ 01834 812282

Accommodation, No Smoking Area

109 Jolly Sailor

Burton, Milford Haven, Pembrokeshire SA73 1NX

☎ 01646 600378

Real Ales, Bar Food

110 The Jubilee Hotel

See panel below

111 Kirkland Arms

34 St James St, Narberth,
Pembrokeshire SA67 7BU

☎ 01834 860423

Real Ales, No Smoking Area

110 The Jubilee Hotel

112 St David's Road, Letterston, Fishguard,
Pembrokeshire SA62 5SJ

☎ 01248 852360

Real Ales, Restaurant Menu, Accommodation,
No Smoking Area

The Jubilee Hotel is an elegant and charming
place with a great deal of character. Owner James
Gwilt has been here since the summer of 2004,
bringing a lot of enthusiasm and zeal to making
this a destination pub for food and ales. A hub of

local activity, the inn is home to local darts teams
and football sides, and locals and visitors alike
happily rub shoulders at the bar. The traditional
bar has roaring fires in winter and a cosy lounge.
Outside, the beer garden is a peaceful haven for
relaxing with a pint or meal. Within the next year
plans are afoot to extend the restaurant to
accommodate more diners. The accommodation is
simply lovely – polished wood floors, tasteful and
attractive décor and furnishings – and there are
many sights and attractions within easy reach
(including a good golf course close by), making this
an excellent touring base.

- 🍺 5 miles from Fishguard off the A40
- 🍺 Worthington Cask
- 🛏 3 en suite rooms
- 🎵 Quiz nights, Tue pool night, Weds & Fri darts nights
- 🏖 Car park, garden
- 🕐 11.30-11 (Sun and Bank Holidays to 10.30)
- 🏛 Golfing, Fishguard 5 miles, Strumble Head 7 miles

112 The Lamb Inn

14 High St, North Beach, Tenby,
Pembrokeshire SA70 7HD

☎ 01834 844958

Real Ales, Bar Food, Restaurant Menu,
No Smoking Area

113 Lamphey Court Hotel

Lamphey, Pembroke, Pembrokeshire SA71 5NT

☎ 01646 672273

Real Ales, Bar Food, Restaurant Menu,
Accommodation, No Smoking Area

114 Lamphey Hall Hotel

Lamphey, Pembroke, Pembrokeshire SA71 5NR

☎ 01646 672394

115 Lawrenny Arms Hotel

Lawrenny Quay, Lawrenny, Kilgetty,
Pembrokeshire SA68 0PR

☎ 01646 651439

Real Ales, Bar Food, Restaurant Menu,
No Smoking Area

116 The Legionaire

Neyland Hill, Neyland, Milford Haven,
Pembrokeshire SA73 1SL

☎ 01646 600230

Real Ales

117 The Lifeboat Tavern

St Julians St, Tenby, Pembrokeshire SA70 7AS

☎ 01834 844948

Real Ales, Bar Food, No Smoking Area

118 Llwyngwair Arms

East St, Newport, Pembrokeshire SA42 0SY

☎ 01239 820267

Real Ales, Bar Food

119 Lydstep Tavern

Hillside Lydstep, Tenby, Pembrokeshire SA70 7SG

☎ 01834 871521

Real Ales, Bar Food

120 Manian Lodge Hotel

Begelly, Kilgetty, Pembrokeshire SA68 0XE

☎ 01834 813273

Restaurant Menu, Accommodation,
No Smoking Area

121 Mariners Inn

Nolton Haven, Haverfordwest,
Pembrokeshire SA62 3NH

☎ 01437 710469

Real Ales, Bar Food, Restaurant Menu,
Accommodation

122 Masons Arms

Cnwce, Cilgerran, Cardigan, Pembrokeshire SA43 2SR

☎ 01239 621660

Real Ales

123 The Milford Arms

Cartlett, Haverfordwest, Pembrokeshire SA61 2LH

☎ 01437 767288

124 The Milton Brewery Inn

Milton, Tenby, Pembrokeshire SA70 8PH

☎ 01646 651202

Real Ales, Bar Food, Restaurant Menu,
No Smoking Area

125 Nags Head Inn

Abercych, Boncath, Pembrokeshire SA37 0HJ

☎ 01239 841200

Real Ales, Bar Food, Restaurant Menu,
No Smoking Area

126 Nantyffin Motel

Llandissilio, Clynderwen, Pembrokeshire SA66 7SU

☎ 01437 563423

Real Ales, Bar Food, Restaurant Menu,
Accommodation, No Smoking Area

127 The Navy Inn

Melville St, Pembroke Dock, Pembrokeshire SA72 6XS

☎ 01646 682300

Real Ales, Bar Food, Restaurant Menu,
Accommodation, No Smoking Area

128 New Hedges Tavern

New Hedges, Tenby, Pembrokeshire SA70 8TR

☎ 01834 842630

129 The Normandie Inn

Upper Frog St, Tenby, Pembrokeshire SA70 7JD

☎ 01834 842227

Real Ales, Bar Food, Restaurant Menu,
Accommodation

130 The Old Chemist Inn

The Strand, Saundersfoot,
Pembrokeshire SA69 9ET

☎ 01834 813982

Real Ales, Bar Food, Restaurant Menu,
Accommodation

131 The Old Coach House

See panel below

132 Old Cross Hotel

Cross Square St, St Davids, Haverfordwest,
Pembrokeshire SA62 6SP

☎ 01437 720387

Bar Food, Restaurant Menu, Accommodation,
No Smoking Area

133 Old Point House

Angle Village, Angle, Pembroke,
Pembrokeshire SA71 5AS

☎ 01646 641205

Real Ales, Bar Food, Restaurant Menu,
Accommodation, No Smoking Area

134 Old Three Crowns

47 High St, Haverfordwest,
Pembrokeshire SA61 2BN

☎ 01437 764613

Real Ales, Bar Food

---

131 The Old Coach House

10 High Street, Fishguard,
Pembrokeshire SA65 9AR

☎ 01348 875429

Real Ales, Bar Food, Restaurant Menu,
No Smoking Area

The Old Coach House began life in the late
1700s as a coaching inn, with more recent
additions (the restaurant and function room)
created in 2000. Paul Mason and Alan Phillips have
been running this fine establishment in the heart
of Fishguard since October of 2002. With up to

five real ales in the summer months supplement-
ing the regular choice of ales, lagers, cider, stout,
wines, spirits and soft drinks, there's something to
quench every thirst. The upstairs restaurant
overlooks the pub, like a minstrels' gallery, and
here guests choose off the menu or specials
board from a range of tempting dishes using the
freshest locally-sourced ingredients. Booking
advised at weekends. There is also more dining
room in the downstairs games room, which
doubles as a function suite.

☛ Fishguard is on the A40/off the A4087, 6½
miles west of Newport

🍺 Rev James and Thomas Watkins plus
changing guest ales

🍴 12-2.30 & 7-9.30; (Jan-Mar no food eves)

🎵 Occasional live entertainment

⚓ Parking, garden, patio, disabled access

💳 Not Amex or Diners

🕐 12-11 (Sun to 10.30, Bank Holidays to 12,
Sat to 1am)

🏛 Dinas 3½ miles, Newport (Pembrokeshires)
6½ miles, Haverfordwest 14 miles, Cardigan
18 miles

135 Pant-Y-Blaidd Inn

Tegryn, Pembrokeshire SA35 0DB
☎ 01239 698356
Real Ales, Bar Food, Restaurant Menu

136 Parsonage Farm Inn

St Florence, Tenby, Pembrokeshire SA70 8LR
☎ 01834 871436
Real Ales, Bar Food, No Smoking Area

137 Pelcomb Inn

See panel below

138 The Pembroke House Hotel

6-7 Spring Gardens, Haverfordwest,
Pembrokeshire SA61 2EJ
☎ 01437 779622
Bar Food, Restaurant Menu, Accommodation

139 The Pembroke Yeoman

11 Hill St, Haverfordwest,
Pembrokeshire SA61 1QQ
☎ 01437 762500
Real Ales, Bar Food

140 The Pendre Inn

High St, Fishguard, Pembrokeshire SA65 9AT
☎ 01348 874128
Real Ales

141 Pendre Inn

High St, Cilgerran, Cardigan,
Pembrokeshire SA43 2SL
☎ 01239 614223
Real Ales, Bar Food, No Smoking Area

142 Penrhiw Inn

Abercych, Boncath, Pembrokeshire SA37 0HA
☎ 01239 682229
Real Ales, Bar Food

---

137 Pelcomb Inn

Pelcomb Cross, Haverfordwest, Pembrokeshire
☎ 01437 710267
e-mail: info@pelcombinn.co.uk
🌐 www.pelcombinn.co.uk

Real Ales, Bar Food, Restaurant Menu, No
Smoking Area

A shining example of what a traditional inn should
be, Pelcomb Inn offers excellent food and drink
and a relaxed and comfortable ambience.

Owner Gareth arrived here in the summer of
2004 – after many years of the farming life, he has
set about refurbishing and renewing this fine inn's
lease of life. Welsh cuisine at its best is the
highlight of a good and varied menu, with
everything from home-made soups, freshly baked
baguettes and smoked paté to fresh fish and
locally-reared beef and lamb.

Everywhere the décor and furnishings speak of
taste and quality, from the to the original artwork,
painted in oils by Carol, adorning the walls.

☛ Pelcomb Cross is on the A487, 2 miles
northeast of Haverfordwest

🍺 Rev James, Worthington Cask

🅿 Car park, disabled access

💳 All major cards

🕐 summer: Mon-Fri 11-3 & 6-11, Sat 11-11,
Sun and Bank Holidays to 10.30

🏛 Haverfordwest 2 miles, Scolton 3 miles, Llys-
y-fran 6 miles, St David's 10 miles

143 Penybryn Arms

Penybryn, Cardigan, Pembrokeshire SA43 3NJ
☎ 01239 612434
Real Ales, Bar Food

144 Picton Inn

Clarbeston Rd, Pembrokeshire SA63 4UN
☎ 01437 731615

145 Pleasant Valley House Hotel

Pleasant Valley Stepaside, Saundersfoot, Narberth,
Pembrokeshire SA67 8NY
☎ 01834 813607
Restaurant Menu, Accommodation,
No Smoking Area

146 The Plough Inn

Sageston, Tenby, Pembrokeshire SA70 8SG
☎ 01646 651557
Real Ales, Bar Food, Restaurant Menu

147 Prince of Wales

1 Laws St, Pembroke Dock,
Pembrokeshire SA72 6DJ
☎ 01646 622700
Real Ales, Bar Food

148 Priory Inn

Lower Priory, Neyland, Milford Haven,
Pembrokeshire SA73 3UA
☎ 01646 695231
Bar Food, Restaurant Menu, No Smoking Area

149 Railway Inn

St Peters Rd, Johnson, Haverfordwest,
Pembrokeshire SA62 3PR
☎ 01437 890355

150 Red Rose Inn

See panel below

---

150 Red Rose Inn

113 High Street, Pembroke Dock,
Pembrokeshire SA72 6PE
☎ 01646 622919

Real Ales, Bar Food

Just a few minutes' walk from the shopping area of Pembroke Dock, the Red Rose Inn is a friendly and welcoming place. The traditional interior boasts exposed beamwork and a brickbuilt bar, and has a relaxed and cosy ambience.

Run by Richard and Denise, ably assisted by their sons Thomas and Eoin, this quality establishment is their first venture in the licensing trade and they have made a real success of it, with a warm welcome for all their guests and a high standard of hospitality. The menu is filled with locally-sourced produce; specialities include the steaks but there is something to please every palate. The real ales are complemented by a good selection of lagers, cider, stout, wines, spirits and soft drinks. Children welcome.

- ☛ Off the A477 at Ferry Lane
- 🍺 Bass, Greene King IPA, rotating guest ale
- 🍴 12-2.30 & 6-9.30 (breakfast available during Summer)
- 🎵 Quiz Mon from 8.30 p.m.
- ♿ Parking, disabled access
- 💳 Not Amex or Diners
- 🕐 Tues/Weds/Fri/Sat 12-3 & daily 6-11 (Sun and Bank Holidays to 10.30)
- 🏛 Pembroke 1½ miles, Bosherston 6 miles, Milford Haven 8 miles

151 The Rising Sun Inn

Pelcomb Bridge, St Davids, Haverfordwest,
Pembrokeshire SA62 6EA

☎ 01437 765171

Bar Food, Restaurant Menu, Accommodation,
No Smoking Area

152 Robins Den

Within The Panorama Hotel, The Esplanade, Tenby,
Pembrokeshire SA70 7DU

☎ 01834 844976

Restaurant Menu, Accommodation,
No Smoking Area

153 Rochgate Motel

Roch, Haverfordwest, Pembrokeshire SA62 6AF

☎ 01437 710435

Real Ales, Restaurant Menu, Accommodation

154 Rose and Crown

71 Queen St, Pembroke Dock,
Pembrokeshire SA72 6JE

☎ 01646 683067

155 Rose and Crown Inn

1 Goodwick Square, Goodwick,
Pembrokeshire SA64 0BP

☎ 01348 872305

Real Ales, Bar Food, Restaurant Menu,
No Smoking Area

156 Royal Gate House Hotel

White Lion St, North Beach, Tenby,
Pembrokeshire SA70 7ET

☎ 01834 842255

Real Ales, Bar Food, Restaurant Menu,
Accommodation, No Smoking Area

157 The Royal Hotel

Trafalgar Terrace, Broad Haven, Haverfordwest,
Pembrokeshire SA62 3JU

☎ 01437 781249

Real Ales, Bar Food, Restaurant Menu,
Accommodation, No Smoking Area

158 Royal Oak

Market Square, Fishguard,
Pembrokeshire SA65 9HA

☎ 01348 872514

Real Ales, Bar Food, Restaurant Menu,
No Smoking Area

159 Royal Oak

West St, Newport, Pembrokeshire SA42 0TA

☎ 01239 820632

Real Ales, Bar Food, Restaurant Menu,
No Smoking Area

160 The Royal Oak Inn

Wogan Terrace, Saundersfoot,
Pembrokeshire SA69 9HA

☎ 01834 812546

Real Ales, Bar Food, Restaurant Menu,
No Smoking Area

161 Salutation Inn

Felindre Farchog, Crymych, Newport,
Pembrokeshire SA41 3UY

☎ 01239 820564

Real Ales, Bar Food, Restaurant Menu,
Accommodation, No Smoking Area

162 The Sherlock Holmes

19 Military Rd, Pennar, Pembroke Dock,
Pembrokeshire SA72 6SH

☎ 01646 687526

Bar Food, Restaurant Menu, No Smoking Area

163 The Ship Aground

Dinas Cross, Newport, Pembrokeshire SA42 0UY

☎ 01348 811261

Real Ales, Bar Food, Restaurant Menu,
No Smoking Area

164 Ship And Anchor

High St, Fishguard, Pembrokeshire SA65 9AR

☎ 01348 872362

Bar Food, Restaurant Menu, No Smoking Area

166 The Ship Inn

Main Street, Solva, Pembrokeshire SA62 6UU

☎ 01437 721247

Real Ales, Bar Food, Restaurant Menu, Accommodation, No Smoking Area

The Ship Inn is a very friendly, family-run pub offering superb food, drink and accommodation. Pristine inside and out, the inn boasts bags of character and a welcoming ambience enhanced by traditional features such as the open fires and exposed beamwork.

Lin Spicer and her family take justified pride in the high standard of food, well-kept ales and

comfortable and attractive accommodation on offer here. Dishes such as T-bone fillet and sirloin steaks from the finest Welsh Black beef and fresh local fish grace the menu, which offers a good range of expertly prepared choices. Food is served either in the bar or the wonderfully quaint 'Matties' restaurant next door. The handsome beer garden leads down to the river. This fine inn is well worth seeking out. Children and dogs welcome.

☛ On the A487 4 miles east of St David's and 12 miles northwest of Haverfordwest

🍺 Buckley IPA, Worthingtons, Tomos Watkins

🍴 12-3 & 6-9 (Sundays lunch only)

🛏 2 double en suite rooms

🎵 Quiz night Weds, singles night, themed nights

🚗 Car park, garden

💳 All major cards

🏅 4 stars Welsh Tourist Board (accommodation)

🕐 11-11 (Sun and Bank Holidays to 10.30)

🏛 St David's 4 miles, Ramsey Island 8 miles, Haverfordwest 12 miles, Fishguard 16 miles

168 Silverdale Inn & Lodges

Vine Road, Johnson, Milford Haven, Pembrokeshire SA62 3NZ

☎ 01437 890943

Bar Food, Restaurant Menu, Accommodation

The Silverdale Inn is a welcoming place with traditional features such as the exposed beamwork and stonebuilt walls, and a long history of providing great food, drink and accommodation. Bar snacks available include tempting morsels such as baked potatoes and cod and chips, while

the restaurant serves up steaks, gammon, chicken and other traditional favourites using the freshest locally-sourced ingredients expertly prepared and presented. Owner Werner Fuchs is also one of the chefs, and brings many years' experience into creating a memorable dining experience for all his guests. The accommodation lodges were completely refurbished in 2004, so that each one is tasteful, comfortable and equipped with every amenity guests could expect. Two of the units are specially equipped for visitors with disabilities.

☛ On the A4076 midway between Haverfordwest and Milford Haven

🍴 12-2 & 7-closing

🛏 21 en suite rooms

🎵 Occasional

🚗 Parking, disabled access, garden

💳 All the major cards

🕐 12-3 & 6-11 (Sun and Bank Holidays to 10.30)

🏛 Haverfordwest 3 miles, Milford Haven 3 miles, Scolton 7 miles, Sandy Haven 11 miles

165 The Ship Inn

Newport Rd, Lower Town, Fishguard,
Pembrokeshire SA65 9NA
☎ 01348 874033

166 The Ship Inn

See panel opposite

167 The Ship Inn

Trefin, Haverfordwest, Pembrokeshire SA62 5AX
☎ 01348 831445
Real Ales, Bar Food, Restaurant Menu,
No Smoking Area

168 Silverdale Inn & Lodges

See panel opposite

169 Sir Benfro Hotel

Herbrandston, Neyland, Milford Haven,
Pembrokeshire SA73 3TD
☎ 01646 694242
Restaurant Menu, Accommodation,
No Smoking Area

170 Sloop Inn

Porthgain, Haverfordwest, Pembrokeshire SA62 5BN
☎ 01348 831449
Real Ales, Bar Food, Restaurant Menu,
No Smoking Area

171 Speculation Inn

Hundleton, Pembroke, Pembrokeshire SA71 5RU
☎ 01646 661306
Real Ales, Bar Food, No Smoking Area

172 The Square and Compass Inn

Trevine, Haverfordwest, Pembrokeshire SA62 5JJ
☎ 01348 831420

173 St Brides Hotel

St Brides Hill, Saundersfoot,
Pembrokeshire SA69 9NH
☎ 01834 812304
Real Ales, Bar Food, Restaurant Menu,
Accommodation, No Smoking Area

176 The Stable Inn

Burton, Milford Haven, Pembrokeshire SA73 1NT
☎ 01646 600622

Real Ales, Bar Food, Restaurant Menu

The Stable Inn in Burton is well worth seeking out. Resembling a cosy and welcoming home more than an anonymous pub, this fine inn has featured in the local press thanks to the quality of its food.

The menus include some 130 tasty items, all freshly served to order and including dishes such as steaks, grills, fresh fish when available (lemon Sole, bass and salmon) and a mouth-watering cheese and broccoli bake. Warm and welcoming inside, work in oils and watercolours by local artists adorns the walls.

There's also a very lovely walled garden area where guests can enjoy their delicious meal or a drink on fine days. Justly popular with families, there is no smoking in the food areas and around the bar.

- Off the A477 north of Pembroke
- Flowers IPA, Bass, Abbott
- Weds-Sun 12-2.30 & daily 6-9
- Parking, disabled access, garden
- All major cards
- Pembrokeshire Food Pub of the Month (August 2004)
- Weds-Sun 12-2.30, daily 6-11 (Sun to 10.30)
- Pembroke 2 miles, Pembroke Dock 1 mile, Milford Haven 5 miles

174 St Brides Inn

St Brides Rd, Little Haven, Haverfordwest,
Pembrokeshire SA62 3UN

☎ 01437 781266

Real Ales, Bar Food, Restaurant Menu,
Accommodation, No Smoking Area

175 St Govans Country Inn

Bosherston, Pembroke, Pembrokeshire SA71 5DN

☎ 01646 661311

Real Ales, Bar Food, Restaurant Menu,
Accommodation, No Smoking Area

176 The Stable Inn

See panel on page 185

177 The Stackpole Inn

See panel below

178 Station Inn

Apple Green, Dimond St, Pembroke Dock,
Pembrokeshire SA72 6HN

☎ 01646 621255

Real Ales, Bar Food, Restaurant Menu,
No Smoking Area

179 The Sun

High St, North Beach, Tenby,
Pembrokeshire SA70 7HD

☎ 01834 845941

Bar Food

180 Sun Inn

See panel opposite

181 The Swan Inn

23 Queen St, Pembroke Dock,
Pembrokeshire SA72 6JH

☎ 01646 686964

Bar Food, Restaurant Menu

177 The Stackpole Inn

Jasons Corner, Stackpole,
Pembrokeshire SA71 5DF

☎ 01646 672324

🌐 www.stackpoleinn.co.uk

Real Ales, Bar Food, Restaurant Menu,
No Smoking Area

Set in a beautiful location just south of Pembroke amid scenic countryside and close to the coast, The Stackpole Inn serves up great food, drink and hospitality. Kim and Chris Jewell offer all their guests a warm welcome and first-class service. The three chefs are devoted to creating superb dishes using the freshest ingredients, with

seasonal menus that include local sausages, home-cooked pies and a selection of fish dishes. Regular food-themed nights are another ongoing attraction at this spacious and attractive inn. Quality is always the byword here.

The interior is traditional in style, with comfortable seating and a relaxed, informal ambience, while outdoors there's a lovely garden and patio area for enjoying a drink or meal on fine days.

🚩 On the B4319, 3 miles south of Pembroke

🍺 Reverend James, Double Dragon, 2 rotating guest ales

🍴 12-2.30 & 6-9

🎵 Quiz night Tues (winter)

♿ Parking, disabled access, garden

💳 All major cards

🏆 Food Pub of the Year 2005 Wales

🕐 12-2.30 & 6-11 (Sun and Bank Holidays to 10.30)

🏛 National Trust park (Stackpole), Barafundel 1 mile, Broadhaven 2 miles, Pembroke 3 miles

180 Sun Inn

St Florence, Tenby, Pembrokeshire SA70 8LS
☎ 01834 871322
Real Ales, Bar Food, Restaurant Menu

Set in the award-winning floral village of St Florence, Sun Inn is a picture-postcard 18th-century Free House decorated with a wealth of memorabilia and serving great food and drink. Upstairs in the no-smoking restaurant, specialities include home-made steak-and-kidney pie, trout and prime steaks. Fish and meat dishes are sourced locally. Children welcome

- 2 miles west of Tenby off the B4318 and a short drive from the A477
- Double Dragon, rotating guest ale
- daily 6-9 & Sundays 12-3
- Quiz night Mon form 9 p.m., occasional live music
- Parking, disabled access
- Credit cards welcome (not Diner's)
- Mon-Sat 5-11, Sun 12-3 & 6-10.30
- Carew 1½ miles, Tenby 2 miles, Upton 5 miles, Pembroke 5½ miles

182 Swan Lake Inn

Jameston, Tenby, Pembrokeshire SA70 8QE
☎ 01834 871262
Real Ales, Bar Food

183 Swn Y Mor Hotel & Restaurant

4 Cambrian Terr, Saundersfoot, Saundersfoot, Pembrokeshire SA69 9ER
☎ 01834 813201
Restaurant Menu

184 Taberna Inn

Herbrandston, Neyland, Milford Haven, Pembrokeshire SA73 3TD
☎ 01646 693498
Real Ales, Bar Food, Restaurant Menu, No Smoking Area

185 Tafarn Sinc Preseli

Rosebush, Clynderwen, Pembrokeshire SA66 7QT
☎ 01437 532214
Real Ales, Bar Food, Restaurant Menu, No Smoking Area

186 Tara Hotel

11 Windy Hall, Fishguard, Pembrokeshire SA65 9DP
☎ 01348 872777
Real Ales, Bar Food, Restaurant Menu, Accommodation, No Smoking Area

187 Teifi Netpool Inn

St Dogmaels, Cardigan, Pembrokeshire SA43 3ET
☎ 01239 612680
Real Ales, Bar Food, Restaurant Menu

188 Tenby House Hotel

See panel on page 188

189 The Three Crowns Inn

42 Laws Street, Pembroke Dock, Pembrokeshire SA72 6DL
☎ 01646 681811
Real Ales, Bar Food, No Smoking Area

Located just off the main street in Pembroke Dock, The Three Crowns Inn is a friendly, comfortable Free House much more spacious inside than it might at first appear from outside. Specialities on the menu include mixed grills and a good range of fish dishes, all freshly prepared to order.

- On the A477, 1¼ miles northwest of Pembroke
- Worthington Cask, Hancocks, Reverend James, rotating guest ale
- 12-2.30 & 6-9
- Occasional music Fri nights
- Parking, disabled access, garden
- 11.30-11 (Sun and Bank Holidays to 10.30)
- Pembroke 1½ miles, Bolsherston 6 miles, Milford Haven 8 miles

188 Tenby House Hotel

Tudor Square, Tenby, Pembrokeshire SA70 7AJ
☎ 01834 842000
⊕ www.tenbyhousehotel.com
e-mail: tenby.house@btconnect.com

Real Ales, Bar Food, Restaurant Menu,
Accommodation, No Smoking Area

The Tenby House Hotel is a truly elegant place
that was once the home of Sir William Paxton,
creator of many of the attractive and important
buildings in the town that made it a Regency
resort of such distinction. The hotel began life in
medieval times as a coaching inn known as The
Globe; Sir William developed the site in 1802 on
his return from India, where he'd made his
fortune as a trading merchant.

Tasteful and gracious throughout, the hotel has
18 bedrooms that echo the hotel's Regency
heritage. Hot and cold meals are served at lunch
and dinner in Paxton's Bistro, with a great variety
of dishes using the freshest local produce.

The Bistro is also open for morning coffee and
afternoon tea.

☛ On the A478, then a few minutes' walk from
the harbour, the Castle and the town's
North and South beaches

⋈ 18 en suite rooms

♫ Resident DJ in the bars at weekends

♿ Disabled access, garden

💳 All the major cards

🏵 3 Stars Welsh Tourist Board

🏛 Tenby, Saundersfoot 2½ miles, Caldey Island
2½ miles, Stepaside 4 miles, Amroth 4½
miles

190 Three Mariners Inn

St George St, Tenby, Pembrokeshire SA70 7JB
☎ 01834 849078
Real Ales, Bar Food, No Smoking Area

191 Travellers Rest

Freystrop Rd, Freystrop, Haverfordwest,
Pembrokeshire SA62 4LD
☎ 01437 890562
Real Ales, Bar Food, Restaurant Menu

192 Tregynon Farmhouse

Gwaun Valley, Fishguard, Pembrokeshire SA65 9TU
☎ 01239 820531
Real Ales, Bar Food, Restaurant Menu,
Accommodation, No Smoking Area

193 Trewern Arms

Nevern, Newport, Pembrokeshire SA42 0NB
☎ 01239 820395
Real Ales, Bar Food, Restaurant Menu,
Accommodation, No Smoking Area

194 Tudor Lodge

Jameston Manorbier, Tenby,
Pembrokeshire SA70 7SS
☎ 01834 871978
Real Ales, Bar Food, Restaurant Menu

195 Victoria Inn

Roch, St Davids, Haverfordwest,
Pembrokeshire SA62 6JU
☎ 01437 710426
Real Ales, Bar Food, Restaurant Menu,
Accommodation, No Smoking Area

196 Wanderers Rest Country Inn

Llanteglos Estate, Llanteg, Narberth,
Pembrokeshire SA67 8PU

☎ 01834 831677

Real Ales, Bar Food, Restaurant Menu,
Accommodation, No Smoking Area

197 Warpool Court Hotel

St Davids, Haverfordwest,
Pembrokeshire SA62 6BN

☎ 01437 720300

Bar Food, Restaurant Menu, Accommodation,
No Smoking Area

198 Webley Waterfront Hotel

Poppit Sands, St Dogmaels, Cardigan,
Pembrokeshire SA43 3LN

☎ 01239 612085

Real Ales, Bar Food, Restaurant Menu,
Accommodation, No Smoking Area

199 Welcome Traveller

Tiers Cross, Haverfordwest,
Pembrokeshire SA62 3DD

☎ 01437 891398

Real Ales, Bar Food, Restaurant Menu,
Accommodation, No Smoking Area

200 Welshmans Arms

Pembroke Dock, Pembrokeshire SA72 6DS

☎ 01646 685643

Real Ales, Bar Food, Restaurant Menu,
Accommodation, No Smoking Area

201 White Hart Inn

Finch St, St Dogmaels, Cardigan,
Pembrokeshire SA43 3EA

☎ 01239 612099

Real Ales, Bar Food, Restaurant Menu

202 Wilton House Hotel

Quay St, Haverfordwest, Pembrokeshire SA61 1BG

☎ 01437 760033

Real Ales, Bar Food, Restaurant Menu,
Accommodation, No Smoking Area

203 Windsor Hotel

6 Church Rd, Johnston, Haverfordwest,
Pembrokeshire SA62 3HD

☎ 01437 890080

Real Ales, Bar Food, Restaurant Menu,
Accommodation, No Smoking Area

204 Wisemans Bridge Inn

Wisemans Bridge, Saundersfoot,
Pembrokeshire SA69 9AU

☎ 01834 813236

Real Ales, Bar Food, Restaurant Menu,
Accommodation, No Smoking Area

205 The Wolfe Inn

Wolfscastle, Haverfordwest,
Pembrokeshire SA62 5LS

☎ 01437 741662

Real Ales, Bar Food, Restaurant Menu,
Accommodation, No Smoking Area

206 Wolfscastle Country Hotel

Wolfscastle, Haverfordwest,
Pembrokeshire SA62 5LZ

☎ 01437 741225

Bar Food, Restaurant Menu, Accommodation, No
Smoking Area

207 Woodridge Inn And Squash Club

The Fold Wooden, Saundersfoot,
Pembrokeshire SA69 9DY

☎ 01834 812259

Bar Food, Restaurant Menu, Accommodation

208 Ye Olde Inn

Camrose, St Davids, Haverfordwest,
Pembrokeshire SA62 6HY

☎ 01437 710293

Bar Food

LOCATION MAP

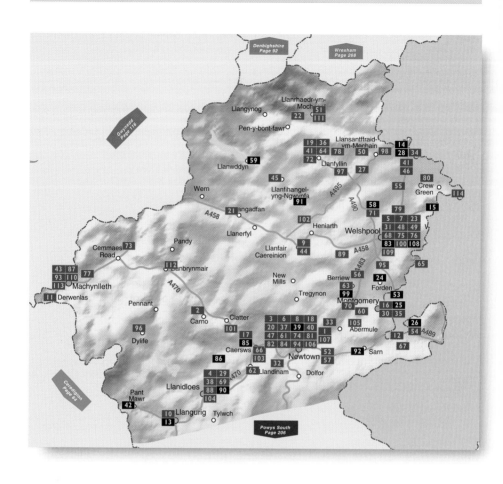

Denbighshire Page 92

Wrexham Page 268

Llangynog

Llanrhaedr-ym-Moch **51** **22** **111**

Pen-y-bont-fawr

Gwynedd Page 116

Llansantffraid-ym-Mechain
19 **36** **14**
41 **64** **78** **50** **98** **28** **34**
72 **59** Llanfyllin **41**
Llanwddyn **97** **27** **46**

45 **80**
Wern Llanfihangel-yng-Ngwynfa **55** Crew Green **114**
91

A495 A490 **58** **71** **79** **15**

A458 angadfan **21**
102 Heniarth **5** **7** **23**
Llanerfyl Welshpool **31** **48** **49**
Pandy **68** **75** **76**
Cemmaes **73** **9** **83** **100** **108**
Road Llanfair **44** **89** A458 **109**
Caereinion A483

112 Llanbrynmair **95** **65**
43 **87** New Berriew **56** **24**
93 **110** **77** Mills **63** Forden
113 Machynlleth A470 Tregynon **99** **53**
11 Derwenlas Montgomery **70** **60** **16** **25**
Pennant **30** **35**
2 **3** **6** **8** **18** **33**
Carno Clatter **20** **37** **39** **40** **105** **26**
101 **47** **61** **74** **81** **1** Abermule **54** A489
96 **17** **107** **12**
Dylife **85** **82** **84** **94** **106** **67**
Caersws **66** **52** **92** Sarn
86 **103** **32** Newtown **57**
4 **29** **62** Llandinam Dolfor
38 **69**
Pant Llanidloes **88** **90**
Mawr **104**
42
10 Llangurig Tylwch
13

Powys South Page 206

11 North Powys Reference Number - Detailed Information

12 North Powys Reference Number - Summary Entry

Ceredigion Page 249 Adjacent area - refer to pages indicated

POWYS - NORTH

WELSHPOOL • LLANIDLOES • MONTGOMERY

Over 2,000 square miles in size, the county of Powys covers the traditional counties of Montgomeryshire, Radnorshire and Brecknockshire. The area is named after the older Welsh kingdom of Powys, which occupied roughly the same area and came to an end when it was absorbed into the kingdom of Gwynedd by Hywel Dda.

North Powys was once part of the old county of Montgomeryshire, and is situated between the high, rugged landscape of Snowdonia and the farmland of Shropshire, a pleasant and gentle region with small towns and villages and a varied landscape. Along with being the home to the highest British waterfall outside Scotland, Pistyll Rhaeadr, one of the Seven Wonders of Wales, there is Lake Vyrnwy, a reservoir that was built in the 1880s to supply water to the burgeoning city of Liverpool.

The major settlement in the north is Welshpool, close to the English border and originally known as Pool – the prefix was added to ensure that the dispute regarding its nationality was resolved once and for all.

Still along the border with England there is the tiny anglicised town of Montgomery, with its superb remains of a borderland castle and also some of the best-preserved sections of Offa's Dyke. To the west lies Machynlleth, home of Owain Glyndwr's parliament in the 15th century. A visit to the Welsh hero's centre tells the story of his struggle against the English.

Lake Vyrnwy

To the south can be found the four spa towns of Llandrindod Wells, Builth Wells, Llangammarch Wells and Llanwrtyd Wells. Still popular tourist centres today, though no longer spas, these places all grew and developed as a result of the arrival of the railway and the Victorians' interest in health. Northeast of Llandrindod Wells, in the town of Knighton, the Offa's Dyke Centre has information about the long-distance footpath that runs from Prestatyn to Chepstow. Glyndwr's Way also begins in Knighton, following the route taken by one of Wales' favourite sons as he fought the English for Welsh independence in the 1400s. This scenic and important route travels westwards to Abbey-cwm-Hir.

To the west of the spas and found up in the Cambrian Mountains are more examples of 19th-century engineering skill: the spectacular reservoirs and dams that make up the Elan Valley are a fascinating sight, and the surrounding countryside is home to one of Britain's rarest and most beautiful birds – the Red Kite.

1   Abermule Hotel

Abermule, Montgomery, Powys SY15 6ND

☎ 01686 630676

Real Ales, Bar Food, Restaurant Menu,
Accommodation, No Smoking Area

2   Aleppo Merchant Inn

Carno, Caersws, Powys SY17 5LL

☎ 01686 420210

Real Ales, Bar Food, Restaurant Menu,
Accommodation, No Smoking Area

3   The Angel

4 High St, Newtown, Powys SY16 2NX

☎ 01686 626809

Bar Food

4   Angel Hotel

High St, Llanidloes, Powys SY18 6BY

☎ 01686 412381

Real Ales, Bar Food, Restaurant Menu,
No Smoking Area

5   The Angel

12 Berriew St, Welshpool, Powys SY21 7SQ

☎ 01938 553473

Real Ales, Bar Food

6   Bell Hotel

Commercial St, Newtown, Powys SY16 2DE

☎ 01686 625540

Real Ales, Bar Food, Restaurant Menu,
Accommodation

7   Best Western Royal Oak Hotel

The Cross, Welshpool, Powys SY21 7DG

☎ 01938 552217

Real Ales, Bar Food, Restaurant Menu,
Accommodation, No Smoking Area

15   The Breidden Inn

Middletown, Welshpool, Powys SY21 8EL

☎ 01938 570250

Real Ales, Bar Food, Restaurant Menu,
No Smoking Area

The Breidden Inn is a large and friendly inn with real ales and a separate restaurant. Once known as the 4 Crosses, the inn dates back to the early 1800s.

Owners Tracey and Wayne Fisher have been here since December of 2003, and bring a wealth of enthusiasm and expertise to their roles. Tracey is the cook, creating a good range of tempting dishes for the menu and specials board.

Meals available include a range of home made dishes such as steak & ale pie, lasagne, chicken ham & leek crumble and curry, as well as a variety of quality steaks and a comprehensive vegetarian selection.

The interior is traditional and comfortable; outdoors there's a nice beer garden and children's play area.

☞ Middletown is on the A458 west of Welshpool towards Shrewsbury

🍺 Tetleys, Black Sheep and a rotating guest ale

12-2, 7-9

♪ Fri live music from 9; quiz night every Thurs from 9.30, folk night last wednesday every month

⋈ Off-road car park, disabled access, garden, children's play area

All major cards

⏀ 12.00-11 (Sun and Bank Holidays to 10.30)
🕐 Open all day during summer

🏛 Offa's Dyke 3 miles, Montgomery 6 miles, Welshpool 5 miles

8 Black Boy Hotel

Broad St, Newtown, Powys SY16 2BQ

☎ 01686 626834

Real Ales, Bar Food, Restaurant Menu,
Accommodation, No Smoking Area

9 The Black Lion

Parsons Bank, Llanfair, Caereinion, Welshpool,
Powys SY21 0RR

☎ 01938 810759

Real Ales

10 The Black Lion Hotel

Llangurig, Llanidloes, Powys SY18 6SG

☎ 01686 440223

Real Ales, Bar Food, Restaurant Menu,
Accommodation, No Smoking Area

13 The Blue Bell Inn

Llangurig, Powys SY18 6SG
☎ 01686 440254
🌐 www.bluebell-inn.co.uk

Real Ales, Bar Food, Restaurant Menu,
Accommodation, No Smoking Area

The Blue Bell Inn is a former coaching inn dating
back to the 1500s., where real ales, great food and
comfortable accommodation are the draws.
Guests choose from a good variety of home-made
favourites expertly prepared by Gwlithyn Price,
who runs this inn with her husband Martin and
business partner Jo Lewis.

- ☞ At the junction of the A44/A470 8 miles
  northeast of Rhayader

- 🍺 Banks Bitter, Cloud Nine

- 🍴 12-2 & 6.30-9 (except Tues in winter)

- 🛏 8 rooms (4 en suite)

- 🎵 Quiz night once a month on a Thurs from 8
  p.m., food-themed evenings

- ♿ Parking, disabled access

- 💳 Not AMEX or Diner's

- 🕐 Mon-Fri 12-3 & 6-11, Sat 12-11, Sun 12-
  10.30

- 🏛 Llanidloes 3 miles, Rhayader 8 miles, Elan
  Village 10 miles

11 The Black Lion Inn

Derwenlas, Machynlleth, Powys SY20 8TN

☎ 01654 703913

Real Ales, Bar Food, Restaurant Menu,
No Smoking Area

12 Blue Bell Hotel

Church Stoke, Montgomery, Powys SY15 6SP

☎ 01588 620231

Real Ales, Bar Food

13 The Blue Bell Inn

See panel adjacent

14 The Bradford Arms

See panel below

15 The Breidden Inn

See panel opposite

14 The Bradford Arms

Llanymynech, Oswestry SY22 6EJ

☎ 01691 830582

🌐 www.bradfordarmshotel.com

Real Ales, Bar Food, Restaurant Menu,
Accommodation, No Smoking Area

- ☞ Llanymynech is adjacent to the A483 on the
  England/Wales border

- 🍺 1 rotating guest ale

- 🍴 12-2 & 7-9.30 (closed Sun and Mon all day)

- 🛏 5 rooms (2 ground-floor) en suite (available
  all year except Xmas & Boxing Day)

- ♿ Off-road car park, disabled access

- 💳 All major cards

- 🍷 AA 4 Red Diamonds

- 🏅 No smoking in restaurant areas

- 🚫 12.00-2.00 & 7.00-11.00(closed Sun Mon all
- 🕐 day)

- 🏛 Oswestry 6 miles, Welshpool 10 miles, Lake
  Vyrnwy 20 miles

16 Brickys

Chirbury Rd, Montgomery, Powys SY15 6QQ

☎ 01686 668177

Real Ales, Restaurant Menu, No Smoking Area

17 The Buck Hotel

Main St, Caersws, Powys SY17 5EL

☎ 01686 688267

Real Ales, Bar Food, Restaurant Menu, Accommodation, No Smoking Area

18 The Buck Inn

19 High St, Newtown, Powys SY16 2NP

☎ 01686 622699

Real Ales, Bar Food, No Smoking Area

19 Cain Valley Hotel

High St, Llanfyllin, Powys SY22 5AQ

☎ 01691 648366

Real Ales, Restaurant Menu, Accommodation, No Smoking Area

25 The Cottage Inn

Pool Road, Montgomery, Powys SY15 6QT

☎ 01686 668348

Real Ales, Restaurant Menu, No Smoking Area

The popular and friendly Cottage Inn is situated between Montgomery Castle to the rear and Offa's Dyke at the front. The bar area has a rustic charm and serves a choice of well kept real ales, while the spacious non smoking restaurant offers a wide range of tempting dishes and an excellent Sunday Carvery – booking is advisable.

🖝 7 miles south of Welshpool on the B4385

🍺 Brains, Duck & Dive

🍴 Tues-Sun 12-2 & 7-9

🎵 Curry evenings; quiz night last Thurs of the month from 9 p.m.

🅿 Parking, garden

💳 Not AMEX or Diner's

🕐 Tues-Sat 12-3 & 6-11, Sun and Bank Holidays 12-3 & 6-10.30

🏛 Montgomery Castle, Offa's Dyke, Newtown 10 miles, Tregynon 12½ miles

20 The Cambrian Vaults

New Rd, Newtown, Powys SY16 1BG

☎ 01686 622501

Real Ales

21 Cann Office Hotel

Llangadfan, Welshpool, Powys SY21 0PL

☎ 01938 820202

Real Ales, Bar Food, Restaurant Menu, Accommodation, No Smoking Area

22 Cefn Coch Inn

Cefn Coch, Welshpool, Powys SY21 0AE

☎ 01938 810247

Bar Food

23 Churchills

38 High St, Welshpool, Powys SY21 7JL

☎ 01938 555740

24 The Cock Hotel

Forden, Welshpool, Powys SY21 8LX

☎ 01938 580226 Fax: 01938 580691

e-mail: cockforden@btconnect.com

Real Ales, Restaurant Menu, No Smoking Area

🖝 The village of Forden lies close to where the B4388 meets the A490

🍺 2 rotating guest ales

🍴 Tues-Sat 12-9; Sun Lunch 12-2.00 then bar food until 8. (last orders half hour before)

🅿 Off-road car park

💳 All major cards

🕐 Mon 6.30-11, Tues – Sat 12.00-11 (Sun 12.00-10.30, (Bank Holidays 12.00-11.00)

🏛 Offa's Dyke 1 mile, Montgomery 3 miles, Powis Castle 3 miles, Welshpool 4 miles, Berriew (Glansevern Hall & Gardens) 4 miles

25 The Cottage Inn

See panel adjacent

26 The Court House Inn

See panel opposite

26 The Court House Inn

Church Stoke, Montgomery, Powys SY15 6AF
☎ 01588 620305
Real Ales, Bar Food, Restaurant Menu,
No Smoking Area

Very close to the English border and located next to the well-known St Nicholas Church in the picturesque village of Church Stoke, The Court House Inn is a friendly place with good food, drink and hospitality. Guests choose off the menu or daily specials board from a good variety of tempting hot and cold dishes.

- ☞ Church Stoke is just off the A490
- 🍺 Tetleys Cask and a rotating guest ale
- 🍴 12-3 & 5-9
- 🛏 2 rooms
- ♿ Off-road parking, some disabled access
- 💳 All the major cards
- 🕐 11.30-11 (Sun and Bank Holidays to 10.30)
- 🏛 Montgomery 2 miles, Newtown 12 miles, Welshpool 9 miles

27 Cross Keys Inn

Gwern Y Ciliau, Llansantffraid, Powys SY22 6XS
☎ 01691 828450
Real Ales, Bar Food, No Smoking Area

28 The Crosskeys Hotel

See panel adjacent

29 The Crown and Anchor

41 Long Bridge St, Llanidloes, Powys SY18 6EF
☎ 01686 412398
Real Ales

30 Crown Hotel

Castle St, Montgomery, Powys SY15 6PW
☎ 01686 668533
Real Ales, Bar Food

31 Crown Hotel

7 Hall St, Welshpool, Powys SY21 7RY
☎ 01938 553897
Real Ales

32 Dolau Inn

Mochdre, Newtown, Powys SY16 4JL
☎ 01686 629538
Real Ales, Bar Food, Restaurant Menu,
No Smoking Area

33 Dolforwyn Hall Hotel

Dolforwyn, Abermule, Montgomery,
Powys SY15 6JG
☎ 01686 630221
Real Ales, Bar Food, Restaurant Menu,
Accommodation, No Smoking Area

28 The Crosskeys Hotel

North Road, Llanymynech, Oswestry SY22 6EA
☎ 01691 831585
🌐 www.crosskeyshotel.info
Real Ales, Restaurant Menu, Accommodation, No Smoking Area

Cross Keys Hotel is an impressive 17th-century inn owned by David and Margaret Humphreys. David is an experienced chef who creates a range of tempting dishes such as stuffed local trout, steaks, grills using the freshest ingredients. Roasts and a vegetarian option are available on Sundays. Booking advised at weekends and is essential for Sunday lunch. Children welcome.

- ☞ Llanymynech is adjacent to the main A483 on the England/Wales border
- 🍺 2 rotating guest ales
- 🍴 April-Oct: Mon 5-10, Tues-Sat 12-10, Sun 12-10
- 🛏 6 rooms (4 en suite)
- 🎵 Live singers Fri eve from 9 – ring for details
- ♿ Car park, disabled access
- 💳 Not Amex or Diner's
- 🕐 April-Oct: Mon 5-11, Tues-Sat 12-11 (Sun and Bank Holidays to 10.30); Nov-Mar: Mon-Thurs 5-11, Fri-Sat 12-11 (Sun and Bank Holidays to 10.30)
- 🏛 Oswestry 6 miles, Welshpool 9 miles, Lake Vyrnwy 10 miles

34 The Dolphin Inn

Llanymynech, Powys SY22 6ER

☎ 01691 831078

Real Ales, Bar Food, Restaurant Menu,
No Smoking Area

35 The Dragon Hotel

Market Square, Montgomery, Powys SY15 6PA

☎ 01686 668359

Real Ales, Bar Food, Restaurant Menu,
Accommodation, No Smoking Area

36 Eagles Nest

Llanfyllin, Powys SY22 5AT

☎ 01691 648334

Real Ales, Bar Food, Restaurant Menu

39 The Exchange Public House

The Regent Centre, Broad Street, Newtown,
Powys SY16 2NA

☎ 01686 621814

🌐 www.theregentcentre.net

Real Ales, Bar Food, Restaurant Menu,
No Smoking Area

The Exchange is located within the Regent
Centre, built in 1827 and has housed the Flannel
Exchange, Court Assizes, Public Rooms, the local
Post Office and there has been a cinema here
since the 1930s. The Exchange boasts an
extensive menu of superb dishes from steaks,
Pasta to sandwiches and soups.

☞ Newtown is on the A483 southwest of
Welshpool

🍺 Courage Directors

🍴 10-9 Sun-Thurs 10-6 Fri & Sat, Lunchtime
carvery Tues & Sun

🎵 Nightclub above-stairs – please ring for
details

🕐 10-11 Mon-Thurs (Sun and Bank Holidays to
10.30); Fri-Sat 10 a.m.-1 a.m.

🏛 Pwll Penarth Nature Reserve, Robert Owen
Museum, Montgomery 10 miles, Welshpool
12 miles

37 Elephant and Castle Hotel

Broad St, Newtown, Powys SY16 2BQ

☎ 01686 626271

Real Ales, Bar Food, Restaurant Menu,
Accommodation, No Smoking Area

38 Elephant Hotel

46 Long Bridge St, Llanidloes, Powys SY18 6EF

☎ 01686 412505

Real Ales, Bar Food, Restaurant Menu,
No Smoking Area

39 The Exchange Public House

See panel adjacent

40 The Flying Shuttle

Llanidloes Rd, Newtown, Powys SY16 1HL

☎ 01686 624688

Real Ales, Bar Food, Restaurant Menu,
No Smoking Area

41 The Four Crosses Inn

Four Crosses, Llanymynech, Powys SY22 6RE

☎ 01691 831643

Real Ales, Bar Food, Restaurant Menu,
No Smoking Area

42 The Glansevern Arms

See panel opposite

43 Glyndwr Hotel

14 Doll St, Machynlleth, Powys SY20 8BQ

☎ 01654 703989

Bar Food, Restaurant Menu, Accommodation

44 The Goat Hotel

High St, Llanfair, Caereinion, Welshpool,
Powys SY21 0QS

☎ 01938 810428

Real Ales, Restaurant Menu, Accommodation,
No Smoking Area

42 The Glansevern Arms

Pantmawr, nr Llangurig, Powys SY18 6SY

☎ 01686 440240

🌐 www.glansevernarms.com

Real Ales, Bar Food, Restaurant Menu,
Accommodation, No Smoking Area

Enjoying a superb position on the banks of the
River Wye, The Glansevern Arms boasts great
food, drink and accommodation. Local produce is
a central feature of the menu here and the guest
bedrooms are charming and welcoming. Has its
own working farm, B&B for horses. Good for
walking and mountain biking.

☞ On the main A44, 4 miles west of Llangurig
and 19 miles inland of Aberystwyth

🍺 Bass

🍴 12-2 & 6.30-9 (closed lunchtimes in winter)

8 en suite rooms

🛏 Parking

Not AMEX or Diner's

No smoking in guest rooms

🚫 12-2.30 & 6-11 (Sun and Bank Hols to
🕐 10.30)

🏛 Llangurig 4 miles, Devil's Bridge 7 miles,
Llanidloes 7 miles, Aberystwyth 19 miles,
Cardigan Bay 19 miles

45 The Goat Inn

Llanfihangel, Llanfyllin, Powys SY22 5JD

☎ 01691 648209

46 The Golden Lion

Four Crosses, Llandysilio, Llangedwyn, Llanymynech,
Powys SY22 6RB

☎ 01691 830295

Real Ales, Bar Food, Restaurant Menu,
Accommodation, No Smoking Area

47 The Grapes

3 Commercial St, Newtown, Powys SY16 2BL

☎ 01686 624488

Real Ales

48 Grapes Hotel

Salop Rd, Welshpool, Powys SY21 7EZ

☎ 01938 553292

Real Ales

49 The Green Dragon

9-10 Mount St, Welshpool, Powys SY21 7LW

☎ 01938 552531

Real Ales

50 Green Inn

Llangedwyn, Llanfyllin, Powys SY22 6UA

☎ 01691 828234

Real Ales, Bar Food, Restaurant Menu,
No Smoking Area

51 Hand Inn

Llanrhaeadr-Ym-Mochnant, Oswestry,
Powys SY10 0JJ

☎ 01691 780413

Real Ales, Bar Food, Restaurant Menu,
No Smoking Area

52 The Herbert Arms

Kerry, Newtown, Powys SY16 4NU

☎ 01686 670638

Real Ales, No Smoking Area

53 The Herbert Arms Hotel

See panel on page 199

54 The Horse And Jockey

Chirbury Rd, Churchstoke, Montgomery,
Powys SY15 6AE

☎ 01588 620060

Bar Food, Restaurant Menu, No Smoking Area

55 Horseshoe Inn

Arddleen, Llangedwyn, Llanymynech,
Powys SY22 6PU

☎ 01938 590318

Real Ales, Bar Food, Restaurant Menu,
Accommodation, No Smoking Area

58 The Kings Head Inn

Guilsfield, Welshpool, Powys SY21 9NJ
☎ 01938 553656
⊕ www.kingshead.uk.com

Real Ales, Bar Food, Restaurant Menu,
No Smoking Area

Built in the 1600s, The Kings Head Inn began life
as a coaching inn for travellers on the road
between London and Holyhead. Retaining a
welcoming traditional ambience and original
features such as exposed beamwork.

The pub serves up real ales together with a
good selection of lagers, stout, wines, spirits and
soft drinks. International Master Chef Henryk
Azanko and his team prepare excellent food;
meals are served at lunch and dinner from a menu
and specials board featuring a good range of
hearty favourites. The restaurant area is spacious
and attractive. Booking is required Saturday
evenings and Sunday lunchtime at this popular
place.

Leaseholder George, who has over 30 years'
experience in catering and the licensing trade, is
assisted by his daughter Zofia and their friendly
staff in offering all their guests a warm and
genuine welcome.

☞ Guilsfield is on the B4392, 4 miles from the
junction with the A483

🍺 Bass, Worthington and a rotating guest ale

🍴 12-9.30 (7 days Easter-Sept)

🅿 Car park, disabled access

💳 All major cards

🕐 Mon-Sat 12.00-11(Easter-Sept); Sun 12.00-
10.30 (Easter-Sept)

🏛 Glynowr Way, Trelyden Hall 1 mile,
Welshpool 2 miles, Powysland Museum 2
miles, Montgomery 9 miles

59 Lake Vyrnwy Hotel

Lake Vyrnwy, Llanwddyn,
Montgomeryshire SY10 0LY
☎ 01691 870692 ⊕ www.lakevyrnwy.com

Real Ales, Bar Food, Restaurant Menu,
Accommodation, No Smoking Area

Superb is the only word for the Lake Vyrnwy
Hotel, long established as the premier place to
stay to enjoy luxurious comfort amid the beauty
and attractions of the region. This outstanding
hotel's reputation precedes it: a magnificent stone
mansion set high on a wooded hillside overlooking the lake and set in 24,000 acres of the Vyrnwy
Estate. Each of the guest bedrooms is individually
furnished and decorated with style and elegance.
In the award-winning restaurant the freshest and
best produce is used to create excellent dishes
such as Welsh Black beef, salmon and herb boudin
and classic pear Belle Hélène. Everything from the
breakfast marmalade to the petits fours is made in
the hotel's kitchens. Booking required at all times.

☞ 14 miles northwest of Welshpool on the
B4393

🍺 Two rotating guest ales

🍴 12-2 & 7-9.30

🛏 35 en suite rooms

🅿 Car park, grounds, disabled access

💳 All major cards

🏵 4 Stars Welsh Tourist Board

🕐 11-11 (Sun and Bank Holidays to 10.30)

🏛 Lake Vyrnwy, Llanwddyn, Pistyll Rhaeadr 1
mile

53 The Herbert Arms Hotel

Chirbury, Montgomery, Powys SY15 6BG

☎ 01938 561216

Real Ales, Bar Food, Restaurant Menu, Accommodation

Real fires, quarry-tiled floors, a warm and welcoming atmosphere – traditional features and comforts abound at the excellent Herbert Arms Hotel. Offering great food, drink and accommodation, the hotel has been run by Peter and Michelle since the Spring of 2004. The menu offers a good choice of home-cooked dishes.

☛ Chirbury can be found at the junction of the A490 and the B4386

🍺 Worthington Cask and a rotating guest ale

🍴 summer: Tues-Sun and Bank Hols 12-2.30, Tues, Wed, Fri, Sat 7-9; winter: Fri-Sat 12-2 & 7-9, Sun 12.30-2.30

🛏 4 rooms (1 en suite)

🅿 Off-road car park, some disabled access, garden

💳 Not AMEX

🕐 Summer only Tues-Thurs 12-2.30 All year Mon-Thurs 7-11, Fri-Sat 12-11 (Sun and Bank Holidays to 10.30)

🏛 Montgomery Castle 2 miles, Fridd Faldwyn 2 miles, Newtown 8 miles

56 Horseshoes Inn

Berriew, Welshpool, Powys SY21 8AW

☎ 01686 640282

Real Ales, Restaurant Menu, No Smoking Area

57 The Kerry Lamb

Kerry, Newtown, Powys SY16 4NP

☎ 01686 670226

Real Ales, Bar Food, Restaurant Menu, Accommodation, No Smoking Area

58 The Kings Head Inn

See panel opposite

59 Lake Vyrnwy Hotel

See panel opposite

60 The Lion Hotel

Caerhowell, Churchstoke, Montgomery, Powys SY15 6HF

☎ 01686 668096

Real Ales, Bar Food, Restaurant Menu, No Smoking Area

61 The Lion Hotel

Short Bridge St, Newtown, Powys SY16 2LR

☎ 01686 625807

Real Ales

62 The Lion Hotel

Llandinam, Powys SY17 5BY

☎ 01686 688233

Real Ales, Bar Food, Restaurant Menu, Accommodation, No Smoking Area

63 The Lion Hotel

Berriew, Welshpool, Powys SY21 8PQ

☎ 01686 640452

Real Ales, Bar Food, Restaurant Menu, Accommodation, No Smoking Area

64 The Lower Cross Keys

High St, Llanfyllin, Powys SY22 5AT

☎ 01691 648890

65 Lowfield Inn

The Lowfields, Marton, Welshpool, Powys SY21 8JX

☎ 01743 891313

Real Ales, Bar Food, Restaurant Menu, Accommodation, No Smoking Area

66 Maesmawr Hall Hotel

Maesmawr Hall, Caersws, Powys SY17 5SF

☎ 01686 688255

Real Ales, Bar Food, Restaurant Menu, Accommodation, No Smoking Area

67 Mellington Hall Hotel

Mellington, Church Stoke, Montgomery, Powys SY15 6HX

☎ 01588 620456

Real Ales, Bar Food, Restaurant Menu, Accommodation, No Smoking Area

83   The Raven Inn

Raven Square, Welshpool, Powys   SY21 7LT

☎ 01938 553070

Real Ales, Bar Food, Restaurant Menu,
No Smoking Area

Adjacent to the start of the Welshpool and
Llanfair Light Railway, The Raven Inn is a superb
place to stop and enjoy a relaxing drink or meal.
Real ale, lagers, wines, spirits and soft drinks are
on hand to quench every thirst, while the accent
is firmly on quality food. Making use of only
organic meats produced by Welsh Farm Organics
in Tyn y Fron, the menu and specials board dishes
include tempting delights such as steaks, lamb,

gammon and home-made curry and vegetarian
selections. There's also a great selection of
sandwiches, toasties and delicious traditional
sweets including sherry trifle and fruit cheesecake.
The chef, Stephen, was awarded Trainee Chef of
Wales in 1999/2000, and has continued to go
from strength to strength. Booking required for
Friday and Saturday evening and Sunday lunchtime,
and at all times for parties of four or more, at this
justly popular place.

☞   On the edge of Welshpool town centre
where the A458 meets the A490

🍺   Worthington Cask

🍴   12-2 & 6-8.30 (closed Mondays in winter)

🅿   Car park, children's play area, garden

🚫   Not Amex or Diners

🏆   Trainee Chef of Wales 1999/2000

🕐   Weekdays 11.30-3 & 6-11; Fri-Sat 11.30-11
(Sun and Bank Holidays to 10.30; closed
Mondays in winter)

🏛   Welshpool & Llanfair Light Railway,
Powysland Museum 3 miles, Powys Castle 5
miles

---

85   The Red Lion

3/4   Main Street, Caersws, Powys   SY17 5EL

☎ 01686 688023

Real Ales, Bar Food, Restaurant Menu,
Accommodation, No Smoking Area

Handsome, pristine and welcoming inside and out,
The Red Lion in Caersws is an excellent place to
enjoy a quiet drink or meal. This cosy, traditional
pub serves up real ales and good food. Dating
back in parts to 1790, it began life as an alehouse,
becoming fully licensed in the mid-1800s. Real
fires and other traditional features add to the

pub's relaxed ambience. The menu features
favourites such as home-made pies (beef and ale,
chicken and mushroom or beef and onion), home-
made chilli, steaks and home-made curry, to name
just a few selections. On Sundays there's a choice
of traditional roasts. Accommodation is on hand in
two en suite double guest bedrooms available all
year round. Owners Jayne and David, ably assisted
by daughter Mandy and her husband Jim, offer all
their guests a warm and genuine welcome. Fishing
and clay-pigeon shooting can be arranged for
guests.

☞   Caersws is just yards from the main A470

🍺   Banks Bitter, Banks Original, rotating guest
ale

🍴   Weds to Mon 12-2 & 6-9; summer: 12-9

🛏   2 en suite rooms

🅿   Car park, disabled access, beer garden,
children's play area

🚭   No smoking in dining room

🕐   11.30-3 & 6-11; summer: 11.30-11 (Sun and
Bank Holidays to 10.30)

🏛   Newtown 3 miles, Gregynon Hall Gardens 6
miles, Welshpool 15 miles

68 ## Mermaid
28 High St, Welshpool, Powys SY21 7JP
☎ 01938 552027
Real Ales

69 ## The Mount Inn
China St, Llanidloes, Powys SY18 6AB
☎ 01686 412247
Real Ales, Bar Food, Restaurant Menu,
Accommodation, No Smoking Area

70 ## The Nags Head Hotel
Garthmyl, Montgomery, Powys SY15 6RS
☎ 01686 640287
Real Ales, Bar Food, Restaurant Menu,
Accommodation, No Smoking Area

71 ## The Oak Inn
Guilsfield, Welshpool, Powys SY21 9NH
☎ 01938 553391
Real Ales, Bar Food, Restaurant Menu,
No Smoking Area

72 ## The Old New Inn
High St, Llanfyllin, Powys SY22 5AA
☎ 01691 648449
Real Ales, Bar Food, Accommodation

73 ## Penrhos Arms Hotel Ltd
Cemmaes, Machynlleth, Powys SY20 9PR
☎ 01650 511243
Real Ales, Bar Food, Accommodation,
No Smoking Area

74 ## The Pheasant Inn
14 Market St, Newtown, Powys SY16 2PQ
☎ 01686 625383
Real Ales, Bar Food, Accommodation,
No Smoking Area

75 ## Pheasant Inn
43 High St, Welshpool, Powys SY21 7JQ
☎ 01938 553104
Real Ales

76 ## Pinewood Tavern
1 Broad St, Welshpool, Powys SY21 7RZ
☎ 01938 553067
Real Ales, Accommodation

77 ## Plas Dolguog
Felingerrig, Machynlleth, Powys SY20 8UJ
☎ 01654 702244
Bar Food, Restaurant Menu, Accommodation,
No Smoking Area

78 ## Plas-Yn-Dinas Inn
Llanfechain, Powys SY22 6UJ
☎ 01691 828380
Real Ales, Bar Food, No Smoking Area

79 ## Powis Arms Hotel
Pool Quay, Welshpool, Powys SY21 9JS
☎ 01938 590253
Real Ales

80 ## Punch Bowl Inn
Llandrinio, Llanymynech, Powys SY22 6SG
☎ 01691 830247
Real Ales, Bar Food, Restaurant Menu,
Accommodation, No Smoking Area

81 ## Queens Head Hotel
Pool Rd, Newtown, Powys SY16 1DG
☎ 01686 626461
Real Ales

82 ## The Railway Tarvern
Old Kerry Rd, Newtown, Powys SY16 1BH
☎ 01686 626156
Real Ales

83 ## The Raven Inn
See panel opposite

84 ## Red Dragon
Plantation Lane, Newtown, Powys SY16 1LH
☎ 01686 625891
Real Ales

85 ## The Red Lion
See panel opposite

86 The Red Lion

Trefeglwys, nr Caersws, Powys SY17 5PH

☎ 01686 430255

⊕ www.redlion-pub.co.uk

Real Ales, Bar Food, Restaurant Menu, No Smoking Area

The Red Lion is a large and pristine traditional inn with original features such as the stonebuilt fireplace and exposed beamwork. David and Lynne Markworth and their daughter Frances, offer a warm welcome to all their guests. There is a separate no-smoking dining room where guests can choose from a good selection of tempting dishes. They also have a games room.

☛ A few miles north of Llandiloes on the B4569

🍺 Traditional Bitter

🍴 Mon-Fri 7-9, Sat 12-9, Sun 12-3 & 7-9

♫ Folk night first Fri of month, monthly quiz

🅿 Parking, garden/patio

💳 All the major cards

🚫 summer: Mon-Fri 12-3 & 6-11, Sat 12-11, Sun 12-3 & 6-10.30; winter: Mon-Fri 6-11, Sat 12-11, Sun 12-3 & 6-10.30 (please see website)

🏛 Llyn Mawr Reserve 3 miles, Llanidloes 5 miles, Newtown 8 miles, Gregynon Hall Gardens 9 miles

87 Red Lion

11 Maengwyn St, Machynlleth, Powys SY20 8AA

☎ 01654 703323

Real Ales, Bar Food, Restaurant Menu

88 Red Lion Hotel

8 Long Bridge St, Llanidloes, Powys SY18 6EE

☎ 01686 412270

Real Ales, Bar Food, Restaurant Menu, Accommodation, No Smoking Area

89 Red Lion Inn

Castle Caereinion, Welshpool, Powys SY21 9AL

☎ 01938 850233

Real Ales, Accommodation

91 The Royal Oak Inn

Pont Robert, Nr Meifod, Powys SY22 6HY

☎ 01938 500243

Real Ales, Bar Food, Restaurant Menu, Accommodation, No Smoking Area

☛ Pont Robert is off the A495 a couple of miles' drive from Meifod

🍺 2 – 4 rotating guest ales

🍴 12.30-11

🛏 2 rooms en suite

🅿 Off-road car park, disabled access

🕐 11.30-11

🏛 Meifod 2 miles, Welshpool 5 miles

92 The Sarn Inn

Sarn, Newtown, Powys SY16 4EJ

☎ 01686 670757

Real Ales, Bar Food, Restaurant Menu, No Smoking Area

Dating to the mid-1700s, The Sarn Inn is a recently refurbished former coaching inn. This popular and friendly pub serves up hearty traditional fare and has a range of thirst-quenchers including real ale, lagers, cider, stout, wines, spirits and soft drinks. Owners Aileen and David have been in the trade for 27 years, and their experience is put to good use here.

☛ Sarn is adjacent to the A489 between Church Stoke and Newtown

🍺 Burtonwood Bitter

🍴 12-3 & 7-9

♫ Occasional entertainment and food-themed eves – ring for details

🅿 Car park, garden

🕐 Mon-Thurs 11.30-3 & 6.30-11, Fri-Sat 11.30-11 (Sun and Bank Holidays to 10.30)

🏛 Clun Forest, Church Stoke 1½ miles, Newtown 1½ miles

90 The Royal Head

See panel below

91 The Royal Oak Inn

See panel opposite

92 The Sarn Inn

See panel opposite

93 Skinners Arms

14 Penrallt St, Machynlleth, Powys SY20 8AJ

☎ 01654 702354

Real Ales, Bar Food, Restaurant Menu,
No Smoking Area

94 The Sportsman

17 Severn St, Newtown, Powys SY16 2AQ

☎ 01686 625885

Real Ales, Bar Food, No Smoking Area

95 Square and Compass

Forden Kilkewydd, Welshpool, Powys SY21 8RU

☎ 01938 580360

Real Ales, Accommodation, No Smoking Area

96 Star Inn

Dylife, Llanbrynmair, Powys SY19 7BW

☎ 01650 521345

Real Ales, Bar Food, Restaurant Menu,
Accommodation, No Smoking Area

97 The Stumble Inn

Bwlch Y Cibau, Llanfyllin, Powys SY22 5LL

☎ 01691 648860

Real Ales, Bar Food, No Smoking Area

98 The Sun Hotel

Llansantffraid, Powys SY22 6AR

☎ 01691 828000

Real Ales, Bar Food, Restaurant Menu,
No Smoking Area

---

90 The Royal Head

Shortbridge Street, Llanidloes, Powys SY18 6AD

☎ 01636 412583

Real Ales, Bar Food, Restaurant Menu,
Accommodation, No Smoking Area

Handsome and immediately welcoming, the Royal Head in Llanidloes is a traditional inn in the best sense of the word. Original features of this fine inn include a wealth of exposed beamwork and exposed stonework walls. Leaseholders Sue and Ian are making a great success of their first venture into the licensing trade. Sue does all the cooking, using the freshest locally-sourced produce to create a range of delicious dishes. During the lifetime of this edition the inn will also have two guest bedrooms available. With activities such as fishing, sailing, golf and clay pigeon shooting on hand locally, together with many sights and attractions in Llanidloes and the surrounding area, the inn makes a perfect place to enjoy a relaxing drink or meal while exploring the region.

🍺 Just off the main A470 10 miles north of Rhayader

🍺 Hancocks HB, three rotating guest ales

🍴 Tues-Sun 12-2 & 6-9

🛏 2 en suite rooms

🎵 Occasional live entertainment

♿ Parking, disabled access

🕐 Tues-Thurs 12-3 & 6-11, Fri-Sat 12-11, Sun and Bank Holidays 12-3 & 6-10.30

🏛 Fan Hill, Llanidloes, Hafren Forest 6 miles, Glaslyn Nature Reserve 8 miles, Rhayader 10 miles

99   The Talbot Hotel

See panel below

100   The Talbot Inn

16 High St, Welshpool, Powys SY21 7JP

☎ 01938 553711

Real Ales, Bar Food, Restaurant Menu

101   Talkhouse

Ty Siarad, Pontdolgoch, Caersws, Powys SY17 5JE

☎ 01686 688919

Real Ales, Restaurant Menu, Accommodation,
No Smoking Area

102   The Tan House Inn

Llangyniew, Welshpool, Powys SY21 0JY

☎ 01938 810056

Real Ales, Bar Food, Restaurant Menu,
Accommodation, No Smoking Area

103   Unicorn Hotel

Bridge St, Caersws, Powys SY17 5DT

☎ 01686 688237

Real Ales, Bar Food, Restaurant Menu,
Accommodation, No Smoking Area

104   Unicorn Hotel

Long Bridge St, Llanidloes, Powys SY18 6EE

☎ 01686 413167

Real Ales, Bar Food, Restaurant Menu,
Accommodation, No Smoking Area

105   Upper House Inn

Llandyssil, Abermule, Montgomery,
Powys SY15 6LQ

☎ 01686 668465

Real Ales, Bar Food, Restaurant Menu

99   The Talbot Hotel

Berriew, Welshpool, Powys SY21 8PJ

☎ 01686 640881

⊕ www.thetalbotberriew.co.uk

Real Ales, Bar Food, Restaurant Menu,
Accommodation, No Smoking Area

Charming and picture-postcard inside and out, The Talbot Hotel in Berriew dates back in parts to the late 1500s and offers a warm welcome to all guests. Home-cooked food, guest ales and en suite accommodation can all be found here. Set near the riverside, the surrounding area is very pretty and offers many sights and attractions. The interior is homely and relaxed, with overstuffed chairs, open fires and traditional beamwork among the many attractive features; the no-smoking restaurant is the place to enjoy a range of home-made daily specials such as steaks, lamb shank, ginger-marinated salmon, Stilton-and-spinach tart and much more. The Sunday lunch is a real treat. Owner Gwyneth does all the cooking, and is a talented and creative chef. Together with her partner Michael she offers all her guests genuine hospitality.

☛ Berriew is just off the A483 at the junction of the B4385 and B4390

🍺 Worthington Cask and a rotating guest ale

🍴 Tues-Fri 6.30-9, Sat-Sun 12-2 & 6.30-9, Bank Holiday Mondays only

🛏 6 en suite rooms (including 2 family rooms)

♫ Singer Sat eves from 8 p.m.

🅿 Parking, disabled access, garden

💳 Not Amex or Diners

🏅 2 stars Welsh Tourist Board

🕐 Mon-Fri 4.30-11, Sat 11-11, Sun and Bank Holidays 11-10.30

🏛 Andrew Logan Museum of Sculpture, Glansevern Hall, Welshpool 5 miles

106 Waggon and Horses

Lower Canal Rd, Newtown, Powys SY16 2JB
☎ 01686 625790
Real Ales, Bar Food, Restaurant Menu

107 Waterloo Arms

Abermule, Montgomery, Powys SY15 6ND
☎ 01686 630528
Bar Food, Restaurant Menu

108 The Wellington Inn

2 Berriew Street, Welshpool, Powys SY21 7SQ
☎ 01938 553315

Real Ales, Bar Food, Restaurant Menu

In the heart of Welshpool, The Wellington Inn dates back to the 1500s and is popular with locals and visitors alike. Cosy and friendly, guests are in safe hands with owner Barbara Jones and her son Paul, who provide a full range of drinks, delicious home-cooked meals and snacks, Sunday lunch and genuine hospitality.

☛ Welshpool is on the A458 and A483

🍺 Theakstons and a rotating guest ale

🍴 12-6

🎵 Karaoke Sat and alternate Sundays

🅿 Parking nearby, disabled access

🕐 11.30-11 (Sun to 10.30, Bank Holidays to Midnight)

🏛 Powysland Museum, Powis Castle, Montgomery Canal Centre, Welshpool and Llanfair Railway

109 Westwood Park Hotel

Salop Rd, Welshpool, Powys SY21 7EA
☎ 01938 553474
Real Ales, Bar Food, Accommodation

110 The White Lion Hotel

10 Heol, Pentrerhedyn, Machynlleth, Powys SY20 8DN
☎ 01654 703455
Real Ales, Bar Food, Restaurant Menu, Accommodation, No Smoking Area

111 Wynnstay Arms Hotel

Market Square, Llanrhaeadr-Ym-Mochant, Oswestry, Powys SY10 0JL
☎ 01691 780210
Real Ales, Bar Food, Restaurant Menu, Accommodation, No Smoking Area

112 Wynnstay Arms Hotel

Maengwyn St, Machynlleth, Powys SY20 8AE
☎ 01654 702941
Real Ales, Bar Food, Restaurant Menu, Accommodation, No Smoking Area

113 Wynnstay Arms Hotel

Llanbrynmair, Powys SY19 7AA
☎ 01650 521431
Real Ales, Bar Food, Restaurant Menu, Accommodation, No Smoking Area

114 Ye Old Hand & Diamond

Coedway, Powys SY5 9AR
☎ 01743 884379
Real Ales, Bar Food, Restaurant Menu, Accommodation

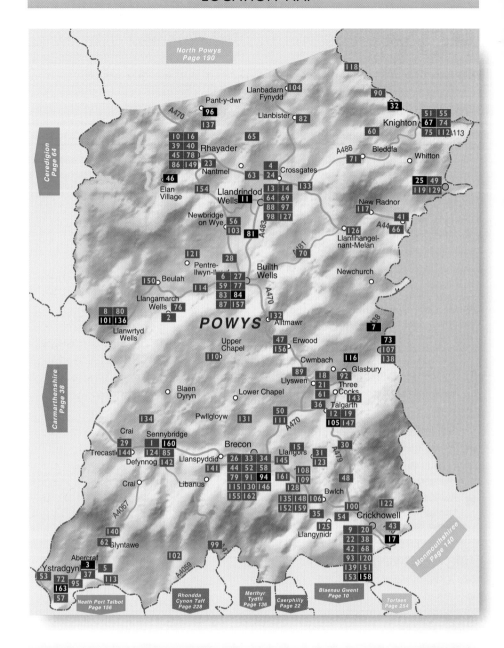

North Powys
Page 190

118

104 Llanbadarn
Fynydd

Pant-y-dwr

96

137

Llanbister 82

90

32

51 55
67 74
75 112 113

Knighton

60

Ceredigion
Page 64

10 16
39 40
45 78
86 149 23

Rhayader

Nantmel

46

Elan
Village

154

Landrindod
Wells II

Newbridge
on Wye

65

63

4
24

Crossgates

A488 Bleddfa

71

Whitton

25 49
119 129

13 14
64 69
88 97
98 127

New Radnor

117

41

A44 66

56
103 81

121

28

Pentre-
llwyn-llwyd

150 Beulah

114

Llangamarch
Wells 76

6 27
59 77
83 84
87 157

2

126

70

Llanfihangel-
nant-Melan

Builth
Wells

Newchurch

8 80
101 136

Llanwrtyd
Wells

POWYS

132

Alltmawr

7

73

Upper
Chapel

110

47
156

Erwood

Cwmbach

116

107
138

89

Blaen
Dyryn

Lower Chapel

18
21
61

92

Three
Cocks

143

Glasbury

Llyswen

36

Talgarth

12 19
105 147

Pwllgloyw

131

50
111

134

Crai

Sennybridge

Brecon

29

1 160

Trecastle 144

Defynnog

124 85

142

Llanspyddid

15

Llangors

31
123

145

30

48

26 33 34
44 52 58
79 91 94
115 130 146
155 162

161

108
109

Crai

Libanus

128

Bwlch

100

122

135 148 106
152 159

35

54

Crickhowell

140

62 Glyntawe

99

102

125

Llangynidr

9 20
22 38
42 68
93 120
139 151
153 158

43

17

Abercraf

Ystradgyn

3

53

72

95

163

57

5

37

113

Neath Port Talbot
Page 156

Rhondda
Cynon Taff
Page 228

Merthyr
Tydfil
Page 136

Caerphilly
Page 22

Blaenau Gwent
Page 10

Torfaen
Page 254

Monmouthshire
Page 140

Carmarthenshire
Page 38

II South Powys Reference Number - Detailed Information

12 South Powys Reference Number - Summary Entry

Ceredigion
Page 249 ▷ Adjacent area - refer to pages indicated

POWYS - SOUTH

BRECON • LLANDRINDOD WELLS • RHAYADER

Over 2,000 square miles in size, the county of Powys covers the traditional counties of Montgomeryshire, Radnorshire and Brecknockshire. The area is named after the older Welsh kingdom of Powys, which occupied roughly the same area and came to an end when it was absorbed into the kingdom of Gwynedd by Hywel Dda.

Much of the southern part of the county of Powys lies within the Brecon Beacons National Park, which takes its name from the distinctively-shaped sandstone mountains of the Brecon Beacons. While the scenery is undoubtedly beautiful and impressive, the National Park has much to offer as, like much of the rest of this part of the county, it is steeped in history that dates back to prehistoric times.

Famous for its ancient cathedral, Georgian architecture and annual Jazz Festival Brecon

Brecon Beacons

lies on the banks of the River Usk, at the confluence of the Rivers Honddu and Tarrell in the heart of the National Park. A walk along the promenade beside the River Usk leads to the remains of medieval Brecon Castle. Close by stands Brecon Cathedral, and impressive and magnificent building that originated from an 11th-century cell of the Benedictine monastery at Battle in Sussex. Brecon is also home to the Monmouthshire and Brecon Canal, a beautiful waterway with attractive walks along the towpath and pleasure cruises on both motorised and horse-drawn barges.

The Canal passes through the 375-yard long Ashford Tunnel before, further south, the Talybont Reservoir is the site of a narrow wooded valley on the southeastern slopes of the Brecons where several forest trails begin.

Lying in the foothills of the Black Mountains, Talgarth is an attractive market town with narrow streets that boasts many historic associations as well as some fine architecture. Hay-on-Wye is another ancient town, tucked between the Black Mountains and the River Wye in the northernmost corner of the National Park. Famed for its plethora of second-hand bookshops, it hosts the annual Festival of Art and Literature every May.

Hay Book Festival, Hay-On-Wye

To the south of the village of Llangorse, some five miles east of Brecon, lies the largest natural lake in South Wales – Llangorse Lake (Llyn Syfaddan). Around four miles in circumference and following its way round a low contour of the Brecon Beacons, it's home to a wide variety of sporting and leisure activities such as fishing, horse-riding and sailing.

Owned by the Brecknock Wildlife Trust, Pwll-y-Wrach Nature Reserve has a waterfall and a great variety of flora, for which it has been designated a Site of Special Scientific Interest.

At Craig-y-nos, 15 miles southwest of Brecon, the Dan-yr-Ogof Showcaves are the largest complex of caverns in northern Europe. Exploring these underground caverns is only one part of this fascinating attraction, as there is also an award-winning Dinosaur Park and A Shire Horse Centre. To the east of the village there's a Country Park where visitors can enjoy the unspoilt countryside and the landscaped country parkland of the upper Tawe Valley.

Sgwd Einion Gam Waterfall, Ystradfellte

1   Abercamlais Arms

Sennybridge, Brecon, Powys LD3 8PH

☎ 01874 636461

Real Ales

2   Aberceiros Inn

Cefngorwydd Rd, Llangammarch Wells,
Powys LD4 4EW

☎ 01591 620227

Real Ales, Bar Food, Accommodation

3   Abercrave Inn

See panel below

4   Allt-Yr-Ynys Country House Hotel

Walterstone, Abergavenny, Powys HR2 0DU

☎ 01873 890307

Real Ales, Bar Food, Restaurant Menu,
Accommodation, No Smoking Area

5   The Ancient Briton Hotel

Brecon Rd Penycae, Penycae, Swansea,
Powys SA9 1YY

☎ 01639 730273

Real Ales, Bar Food, Restaurant Menu,
Accommodation, No Smoking Area

---

3   Abercrave Inn

145 Heol Tawe, Abercrave, Swansea SA9 1XS

☎ 01639 731002

🌐 www.abercraveinn.co.uk

Real Ales, Bar Food, Restaurant Menu,
Accommodation, No Smoking Area

The Abercrave Inn is a large and spacious traditional inn dating back in parts to the 16th century. The lounge is a case in point, where exposed beams and the large stonebuilt fireplace add to the welcoming and friendly atmosphere.

Well-known for its excellent food, the Michelin-star head chef and his expert staff prepare everything from simple snacks to a superb range of justly popular dishes at lunch and dinner that make use of the freshest local produce. Booking advised. The restaurant overlooks the gardens, where the River Tawe flows through the beautiful landscaping. It's the perfect place to enjoy a relaxing drink or meal on fine days.

Close to the Brecon Beacons and Swansea, the inn is a wonderful base from which to explore the region.

☛ Off the A4067 14 miles southwest of Brecon

🍺 Brains SA, Buckleys Best and 2 rotating guest ales

🍴 12-2.30 & 6-9.30

🛏 12 en suite rooms

🅿 Parking, garden

🍻 12-11 (Sun and Bank Holidays to 10.30)

🕐 Craig-y-Nos 2 miles, Ystradfellte 5 miles, Libanus 10 miles, Brecon 14 miles

6 Barley Mow Inn

1 West St, Builth Wells, Powys LD2 3AH

☎ 01982 553648

Bar Food, Restaurant Menu

7 The Baskerville Arms Hotel

Clyro, nr Hay-on-Wye, Herefordshire HR3 5RZ

☎ 01497 820670

⊕ www.baskervillearms.co.uk

Real Ales, Bar Food, Restaurant Menu, Accommodation, No Smoking Area

Documented as 'The Swan' in the diaries of the Reverend Francis Kilvert in the late 1800s, The Baskerville Arms is a handsome Georgian hotel and restaurant. Gracious and elegant throughout, the inn provides an extensive menu of delicious home-made dishes using the freshest locally-sourced ingredients.

☛ Just off the A438 15 miles southeast of Llandrindod Wells

🍺 Bass, an ale from the Wye Valley Brewery and a rotating guest ale

🍴 Fri-Sun 12-2.30 & every evening 6-9

🛏 13 en suite rooms

♫ Monthly quiz, occasional food-themed evenings

🅿 Parking

💳 Not AMEX

🏆 2 Stars Welsh Tourist Board

🕐 12-3 & 6-11 (Sun and Bank Holidays to 10.30)

🏛 Hay-on-Wye 1 mile, Builth Wells 10 miles, Llandrindod Wells 15 miles

8 Basselke Brasserie and Bar

The Square, Llanwrtyd Wells, Powys LD5 4SP

☎ 01591 610564

Bar Food, Restaurant Menu, Accommodation, No Smoking Area

9 Bear Hotel

High St, Crickhowell, Powys NP8 1BW

☎ 01873 810408

Real Ales, Bar Food, Restaurant Menu, Accommodation, No Smoking Area

10 The Bears Head Inn

East St, Rhayader, Powys LD6 5DN

☎ 01597 810289

Real Ales, Bar Food

11 The Bell Country Inn

Llanyre, Llandrindod Wells, Powys LD1 6DY

☎ 01597 823959

⊕ www.bellcountryinn.co.uk

Real Ales, Restaurant Menu, Accommodation, No Smoking Area

Strikingly handsome and traditional, The Bell Country Inn lives up to its motto: 'The best – first time'. Three menus plus the specials board use local produce to create a variety of meals including home-made pies and puddings. The 'Taste of Five Continents' – an array of dishes from around the world, served tapas-style – is particularly popular. The accommodation is comfortable and attractive.

☛ 1½ miles northwest of Llandrindod Wells off the A4081

🍺 Hancock HB and 3 changing guest ales including another Welsh-brewed ale

🍴 12-2.30 & 6.30-9.30

🛏 10 en suite rooms karaoke

🅿 Off-road car park, some disabled access, garden

💳 All the major cards

🕐 12-3 & 6.30-11 (Sun and Bank Holidays to 10.30)

🏛 Llandrindod Wells 1½ miles, fishing, golf, riding, bird-watching, walking, climbing

12 Bell Hotel

High St, Talgarth, Brecon, Powys LD3 0BP

☎ 01874 711467

Real Ales, Bar Food, Accommodation

13 Belle Vue Hotel

Belle Vue Terrace, Llanwrtyd Wells, Powys LD5 4RE

☎ 01591 610237

Real Ales, Bar Food, Restaurant Menu,
Accommodation, No Smoking Area

14 Best Western Metropole Hotel

Temple St, Llandrindod Wells, Powys LD1 5DY

☎ 01597 823700

Real Ales, Bar Food, Restaurant Menu,
Accommodation, No Smoking Area

15 Black Cock Inn

Llanfihangel Talyllyn, Brecon, Powys LD3 7TL

☎ 01874 658697

Real Ales, Bar Food, Restaurant Menu,
Accommodation, No Smoking Area

16 Black Lion Hotel

North St, Rhayader, Powys LD6 5BU

☎ 01597 810271

Real Ales, Bar Food

17 The Bluebell Inn

See panel below

18 The Boat Inn

Boughrood, Brecon, Powys LD3 0YD

☎ 01874 754359

Real Ales

19 Bridge End Inn

Bridge St, Crickhowell, Powys NP8 1AR

☎ 01873 810338

Real Ales, Bar Food, Restaurant Menu

---

17 The Bluebell Inn

Glangrwyney, nr Crickhowell, Powys

☎ 01873 810247

Real Ales, Bar Food, Restaurant Menu,
Accommodation, No Smoking Area

The Bluebell Inn is a truly lovely 17th-century coaching inn with great food, drink and accommodation. In the warm and cosy bar and lounge, guests can enjoy a selection of snacks, light lunches and bar meals, while the spacious and attractive restaurant has a full menu and daily specials making the best use of locally-sourced meats and produce, cooked to order by the inn's experienced professional chef. Booking essential for Sunday lunch.

The accommodation comprises five en suite guest bedrooms, including one with a four-poster bed, and the inn makes an excellent base from which to explore Sugar Loaf Mountain and to sample the many outdoor pursuits (including golfing) which can be arranged by friendly and helpful tenants Paul and Louise.

☛ Off the A40 between Abergavenny and Crickhowell

🍺 Brains and rotating guest ale

🍴 12-2 & Mon-Thurs 6-9, Fri-Sat 6-10

🛏 5 en suite rooms

🅿 Parking, garden, patio, disabled access

💳 All major cards

🕐 summer: 12-11; winter: 12-3 & 6-11 (Sun and Bank Holidays to 10.30)

🏛 Golfing (nearby), Sugarloaf Mountain 4 miles, Abergavenny 6 miles, Crickhowell 6 miles

20 Bridge End Inn

Bell St, Talgarth, Brecon, Powys LD3 0BP

☎ 01874 711936

Real Ales, Restaurant Menu, No Smoking Area

21 Bridgend Inn

Llyswen, Brecon, Powys LD3 0YB

☎ 01874 754225

Real Ales, Bar Food, No Smoking Area

22 Britannia Inn

20 High St, Crickhowell, Powys NP8 1BD

☎ 01873 810553

23 Brynafon Country House Hotel

South St, Rhayader, Powys LD6 5BL

☎ 01597 810735

Real Ales, Restaurant Menu, Accommodation, No Smoking Area

24 The Builders Arms

Crossgates, Llandrindod Wells, Powys LD1 6RB

☎ 01597 851235

Real Ales, Bar Food, Accommodation

25 The Bull Hotel

See panel below

26 The Bulls Head

86 The Struet, Brecon, Powys LD3 7LS

☎ 01874 622044

Real Ales, Bar Food, Accommodation

27 Caer Beris Manor Hotel

Garth Rd, Builth Wells, Powys LD2 3NP

☎ 01982 552601

Real Ales, Bar Food, Restaurant Menu, Accommodation, No Smoking Area

---

25 The Bull Hotel

St David's Street, Presteigne, Powys LD8 2BP

☎ 01544 267488

Real Ales, Bar Food, Restaurant Menu, Accommodation, No Smoking Area

The Bull Hotel is a family-run establishment in the capable hands of Tony and Jeanette Jalland and their daughter Chloe. Occupying a Grade II listed building dating back to the early 1700s, a bull-baiting post once stood in the old market square where the inn now stands, from which it takes its name. The surrounding countryside is breath-

taking. Inside, the lounge bar is comfortable and welcoming, with two log fires and other traditional features. The no-smoking restaurant seats 28. Sunday roasts are added to the main extensive menu on Sundays. Booking advised. The inn's six upstairs guest bedrooms are available all year round. Private fishing along a beautiful stretch of the River Lugg is available to hotel guests, while painting holidays and short breaks are held throughout the year.

☛ At the junction of the B4362/B4356/B4355, 16½ miles east of Llandrindod Wells

2-3 rotating guest ales

12-2.30 & 7.30-8.30

6 en suite rooms

Folk night second Weds of the month

Parking

Not Amex or Diners

11-3 & 5-11 (Sun and Bank Holidays to 10.30); closed all day Mon and Tues-Thurs lunchtimes in winter

The Judge's Lodging (Presteigne), Knighton 5 miles, Llandrindod Wells 16½ miles

28 Cambrian Arms

Builth Rd, Builth Wells, Powys LD2 3RG

☎ 01982 553200

Real Ales, No Smoking Area

29 Castle Coaching Inn

Trecastle, Brecon, Powys LD3 8UH

☎ 01874 636354

Real Ales, Bar Food, Restaurant Menu,
Accommodation, No Smoking Area

30 Castle Inn

Llangorse, Brecon, Powys LD3 7UB

☎ 01874 658225

Real Ales, Bar Food, Restaurant Menu

31 Castle Inn

Pengenffordd, Talgarth, Brecon, Powys LD3 0EP

☎ 01874 711353

Real Ales, Bar Food, Restaurant Menu,
Accommodation, No Smoking Area

32 The Castle Inn

Knucklas, Knighton, Powys LD7 1PW

☎ 01547 528150   ⊕ www.castleinn.org.uk

**Real Ales, Bar Food, Restaurant Menu,
Accommodation, No Smoking Area**

Unassuming from the outside, this welcoming
17th century inn offers a wealth of beams, wood
panelling, exposed stone walls and flagstone
flooring as well as real fires in each room. Home-
made dishes including steak and ale pie and
chicken tikka can be taken in the bar or non-
smoking lounge. Excellent carvery with local
meats served Sunday lunchtimes 12-2.

☛ A few miles northwest of Knighton on the
   B4355

🍺 2-4 real ales, depending on season

🍴 Sun 12-2; 7-9, Tues-Sat 6.30-9

🛏 5 en suite rooms

🅿 Parking, Beer Garden

🕐 Mon-Sat 6.30-11, Sun 12-3 & 7-10.30

🏛 Offa's Dyke Centre, Glyndwr's Way, Pinners
   Hole, Kinsley Wood (all Knighton), 4 miles

33 Castle of Brecon Hotel

The Castle Square, Brecon, Powys LD3 9DB

☎ 01874 624611

Real Ales, Bar Food, Restaurant Menu,
Accommodation, No Smoking Area

34 Chweraepeg

21 The Watton, Brecon, Powys LD3 7ED

☎ 01874 624555

Real Ales, Restaurant Menu, Accommodation,
No Smoking Area

35 Coach and Horses

Cwmcrawnon Rd, Llangynidr, Crickhowell,
Powys NP8 1LS

☎ 01874 730245

Real Ales, Bar Food, Restaurant Menu,
Accommodation

36 Cock Hotel

Bronllys, Brecon, Powys LD3 0LE

☎ 01874 711151

Real Ales, Bar Food, No Smoking Area

37 The Copper Beech Inn

133 Heol Tawe, Abercraf, Swansea, Powys SA9 1XS

☎ 01639 730269

Real Ales, Bar Food, Restaurant Menu,
Accommodation, No Smoking Area

38 The Corn Exchange

High St, Crickhowell, Powys NP8 1BH

☎ 01873 810699

Real Ales, Bar Food

39 The Cornhill Inn

13 West St, Rhayader, Powys LD6 5AB

☎ 01597 811015

Real Ales, Bar Food, Restaurant Menu,
Accommodation, No Smoking Area

40 The Crown Inn

North St, Rhayader, Powys LD6 5BT

☎ 01597 811099

Real Ales, Bar Food, Accommodation,
No Smoking Area

41 Crown Inn

Walton, Presteigne, Powys LD8 2PY

☎ 01544 350663

Real Ales, Bar Food, Restaurant Menu, Accommodation, No Smoking Area

42 Dragon Hotel

High St, Crickhowell, Powys NP8 1BE

☎ 01873 811087

Real Ales, Bar Food, Restaurant Menu, Accommodation

43 The Dragons Head

Llangenny, Crickhowell, Powys NP8 1HD

☎ 01873 810350

Real Ales, Bar Food, Restaurant Menu, No Smoking Area

44 Drovers Arms

Newgate St, Llanfaes, Brecon, Powys LD3 8DN

☎ 01874 623377

Real Ales, Bar Food, No Smoking Area

45 Elan Hotel

West St, Rhayader, Powys LD6 5AF

☎ 01597 810109

Restaurant Menu, Accommodation, No Smoking Area

46 Elan Valley Hotel

See panel below

47 The Erwood Inn

Erwood, Builth Wells, Powys LD2 3EZ

☎ 01982 560218

Real Ales, Bar Food, Restaurant Menu, No Smoking Area

48 Farmers Arms

Cwmdu, Crickhowell, Powys NP8 1RU

☎ 01874 730464

Real Ales, Bar Food, Restaurant Menu, No Smoking Area

---

46 Elan Valley Hotel

Elan Valley, near Rhayader, Powys LD6 5HN

☎ 01597 810448

🌐 www.elanvalleyhotel.co.uk

Real Ales, Restaurant Menu, Accommodation, No Smoking Area

Elan Valley Hotel began life in the late-1800s as a fishing lodge; it is now a cosy and welcoming family-run hotel set amid an area of great scenic beauty abounding in varied plant, animal and bird life. The outstanding, intimate restaurant has a menu packed with tempting home-cooked delights with an emphasis on the freshest locally-sourced ingredients such as Welsh Black steaks, local lamb and wild mushroom dishes. Booking advised for non-residents. The hotel also has a range of bar meals and a children's menu. The excellent accommodation is available on a B&B or B&B and dinner basis. This superior hotel also offers activity weekends throughout the year, offering cycling, birdwatching, walking, pony trekking and 'Fungi Forays' (the hotel's special mushroom-foraging weekends). Ideal Wedding and Conference venue.

☛ 2 miles southwest of Rhayader off the A470

🍺 Hancocks Bitter and Timothy Taylor Landlord

🍴 Mon-Sat 7-9 p.m., Sun 12-2 & 7-9

🛏 10 en suite rooms

🎵 Special activity breaks throughout the year – please ring for details

🅿 Parking, garden, disabled access

💳 All major cards

🎖 2 Stars Welsh Tourist Board

🕐 6-11 (Sun and Bank Holidays to 10.30) and Sunday 12-3

🏛 Elan Valley, Rhayader (Welsh Royal Crystal, Gigrin Farm, Wye Valley Walk) 2 miles

49 The Farmers Inn

Hereford St, Presteigne, Powys LD8 2AW
☎ 01544 267389
Real Ales, Bar Food, No Smoking Area

50 The Felinfach Griffin

Felinfach, Brecon, Powys LD3 0UB
☎ 01874 620111
Real Ales, Bar Food, Restaurant Menu,
No Smoking Area

51 George and Dragon

Broad St, Knighton, Powys LD7 1BL
☎ 01547 528532
Real Ales, Bar Food, Restaurant Menu,
No Smoking Area

52 The George Hotel

George St, Brecon, Powys LD3 7LD
☎ 01874 623421
Real Ales, Bar Food, Restaurant Menu,
Accommodation, No Smoking Area

53 George IV Inn

Heol Gwys, Swansea, Powys SA9 2XH
☎ 01639 830938
Real Ales, Bar Food, Restaurant Menu,
No Smoking Area

54 Gliffaes Country House
Hotel

Gliffaes Rd, Crickhowell, Powys NP8 1RH
☎ 01874 730371
Real Ales, Bar Food, Restaurant Menu,
Accommodation, No Smoking Area

55 Golden Lion

High St, Knighton, Powys LD7 1AT
☎ 01547 528757
Real Ales

56 Golden Lion Hotel

Newbridge On Wye, Llandrindod Wells,
Powys LD1 6LN
☎ 01597 860392
Real Ales

57 Gough Arms Hotel

Glantawe Row, Ystradgynlais, Swansea,
Powys SA9 1ES
☎ 01639 843292
Real Ales, Bar Food, Restaurant Menu,
Accommodation, No Smoking Area

58 The Gremlin Hotel

48 The Watton, Brecon, Powys LD3 7EG
☎ 01874 623829
Real Ales, Bar Food, Restaurant Menu,
Accommodation, No Smoking Area

59 Greyhound Hotel

3 Garth Rd, Builth Wells, Powys LD2 3AR
☎ 01982 553255
Real Ales, Restaurant Menu, Accommodation,
No Smoking Area

60 Greyhound Inn

Llangunllo, Knighton, Powys LD7 1SP
☎ 01547 550241
Real Ales

61 Griffin Inn

Llyswen, Brecon, Powys LD3 0UR
☎ 01874 754241
Real Ales, Bar Food, Restaurant Menu,
Accommodation

62 The Gwyn Arms

Penycae, Swansea, Powys SA9 1GP
☎ 01639 730310
Real Ales, Bar Food, Restaurant Menu,
Accommodation, No Smoking Area

63 Gwystre Country Inn

Gwystre, Llandrindod Wells, Powys LD1 6RN
☎ 01597 851650
Real Ales, Bar Food, Restaurant Menu,
No Smoking Area

64 Hampton Hotel

Temple St, Llandrindod Wells, Powys LD1 5HF
☎ 01597 822585
Real Ales, Bar Food, Accommodation

65 Happy Union Inn

Abbey Cwmhir, Llandrindod Wells,
Powys LD1 6PH
☎ 01597 851203
Real Ales

66 The Harp Inn

Old Radnor, Presteigne, Powys LD8 2RH
☎ 01544 350655
Real Ales, Bar Food, Restaurant Menu,
No Smoking Area

67 The Horse & Jockey Inn

See panel below

68 The Horseshoe Inn

Llangattock, Crickhowell, Powys NP8 1PA
☎ 01873 810393
Real Ales, Bar Food, Restaurant Menu

69 Hotel Commodore

Spa Rd, Llandrindod Wells, Powys LD1 5ER
☎ 01597 822288
Bar Food, Restaurant Menu, Accommodation,
No Smoking Area

70 Hundred House Inn

Bleddfa, Knighton, Powys LD7 1PA
☎ 01547 550333
Real Ales, Bar Food, Restaurant Menu,
No Smoking Area

71 Hundred House Inn

Hundred House, Llandrindod Wells,
Powys LD1 5RY
☎ 01982 570231
Real Ales, Bar Food, Restaurant Menu,
Accommodation, No Smoking Area

67 The Horse & Jockey Inn

Wylcum Place, Station Road, Knighton,
Powys LD7 1AE
☎ 01547 520062
⊕ www.thehorseandjockeyinn.co.uk
Real Ales, Restaurant Menu, Accommodation,
No Smoking Area

Here in Knighton, The Horse and Jockey Inn is a Free House with real ales and a varied menu of expertly prepared dishes. Well recommended for its hospitality and cuisine, specialities include steak dishes and chicken-and-bacon enchiladas, together with tempting delights such as

chargrilled seabass, calamari and aubergine parmigiana. Booking required Saturday and Sunday. Owners Gary and Jacqui have been here since 1989, and are justly proud of their traditional inn, parts of which date back to Medieval times. The interior has a great deal of character and charm, with huge open fires and a cosy and welcoming ambience. The comfortable accommodation is available on a room-only basis. Children welcome.

☛ On the Welsh/Shropshire border, 16 miles northeast of Llandrindod Wells where the A488 meets the A4113

🍺 Speckled Hen and rotating guest ale

🍴 12-2 & 6-9 (Sun 12-2 & 7-9)

🛏 1 en suite room

🎵 Disco Fri and Sat from 9 p.m.

🅿 Parking, courtyard with seating, some disabled access

💳 Not Amex or Diners

🕐 11-11 (Sun and Bank Holidays to 10.30)

🏛 Glyndwr's Way, Offa's Dyke Centre, Kinsley Wood, Pinners Hole

72 Jeffreys Arms

108 Brecon Rd, Ystradgynlais, Swansea,
Powys SA9 1QL

☎ 01639 843319

Bar Food

73 Kilverts Inn

See panel below

74 The Kinsley

Station Rd, Knighton, Powys LD7 1DT

☎ 01547 520753

Real Ales

75 The Knighton Hotel

Broad St, Knighton, Powys LD7 1BL

☎ 01547 520530

Real Ales, Bar Food, Restaurant Menu,
Accommodation, No Smoking Area

76 Lake Country House Hotel

Llangammarch Wells, Powys LD4 4BS

☎ 01591 620202

Bar Food, Restaurant Menu, Accommodation,
No Smoking Area

77 The Lamb

12 Broad St, Builth Wells, Powys LD2 3DT

☎ 01982 552332

Real Ales, Bar Food

78 Lamb And Flag Inn

North St, Rhayader, Powys LD6 5BU

☎ 01597 810819

Real Ales, Bar Food, Restaurant Menu,
Accommodation, No Smoking Area

---

73 Kilverts

The Bullring, Hay-on-Wye, Herefordshire HR3 5AG

☎ 01497 821042 🌐 www.kilverts.co.uk

Real Ales, Bar Food, Restaurant Menu,
Accommodation, No Smoking Area

Set in the heart of Hay-on-Wye, Kilverts is an excellent inn dating back to 1860. Owner Colin Thomson has been here some 12 years and he offers all his guests a warm welcome and genuine hospitality. Guests choose off the bar or restaurant menus, or daily specials board, from a range of tempting dishes. Booking is essential for Friday and Saturday evening at this justly popular place. The restaurant interior is stylish and modern, with polished wood floors and tasteful décor and furnishings.

The accommodation is comfortable and attractive. When the weather is fine, guests can take advantage of Kilverts' garden – one of Hay-on-Wye's best-kept secrets: half an acre of lawns and flower beds with a pond and fountain area.

☛ 14½ miles northeast of Brecon on the B4350

🍺 3 rotating guest ales (1 always from local Wye Valley Brewery)

🍴 12-2 & 7-9.30 (12-10 during Festival)

🛏 12 en suite rooms

🅿 Parking, disabled access, garden

🚫 Not Diner's

🏅 2 Stars AA, 2 Stars Welsh Tourist Board

🕐 12-11 (Sun and Bank Holidays to 10.30)

🏛 Hay-on-Wye Craft Centre, Talgarth 7 miles, Brecon 14½ miles, Llangorse 12 miles

79 Lansdowne Hotel and Restaurant

39 The Watton, Brecon, Powys LD3 7EG

☎ 01874 623321

Restaurant Menu, Accommodation,
No Smoking Area

80 Lasswade Country House Hotel

Station Rd, Llanwrtyd Wells, Powys LD5 4RW

☎ 01591 610515

Bar Food, Restaurant Menu, Accommodation

81 The Laughing Dog

Howey, Llandrindod Wells, Powys LD1 5PT

☎ 01597 822406

⊕ www.thelaughingdog.ukpub.net

Real Ales, Bar Food, Restaurant Menu, No Smoking Area

The Laughing Dog is a friendly family pub with bags of charm and atmosphere. Built in the early 1700s, this welcoming Free House serves up a range of ales and great food. Booking advised Friday and Saturday at this justly popular inn.

☞ Just off the main A483 a few miles south of Llandrindod Wells

🍺 Woods Bitter, Wye Valley Bitter, rotating guest

🍴 Tues-Sat & Bank Hols 12-2.30 & 6-9.30, Sun 12-2.30

♫ Folk music first Weds in month from 8.30 p.m.

🏛 Parking, garden, disabled access

🕐 summer: 11-11 (Sun and Bank Holidays to 10.30); rest of year: 11-3 & 6.30-11 (Sun and Bank Holidays to 10.30)

🏛 Llandrindod Wells 2 miles, Builth Wells 5 miles, Cwmhir Cistercian Abbey 12 miles

82 Lion Hotel

Llanbister, Llandrindod Wells, Powys LD1 6TN

☎ 01597 840244

Real Ales, Bar Food, Accommodation,
No Smoking Area

83 The Lion Hotel

Builth Wells, Powys LD2 3DT

☎ 01982 550670

Real Ales, Bar Food, Restaurant Menu,
Accommodation, No Smoking Area

84 The Lion Hotel

See panel opposite

85 The Lion Inn

Defynnog, Brecon, Powys LD3 8SB

☎ 01874 636895

Real Ales, Bar Food, Restaurant Menu

86 Lion Royal Hotel

West St, Rhayader, Powys LD6 5AB

☎ 01597 810202

Real Ales, Bar Food, Restaurant Menu

87 Llanelwedd Arms

Llanelwedd, Builth Wells, Powys LD2 3SR

☎ 01982 553282

Real Ales, Bar Food, Restaurant Menu,
No Smoking Area

88 Llanerch Inn

Waterloo Rd, Llandrindod Wells, Powys LD1 6BG

☎ 01597 822086

Real Ales, Bar Food, Restaurant Menu,
Accommodation, No Smoking Area

89 Llangoed Hall

Llyswen, Brecon, Powys LD3 0YP

☎ 01874 754525

Real Ales, Bar Food, Restaurant Menu,
Accommodation, No Smoking Area

90 Lloyney Inn

Lloyney, Knighton, Powys LD7 1RG

☎ 01547 528498

Real Ales, Bar Food

91 The Lounge Cafe Bar

21A High St, Brecon, Powys LD3 7LA

☎ 01874 611189

Real Ales, Bar Food, No Smoking Area

84 The Lion Hotel

2 Broad Street, Builth Wells, Powys LD2 3DT

☎ 01982 553311

⊕ www.thelionbuilthwells.com

Real Ales, Restaurant Menu, Accommodation, No Smoking Area

Handsome and stylish, The Lion Hotel has recently undergone tasteful refurbishment to offer a high standard of comfort and quality. Set in the heart of Builth Wells, handy for the many sights and attractions of the region, the hotel is family-run by the Pattersons. With a wealth of

experience – they have been in the trade for over 20 years – they provide a high level of service and attention to the little details that can add so much to guests' enjoyment and comfort.

The spacious and elegant restaurant is the setting for a selection of delicious and freshly made dishes. Booking advised at all times. The accommodation includes two elegant suites; all 18 en suite rooms are located upstairs, but the hotel is fitted with a lift.

☛ In the heart of Builth Wells, 7 miles south of Llandrindod Wells on the A483

🍺 Rotating guest ales

🍴 9-9.30

🛏 18 en suite rooms

🅿 Parking

💳 Not Amex

🚭 No smoking in restaurant or guest rooms

🕐 12-3 & 6-11 (Sun and Bank Holidays to 10.30)

🏛 Builth Wells (Wayside Arts Centre, Groe Park, Cefn Carn Cafall), Llandrindod Wells 7 miles

94 The Markets Tavern Hotel

Free Street, Brecon, Powys LD3 7BL

☎ 01874 623595 ⊕ www.innfood.com

Real Ales, Bar Food, Restaurant Menu, Accommodation, No Smoking Area

Dating back to the late 1700s, the impressive Markets Tavern Hotel is a large and spacious inn bursting with character and a warm, welcoming ambience. Here in the heart of Brecon, the inn boasts a separate restaurant that is very charming. Specialities include home-made steak-and-kidney pie, lasagne and Welsh stew, from a full menu of

delicious dishes. Guests can also enjoy their relaxing drink or meal outside on the sun-drenched patio or garden on fine days. Richard and Jacky Edwards have been here since 2003 as leaseholders. Richard and Jacky have over 20 years' experience in the trade, and it shows in the expert service and hospitality they and their friendly staff provide. The hotel's 10 comfortable and attractive guest bedrooms are available all year round.

☛ On the A40/A470 14½ miles southwest of Hay-on-Wye

🍺 Real ales from the Thomas Watkins brewery

🍴 12-3 & 6.30-10 (no food Mon eve in winter)

🛏 10 rooms

🎵 Live music monthly on a Saturday eve; food-themed eves from 7 p.m Wednesday. Parking, disabled access, garden, patio

💳 Not Amex

🕐 12-11 (Sun and Bank Holidays to 10.30)

🏛 Brecon Cathedral and Heritage Centre, Brecknock Wildlife Trust, Talgarth 7½ miles, Hay-on-Wye 14½ miles

92 The Maesllwch Arms Hotel

Glasbury-On-Wye, Herefordshire, Powys HR3 5LH
☎ 01497 847637
Real Ales, Bar Food, Restaurant Menu, Accommodation, No Smoking Area

93 The Manor Hotel

Brecon Rd, Crickhowell, Powys NP8 1SE
☎ 01873 810212
Real Ales, Bar Food, Restaurant Menu, Accommodation, No Smoking Area

94 The Markets Tavern Hotel

See panel on page 219

95 Merlyns

44-46 Commercial St, Ystradgynlais, Swansea, Powys SA9 1JH
☎ 01639 845670
Bar Food, Restaurant Menu, Accommodation, No Smoking Area

96 Mid Wales Inn

See panel below

97 Middleton Arms Hotel

Tremont Rd, Llandrindod Wells, Powys LD1 5EB
☎ 01597 822066

98 Montpellier Hotel

Temple St, Llandrindod Wells, Powys LD1 5HW
☎ 01597 822388
Real Ales, Bar Food, Restaurant Menu, Accommodation, No Smoking Area

---

96 Mid Wales Inn

Pant-y-Dwr, Rhayader, Powys LD6 5LL
☎ 01597 870076
⊕ www.mid-wales-inn.co.uk

Real Ales, Bar Food, Restaurant Menu, Accommodation

Set along a designated prime scenic route, the Mid Wales Inn is a welcoming place to enjoy great food, drink and accommodation.

Having been the licensee at the Oval cricket ground between 1995 and 2001, manager Arthur has a wealth of experience at pleasing his guests

with well-kept ales and great food. He has run this Free House with able assistance from his business partner Andy since July of 2004.

Booking is advised at all times for the restaurant, where the dishes on the menu make use of locally-sourced produce. Specialities include mouth-watering steaks and curries.

Accommodation is available all year round in five well-appointed guest bedrooms, and the area boasts a number of attractions including good walking, cycling and the sights of Aberystwyth, Llandrindod Wells and Builth Wells.

☛ On the B4518 3 miles north of Rhayader

🍺 Buckley's Best

🍴 As for opening hours

🛏 5 rooms (4 en suite, 1 with private bath)

♿ Parking, disabled access

💳 Not Amex

🕐 Mon-Fri 5-11, Sat 12-11, Sun and Bank Holidays 12-10.30

🏛 Red Kite Centre, Rhayader 3 miles, Llanidloes 7 miles

99 Nant Ddu Lodge Hotel

Cwm Taf, Merthyr Tydfil, Powys CF48 2HY

☎ 01685 379111

Bar Food, Restaurant Menu, Accommodation,
No Smoking Area

100 Nantyffin Cider Mill

Talgarth Rd, Crickhowell, Powys NP8 1SG

☎ 01873 810775

Real Ales, Bar Food, Restaurant Menu,
No Smoking Area

101 The Neuadd Arms Hotel

Llanwrtyd Wells, Powys LD5 4RB

☎ 01591 610236

🌐 www.neuaddarmshotel.co.uk

Real Ales, Bar Food, Restaurant Menu,
Accommodation, No Smoking Area

☞ On the A483 about 10 miles northeast of
Llandovery

🍺 Felinfoel, Double Dragon and 3 rotating
guest ales; micro-brewery on site

🍴 12-2.30 & 6-8.30

🛏 21 en suite rooms

🎵 Regular beer festivals – please ring for
details

⚒ Parking, garden

✦ Not AMEX

🚭 No smoking in residents' lounge

🕐 11.30-11 (Sun and Bank Holidays to 10.30)

🏛 Local events ; Cambrian Woollen Mill

102 New Inn

Ystradfellte, Aberdare, Powys CF44 9JE

☎ 01639 720211

Real Ales

103 The New Inn

Newbridge on Wye, Llandrindod Wells, Powys LD1 6HY

☎ 01597 860211

Real Ales, Bar Food, Restaurant Menu,
No Smoking Area

104 The New Inn

Llanbadarnfynydd, Llandrindod Wells, Powys LD1 6YA

☎ 01597 840378

Real Ales, Bar Food, Restaurant Menu,
Accommodation, No Smoking Area

105 The New Inn

Bronllys Road, Talgarth, Brecon, Powys LD3 0HH

☎ 01874 711581

🌐 www.newinntalgarth.com

Real Ales, Bar Food, Restaurant Menu,
No Smoking Area

☞ On the A479 close to the junction with the
A4078, 7½ miles northeast of Brecon

🍺 Brains Bitter and a rotating guest ale

🍴 Mon-Sat 12-3 & 6-10, Sun 12-3 & 6-9.30

🎵 Occasional live music

⚒ Parking, disabled access

🕐 11.30-11 (Sun and Bank Holidays to 10.30)

🏛 Bronllys Castle, Brecon 7½ miles, Hay-on-
Wye 7 miles

106 The New Inn

Bwlch, Brecon, Powys LD3 7RQ

☎ 01874 730215

Real Ales, Bar Food, Accommodation,
No Smoking Area

107 Old Black Lion

Lion St, Hay-on-Wye, Powys HR3 5AD

☎ 01497 820841

Real Ales, Bar Food, Restaurant Menu,
Accommodation, No Smoking Area

108 Old Ford Inn

Llanhamlach, Brecon, Powys LD3 7YB

☎ 01874 665220

Real Ales, Bar Food, Restaurant Menu,
Accommodation, No Smoking Area

109 Peterstone Court Hotel

Llanhamlach, Brecon, Powys LD3 7YB

☎ 01874 665387

Real Ales, Bar Food, Restaurant Menu,
Accommodation, No Smoking Area

110 The Plough And Harrow

Upper Chapel, Brecon, Powys LD3 9RG
☎ 01874 690355

111 Plough And Harrow Inn

Felinfach, Brecon, Powys LD3 0UB
☎ 01874 622709
Real Ales, Bar Food, Accommodation,
No Smoking Area

112 The Plough Hotel

40 Market St, Knighton, Powys LD7 1EY
☎ 01547 528041
Real Ales, Accommodation

113 Prices Arms

Station Rd, Coelbren, Neath, Powys SA10 9PN
☎ 01639 700370
Real Ales, Bar Food, Restaurant Menu,
No Smoking Area

114 Prince Llewelyn Inn

Cilmery, Builth Wells, Powys LD2 3NU
☎ 01982 552694
Real Ales, Bar Food, Restaurant Menu,
Accommodation, No Smoking Area

115 The Puzzle Tree

The Watton, Brecon, Powys LD3 7EG
☎ 01874 610005
Bar Food, Restaurant Menu

116 The Radnor Arms

See panel below

117 Radnor Arms

Broad St, New Radnor, Presteigne, Powys LD8 2SP
☎ 01544 350232
Real Ales, Bar Food, Restaurant Menu,
Accommodation, No Smoking Area

---

116 The Radnor Arms

Llowes, Herefordshire HR3 5JA
☎ 01497 847460

Real Ales, Bar Food, Restaurant Menu

Brian Gorringe MBE and his wife Tina are the proud proprietors of The Radnor Arms, originally a drovers' inn dating back over 400 years. This handsome stonebuilt inn is set against a stunning backdrop of the Black Mountains, with magnificent scenery in all directions including the Begwins, the Brecon Beacons and the Wye Valley. The atmosphere is always warm and friendly at this award-winning Restaurant and Free House,

which is tastefully decorated with plates and paintings by local artists. The Radnor Arms serves excellent French and English style cuisine but also offers light bar snacks, traditional Sunday Roasts and a very extensive range of Vegetarian dishes. The Dessert menu is wide and varied with choices of hot desserts, icecream dishes and other mouthwatering delights. An extensive wine list compliments the high standard of quality with choices from various parts of the world. All the dishes are prepared using as much local produce as possible. Booking essential.

☛ Adjacent to the A438 at Llowes, 2 miles west of Hay-on-Wye

🍺 Double Dragon

🍴 Tues-Sun and Bank Hols 12.30-2.30; Tues-Sat and Bank Hols 6-9

🅿 Parking, garden, disabled access

💳 All major cards

🕐 12-3 & 6-11 (Sun and Bank Holidays to 10.30)

🏛 Hay-on-Wye 2 miles, Clyro 2 miles, Talgarth 7 miles

118 The Radnorshire Arms

Beguildy, Knighton, Powys LD7 1YE
☎ 01547 510634
Real Ales, Restaurant Menu, No Smoking Area

119 Radnorshire Arms Hotel

High St, Presteigne, Powys LD8 2BE
☎ 01544 267406
Real Ales, Bar Food, Restaurant Menu,
Accommodation, No Smoking Area

120 The Rectory Hotel

Llangattock, Crickhowell, Powys NP8 1PH
☎ 01873 810373
Real Ales, Bar Food, Restaurant Menu,
Accommodation, No Smoking Area

121 Red Lion

Llanbedr, Crickhowell, Powys NP8 1SR
☎ 01873 810754
Real Ales, Bar Food, No Smoking Area

122 The Red Lion

Llanafanfawr, Builth Wells, Powys LD2 3PN
☎ 01597 860204
Real Ales, Bar Food, Restaurant Menu,
Accommodation, No Smoking Area

123 Red Lion Hotel

Llangorse, Brecon, Powys LD3 7TY
☎ 01874 658238
Real Ales, Bar Food, Restaurant Menu,
Accommodation, No Smoking Area

124 The Red Lion Hotel

High St, Sennybridge, Brecon, Powys LD3 8PH
☎ 01874 636346
Real Ales, Bar Food, Restaurant Menu

125 Red Lion Hotel

Duffryn Rd, Llangynidr, Crickhowell,
Powys NP8 1NT
☎ 01874 730223
Bar Food, Restaurant Menu, Accommodation

126 Red Lion Inn

Llanfihangel-Nant-Melan, New Radnor, Presteigne,
Powys LD8 2TN
☎ 01544 350220
Real Ales, Bar Food, Restaurant Menu,
Accommodation, No Smoking Area

127 Ridgebourne Inn

Wellington Rd, Llandrindod Wells, Powys LD1 5NH
☎ 01597 822144
Real Ales, Bar Food

128 The Royal Oak

Pencelli, Brecon, Powys LD3 7LX
☎ 01874 665396
Real Ales, Bar Food, Restaurant Menu,
No Smoking Area

129 The Royal Oak

High St, Presteigne, Powys LD8 2BB
☎ 01544 260842
Bar Food, Restaurant Menu

130 Sarah Siddons Inn

47 High St, Brecon, Powys LD3 7AP
☎ 01874 610666
Real Ales

131 Seland Newydd

Pwllgloyw, Brecon, Powys LD3 9PY
☎ 01874 690282
Real Ales, Bar Food, Accommodation,
No Smoking Area

132 The Seven Stars Inn

Aberedw, Builth Wells, Powys LD2 3UW
☎ 01982 560494
Real Ales, Bar Food, Restaurant Menu,
Accommodation, No Smoking Area

133 Severn Arms Hotel

Penybont, Llandrindod Wells, Powys LD1 5UA
☎ 01597 851224
Real Ales, Bar Food, Accommodation

134 Shoemakers Arms

Pentre-Bach, Brecon, Powys LD3 8UB

☎ 01874 636508

Bar Food

135 The Star Inn

Talybont-On-Usk, Brecon, Powys LD3 7YX

☎ 01874 676635

Real Ales, Bar Food, Restaurant Menu,
Accommodation, No Smoking Area

136 Stonecroft Inn

Dolecoed Road, Llanwrtyd Wells, Powys LD5 4RA

☎ 01591 610327

⊕ www.stonecroft.co.uk

**Real Ales, Bar Food, Restaurant Menu,
Accommodation, No Smoking Area**

Stonecroft Inn and the adjoining Stonecroft Lodge
are well worth seeking out. Well-kept ales and a
good range of great food, can be enjoyed in the
convivial, attractive bar or, on fine days, in the large
riverside garden. The accommodation caters for
everything from individuals and families to large
groups.

☞ On the A483 10 miles northeast of
Llandovery

🍺 At least 4 rotating guest ales

🍴 Mon-Thurs 5-9.30, Fri-Sat 12-9.30, Sun 12-
9.30

🛏 Private and shared in 9 rooms of the self-
catering guest house

🎵 Live music Sat, annual beer festival (Novem-
ber)

⚒ Parking, disabled access

💳 All the major cards

🕐 Mon-Thurs 5-11, Fri-Sat 12-11, Sun 12-10.30

🏛 Cambrian Woollen Mill, Llyn Brianne
(Llanwrtyd Wells), Builth Wells 8 miles,
Llandovery 8 miles, Elan Village 12 miles,
Rhayader 14½ miles

137 The Sun Inn

St Harmon, Rhayader, Powys LD6 5LH

☎ 01597 870366

Real Ales, Bar Food, Restaurant Menu,
Accommodation, No Smoking Area

138 Swan At Hay

Church St, Hay-On-Wye, Powys HR3 5DQ

☎ 01497 821188

Real Ales, Bar Food, Restaurant Menu,
Accommodation, No Smoking Area

139 The Swan Inn

10 Llanbedr Rd, Crickhowell, Powys NP8 1BT

☎ 01873 810858

Real Ales

140 Tafarn-Y-Garreg

Penycae, Swansea, Powys SA9 1GS

☎ 01639 730267

Real Ales

141 The Tair Bull Inn

Libanus, Brecon, Powys LD3 8EL

☎ 01874 625849

Real Ales, Bar Food, Restaurant Menu,
Accommodation, No Smoking Area

142 Tanners Arms

Defynnog, Brecon, Powys LD3 8SF

☎ 01874 638032

Real Ales, Bar Food, Restaurant Menu,
No Smoking Area

143 Three Horse Shoes

Velindre, Brecon, Powys LD3 0SU

☎ 01497 847304

Real Ales, Bar Food

144 The Three Horse Shoes

Trecastle, Brecon, Powys LD3 8UP

☎ 01874 638057

Bar Food, No Smoking Area

145 The Three Horseshoes

Groesffordd, Brecon, Powys LD3 7SN

☎ 01874 665672

Real Ales, Bar Food, Restaurant Menu,
Accommodation, No Smoking Area

146 Three Horseshoes Inn

47 Orchard St, Llanfaes, Brecon, Powys LD3 8AL

☎ 01874 622874

Real Ales, Bar Food, Restaurant Menu,
No Smoking Area

147 Tower Hotel

The Square, Talgarth, Brecon, Powys LD3 0BW

☎ 01874 711253

Real Ales, Restaurant Menu, Accommodation,
No Smoking Area

148 Travellers Rest

Talybont On Usk, Brecon, Powys LD3 7YP

☎ 01874 676233

Real Ales, Bar Food, Restaurant Menu,
Accommodation, No Smoking Area

149 Triangle Inn

Triangle Cwmdauddwr, Rhayader, Powys LD6 5AR

☎ 01597 810537

Real Ales, Bar Food, Accommodation,
No Smoking Area

150 The Trout Inn

Beulah, Llanwrtyd Wells, Powys LD5 4UU

☎ 01591 620235

Real Ales, Bar Food, Restaurant Menu,
Accommodation

151 Ty Croeso Hotel

The Dardy, Crickhowell, Powys NP8 1PU

☎ 01873 810573

Real Ales, Bar Food, Restaurant Menu,
Accommodation, No Smoking Area

152 Usk Inn

Talybont-On-Usk, Brecon, Powys LD3 7JE

☎ 01874 676251

Real Ales, Bar Food, Restaurant Menu,
Accommodation, No Smoking Area

158 The White Hart

Crickhowell, Powys NP8 1DL

☎ 01873 810473

Bar Food, Restaurant Menu, No Smoking Area

Quality is the hallmark of The White Hart in Crickhowell. This handsome inn is run by David and Judy Rees – they have been here some six years – with David looking after the bar and Judy and her team doing the cooking. Dating back to the 16th century, the inn boasts many original features and is full of character and charm. Built on the site of the old village tollgate, and there's an interesting plaque on the wall displaying ancient charges ('a score of pigs, 2p'). David and Judy take justifiable pride in the food and ale served here. Real ale is accompanied by a good range of lagers, ciders, stout, wines, spirits and soft drinks. Everything on the menu and specials board is home-cooked to order. Welsh lamb is just one of the delicious specialities, as is Glamorgan sausage (a vegetarian dish). Judy uses the freshest locally-sourced ingredients.

- In the heart of Crickhowell, 6 miles northwest of Abergavenny on the A40
- Reverend James
- 12-2.30 & 6-9.30 (Sunday 6.30-9)
- Quiz night Mon
- Parking, gardens
- All major cards
- No pets
- 12-3 & 6-11 (Sun and Bank Holidays to 10.30)
- Brecon Beacons National Park, Tretower 2 miles, Abergavenny 6 miles, Big Pit Mining Museum 7 miles

153 Vine Tree Inn

Legar Rd, Llangattock, Crickhowell, Powys NP8 1HG

☎ 01873 810514

Real Ales, Bar Food, Restaurant Menu,
No Smoking Area

154 The Vulcan Arms

Llanwrthwl, Llandrindod Wells, Powys LD1 6NN

☎ 01597 811152

Real Ales, Bar Food, Restaurant Menu

155 The Wellington Hotel

The Bulwark, Brecon, Powys LD3 7AD

☎ 01874 625225

Real Ales, Bar Food, Restaurant Menu,
Accommodation, No Smoking Area

156 Wheelwright Arms

Erwood, Builth Wells, Powys LD2 3EQ

☎ 01982 560740

Real Ales, Restaurant Menu, No Smoking Area

157 The White Hart Inn

19 High St, Builth Wells, Powys LD2 3DL

☎ 01982 553639

Real Ales, Bar Food, Restaurant Menu

158 The White Hart Inn

See panel on page 225

159 The White Hart Inn & Bunkhouse

Talybont-On-Usk, Brecon, Powys LD3 7JD

☎ 01874 676227

Real Ales, Bar Food, Restaurant Menu,
Accommodation, No Smoking Area

160 The White House Inn

See panel below

---

160 The White House Inn

Sennybridge, nr Brecon, Powys LD3 8RP

☎ 01874 636396

⊕ www.thewhitehouseinn.co.uk

Real Ales, Bar Food, Restaurant Menu,
Accommodation, No Smoking Area

The White House Inn in Sennybridge is gaining a well-deserved reputation for the quality of its food. The restaurant seats 60; guests choose from the menus or specials board from a range of tempting dishes such as the 'seafood carousel' with prawn, crab and smoked salmon, venison, a selection of steaks and much more. Owner Hilary Rees has been here since 2004, ably assisted by manager Peter and a dedicated and loyal staff who offer all their guests great service and warm hospitality. The seven guest bedrooms upstairs are charming and comfortable, tastefully decorated and furnished. With cycling, walking, fishing, caving, canoeing, pony-trekking and golf all within easy reach, as well as the many other sights and attractions of the region, the inn makes an ideal touring base.

☛ Alongside the A40 at Sennybridge, 7½ miles west of Brecon

🍺 Worthington, Double Dragon

🍴 12-2 & 6.30-9.30

🛏 7 en suite rooms

🅿 Parking, some disabled access, garden, children's play area

💳 All major cards

🌟 2 stars Welsh Tourist Board

🕐 summer: 11.30-11; winter: 12-2.30 & 6-11 (Sun and Bank Holidays to 10.30)

🏛 Castell Ddu, Disgwylfa Conservation Centre (Sennybridge), Libanus 5 miles, Brecon 7½ miles, Dan-yr-Ogof Showcaves 12 miles

163 Ynyscedwyn Arms

53 Commercial Street, Ystradgynlais,
Swansea SA9 1LA
☎ 01639 841000

Bar Food, Restaurant Menu, Accommodation, No
Smoking Area

Set along the river that runs through the
charming village of Ystradgynlais, close to the
Dan-yr-Ogof Showcaves and at the gateway to the
Brecon Beacons National Park, Ynyscedwyn Arms
is a cosy and very tastefully decorated pub with a
large restaurant and conservatory extension.
Landlords Jay and Charlotte Morrell have made
their first venture into the trade a great success.

Jay looks after the beer, while Charlotte cooks up
an extensive range of home-made dishes at lunch
and dinner, including steaks, lamb, chicken, seafood
and vegetarian meals including tempting pies and
curries. The delicious desserts are well worth
leaving room for. The four good-sized and modern
guest bedrooms offer very comfortable accommodation, and the inn makes an ideal base from
which to explore the exciting range of attractions
in the region.

🍺 19½ miles southwest of Brecon off the
A4067 and on the B4599

🍺 Reverend James, Buckleys Best and a rotating
guest ale

🍴 12-2 & Weds-Sat 6-9

🛏 4 en suite rooms

🎵 Quiz night Fri, occasional theme nights

🅿 Parking, garden, disabled access

💳 All major cards

🕐 12-11 (Sun and Bank Holidays to 10.30)

🏛 Y Garn Goch ½ mile, Dan-yr-Ogof Caves 4
miles, Ystradfellte 7 miles, Libanus 15 miles

161 The White Swan Inn

Llanfrynach, Brecon, Powys LD3 7BZ
☎ 01874 665276
Real Ales, Bar Food, Restaurant Menu

162 Ye Olde Cognac

50 High St, Brecon, Powys LD3 7AP
☎ 01874 622725
Bar Food, Restaurant Menu

163 Ynyscedwyn Arms

See panel above

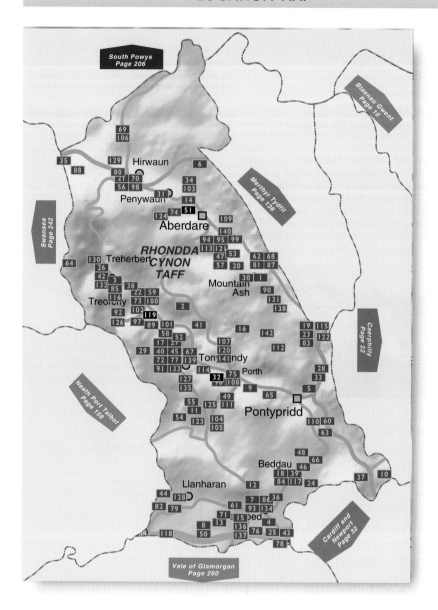

South Powys
Page 206

Blaenau Gwent
Page 10

69
106

35   129   Hirwaun   6
88
80
27 70   34
56 98   103
31   14
Penywaun
124 74 51   109
Aberdare   140
94 95 99
RHONDDA   113 121
Treherbert CYNON   47 53   62 68
TAFF   57 20   81 87
26
42   Mountain 30 1
132 3   Ash   90
85 38
116 22 59   131
Treorchy 73 100   138
92 102   2
126 97 119
89 101   41
58 52   16   142   19 115
17 27   23 122
29 40 45 67   107   83
72 77 139 Tonypandy 120   112
91 133   114
32 75 Porth   28
127   33
135   5
55 125 111
11   49
54 123 104 111
105   Pontypridd   110 60
63

48
66
Beddau 18 39 46
84 117 24   37 10
Llanharan   12
7 8 36
61 93 134
71 15
8 13 136 4
118 50 137 76 25 43
78

Merthyr Tydfil
Page 136

Swansea
Page 242

Caerphilly
Page 22

Neath Port Talbot
Page 156

Cardiff and
Newport
Page 32

Vale of Glamorgan
Page 260

11 Rhondda Cynon Taff Reference Number - Detailed Information

12 Rhondda Cynon Taff Reference Number - Summary Entry

Ceredigion
Page 249   Adjacent area - refer to pages indicated

228

RHONDDA CYNON TAFF
ABERDARE • PONTYPRIDD • LLANTRISANT

Rhondda Cynon Taff (in Welsh, the final word is Taf) is a county borough in Glamorgan, South Wales with all the necessary ingredients for a wonderful get-away-from-it-all holiday. Taking its name from three rivers, which together with several smaller streams have cut deep into the high plateau, creating a distinctive landscape to explore, here can be discovered bustling towns and villages strung together with necklaces of traditional homes and buildings of historic significance, offering locally-produced crafts and produce. The northern aspect of Rhondda Cynon Taf stretches to the breathtaking Brecon Beacons

Rhondda Valley

National Park, while the south extends to just north of Wales' capital city, Cardiff.

The district borders Merthyr Tydfil and Caerphilly to the east, Cardiff and the Vale of Glamorgan to the south, Bridgend and Neath Port Talbot to the west and Powys to the north. Its main towns are Aberdare, Mountain Ash and Pontypridd.

Settlements in the district include Aberdare, Hirwaun, Llanharan, Llantrisant, Maerdy, Miskin, Mountain Ash, Pontypridd, Porth Tonypandy, Tonyrefail and Treherbert. The county borough was formed on April 1, 1996 by the merger of the former districts of Cynon Valley, Rhondda and part of Taff-Ely.

Pontypridd's famous sons include Evan and James James, composers of the Welsh national anthem *Land of My Fathers* (*Hen Wlad fy Nhadau*), and the perennial Tom Jones. Just outside Pontypridd, at Fforest Uchaf Farm, Penyoedcae, is the Pit Pony Sanctuary, where visitors can meet with more than 25 horses and ponies together with memorabilia and a reconstruction of a typical pony-powered Welsh drift coal mine.

In the Rhondda Valley alone there were once 53 working

Royal Mint, Llantrisant

mines in just 16 square miles; though they have now gone, the traditions of the colliery live on. When the Lewis Merthyr Colliery closed in 1983, it reopened as the Rhondda Heritage Park.

Just a short distance from the busy centre of Aberdare is Dare Valley Country Park.

1 Aberdare Hotel
Ffrwd Crescent, Mountain Ash,
Rhondda Cynon Taff CF45 4AA
☎ 01443 475801
Real Ales

2 Anchor Hotel
The Strand, Ferndale,
Rhondda Cynon Taff CF43 4RS
☎ 01443 756261
Bar Food, Restaurant Menu, Accommodation,
No Smoking Area

3 Baglan Hotel
30 Baglan St, Treherbert, Treorchy,
Rhondda Cynon Taff CF42 5AW
☎ 01443 776111
Real Ales, Bar Food, Restaurant Menu,
Accommodation, No Smoking Area

4 The Barn at Mwyndy
Cardiff Rd, Mwyndy, Pontyclun,
Rhondda Cynon Taff CF72 8PJ
☎ 01443 222333
Real Ales, Bar Food, Restaurant Menu,
No Smoking Area

5 Bassett Hotel
Pontshonnorton Rd, Pontypridd,
Rhondda Cynon Taff CF37 4NA
☎ 01443 493120
Bar Food

6 The Baverstock Hotel
Llwydcoed, Aberdare,
Rhondda Cynon Taff CF44 0LX
☎ 01685 386221
Real Ales, Bar Food, Restaurant Menu,
Accommodation, No Smoking Area

7 The Bear Inn
Heol-Y-Sarn, Llantrisant, Pontyclun,
Rhondda Cynon Taff CF72 8DA
☎ 01443 222271
Bar Food, Restaurant Menu, Accommodation

8 The Bear Inn
Llanharry, Pontyclun,
Rhondda Cynon Taff CF72 9LH
☎ 01443 225425
Bar Food, Restaurant Menu, No Smoking Area

9 The Bertie
1-3 Phillips Terrace, Trehafod, Pontypridd,
Rhondda Cynon Taff CF37 2NW
☎ 01443 688204
Bar Food, Restaurant Menu, Accommodation,
No Smoking Area

10 Black Cock Inn
Caerphilly Mountain, Caerphilly,
Rhondda Cynon Taff CF83 1NF
☎ 02920 880534
Real Ales, Bar Food, Restaurant Menu,
No Smoking Area

11 Black Diamond
Edmondstown Rd, Tonypandy,
Rhondda Cynon Taff CF40 1NR
☎ 01443 432860
Bar Food, Restaurant Menu, No Smoking Area

12 Black Prince Hotel
Llantrisant business park, Llantrisant, Pontyclun,
Rhondda Cynon Taff CF72 8LF
☎ 01443 227723
Real Ales, Bar Food, Restaurant Menu,
Accommodation, No Smoking Area

13 Boars Head
Tyla Garw, Pontyclun,
Rhondda Cynon Taff CF72 9EZ
☎ 01443 225400
Real Ales, Bar Food, Restaurant Menu

14 Bridgend Inn
Harriet St, Trecynon, Aberdare,
Rhondda Cynon Taff CF44 8PL
☎ 01685 871340
Accommodation, No Smoking Area

15 Brunel Arms
Station Approach, Pontyclun,
Rhondda Cynon Taff CF72 9DS
☎ 01443 227688
Real Ales

16 Brynffynon Hotel
Llanwonno, Pontypridd,
Rhondda Cynon Taff CF37 3PH
☎ 01443 790272
Real Ales, Bar Food, Restaurant Menu,
No Smoking Area

17 The Bush Hotel
Clydach Rd, Blaenclydach, Tonypandy,
Rhondda Cynon Taff CF40 2DG
☎ 01443 432807
Real Ales, Bar Food, Restaurant Menu

18 Bush Inn
Bryn Terrace Llantwit Fardre, Pontypridd,
Rhondda Cynon Taff CF38 2EP
☎ 01443 203958
Real Ales, Bar Food, No Smoking Area

19 Butchers Arms
10 Allen St, Abercynon, Mountain Ash,
Rhondda Cynon Taff CF45 4BD
☎ 01443 473435
Real Ales

20 The Cap Coch Inn
John St, Abercwmboi, Aberdare,
Rhondda Cynon Taff CF44 6BN
☎ 01443 475777

21 Cardiff Arms Hotel
High St, Hirwaun, Aberdare,
Rhondda Cynon Taff CF44 9SL
☎ 01685 812540

22 Cardiff Arms Hotel
Bute St, Treorchy, Rhondda Cynon Taff CF42 6BS
☎ 01443 772849
Real Ales, Bar Food, Restaurant Menu

23 Carne Park Hotel
1 Park St, Abercynon, Mountain Ash,
Rhondda Cynon Taff CF45 4PF
☎ 01443 740258
Bar Food, Restaurant Menu, No Smoking Area

24 Carpenters Arms
Heol Ffrwd Philip Efail Isaf, Pontypridd,
Rhondda Cynon Taff CF38 1AR
☎ 01443 202426
Real Ales

25 Castell Mynach
Llantrisant Rd, Groesfaen, Pontyclun,
Rhondda Cynon Taff CF72 8NH
☎ 01443 220940
Real Ales, Bar Food, Restaurant Menu,
No Smoking Area

26 Castle Hotel
Treorchy, Rhondda Cynon Taff CF42 5PD
☎ 01443 776439

27 The Central Hotel
Clydach Rd, Tonypandy,
Rhondda Cynon Taff CF40 2DG
☎ 01443 432832
Accommodation

28 Cilfynydd Inn
Cilfynydd Rd Clifynydd, Clifynydd, Pontypridd,
Rhondda Cynon Taff CF37 4NN
☎ 01443 402052
Real Ales, Restaurant Menu, No Smoking Area

29 Clydach Vale Hotel
Wern St, Clydale Vale, Tonypandy,
Rhondda Cynon Taff CF40 2DJ
☎ 01443 432310

30 Colliers Arms
Lower Fforest Level, Newton, Abercynon,
Mountain Ash, Rhondda Cynon Taff CF45 4HP
☎ 01443 474432
Bar Food, Restaurant Menu, No Smoking Area

31 Colliers Arms

Bronllys, Aberdare, Rhondda Cynon Taff CF44 9AS

☎ 01685 811270

Bar Food

32 The Colliers Arms

See panel below

33 The Commercial Hotel

35 Cilfynydd Rd, Pontypridd,
Rhondda Cynon Taff CF37 4NL

☎ 01443 491176

Bar Food, Restaurant Menu, No Smoking Area

34 Corner House

Corner House St, Aberdare,
Rhondda Cynon Taff CF44 0YA

☎ 01685 879739

Bar Food, Restaurant Menu

35 Craig-Y-Ddinas Hotel

Dinas Rd, Pontneathvaughan, Neath,
Rhondda Cynon Taff SA11 5NH

☎ 01639 720378

Real Ales, Bar Food, Restaurant Menu,
Accommodation, No Smoking Area

36 Cross Inn Hotel

Main Rd, Cross Inn, Llantrisant, Pontyclun,
Rhondda Cynon Taff CF72 8AZ

☎ 01443 223431

37 The Cross Keys

Cardiff Rd, Nantgarw, Cardiff,
Rhondda Cynon Taff CF15 7SR

☎ 01443 843262

Real Ales, Bar Food, Restaurant Menu,
Accommodation, No Smoking Area

---

32 Colliers Arms

Glynfach Road, Cymmer Porth, Rhondda CF39 9LF

☎ 01443 684424

🌐 www.thecolliersarms.co.uk

Real Ales, Bar Food, Restaurant Menu, No
Smoking Area

The Colliers Arms is a distinctive and distinguished inn just off the main street in the village
of Cymmer Porth. A happy mix of traditional and

modern comforts make up the interior, with
warm woods and tasteful décor adding to the
inn's warm and welcoming ambience. At the time
of writing, renovations are well in progress
creating an extension to the restaurant, to meet
demand at this, one of the most popular pubs in
the Rhondda Valley. Owners Dave and Lynne
Williams are justly proud of the inn's enviable
reputation for quality and service. The inn's menu
boasts a range of tempting dishes using locally-
sourced produce; specialities include Welsh Black
steaks, Welsh lamb and steak-and-ale pie, together
with a good variety of vegetarian dishes. There's
something to please every palate here, and food-
themed nights are a regular feature.

🍺 HB Hancocks

🍴 Mon 6-11, Tues-Sun 12-2.30 & 6-9

🎵 Food-themed nights

♿ Disabled access

💳 All major cards

🚫 No smoking in restaurants

🕐 Mon 6-11, Tues-Sat 12-11, Sun 12-10.30,
Bank Holidays 12-12

38 Crown Hotel

Ynyswen Rd, Treorchy,
Rhondda Cynon Taff CF42 6EG
☎ 01443 772805
Real Ales

39 Crown Inn

Llantwit Fardre, Pontypridd,
Rhondda Cynon Taff CF38 2HL
☎ 01443 208531
Real Ales, Bar Food, Restaurant Menu,
No Smoking Area

40 De Winton Hotel

De Winton St, Tonypandy,
Rhondda Cynon Taff CF40 2QZ
☎ 01443 442276
Bar Food, No Smoking Area

41 Duke of York Hotel

East Rd, Tylorstown, Ferndale,
Rhondda Cynon Taff CF43 3BS
☎ 01443 732620
Bar Food, Restaurant Menu, No Smoking Area

42 The Dunraven Hotel

13 Dunraven St, Treherbert, Treorchy,
Rhondda Cynon Taff CF42 5BG
☎ 01443 778222
Real Ales, Bar Food, Restaurant Menu,
Accommodation, No Smoking Area

43 Dynevor Arms

Groesfaen, Pontyclun,
Rhondda Cynon Taff CF72 8NS
☎ 02920 890530
Real Ales, Bar Food, Restaurant Menu, No Smoking
Area

44 The Eagle Inn

Southall St, Brynna, Pontyclun,
Rhondda Cynon Taff CF72 9QH
☎ 01443 222103

45 Embassy Bar and Restaurant

60 Gelli Rd, Tonypandy,
Rhondda Cynon Taff CF40 1DB
☎ 01443 421555

46 Fagins Bar and Restaurant

Main Rd, Church Village, Pontypridd,
Rhondda Cynon Taff CF38 1PY
☎ 01443 202419
Real Ales, No Smoking Area

47 Falcon Hotel

1 Incline Row, Cwmaman, Aberdare,
Rhondda Cynon Taff CF44 6LU
☎ 01685 873758
Real Ales, Bar Food, Accommodation,
No Smoking Area

48 Farmers Arms

St Illtyds Rd, Church Village, Pontypridd,
Rhondda Cynon Taff CF38 1EB
☎ 01443 205766
Real Ales, Bar Food, No Smoking Area

49 The Farmers Arms

Trebanog Rd, Trebanog, Porth,
Rhondda Cynon Taff CF39 9EL
☎ 01443 688210
Bar Food

50 Fox and Hounds

Llanharan Rd, Llanharry, Pontyclun,
Rhondda Cynon Taff CF72 9LL
☎ 01443 222124
Bar Food

51 The Full Moon

See panel opposite

52 Gelligaled Hotel

Gelligaled Rd, Ystrad, Pentre,
Rhondda Cynon Taff CF41 7RQ
☎ 01443 438737
Real Ales, Bar Food

51 The Full Moon

59 Hariet Street, Trecynon, Aberdare CF44 8PL
☎ 01685 871012

Real Ales, Bar Food, Restaurant Menu

The Full Moon is a delightful and charming pub, run by Stephen Richards and his family. Stephen is an accomplished chef who takes justified pride in providing all his guests with a range of

tempting and expertly prepared dishes at lunch and dinner.

The menu and daily specials board offer a selection of tasty snacks and meals using only the freshest local produce including locally-reared beef and lamb and locally-caught fish and seafood.

As well as the real ales on tap there's a good choice of lagers, cider, stout, wines, spirits and soft drinks to enjoy.

Spacious, comfortable and welcoming, the interior has bags of character and charm, while outside there's a terraced area to the front of the pub and a safe children's play area.

☛ Off the A465 close to Aberdare

🍺 Brains Creamflow

🍴 Tues-Sun 12-2.30 & Tues-Sat 6.30-9

🅿 Parking, some disabled access, play area

🕐 12-11 (Sun and Bank Holidays to 10.30)

🏛 Aberdare 2 miles, Pontypridd 12 miles

53 The General Picton Inn

134 Cardiff Rd, Aberaman, Aberdare,
Rhondda Cynon Taff CF44 6UY
☎ 01685 877556
Bar Food, Restaurant Menu, No Smoking Area

54 Gilfach Goch Wine Bar

20 High St, Gilfach Goch, Porth,
Rhondda Cynon Taff CF39 8SP
☎ 01443 674155

55 The Glamorgan Hotel

Brook St, Williamstown, Tonypandy,
Rhondda Cynon Taff CF40 1PU
☎ 01443 441433
Real Ales, Bar Food, Restaurant Menu

56 Glancynon Inn

Swansea Rd, Hirwaun, Aberdare,
Rhondda Cynon Taff CF44 9PE
☎ 01685 811043
Real Ales, Bar Food, Restaurant Menu,
No Smoking Area

57 The Globe Inn

Fforchneol Row, Cwmaman, Aberdare,
Rhondda Cynon Taff CF44 6HD
☎ 01685 884984
No Smoking Area

58 Greenfield

13-14 William St, Ystrad, Pentre,
Rhondda Cynon Taff CF41 7QR
☎ 01443 435953
Real Ales, Bar Food, Restaurant Menu, No Smoking Area

59 The Griffin

Carne St, Pentre, Rhondda Cynon Taff CF41 7LD
☎ 01443 432879
Bar Food, Restaurant Menu, No Smoking Area

60 The Griffin Inn

37 Dyffryn Rd Rhydyfelin, Rhydyfelin, Pontypridd,
Rhondda Cynon Taff CF37 5NR
☎ 01443 403617

61 Hand and Squirrel

19 Ely Valley Rd, Talbot Green, Pontyclun,
Rhondda Cynon Taff CF72 8AL

☎ 01443 222164

62 The Harp Hotel

3 Jeffrey St, Mountain Ash,
Rhondda Cynon Taff CF45 4AD

☎ 01443 477147

Real Ales

63 Hawthorn Inn

Spencers Place, Hawthorn, Pontypridd,
Rhondda Cynon Taff CF37 5AE

☎ 01443 842394

Real Ales, Bar Food, Restaurant Menu,
No Smoking Area

64 Hendre-Wen Hotel

Hendre-Wen Rd, Blaencwm, Treorchy,
Rhondda Cynon Taff CF42 5DR

☎ 01443 771679

Real Ales, Bar Food, Restaurant Menu,
Accommodation, No Smoking Area

65 The Hollybush

Ty Mawr Rd, Hopkinstown, Pontypridd,
Rhondda Cynon Taff CF37 2SF

☎ 01443 402325

Real Ales, Bar Food, No Smoking Area

66 Hollybush Inn

Main Rd, Church Village, Pontypridd,
Rhondda Cynon Taff CF38 1PS

☎ 01443 202076

Bar Food, Restaurant Menu

67 Ivor Hael Hotel

Salem Terrace, Llwynypia, Tonypandy,
Rhondda Cynon Taff CF40 2JJ

☎ 01443 421547

Bar Food, Restaurant Menu, No Smoking Area

68 Jeffreys Arms Hotel

Jeffrey St Caegarw, Mountain Ash,
Rhondda Cynon Taff CF45 4AD

☎ 01443 472976

Real Ales, Bar Food, Restaurant Menu,
No Smoking Area

69 Lamb Hotel

Chapel Rd, Penderyn, Aberdare,
Rhondda Cynon Taff CF44 9JX

☎ 01685 811357

70 Lamb Inn

78 Brecon Rd, Hirwaun, Aberdare,
Rhondda Cynon Taff CF44 9NL

☎ 01685 811242

Real Ales, Bar Food

71 Legends Hotel & Carvery

Pontyclun, Rhondda Cynon Taff CF72 9EW

☎ 01443 225285

Bar Food, Restaurant Menu, Accommodation,
No Smoking Area

72 Liberal Club (Tonypandy)

11-12 Maddox St, Tonypandy,
Rhondda Cynon Taff CF40 2RR

☎ 01443 432829

73 Lion Hotel

102 Bute St, Treorchy,
Rhondda Cynon Taff CF42 6AH

☎ 01443 772123

Bar Food, Restaurant Menu, No Smoking Area

74 Llwyncelyn Inn

51 Cemetery Rd, Aberdare,
Rhondda Cynon Taff CF44 8HT

☎ 01685 872347

75 The Lodge

Eirw Rd, Britannia, Porth,
Rhondda Cynon Taff CF39 9LT

☎ 01443 685393

Bar Food, Restaurant Menu

76 Miskin Arms

Hensol Rd, Miskin, Pontyclun,
Rhondda Cynon Taff CF72 8JT

☎ 01443 224346

Real Ales, Bar Food, Restaurant Menu,
No Smoking Area

77 Miskin Hotel

Miskin Rd, Trealaw, Tonypandy,
Rhondda Cynon Taff CF40 2QN

☎ 01443 430058

Bar Food, Accommodation

78 Miskin Manor

Pendoylan Rd, Groesfaen, Pontyclun,
Rhondda Cynon Taff CF72 8ND

☎ 01443 224204

Real Ales, Bar Food, Restaurant Menu,
Accommodation, No Smoking Area

79 Morgans at Fagins

Bridgend Rd, Bryncae, Pontyclun,
Rhondda Cynon Taff CF72 9RP

☎ 01443 231671

Real Ales, Bar Food, No Smoking Area

80 Mount Pleasant Inn

Penderyn Rd, Hirwaun, Aberdare,
Rhondda Cynon Taff CF44 9RT

☎ 01685 811944

Bar Food, Restaurant Menu, No Smoking Area

81 Mountain Ash Inn

Commercial St, Mountain Ash,
Rhondda Cynon Taff CF45 3PS

☎ 01443 472678

Real Ales

82 Mountain Hare Inn

Bridgend, Rhondda Cynon Taff CF35 6PG

☎ 01656 860453

Real Ales, Bar Food

83 Navigation House

Cardiff Rd, Abercynon, Mountain Ash,
Rhondda Cynon Taff CF45 4RR

☎ 01443 740196

Bar Food, Restaurant Menu, No Smoking Area

84 New Inn

Llantwit Fardre, Pontypridd,
Rhondda Cynon Taff CF38 2HA

☎ 01443 202017

Real Ales, Bar Food, Restaurant Menu,
No Smoking Area

85 New Inn

Baglan St, Treherbert, Treorchy,
Rhondda Cynon Taff CF42 5AG

☎ 01443 772376

86 The New Inn

Swan St, Llantrisant, Pontyclun,
Rhondda Cynon Taff CF72 8ED

☎ 01443 222232

Real Ales, Bar Food, Accommodation

87 The New Inn

8 Oxford St, Mountain Ash,
Rhondda Cynon Taff CF45 3PL

☎ 01443 472320

88 The New Inn

Smiths Avenue, Rhigos, Aberdare,
Rhondda Cynon Taff CF44 9YU

☎ 01685 811071

Real Ales, Bar Food, Restaurant Menu,
No Smoking Area

89 The New Inn Hotel

Church Rd, Ton Pentre, Pentre,
Rhondda Cynon Taff CF41 7ED

☎ 01443 434660

Restaurant Menu, No Smoking Area

90 Osborne Hotel

Rheola St, Penrhiwceiber, Mountain Ash,
Rhondda Cynon Taff CF45 3TA

☎ 01443 473737

Real Ales

91 Paddys Goose Inn

Trealaw Rd, Trealaw, Tonypandy,
Rhondda Cynon Taff CF40 2NX

☎ 01443 434679

92 Parc Hotel

Park Rd, Treorchy, Rhondda Cynon Taff CF42 6LD

☎ 01443 776512

93 Penny Farthings

Cardiff Rd, Llantrisant, Pontyclun,
Rhondda Cynon Taff CF72 8DG

☎ 01443 228838

Real Ales, Bar Food

94 The Penylan Inn
69 Regent St, Aberaman, Aberdare,
Rhondda Cynon Taff CF44 6ET
☎ 01685 872365

95 Plough Inn
Lewis St, Aberaman, Aberdare,
Rhondda Cynon Taff CF44 6PY
☎ 01685 884880
Real Ales, No Smoking Area

96 The Porth Hotel
Pontypridd Rd, Porth,
Rhondda Cynon Taff CF39 9PH
☎ 01443 682013
Real Ales, Bar Food, Restaurant Menu

97 The Prince of Wales
21 High St, Treorchy, Rhondda Cynon Taff CF42 6AA
☎ 01443 773121
Real Ales, Bar Food, Restaurant Menu

98 Prince of Wales
1 Harris St, Hirwaun, Aberdare,
Rhondda Cynon Taff CF44 9NP
☎ 01685 811048

99 Queen Victoria Inn
Bridge Rd, Cwmbach, Aberdare,
Rhondda Cynon Taff CF44 0AL
☎ 01685 871795
No Smoking Area

100 The Queens Hotel
101-102 Llewellyn St, Pentre,
Rhondda Cynon Taff CF41 7BU
☎ 01443 430338
Bar Food, Restaurant Menu

101 The Railway Inn
Ystrad Rd, Pentre, Rhondda Cynon Taff CF41 7PP
☎ 01443 441691
Bar Food, Restaurant Menu

102 Red Cow Hotel
High St, Treorchy, Rhondda Cynon Taff CF42 6NY
☎ 01443 773032
Bar Food, Restaurant Menu, No Smoking Area

103 Red Cow Inn
6 Merthyr Rd, Llwydcoed, Aberdare,
Rhondda Cynon Taff CF44 0YE
☎ 01685 873924
Real Ales, Restaurant Menu, No Smoking Area

104 Red Cow Inn
Llantrisant Rd, Tonyrefail, Porth,
Rhondda Cynon Taff CF39 8PP
☎ 01443 670419

105 The Red Gate Hotel
High St, Tonyrefail, Porth,
Rhondda Cynon Taff CF39 8PL
☎ 01443 670470

106 The Red Lion Inn
Church Rd, Penderyn, Aberdare,
Rhondda Cynon Taff CF44 9JR
☎ 01685 811914
Real Ales, Restaurant Menu, Accommodation

107 Rheola Hotel
Rheola Rd, Porth, Rhondda Cynon Taff CF39 0LE
☎ 01443 682633
Real Ales

108 Rhondda Hotel
High St, Cymmer, Porth,
Rhondda Cynon Taff CF39 9AD
☎ 01443 682388
Bar Food, Restaurant Menu, No Smoking Area

109 Rhoswenallt Inn
Werfa, Aberdare, Rhondda Cynon Taff CF44 0YS
☎ 01685 875851
Bar Food, Restaurant Menu

110 The Rhydyfelin Arms
Cardiff Rd Rhydyfelin, Rhydyfelin, Pontypridd,
Rhondda Cynon Taff CF37 5HP
☎ 01443 485677

111 Rickards Arms
Trebanog Rd, Trebanog, Porth,
Rhondda Cynon Taff CF39 9EP
☎ 01443 688023

112 Robertown Hotel

Robert St, Ynysybwl, Pontypridd,
Rhondda Cynon Taff CF37 3DU

☎ 01443 791574

113 Rock Inn

167 Cardiff Rd, Aberaman, Aberdare,
Rhondda Cynon Taff CF44 6RB

☎ 01685 872906

Real Ales, Restaurant Menu

114 Royal Hotel

61 Brithweunydd Rd, Tonypandy,
Rhondda Cynon Taff CF40 2UD

☎ 01443 435293

Accommodation

115 Royal Oak

Incline Top, Abercynon, Mountain Ash,
Rhondda Cynon Taff CF45 4EW

☎ 01443 742229

Real Ales, Bar Food, Restaurant Menu,
No Smoking Area

116 Royal Oak Hotel

Treorchy, Rhondda Cynon Taff CF42 5AS

☎ 01443 772592

Restaurant Menu

117 The Ship Inn

Efail Isaf, Pontypridd,
Rhondda Cynon Taff CF38 1BH

☎ 01443 202341

Real Ales, Bar Food, Restaurant Menu,
No Smoking Area

118 St Marys Hotel Golf & Country Club

St mary hill, Pencoed, Bridgend,
Rhondda Cynon Taff CF35 5EA

☎ 01656 860280

Real Ales, Bar Food, Restaurant Menu,
Accommodation, No Smoking Area

119 The Stag Hotel

See panel below

119 The Stag Hotel

26 High Street, Treorchy, Rhondda CF42 6AT

☎ 01443 773571

Real Ales, Restaurant Menu, No Smoking Area

The Stag Hotel is a very large stonebuilt inn that occupies a busy crossroads on the A4061. Right in the heart of the Rhondda Valley, landlady Ann Rich, her husband Handel and their friendly,

efficient staff offer all their guests a warm welcome.

Locals and visitors alike enjoy the relaxed and informal atmosphere. The interior is cosy and welcoming, while outside there is an attractive beer garden.

The real ales on tap are complemented by a range of lagers, cider, stout, wines, spirits and soft drinks. The chef here has quickly built up a reputation for hearty, expertly prepared dishes such as home-made chillies, curries, steak pies and more.

Everything on the menu is made using the freshest ingredients, locally sourced whenever possible.

☛ On the B4061

🍺 HB Hancocks and changing guest ales

🍴 daily 12-2 & Fri-Sat 7-9

🎵 Quiz Sun night

♿ Garden, disabled access

🕐 11-11 (Sun and Bank Holidays to 10.30)

120 The Station Hotel

Ynyshir Rd, Ynyshir, Porth,
Rhondda Cynon Taff CF39 0EN

☎ 01443 687792

Bar Food, Accommodation, No Smoking Area

121 Temple Bar Vaults

Cardiff Rd, Aberaman, Aberdare,
Rhondda Cynon Taff CF44 6UU

☎ 01685 876137

Real Ales

122 Thorn Hotel

Mountain Ash Rd, Abercynon, Mountain Ash,
Rhondda Cynon Taff CF45 4PR

T01443 742284

123 The Three Horseshoes

Gilfach Rd, Tonyrefail, Porth,
Rhondda Cynon Taff CF39 8HE

T01443 670231

124 Ton Glwyd Fawr Inn

Dare Rd, Cwmdare, Aberdare,
Rhondda Cynon Taff CF44 8UB

T01685 870870

125 Trebanog Arms

Trebanog Rd, Trebanog, Porth,
Rhondda Cynon Taff CF39 9DU

☎ 01443 686161

Real Ales, Bar Food

126 Tremains Hotel

Park Rd, Treorchy, Rhondda Cynon Taff CF42 6LG

☎ 01443 775089

Real Ales, No Smoking Area

127 Turberville Arms

Tylacelyn Rd, Penygraig, Tonypandy,
Rhondda Cynon Taff CF40 1LA

☎ 01443 432843

Real Ales, No Smoking Area

128 Turberville Hotel

Chapel Rd, Llanharry, Pontyclun,
Rhondda Cynon Taff CF72 9QA

☎ 01443 222143

Real Ales, No Smoking Area

129 Ty Newydd Country Hotel And Restaurant

Penderyn Rd, Hirwaun, Aberdare,
Rhondda Cynon Taff CF44 9SX

☎ 01685 813433

Real Ales, Bar Food, Restaurant Menu,
Accommodation, No Smoking Area

130 Tynewydd Hotel

Scott St, Treherbert, Treorchy,
Rhondda Cynon Taff CF42 5NA

☎ 01443 771779

Real Ales

131 Tynte Hotel

Main Rd, Penrhiwceiber, Mountain Ash,
Rhondda Cynon Taff CF45 4YH

☎ 01443 478931

132 The Village Tavern

25 Bute St, Treherbert, Treorchy,
Rhondda Cynon Taff CF42 5NP

☎ 01443 777611

Real Ales, Bar Food, Restaurant Menu,
Accommodation, No Smoking Area

133 Welcome Inn

Dunraven St, Tonypandy,
Rhondda Cynon Taff CF40 1AW

☎ 01443 434695

Real Ales, Bar Food

134 Wheatsheaf Hotel

High St, Llantrisant, Pontyclun,
Rhondda Cynon Taff CF72 8BQ

☎ 01443 222249

Real Ales

135 White Rock Hotel
Swan Terrace, Tonypandy,
Rhondda Cynon Taff CF40 1HJ

☎ 01443 434697

136 Windsor Hotel
Llantrisant Rd, Pontyclun,
Rhondda Cynon Taff CF72 9DQ

☎ 01443 223800

Real Ales, Bar Food, Restaurant Menu,
No Smoking Area

137 Y Draenog
Cowbridge Rd, Brynsadler, Pontyclun,
Rhondda Cynon Taff CF72 9BT

☎ 01443 222287

Real Ales, Bar Food, Restaurant Menu,
No Smoking Area

138 Ynysboeth Hotel
Main Rd, Abercynon, Mountain Ash,
Rhondda Cynon Taff CF45 4BX

☎ 01443 740832

139 Ynyscynon Hotel
Ynyscynon Rd, Trealaw, Tonypandy,
Rhondda Cynon Taff CF40 2LL

☎ 01443 433084

Bar Food, Restaurant Menu

140 The Ynyscynon Inn
Cwmbach Rd, Aberdare,
Rhondda Cynon Taff CF44 0PA

☎ 01685 883846

Bar Food, Restaurant Menu

141 Ynyshir Hotel
Ynyshir Rd, Ynyshir, Porth,
Rhondda Cynon Taff CF39 0EL

☎ 01443 686791

142 The Ynysybwl Inn
Mill Rd, Ynysybwl, Pontypridd,
Rhondda Cynon Taff CF37 3LS

☎ 01443 790999

Bar Food, Restaurant Menu, No Smoking Area

LOCATION MAP

Pontarddulais

M4

Gorseinon

Swansea

Llanmadoc

Llangennith

Llanrhidian

SWANSEA

Rhossili

Pennard

Oxwich

Port Einon

Mumbles

11 Swansea Reference Number - Detailed Information

12 Swansea Reference Number - Summary Entry

Ceredigion Page 249   Adjacent area - refer to pages indicated

SWANSEA

SWANSEA • CLYDACH • GOWER PENINSULA

Swansea (Welsh: *Abertawe*) is a city and administrative county in south Wales, situated on the coast immediately to the east of the Gower peninsula in the traditional county of Glamorgan. The English name is believed to come from 'Sweyn's Ey' ('ey' being a Germanic word for 'island') and to have originated in the period when the Vikings plundered the south Wales coast. The city boundaries are widely drawn and include a large amount of open countryside, and towns like Gorseinon and Loughor, along with the Gower peninsula. Swansea is Wales's second city, and it grew to its present importance during the 18th and 19th centuries, becoming a centre of heavy industry. However, it did not enjoy the same degree of immigration as Cardiff and the eastern valleys. Consequently it retains close links with agriculture and rural life, and a healthy proportion of the population are Welsh speakers

The Mumbles

(13.4% at the 2001 census, as compared with 11% for the capital city, Cardiff).

Today, much of Swansea Bay is hailed as one of the UK's premier coastal locations. Much of the traditional industry has disappeared as the old dock area has been transformed into a marina surrounded by stylish waterfront buildings. This Maritime Quarter is arguably the most impressive part of the town and is alive with cafés, pubs and restaurants. Here can also be found the Abbey Woollen Mill, where visitors can see woollen goods produced by traditional means on machinery dating mainly from before 1900. Swansea is rich in

Three Cliffs Bay

gardens and parks and has its own Botanical Garden, housed in the walled garden of Singleton Park. At Plantasia, visitors can wander round a giant hot house and discover a wide range of colourful exotics. Clyne Gardens, at Blackpill off the A4067 Mumbles road, are known in particular for their marvellous rhododendrons, including National Collections, their imposing magnolias and an extensive bog garden.

Weobley Castle

The sheltered Bishopston Valley contains a large area of ancient woodland that supports a wide variety of plants and birds. A two-mile footpath leads along the valley from Kittle to Pwll Du.

The Mumbles is well known as a charming Victorian resort, now a popular sailing centre. Other natural beauties of the Gower Peninsula include the coastal treasures of Three Cliffs Bay in Penmaen, Llanrhidian where can be found some of the finest beaches in the country, and, to the west of Rhossili, Worm's Head, an island which is a National Nature Reserve.

1 Antelope Hotel

628 Mumbles Rd, Mumbles, Swansea SA3 4EA

☎ 01792 366835

Real Ales

2 Beaufort Arms

18 Pennard Rd, Kittle, Swansea SA3 3JS

☎ 01792 234521

Real Ales, Bar Food, Restaurant Menu,
No Smoking Area

3 Beaufort Arms

1 Castle Rd, Norton, West Cross, Swansea SA3 5TF

☎ 01792 401319

Real Ales, Bar Food, Restaurant Menu

4 Bevans Arms

63 Woodfield St, Morriston, Swansea SA6 8BW

☎ 01792 797552

5 Birchgrove Inn

396 Heol Las Close, Birchgrove, Swansea SA7 9DP

☎ 01792 771181

Real Ales

6 Bird In Hand

15 Clase Rd, Morriston, Swansea SA6 8DS

☎ 01792 771302

7 Black Boy

444 Gower Rd, Killay, Swansea SA2 7AJ

☎ 01792 299469

Real Ales, Bar Food, Restaurant Menu

8 Bonymaen Inn

Talfan Rd, Bonymaen, Swansea SA1 7HD

☎ 01792 653453

9 The Bowen Arms

See panel below

10 Britannia Inn

Swansea, Swansea SA3 1DB

☎ 01792 386624

Bar Food, Restaurant Menu, Accommodation, No Smoking Area

---

9 The Bowen Arms

Birchgrove Road, Birchgrove, Swansea SA7 9JR

☎ 01792 812321

Real Ales, Bar Food, Restaurant Menu, No Smoking Area

Spacious and welcoming, The Bowen Arms dates back to the 1860s, when it was one of Swansea's busiest pubs. Now with a more relaxed and informal atmosphere, the inn continues to uphold its long tradition of offering excellent hospitality.

Hearty and simple food is the hallmark here, with a range of snacks served all day together with other traditional favourites cooked to order at lunchtime (and in the evenings by arrangement).

The lovely beer garden has been re-landscaped recently and includes a children's play area. Owner Karen Cook has only recently taken over the running of the pub, and has the enthusiasm and verve to make it a success. She and her friendly, attentive staff make all their guests feel very welcome indeed.

☛ Off J44 of the M4 (midway between Neath and Swansea), then into Swansea on the A4118

🍺 Courage Best

🍴 12-2.30; eves by arrangement

🎵 Karaoke and live music at weekends

🅿 Car park, disabled access

🕐 12-11 (Sun and Bank Holidays to 10.30)

🏛 Swansea 1 mile, Neath 5 miles

11 The Bryngwyn
1 High St, Gorseinon, Swansea SA4 4BX
☎ 01792 893560
Real Ales, Bar Food, Restaurant Menu

12 Carlton Hotel
654-656 Mumbles Rd, Mumbles, Swansea SA3 4EA
☎ 01792 360450
Bar Food, Restaurant Menu, Accommodation,
No Smoking Area

13 Carpenters Arms
High St, Clydach, Swansea SA6 5LN
☎ 01792 843333
Real Ales, Bar Food, Restaurant Menu,
No Smoking Area

14 Castellamare
Bracelet Bay, Mumbles, Swansea SA3 4JT
☎ 01792 369408
Bar Food, Restaurant Menu, No Smoking Area

15 Champion Brewer
106 Martin St, Morriston, Swansea SA6 7BL
☎ 01792 411181
Real Ales, No Smoking Area

16 CJs Wine Bar and Restaurant
135 Mumbles Rd, Mumbles, Swansea SA3 4DN
☎ 01792 361246
Restaurant Menu, No Smoking Area

17 Colliers Arms
450 Jersey Rd, Bonymaen, Swansea SA1 7DW
☎ 01792 702337
Bar Food, Restaurant Menu, No Smoking Area

18 Commercial Hotel
Station Rd, Gowerton, Swansea SA4 3AJ
☎ 01792 872072
Real Ales

19 Crofty Inn
71 Pencaerfenni Lane, Crofty, Swansea SA4 3SW
☎ 01792 850494
Real Ales, Bar Food, Restaurant Menu,
No Smoking Area

20 Cross Keys Inn
70 Glebe Rd, Loughor, Swansea SA4 6SR
☎ 01792 897744

21 The Crown Inn
79 Woodfield St, Morriston, Swansea SA6 8BQ
☎ 01792 411005

22 Deer's Leap
Heol Maes Eglwys, Cwmrhydyceirw,
Swansea SA6 6SG
☎ 01792 704901
Bar Food, Restaurant Menu, No Smoking Area

23 The Dukes Arms
556 Neath Rd, Morriston, Swansea SA6 8HG
☎ 01792 411178
Bar Food, Restaurant Menu, No Smoking Area

24 Farmers Arms
152 St Teilo St, Pontardulais, Swansea SA4 8RA
☎ 01792 886010
Real Ales, Bar Food, Restaurant Menu

25 Farmers Arms
284 Swansea Rd, Waunarlwydd, Swansea SA5 4SL
☎ 01792 872333
Real Ales, No Smoking Area

26 The Fendrod
Fendrod Way, Llansamlet, Swansea SA7 9DG
☎ 01792 701950
Restaurant Menu, No Smoking Area

27 Found Out Inn
8 Killan Rd, Dunvant, Swansea SA2 7TD
☎ 01792 203596
Real Ales, Bar Food, Restaurant Menu, No Smoking
Area

28 Fountain Inn
Bolgoed Rd, Pontardulais, Swansea SA4 8JF
☎ 01792 882501
Real Ales, Bar Food, Restaurant Menu,
Accommodation, No Smoking Area

29 The Fountain Inn

12 Woodfield St, Morriston, Swansea SA6 8AQ

☎ 01792 411484

Real Ales, Bar Food, Restaurant Menu,
No Smoking Area

30 Glamorgan Arms

Bryntirion Rd, Pontlliw, Swansea SA4 9DY

☎ 01792 882409

Real Ales, Bar Food, Restaurant Menu,
No Smoking Area

31 The Globe Inn

Birchgrove Rd, Glais, Swansea SA7 9EN

☎ 01792 842655

Real Ales, Bar Food, Restaurant Menu,
No Smoking Area

32 Gower Inn

Parkmill, Swansea SA3 2EQ

☎ 01792 233116

Real Ales, Bar Food, Restaurant Menu

33 The Greyhound

See panel below

34 Hillcrest House Hotel

1 Higher Lane, Langland, Swansea SA3 4NS

☎ 01792 363700

Accommodation, No Smoking Area

35 Hungry Horse

The Dunvant 234, Dunvant, Swansea SA2 7SR

☎ 01792 208112

Real Ales, Bar Food, Restaurant Menu,
No Smoking Area

36 Imperial Hotel

1125 Neath Rd, Plasmarl, Swansea SA6 8JW

☎ 01792 771205

Real Ales, No Smoking Area

37 Jersey Arms

Swansea, Swansea SA1 7DG

☎ 01792 654512

Bar Food, No Smoking Area

---

33 The Greyhound

Old Walls, Llanrhidian, Gower, Swansea SA3 1HA

☎ 01792 391027

Real Ales, Bar Food, Restaurant Menu,
Accommodation, No Smoking Area

The Greyhound is a 19th-century roadhouse inn with a good selection of cask ales and bitters together with bottled beers, lagers, cider, stout, wines, spirits and soft drinks – something to quench every thirst.

The accent's on the excellent food at this handsome pub: Blackboard daily specials include a variety of hot and cold snacks and main courses with dishes from all parts of the world including Asian and Italian specialities. Other dishes make the most of the freshest local produce, including Welsh beef and lamb.

Inside and out, the pub is cheerful and welcoming, with comfortable seating and an outside patio area and beer garden.

Located at the most westerly tip of the Gower Peninsula, this fine pub is popular with walkers and lovers of nature's beauty, as the region offers splendid views along the coast.

☞ Llanrhidian is 10 miles west of Swansea off the B4295

🍴 as per opening hours

⚒ Parking, garden, patio

💳 All major cards

🕐 11-11 (Sun and Bank Holidays 12-10.30)

🏛 Coast 1 mile, Rhossili 4 miles, Loughor 4 miles, Swansea 10 miles

38 The Joiners Arms

27 Joiners Rd, Three Crosses, Swansea SA4 3NY

☎ 01792 872889

Real Ales, Bar Food, Restaurant Menu

39 Joiners Arms

62 Ystrad Rd, Fforestfach, Swansea SA5 4BU

☎ 01792 588248

Bar Food, Restaurant Menu

40 King Arthur Hotel

Higher Green, Reynoldston, Swansea SA3 1AD

☎ 01792 390775

Bar Food, Restaurant Menu, Accommodation, No Smoking Area

41 The King Hotel

240 St Teilo St, Pontardulais, Swansea SA4 8LQ

☎ 01792 882308

Real Ales, Bar Food, Restaurant Menu

42 The Kings Head Hotel

See panel below

43 Kingsbridge Inn

Swansea Rd, Gorseinon, Swansea SA4 4AS

☎ 01792 892229

Real Ales, Bar Food, Restaurant Menu, No Smoking Area

44 Ludwigs

17 Pontardawe Rd, Clydach, Swansea SA6 5NS

☎ 01792 842524

45 The Mardy

High St, Gorseinon, Swansea SA4 4BR

☎ 01792 892616

Real Ales, Bar Food, No Smoking Area

46 Marquis Arms

Carmarthen Rd, Fforestfach, Swansea SA5 4AA

☎ 01792 560911

Real Ales, Bar Food, No Smoking Area

47 The Masons Arms

Rhydypandy Rd, Rhydypandy, Swansea SA6 6PB

☎ 01792 842535

Real Ales, Bar Food, Restaurant Menu

---

42 The King's Head Hotel

Llangennith, Gower, Swansea SA31 2HX

☎ 01792 386212

Real Ales, Bar Food, Restaurant Menu, Accommodation, No Smoking Area

The King's Head is a traditional 16th-century coaching inn with many original features including the black and amber tiled floor in the main bar and the huge oak beam sunk into the exposed brick over the roaring fire.

There's a full range of cask ales and bitters, together with lagers, cider, bottled beers, stout, wines, spirits and soft drinks.

Blackboard daily specials include a tempting range of hot and cold dishes including ones from all over the globe: Italian foods, curries and home-grown favourites such as pure Welsh beef and lamb.

Located at the most westerly tip of the stunning peninsula, the pub is set amid a walker's and nature-lover's paradise, with fabulous coastal views and, here at this fine pub, a warm and genuine welcome.

☞ Llangennith is 14½ miles west of Swansea off the B4271

❚ as per opening hours

🅿 Parking, garden, patio

💳 All major cards

🕐 11-11 (Sun and Bank Holidays 12-10.30)

🏛 Coast 1 mile, Rhossili 2 miles, Swansea 14½ miles

48 The Masons Arms
104 Swansea Rd, Waunarlwydd, Swansea SA5 4SU
☎ 01792 879739
Bar Food, Restaurant Menu, No Smoking Area

49 The Midland
115 Clydach Rd, Morriston, Swansea SA6 6QB
☎ 01792 781550

50 Millers Arms
See panel below

51 The Millhouse
Cwmbath Rd, Morriston, Swansea SA6 7AU
☎ 01792 799309

52 Mumbles Pier Hotel
Mumbles Pier, Mumbles, Swansea SA3 4EN
☎ 01792 365230
Real Ales, Bar Food, Restaurant Menu,
No Smoking Area

53 The New Inn
The Lone, Clydach, Swansea SA6 5SU
☎ 01792 842839
Real Ales, Bar Food, Restaurant Menu,
No Smoking Area

54 The Newton Inn
New Well Lane, Newton, Swansea SA3 4SR
☎ 01792 363226
Real Ales, Bar Food, Restaurant Menu

55 North Gower Hotel
Llanrhidian, Swansea SA3 1EE
☎ 01792 390042
Real Ales, Bar Food, Restaurant Menu,
Accommodation, No Smoking Area

56 The Old Barn Inn and Restaurant
Cefn Velindre Farm, Pontlasau, Swansea SA6 6PX
☎ 01792 774411
Real Ales, Bar Food, Restaurant Menu,
Accommodation, No Smoking Area

---

50 Millers Arms

Glydach Road, Ynystawe, Swansea SA6 5AY
☎ 01792 842614

**Real Ales, Bar Food, Restaurant Menu,
No Smoking Area**

Pristine and welcoming, the Millers Arms is eye-catching for its whitewashed exterior and hanging baskets overflowing with blooms at the downstairs windows and above the entrance. Inside it's just as pleasant, with a tasteful, understated décor and classic features such as the exposed

beamwork. The Inn is known also as the Teapot Pub as it has a fine collection of teapots. The inn dates back to 1843 and is located next to the site of an old mill, which gives it its name.

Licensees Steven and Delyth Jones offer all their guests a high standard of service and hospitality. The finest produce goes into creating an excellent range of tempting dishes on the menu and specials board, including home-made steak-and-kidney pie, minted lamb shanks, hand cut chips and daily roasts.

The inn has a well-deserved reputation for the quality of its food, which is expertly prepared and presented.

☛ From J45 of the M4 take the B4603 into Ynystawe and the Millers arms is on th right.

🍺 Welsh Smooth, Abbot, Greene King IPA, rotating guest ales

🍴 daily 12-2; Mon-Sat 6-9

🅿 Parking, garden, patio, disabled access

💳 All major cards

🕐 Mon-Fri 11.30-3 & 6-11, Sat 11.30-3 & 5.15-11, Sun and Bank Holidays 12-3 & 7-10.30

57 Old Glais Inn

Glais, Swansea SA7 9EN

☎ 01792 843316

Real Ales, Bar Food, Restaurant Menu,
No Smoking Area

58 The Old Inn

Swansea Rd, Penllergaer, Swansea SA4 9AQ

☎ 01792 894097

Real Ales, Bar Food, Restaurant Menu,
No Smoking Area

59 Oxwich Bay Hotel

Oxwich, Swansea SA3 1LS

☎ 01792 390329

Real Ales, Bar Food, Restaurant Menu,
Accommodation, No Smoking Area

60 Park Inn

23 Park St, Mumbles, Swansea SA3 4DA

☎ 01792 366738

Real Ales

61 Patricks With Rooms

636-638 Mumbles Rd, Mumbles, Swansea SA3 4EA

☎ 01792 360199

Restaurant Menu, Accommodation,
No Smoking Area

62 The Penplas Inn

Leos Shopping Complex Penlan, Swansea SA5 7JR

☎ 01792 581288

63 Pier Hotel

Mumbles Pier, Mumbles, Swansea SA3 4EN

☎ 01792 366920

Real Ales, No Smoking Area

64 Pilot Inn

726 Mumbles Rd, Mumbles, Swansea SA3 4EL

☎ 01792 366643

Real Ales, Bar Food, Restaurant Menu,
No Smoking Area

65 Plough and Harrow

88 Oldway Rd, Murton, Swansea SA3 3DJ

☎ 01792 234459

Bar Food, Restaurant Menu

66 Plough and Harrow

57 Church Rd, Llansamlet, Swansea SA7 9RL

☎ 01792 772263

Real Ales, Bar Food, Restaurant Menu,
No Smoking Area

67 Plough and Harrow Inn

Swansea Rd, Llangyfelach, Llangyselach,
Swansea SA5 7JA

☎ 01792 771816

Real Ales, Restaurant Menu, No Smoking Area

68 Poundffald Inn

Tirmynydd Rd, Three Crosses, Swansea SA4 3PB

☎ 01792 873428

Real Ales, Bar Food, Restaurant Menu,
No Smoking Area

69 The Pub On The Pond

Singleton Park, Mumbles Rd, Swansea SA2 8PY

☎ 01792 298023

Real Ales, Bar Food, Restaurant Menu,
No Smoking Area

70 The Railway Inn

553 Gower Rd, Killay, Swansea SA2 7DS

☎ 01792 203946

Real Ales

71 The Railway Inn

Bellevue, Penclawdd, Swansea SA4 3YE

☎ 01792 851692

72 Ramada Jarvis Hotel

Phoenix Way, Enterprise Park, Swansea SA7 9EG

☎ 01792 310330

Real Ales, Bar Food, Restaurant Menu,
Accommodation, No Smoking Area

73 Red Lion Hotel

See panel opposite

74 The Red Lion Hotel

49 Sway Rd, Morriston, Swansea SA6 6JA

☎ 01792 773206

Real Ales, Bar Food, Restaurant Menu,
Accommodation, No Smoking Area

75 The Reverend James

180 Borough Rd, Loughor, Swansea SA4 6RZ
☎ 01792 516231
Real Ales, Bar Food, Restaurant Menu,
No Smoking Area

76 The Rock and Fountain

147-149 Newton Rd, Newton, Swansea SA3 4ST
☎ 01792 369142
Real Ales

77 Rock and Fountain Inn

Rhyddwen Rd, Craig-Cefn-Parc, Swansea SA6 5RA
☎ 01792 843347
Real Ales

78 The Royal Oak

Beach Rd, Penclawdd, Swansea SA4 3YN
☎ 01792 850642
Bar Food, Restaurant Menu, No Smoking Area

79 Sea Garden Chinese Restaurant and Bar

Penclawdd Rd, Penclawdd, Swansea SA4 3RB
☎ 01792 872886
Real Ales, Restaurant Menu, No Smoking Area

80 The Shepherds Country Inn

See panel on page 252

81 The Ship and Castle

80 Castle St, Loughor, Swansea SA4 6TS
☎ 01792 894873
Real Ales, Bar Food, Restaurant Menu

82 Smiths Arms

141 Samlet Rd, Llansamlet, Swansea SA7 9AQ
☎ 01792 773270
Real Ales

73 Red Lion Hotel

Glebe Road, Lochar, nr Swansea SA4 6SR
☎ 01792 892983
Real Ales, Bar Food, Restaurant Menu,
No Smoking Area

The Red Lion Hotel is a traditional inn that has recently undergone tasteful refurbishment. The smart frontage bodes well for the warm welcome guests can expect inside, where the ambience is always convivial and friendly. Together with the

real ales here there's a good range of lagers, cider, stout, wines, spirits and soft drinks. Licensees Tina Arianna and Wynford Jones arrived in 2004, and have made a real success of the venture thanks to their dedication and enthusiasm for providing excellent service and warm hospitality.

Food is served all day at this friendly and appealing pub, where the choice includes a good range of traditional favourites. Sunday lunch is justly popular here, as it is a hearty and delicious meal expertly prepared and presented. Another boon is the take-away menu; home delivery is also available.

- Off J47 of the M4
- Mon-Sat 10-8, Sun 12-5
- Bingo Tues, quiz Weds, karaoke and disco Thurs-Sat, live music Sun
- Parking, garden, disabled access
- Mon-Sat 10 a.m.-11 p.m., Sun and Bank Holidays 11-10.30
- Swansea, Gorseinon, Loughor

83 Spinning Wheel

Sketty Park Drive, Sketty, Swansea SA2 8JH

☎ 01792 205362

Real Ales, Bar Food, Restaurant Menu,
No Smoking Area

84 St Annes Hotel

Western Lane, Mumbles, Swansea SA3 4EY

☎ 01792 369147

Bar Food, Restaurant Menu, Accommodation,
No Smoking Area

85 The Star Inn

1070 Carmarthen Rd, Fforestfach,
Swansea SA5 4BP

☎ 01792 586910

Bar Food, Restaurant Menu, No Smoking Area

86 Station Hotel

17 High St, Gorseinon, Swansea SA4 4BX

☎ 01792 896844

87 The Swn-Y-Mor Village Inn

Burry House, Burry View, Penclawdd,
Swansea SA4 3XS

☎ 01792 850502

No Smoking Area

88 Tafarn Trap

Swansea Rd, Gorseinon, Swansea SA4 4AS

☎ 01792 892733

Bar Food, Restaurant Menu, No Smoking Area

89 Terrace Inn

205 Birchgrove Rd, Birchgrove, Swansea SA7 9JU

☎ 01792 813123

90 Three Compasses Hotel

Hebron Rd, Swansea SA6 5EJ

☎ 01792 843371

---

80 Shepherds Country Inn

18 Heol Myddfai, Felindre, Swansea SA5 7ND

☎ 01792 794715

Real Ales, Bar Food, Restaurant Menu,
Accommodation, No Smoking Area

The Shepherds Country Inn is a fabulous country pub and well worth seeking out for its superb food, drink and accommodation. Everything on the menu and specials board is home-made using the freshest ingredients, including tasty steaks and traditional favourites. The inn has a cosy, homely feel and looks more like a family home from outside. There's a covered porch area to the front

and a handsome beer garden complete with children's play area to the rear. The accommodation comprises four recently refurbished rooms, tastefully decorated and furnished. The inn is run by husband-and-wife team Rob and Joanne Davies, who have a wealth of experience having run some of London's landmark pubs in the past.

☛ Leave the M4 at J46 and follow the signs for Felindre, turn right after the mill then right again after 20 metres, pass the chapel on the right. The inn will be on your right.

🍺 Abbots and Double Dragon

🍴 12-2.30 & 6-9

🛏 4 en suite rooms

🎵 Occasional live music

♿ Parking, disabled access, garden, children's play area

💳 All major cards

🕐 Mon-Thurs 11.30-3 & 6-11, Fri-Sat 11.30-11, Sun and Bank Holidays 11.30-10.30 (open every day from 11.30 in summer)

🏛 Swansea, Gorseinon, Gowerton, Bishopston, Pontarddulais

91 Ty Gwyn Mawr
71 Sterry Rd, Gowerton, Swansea SA4 3BN
☎ 01792 873931
Real Ales, No Smoking Area

92 The Valley Hotel
41 Bishopston Rd, Bishopston, Swansea SA3 3EJ
☎ 01792 234820
Bar Food, Restaurant Menu, Accommodation,
No Smoking Area

93 The Vardre Hotel
2 Heol Eithrim, Clydach, Swansea SA6 5ES
☎ 01792 842359

94 The Victoria Inn
21 Westbourne Place, Mumbles, Swansea SA3 4DB
☎ 01792 360111
Real Ales, Accommodation

95 The Village Inn
5-6 The Precinct, Killay, Swansea SA2 7BA
☎ 01792 203311
Bar Food, Restaurant Menu, No Smoking Area

96 The Village Inn
580 Mumbles Rd, Mumbles, Swansea SA3 4DL
☎ 01792 368308
Real Ales, Bar Food, Restaurant Menu

97 The Village Tavern
93-94 High St, Clydach, Swansea SA6 5LN
☎ 01792 843244
Accommodation

98 The Welcome Inn
Mynyddbach Common, Llangyselach,
Swansea SA5 7HT
☎ 01792 793548
Real Ales, Bar Food, Restaurant Menu,
No Smoking Area

99 Welcome To Gower
2 Mount St, Gowerton, Swansea SA4 3EJ
☎ 01792 872611
Real Ales, Bar Food, Restaurant Menu,
Accommodation, No Smoking Area

100 West Cross Inn and Restaurant
43 Mumbles Rd, West Cross, Swansea SA3 5AB
☎ 01792 401143
Bar Food, Restaurant Menu

101 West End
1 West St, Gorseinon, Swansea SA4 4AA
☎ 01792 894217
Real Ales, No Smoking Area

102 Wheatsheaf Hotel
38 St Teilo St, Pontardulais, Swansea SA4 8SZ
☎ 01792 884748

103 White Rose
Newton Rd, Mumbles, Swansea SA3 4AR
☎ 01792 365121
Real Ales, Bar Food, No Smoking Area

104 The William Hancock
2 Western Lane, Mumbles, Swansea SA3 4DX
☎ 01792 362133
Real Ales

105 Winston Hotel
11 Church Lane, Bishopston, Swansea SA3 3JT
☎ 01792 232074
Bar Food, Restaurant Menu, Accommodation,
No Smoking Area

106 Worms Head Hotel
Rhossili, Swansea SA3 1PP
☎ 01792 390512
Real Ales, Bar Food, Restaurant Menu,
Accommodation, No Smoking Area

107 The Wychtree Inn
924 Neath Rd, Morriston, Swansea SA6 8ES
☎ 01792 413017

TORFAEN

CWMBRAN • PONTYPOOL • BLAENAVON

The county borough of Torfaen lies within the traditional boundaries of Monmouthshire. The district borders Newport to the south, Monmouthshire to the east, and Blaenau Gwent and Caerphilly to the west. Its main towns are Abersychan, Blaenavon, Cwmbran and Pontypool. Monuments to the great industrial age include Blaenavon's Big Pit Mine and Ironworks. The Big Pit Mine closed in 1980 but was the oldest colliery in Wales; it has now been reopened as a monument to the past. The Blaenavon Ironworks were built against a cliff-face in the 1780s; visitors can see the whole process of production.

Cwmbran is home to the Llanyrafon Mill and Farm Museum and the Llamtarnam Grange Arts Centre. Greenmeadow Community Farm, set within the town's planned green belt, is home to all manner of farm animals as well as farm trails, a children's adventure playground and an unusual dragon sculpture.

Pontypool is credited with being the home of the Welsh iron industry. The first forge here is believed to have been in operation as early as 1425, while the first ironworks opened in 1577. This valley also prides itself on being the earliest place in Britain to have successfully produced tin plate, in 1720. Today, the town's industrial heritage can be explored at the Pontypool Valley Inheritance Centre, where both the industrial and social history of the town and the surrounding Torfaen Valley is detailed. The museum is located in the late-Georgian stables of Pontypool Park, a 19th-century landscaped affair with attractions that include a shell grotto and a unique double-chambered ice house. Canals, too, have played an important part in the development of Pontypool, and this legacy is recalled at Junction Cottage, a tollkeeper's cottage of 1814 lying at the junction of the Monmouthshire and Brecon Canal and the River Lwyd. At Llandegfedd Reservoir, to the east of Pontypool, the lake and surrounding countryside provide numerous opportunities for fishing, sailing, walking and bird-watching.

11   Torfaen Reference Number   - Detailed Information

12   Torfaen Reference Number   - Summary Entry

Ceredigion Page 249   Adjacent area - refer to pages indicated

1   Ashbridge Inn

Avondale Rd, Rhydyrun Cwmbran, Cwmbran,
Torfaen NP44 1DE

☎ 01633 876678

Real Ales, Bar Food, No Smoking Area

2   Best Western Parkway Hotel

Ty Coch Lane, Llantarnam Park Way, Cwmbran,
Torfaen NP44 3UW

☎ 01633 871199

Real Ales, Bar Food, Restaurant Menu,
Accommodation, No Smoking Area

3   The Bridgend Inn

See panel below

4   British Constitution Inn

41 Commercial Rd, Talywain, Pontypool,
Torfaen NP4 7HT

☎ 01495 772768

Real Ales

5   Buck Inn

8 Station St, Abersychan, Pontypool,
Torfaen NP4 8PH

☎ 01495 772152

Real Ales, Bar Food, No Smoking Area

6   The Bush Inn

Graig Rd, Upper Cwmbran, Cwmbran,
Torfaen NP44 5AN

☎ 01633 483764

7   Butterflies

31-33 Queen St, Blaenavon, Pontypool,
Torfaen NP4 9PN

☎ 01495 791044

Real Ales, Bar Food, Restaurant Menu

8   Cambrian Inn

81-82 Llanover Rd, Blaenavon, Pontypool,
Torfaen NP4 9HR

☎ 01495 790327

Real Ales

---

3   The Bridgend Inn

23 Hanbury Road, Pontnewynydd, Pontypool,
Torfaen NP4 6QN

☎ 01495 757435

Real Ales, Bar Food

Cosy and welcoming, The Bridgend Inn began life as cottages built in the late 17th century, which were later converted to create this fine traditional ale house. The inn exudes a very inviting, hospitable atmosphere (even the two resident

ghosts are quite personable!), and owners Rick and Wendy Aldridge have built up an enviable reputation for service and quality since taking over here in 2002.

The real ales come from the local Wye Valley Brewery, complemented by a good selection of lagers, cider, stout, wines, spirits and soft drinks. On request, Wendy will whip up some fresh tasty sandwiches, curries, soup or other snacks, while local places of interest include a pleasant country walk along the old railway line from here right up to Blaenavon.

☞   The village is just off the A4043 about 1 mile north of Pontypool

🍺   Wye Valley ales

🍴   by arrangement

🎵   Live music Fri & Sat, piano, pool table, darts

🅿   Parking, patio

🕐   12-11 (Sun and Bank Holidays to 10.30)

🏛   Pontypool 1 mile, Blaenavon (Big Pit Mine, Ironworks, Pontypool & Blaenavon Railway) 5 miles

9 Castle Hotel

94 Broad St, Blaenavon, Pontypool,
Torfaen NP4 9ND
☎ 01495 792477
Accommodation, No Smoking Area

10 Commodore Hotel

Mill Lane, Llanyravon, Cwmbran, Torfaen NP44 8SH
☎ 01633 484091
Real Ales, Bar Food, Restaurant Menu,
Accommodation, No Smoking Area

11 The Cross Keys

55 Five Locks Rd, Pontnewydd, Cwmbran,
Torfaen NP44 1BT
☎ 01633 861545
Bar Food, Restaurant Menu, Accommodation,
No Smoking Area

12 Crown Inn

Greenhill Rd, Sebastopol, Pontypool,
Torfaen NP4 5BQ
☎ 01495 764197

13 The Crows Nest

Llangorse Rd, Llanyrafon, Cwmbran,
Torfaen NP44 8HU
☎ 01633 480971
Bar Food, Restaurant Menu

14 Cwrt Henllys

Henllys Village Rd, Henllys, Cwmbran,
Torfaen NP44 6HX
☎ 01633 484697
Bar Food, Restaurant Menu, Accommodation

15 Dorallt Inn

Henllys, Cwmbran, Torfaen NP44 6HX
☎ 01633 869697
Bar Food, Restaurant Menu

16 Fountain Inn

17-18 King St, Blaenavon, Pontypool,
Torfaen NP4 9QQ
☎ 01495 792532

17 The Globe Inn

Commercial Rd, Talywain, Pontypool,
Torfaen NP4 7JH
☎ 01495 772053
Real Ales, Bar Food

18 The Greenhouse

Newport Rd, Llantarnam, Cwmbran,
Torfaen NP44 3BP
☎ 01633 482859
Real Ales, Bar Food, Restaurant Menu,
No Smoking Area

19 Halfway Hotel

Commercial St, Cwmbran, Torfaen NP44 3LR
☎ 01633 766982

20 Hanbury Arms

Herberts Rd, Garndiffaith, Pontypool,
Torfaen NP4 7QJ
☎ 01495 772300
Real Ales, Bar Food, Restaurant Menu,
No Smoking Area

21 Horse and Jockey

Usk Rd, Pontypool, Torfaen NP4 8AF
☎ 01495 762721
Real Ales, Bar Food, Restaurant Menu

22 The Horseshoe

Hill St, Pontnewynydd, Pontypool, Torfaen NP4 6NL
☎ 01495 762188
Real Ales, Bar Food

23 Lamb Inn

Penyrheol, Pontypool, Torfaen NP4 5XS
☎ 01495 763718
Real Ales, Bar Food, No Smoking Area

24 Lion Hotel

41 Broad St, Blaenavon, Pontypool,
Torfaen NP4 9NH
☎ 01495 791642
Real Ales

25 Market Tavern

Broad St, Blaenavon, Pontypool, Torfaen NP4 9NE
☎ 01495 792100
Real Ales, Accommodation

26 Masons Arms

Hill St, Pontnewynydd, Pontypool, Torfaen NP4 6NL
☎ 01495 753500

27 Masons Arms

Folley Lane, Trevethin, Pontypool, Torfaen NP4 8JB
☎ 01495 763785

28 New Bridgend Inn

Greenhill Rd, Cwmbran, Torfaen NP44 3DG
☎ 01633 484596

29 The New Inn

130 High St, Abersychan, Pontypool,
Torfaen NP4 7AE
☎ 01495 773706

30 Oddfellows Arms

20 Commercial St, Pontnewydd, Cwmbran,
Torfaen NP44 1DZ
☎ 01633 483091
Real Ales, Bar Food

31 Old Bridgend Inn

Commercial St, Pontnewydd, Cwmbran,
Torfaen NP44 1AE
☎ 01633 483678
Real Ales

32 The Old Castle Inn

High St, Abersychan, Pontypool, Torfaen NP4 7AB
☎ 01495 772649
Real Ales

33 Open Hearth Inn

Wern Rd, Sebastopol, Pontypool, Torfaen NP4 5DR
☎ 01495 763752
Real Ales, Bar Food, Restaurant Menu,
No Smoking Area

36 The Queen Inn

Upper Cwmbran, Cwmbran, Torfaen NP44 1SN
☎ 01633 484252

Real Ales, Bar Food, Restaurant Menu,
No Smoking Area

The Queen Inn is a very handsome and welcoming establishment set amid some lovely countryside in Upper Cwmbran. This pristine whitewashed inn began life in 1824 as three cottages.

The interior décor and furnishings are a

tasteful mix of traditional and modern. Owners Gareth and Jane Edwards and their helpful, friendly staff offer a high standard of quality and service. There are always two regularly changing real ales on tap, together with a good selection of lagers, wines, spirits, cider, stout and soft drinks.

Everything from bar meals to full meals, including specialities such as steaks and the hearty and delicious Sunday lunch, make up a menu with something to suit every taste. The superb garden includes an impressive children's adventure playground.

☛ 3 miles south of Pontypool on the A4051

🍺 2 rotating guest ales

🍴 Tues-Sun 12-3 & 6-9

♫ Live music occasionally

⛱ Parking, garden, patio, children's play area, disabled access

💳 All major cards

🕐 12-11 (Sun and Bank Holidays to 10.30)

🏛 Green Meadow Community Farm, Pontypool 3 miles, Blaenavon 9 miles

34 Ponthir House Inn

Ponthir, Newport, Torfaen NP18 1PG

☎ 01633 420479

Real Ales, Bar Food, No Smoking Area

35 The Pottery

Llanover Rd, Blaenavon, Pontypool,
Torfaen NP4 9HT

☎ 01495 790395

Real Ales, Bar Food

36 The Queen Inn

See panel on page 257

37 Queen Victoria Inn

Prince St, Blaenavon, Pontypool, Torfaen NP4 9BD

☎ 01495 791652

Real Ales, Bar Food, Restaurant Menu,
Accommodation, No Smoking Area

38 The Rhydspence Inn

Whitney-on-Wye, Hereford, Pontypool,
Torfaen NP4 9RN

☎ 01497 831262

Real Ales, Bar Food, Restaurant Menu,
Accommodation, No Smoking Area

39 Riflemans Arms

Rifle St, Blaenavon, Pontypool, Torfaen NP4 9QS

☎ 01495 792297

Real Ales, Bar Food, Accommodation,
No Smoking Area

40 Rising Sun Inn

Cwmavon Rd, Abersychan, Pontypool,
Torfaen NP4 8PP

☎ 01495 773256

Real Ales, Bar Food, Restaurant Menu,
No Smoking Area

46 The Star

Caerleon Road, Porthir NP18 1GZ

☎ 01633 420580

Real Ales, Bar Food, Restaurant Menu

Tucked away just a couple of miles off junction 25A of the M4, The Star inn is a welcoming establishment that is well worth seeking out.

This cosy and friendly pub is run by mother-

and-son team Jean and Michael Davies. They've been here since late 2004 – it's their first venture into the licensing trade and they bring a wealth of enthusiasm to their task.

The interior of this fine inn is a happy marriage of traditional and modern, with exposed beamwork and brickbuilt walls as well as light paintwork and polished wood tables and chairs.

Fresh, locally-sourced ingredients go into the range of delicious dishes served. The real ale on tap is complemented by a very good variety of lagers, cider, stout, wines, spirits and soft drinks.

☛ 2 miles off J25A of the M4 on the A4236

🍺 Rev James

🍴 Tues-Sat 12-2 & 5.30-9, Sun 12-2.30

♫ Quiz Sun night from 8.30 p.m.

🅿 Parking, garden, disabled access

💳 All major cards

🕐 12-11 (Sun and Bank Holidays to 10.30)

🏛 Caerleon 1½ miles, Newport 4 miles,
Penhow 5 miles

41 The Rolling Mill
45 Broad St, Blaenavon, Pontypool,
Torfaen NP4 9NH
☎ 01495 790256
Real Ales

42 Rose & Crown
Victoria St, Cwmbran, Torfaen NP44 3JS
☎ 01633 866700

43 The Sally
Tranch Rd, Tranch, Pontypool, Torfaen NP4 6AN
☎ 01495 753477
Real Ales

44 Six In Hand
Edlogan Square, Croesyceiliog, Cwmbran,
Torfaen NP44 2NR
☎ 01633 482263

45 Square Inn
47-49 Gwent Square, Cwmbran, Torfaen NP44 1PL
☎ 01633 867587
Real Ales, Bar Food, Restaurant Menu

46 The Star Inn
See panel opposite

47 Three Blackbirds Inn
Llantarnam, Cwmbran, Torfaen NP44 3AY
☎ 01633 483130
Real Ales, Bar Food, No Smoking Area

48 Upper Cock Inn
The Highway, Croesyceiliog, Cwmbran,
Torfaen NP44 2HE
☎ 01633 483218
Bar Food, Restaurant Menu, No Smoking Area

49 The Waterloo
Llandowlais St, Oakfield, Cwmbran,
Torfaen NP44 7HD
☎ 01633 485206

50 Waterloo Inn
Avondale Rd, Sebastapol, Pontypool,
Torfaen NP4 5EL
☎ 01495 759588
Bar Food, Restaurant Menu, No Smoking Area

51 Westlake Arms
Cwmavon, Pontypool, Torfaen NP4 8UZ
☎ 01495 772571
Real Ales, Bar Food

52 The Wheatsheaf Inn
Cwmnyscoy Rd, Cwmnyscoy, Pontypool,
Torfaen NP4 5SG
☎ 01495 755561

53 The Whistle Inn
Garn Yr Erw, Pontypool, Torfaen NP4 9SJ
☎ 01495 790403
Real Ales, Restaurant Menu, No Smoking Area

54 White Hart Inn
Broad St, Abersychan, Pontypool,
Torfaen NP4 7BQ
☎ 01495 772378

55 Yew Tree Inn
Penygarn Rd, Penygarn, Pontypool,
Torfaen NP4 8JA
☎ 01495 763742

56 Yew Tree Inn
Maendy Way West, Pontnewydd, Cwmbran,
Torfaen NP44 1LE
☎ 01633 771899
Bar Food, Restaurant Menu, No Smoking Area

VALE OF GLAMORGAN

PENARTH • BARRY • LLANTWIT MAJOR

The Vale of Glamorgan (Welsh: *Dyffryn Morgannwg*) is an exceptionally rich agricultural area in the southern part of Glamorgan, Wales. It has a rugged coastline, but its rolling countryside is quite untypical of Wales as a whole. It has been a county borough since 1996, previously being part of South Glamorgan. The main town and largest centre of population is Barry. Other small towns are Cowbridge, Llantwit Major and Penarth, but a large proportion of the population inhabits villages, hamlets and individual farms. The district borders Cardiff, Rhondda Cynon Taf and Bridgend to the north, and the Bristol Channel to the south. Villages of the Vale include Aberthin, Bonvilston, Colwinston, Corntown, Ewenny, Llanblethian, Llancarfan, Llandough, Llandow, Llanmaes, Llansannor, Llantrithyd, Llysworney, Ogmore-by-Sea, Pendoylan, Penllyn, Penmark, Peterston-super-Ely, Rhoose, Sigginstone, St Athan, St Donat's, St Hilary, St Mary Church, St Nicholas, Sully, Wenvoe, Wick and Ystradowen.

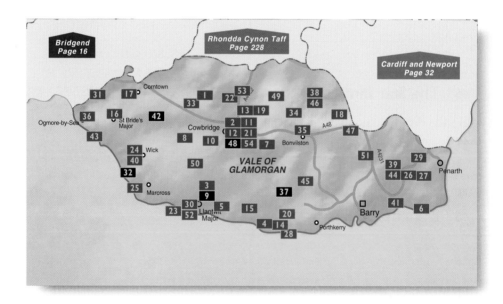

■ Vale of Glamorgan Reference Number - Detailed Information

■ Vale of Glamorgan Reference Number - Summary Entry

Ceredigion Page 249 ▶ Adjacent area - refer to pages indicated

Often described as 'the garden by the sea', Penarth (the name means 'bear's head' in Welsh) is an unspoilt seaside resort that developed in Victorian and Edwardian times. Just south of the town lies a Medieval Village located in Cosmeston Country Park, an area of lakes, woodlands and meadows created from a disused limestone quarry. A peaceful and tranquil habitat for many birds and animals, with a wide range of plant life, the country park has a visitor centre, picnic areas and a café.

Cosmeston Country Park, Penarth

A tiny island with a wealth of wildlife, Flat Holm has a history that dates back to the Dark Ages, when it was used by monks as a retreat. Meanwhile, Barry Island is not in fact an island but a peninsula, facing Barry, whose natural, sheltered harbour has been used since Roman times. The Barry Island Railway Heritage Centre has opened its extended line from Barry Island into the neighbouring Waterfront Dock Development. To the north of the resort is the Welsh Hawking Centre.

To the west of the village of St Donat's lies Nash Point, a headland with two lighthouses and the remnants of an Iron Age fort. This area of the coast is overlooked by limestone cliffs that, through wind erosion, have begun to resemble giant building blocks.

Southerndown is a popular holiday centre overlooking Dunraven Bay and home to the Glamorgan Heritage Coast Centre with its displays and information on the 14-mile long stretch of wild and beautiful coastline which begins in the west at Newton.

To the south of the village of St Nicholas lie Dyffryn Gardens, part of the Dyffryn estate and landscaped in the 1800s. One of the finest surviving Thomas Mawson gardens in Britain, Dyffryn offers a series of broad sweeping lawns, Italianate terraces, a paved court, a physick garden and a rose garden as well as a vine walk and arboretum, and the very impressive Pompeian Garden and Theatre Garden, where open-air plays and concerts are held.

1 Barley Mow Inn

Craig Penllyne, Wick, Cowbridge,
Vale of Glamorgan CF71 7RT

☎ 01446 772558

Real Ales, Bar Food, Restaurant Menu,
No Smoking Area

2 Bear Hotel

63 High St, Cowbridge,
Vale of Glamorgan CF71 7AF

☎ 01446 774814

Real Ales, Bar Food, Restaurant Menu,
Accommodation, No Smoking Area

3 The Blacksmiths Arms

Llanmaes, Llantwit Major,
Vale of Glamorgan CF61 2XR

☎ 01446 792393

Real Ales, Bar Food, Restaurant Menu,
No Smoking Area

4 Blue Anchor Inn

East Aberthaw, Rhoose, Barry,
Vale of Glamorgan CF62 3DD

☎ 01446 750329

Bar Food, Restaurant Menu, Accommodation

5 Boverton Castle

Boverton, Llantwit Major,
Vale of Glamorgan CF61 1UH

☎ 01446 792428

Real Ales, Bar Food, Restaurant Menu,
Accommodation

6 Brewers Fayre

Captains Wife Beach Rd, Swanbridge, Penarth,
Vale of Glamorgan CF64 5UG

☎ 02920 530066

Real Ales, Bar Food, Restaurant Menu,
No Smoking Area

9 The Carpenters Arms

Ewlys Brewis Road, Llantwit Major,
Vale of Glamorgan CF61 2XR

☎ 01466 792063

Real Ales, Bar Food, Restaurant Menu,
Accommodation, No Smoking Area

Set right on the coast, Llantwit Major is a historic settlement, home to the oldest learning centres in the nation, founded by St Illtud in AD500. The Carpenters Arms is another of the town's venerable institutions, featuring many traditional elements such as the stonebuilt walls and exposed beamwork. Having recently undergone a tasteful and sensitive refurbishment, the inn is spacious and welcoming, with a comfortable and eye-pleasing lounge and bar and five attractive guest bedrooms. The food and drink are also impressive, with a range of tasty dishes at lunch and dinner and a good selection of beers, wines, spirits and soft drinks. Owner Tanya Forsyth is also an accomplished cook, and it shows in the excellent dishes she creates.

☛ Off the A48 southwest of Cowbridge

🍺 Brains Smooth and a rotating guest ale

🍴 Mon-Sun 12-3 & Mon-Sat 5-9

🛏 5 en suite rooms

🎵 Karaoke Fri night, disco Sat night

♿ Parking, garden, disabled access

💳 All major cards

🕐 12-11 Mon/Tues/Weds, 12-12.30 a.m. Thu/Fri/Sat (Sun and Bank Holidays to 10.30)

🏛 St Donat's 2 miles, Penmark 6 miles, Cowbridge 7 miles

7 The Bush Inn

St Hilary, Cowbridge, Vale of Glamorgan CF71 7DP
☎ 01446 772745
Real Ales, Bar Food, Restaurant Menu,
Accommodation

8 The Carne Arms

Llysworney, Cowbridge,
Vale of Glamorgan CF71 7NQ
☎ 01446 773553
Real Ales, Bar Food, Restaurant Menu

9 The Carpenters Arms

See panel opposite

10 The Cross Inn

Church Rd, Llanblethian, Cowbridge,
Vale of Glamorgan CF71 7JF
☎ 01446 772995
Bar Food, Restaurant Menu

11 The Duke of Wellington

48 High St, Cowbridge,
Vale of Glamorgan CF71 7AG
☎ 01446 773592
Real Ales, Bar Food, Restaurant Menu,
No Smoking Area

12 Edmondes Arms

Cardiff Rd, Cowbridge,
Vale of Glamorgan CF71 7EP
☎ 01446 773192

13 Farmers Arms

Cowbridge Rd, Aberthin, Cowbridge,
Vale of Glamorgan CF71 7HB
☎ 01446 773429
Bar Food, Restaurant Menu, No Smoking Area

14 The Fontygary Inn

Fonmon Rd, Rhoose, Barry,
Vale of Glamorgan CF62 3DU
☎ 01446 711221
Real Ales, Bar Food

15 The Four Bells Inn

Rock Rd, St Athan, Barry,
Vale of Glamorgan CF62 4PG
☎ 01446 750383
Real Ales

16 Fox and Hounds

Ewenny Rd, St Brides Major, Bridgend,
Vale of Glamorgan CF32 0SA
☎ 01656 880285
Real Ales, Bar Food, No Smoking Area

17 Golden Mile Inn

Corntown, Bridgend, Vale of Glamorgan CF35 5BA
☎ 01656 654884
Real Ales, Bar Food, Restaurant Menu,
No Smoking Area

18 Greendown Inn Hotel

Cardiff, Vale of Glamorgan CF5 6EP
☎ 01446 760310
Bar Food, Restaurant Menu, Accommodation,
No Smoking Area

19 Hare and Hounds Inn

Aberthin, Cowbridge, Vale of Glamorgan CF71 7HB
☎ 01446 774892
Real Ales, Bar Food

20 The Highwayman Inn

Rhoose, Barry, Vale of Glamorgan CF62 3BH
☎ 01446 710205
Real Ales, Bar Food, Restaurant Menu,
Accommodation

21 Horse and Groom

19 High St, Cowbridge,
Vale of Glamorgan CF71 7AD
☎ 01446 772253
Real Ales, No Smoking Area

22 Jane Hodge Resort Hotel

Cowbridge, Vale of Glamorgan CF71 7TN
☎ 01446 772608
Bar Food, Restaurant Menu, Accommodation,
No Smoking Area

23 Kings Head

East St, Llantwit Major, Vale of Glamorgan CF61 1XY
☎ 01446 792697
Real Ales, Bar Food, Restaurant Menu

24 Lamb and Flag Inn

Church St, Wick, Cowbridge,
Vale of Glamorgan CF71 7QE
☎ 01656 890278
Real Ales, Bar Food, Restaurant Menu

25 Lighthouse Inn

Marcross, Llantwit Major,
Vale of Glamorgan CF61 1ZG
☎ 01656 890568
Real Ales, Bar Food, Restaurant Menu

26 The Malthouse

The Parade, Castle Drive, Dinas Powys,
Vale of Glamorgan CF64 4NR
☎ 02920 512445
Real Ales

27 Manor House Hotel

Sully Rd, Penarth, Vale of Glamorgan CF64 2TQ
☎ 02920 709309
Bar Food, Restaurant Menu, Accommodation,
No Smoking Area

28 Mayflower Hotel

88 Fontygary Rd, Rhoose, Barry,
Vale of Glamorgan CF62 3DT
☎ 01446 711130
Real Ales

29 The Merrie Harrier

117 Penlan Rd, Llandough, Penarth,
Vale of Glamorgan CF64 2NY
☎ 02920 303994
Real Ales, Bar Food, No Smoking Area

30 Old Swan Inn

Church St, Llantwit Major, Vale of Glamorgan CF61 1SB
☎ 01446 792230
Bar Food, Restaurant Menu

---

32 The Plough and Harrow

Monknash, nr Cowbridge,
Vale of Glamorgan CF71 7QQ
☎ 01656 890209
Real Ales, Bar Food, Restaurant Menu

One of the best pubs in Wales, The Plough and
Harrow is set near the coast and not far from
centres such as Bridgend and Cowbridge. Setting
the standard for fine food and drink, the inn is
welcoming inside and out, with a handsome décor

and furnishings and an impressive garden for
outdoor dining.

Cosy and welcoming, with roaring log fires the
inn dates back to 1383 and is well worth seeking
out. Wholesome and hearty food is served at
lunch and dinner, while there are always up to
eight real ales (four on tap) together with a full
complement of lagers, cider, stout, wines, spirits
and soft drinks.

New owners Paula Jones and Dai and Debbie
Woodman have made a real sucess of this fine
pub.

- ☛ Off the A48 5 miles south of Cowbridge
- 🍺 Eight real ales
- 🍴 Mon-Sun 12-2.30 & Mon-Sat 6-9
- 🎵 Live folk music Sun night
- 🅿 Parking, garden.
- 💳 All major cards (except Amex)
- 🏆 Eat Out In Wales 2004; CAMRA 2004
- 🕐 12-11 (Sun and Bank Holidays to 10.30)
- 🏛 coast, Cowbridge 5 miles, Barry Island 10 miles

31 The Pelican Inn
Ewenny Rd, Ogmore By Sea, Bridgend,
Vale of Glamorgan CF32 0QP
☎ 01656 880049
Real Ales, Bar Food, Restaurant Menu,
No Smoking Area

32 The Plough & Harrow
See panel opposite

33 The Red Fox Inn
Penllyn, Wick, Cowbridge,
Vale of Glamorgan CF71 7RQ
☎ 01446 772352
Real Ales, Bar Food, Restaurant Menu,
No Smoking Area

34 Red Lion Inn
Pendoylan, Cowbridge,
Vale of Glamorgan CF71 7UJ
☎ 01446 760332
Real Ales, Bar Food, Restaurant Menu,
No Smoking Area

35 The Red Lion Inn
Bonvilston, Cardiff, Vale of Glamorgan CF5 6TR
☎ 01446 781208
Real Ales, Bar Food, Restaurant Menu,
No Smoking Area

36 Sea Lawns Hotel
Slon Lane, Ogmore-By-Sea, Bridgend,
Vale of Glamorgan CF32 0PN
☎ 01656 880311
Real Ales, Bar Food, Restaurant Menu,
Accommodation, No Smoking Area

37 The Six Bells Inn
See panel below

38 The Sportsmans Rest
Peterston-Super-Ely, Cardiff,
Vale of Glamorgan CF5 6LH
☎ 01446 760675
Real Ales

---

37 The Six Bells

Penmark, nr Rhoose, Vale of Glamorgan CF62 3BP
☎ 01446 710229
⊕ www.sixbellspenmark.co.uk

Bar Food, Restaurant Menu, No Smoking Area

The Six Bells in Penmark is a large, convivial and welcoming place offering superb food, drink and hospitality. Owners Norman and Mell Lacey took over back in 2004, and have made a great success of the venture. The expansive floor space is

divided into three areas – the public bar with its black and amber tiles and big log fire, the lounge/restaurant, which is elegant and tastefully decorated and furnished, and the function suite, spacious and attractive. As well as the function suite there's a marquee available for those special celebrations.

The food is home-made, simple and simply delicious, with a range of traditional favourites expertly prepared and cooked to perfection – the many diners who come back again and again attest to the quality of the food and service.

☛ Off the A48 ½ mile from Cardiff airport

🍺 HB Hancocks and a rotating guest ale

🍴 Mon-Sat 12-9; Sun 12-6

🎵 Live music Fri night

🅿 Parking, disabled access, outdoor patio area

💳 All major cards

🏆 HB Hancocks Best Bitter Award 2003

🕐 12-11 (Sun and Bank Holidays to 10.30)

🏛 Barry Island 4 miles, Penarth 8 miles, Southerndown 11 miles

39 The Star

Station Rd, Dinas Powys,
Vale of Glamorgan CF64 4DE
☎ 02920 514245
Real Ales, Bar Food, Restaurant Menu

40 The Star Inn

Ewenny Rd, Wick, Cowbridge,
Vale of Glamorgan CF71 7QA
☎ 01656 890519
Real Ales, Bar Food, Restaurant Menu,
No Smoking Area

41 The Sully Inn

4 Cog Rd, Penarth, Vale of Glamorgan CF64 5TD
☎ 02920 530176
Real Ales, Bar Food

42 The Sycamore Tree Inn

See panel below

43 The Three Golden Cups

Southerndown, Bridgend,
Vale of Glamorgan CF32 0RW
☎ 01656 880432
Real Ales, Bar Food, Restaurant Menu,
No Smoking Area

44 Three Horse Shoes

Station Rd, Dinas Powys, Vale of Glamorgan CF64 4DE
☎ 02920 516011
Real Ales

45 Three Horse Shoes Inn

Moulton, Barry, Vale of Glamorgan CF62 3AB
☎ 01446 710428
Real Ales, Bar Food

46 Three Horseshoes Inn

Peterston-Super-Ely, Vale of Glamorgan CF5 6LH
☎ 01446 760388
Real Ales, Bar Food, Restaurant Menu,
No Smoking Area

42 The Sycamore Tree Inn

Coed Masarnen, Colwinston, nr Cowbridge,
Vale of Glamorgan CF71 7NG
☎ 01656 652827 e-mail: sycamoretreeinn
@colwinston.wanadoo.co.uk
Real Ales, Bar Food, Restaurant Menu

Here in a village that's one of the most desirable addresses in the region, The Sycamore Tree Inn is a distinguished and distinctive inn offering superior food, drink and hospitality. This 15th-century village pub is elegant and tasteful. The range of beers, spirits and soft drinks is complemented by an excellent wine list. Simple and delicious light bites are served, together with superb seasonal menus boasting food for the finest palate, cooked from fresh ingredients: oven-roasted cod, roast breast of Barbary duck, noisettes of lamb and medallions of beef are just a few of the many marvellous selections available. The Sunday roast is one of the best in the Vale, featuring Colwinston-reared meats from nearby Pwllywrach Farm. Booking advised at all times.

🍺 1 mile off the A48 3 miles from Cowbridge

🍺 Brains

🍴 summer: 12-2.30 & 6-9; winter: no food Mondays except Bank Holidays

🎵 Quiz night second Sunday of the month

🪑 Parking, garden

💳 All major cards

🕐 12-2.30 & 6-11 (10.30 Sundays), Monday lunch-open Bank Holidays only

🏛 Cowbridge 3 miles, Bridgend 3 miles, Cardiff 15 miles

47 Treharne Arms

The Tumble, St Nicholas, Vale of Glamorgan CF5 6SA

☎ 02920 597707

Restaurant Menu, No Smoking Area

48 The Vale of Glamorgan

See panel below

49 Vale of Glamorgan Golf Club

Hensol Park, Hensol, Vale of Glamorgan CF72 8JY

☎ 01443 665899

Real Ales, Bar Food, Restaurant Menu, Accommodation, No Smoking Area

50 Victoria Inn

Sigingstone, Cowbridge,
Vale of Glamorgan CF71 7LP

☎ 01446 773943

Real Ales, Bar Food, Restaurant Menu

51 Wenvoe Arms

Old Port Rd Wenvoe, Vale of Glamorgan CF5 6AN

☎ 02920 591129

Real Ales, Bar Food

52 White Lion Hotel

East St, Llantwit Major, Vale of Glamorgan CF61 1XY

☎ 01446 792240

Real Ales, Bar Food, Restaurant Menu

53 White Lion Inn

Ystradowen, Wick, Cowbridge,
Vale of Glamorgan CF71 7SY

☎ 01446 775591

Real Ales, Bar Food, Restaurant Menu,
No Smoking Area

54 Ye Olde Masons Arms

66 High St, Cowbridge, Vale of Glamorgan CF71 7AH

☎ 01446 771989

Real Ales, Bar Food, Accommodation,
No Smoking Area

---

48 The Vale of Glamorgan

53 High Street, Cowbridge,
Vale of Glamorgan CF71 7AR

☎ 01446 772252

Bar Food, Restaurant Menu

Set in the heart of the handsome and prosperous town of Cowbridge, The Vale of Glamorgan is a welcoming inn with a convivial and warm ambience. Owner Alister Sarjeant presides over this justly popular place, and he and his staff offer friendly, efficient service to all their customers. Speckled Hen and Bass are among the four resident ales, while there's also a fifth, rotating guest ale. Hearty and traditional food from the menu and daily specials board is served at lunchtime: home-made pies, liver and onions, gammon and more, all cooked to perfection and using the freshest locally-sourced ingredients. The accommodation comprises three double rooms, a single and a family room, all comfortably furnished.

☛ In the centre of Cowbridge off the A48

🍺 5 cask ales including changing guest ale

🍴 12-2.30

🛏 5 en suite rooms

🎵 Occasional live music

⚜ Garden, disabled access

💳 All major cards

🕐 11.30-11 (Sun and Bank Holidays to 10.30)

🏛 St Hilary 2 miles, St Nicholas 4 miles, Ewenny 5 miles, Penarth 12½ miles

WREXHAM

WREXHAM • RUABON • COEDPOETH

Wrexham county borough in northern Wales covers parts of the traditional counties of Denbighshire and Flintshire. It is named after Wrexham, its main town, and has a population of 130,000 inhabitants. The county borough was formed on April 1, 1996. Most of the area was previously part of the Welsh district of Wrexham Maelor - with a few areas coming from Glyndwr.

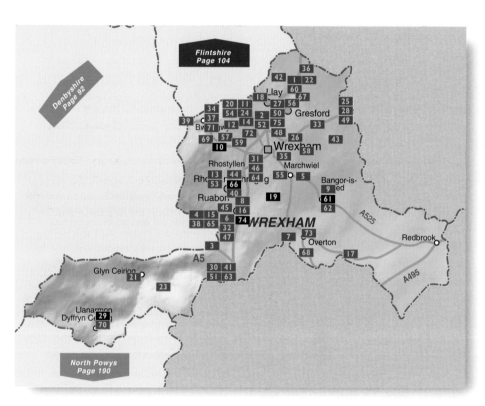

Flintshire
Page 104

Denbyshire
Page 92

North Powys
Page 190

■ Wrexham Reference Number - Detailed Information

■ Wrexham Reference Number - Summary Entry

Ceredigion
Page 249
Adjacent area - refer to pages indicated

The once-small market town of Wrexham, considered the unofficial capital of North Wales, is now a busy place with plenty to offer the visitor. The largest town in North Wales, it has grown and prospered around the commercial importance of its brick and tile

Chirk Castle

manufacturing, brewing, steel and coal. Wrexham still holds a variety of markets today, including a weekly cattle market held on Saturdays. Wrexham County Borough Museum traces the town's history from Bronze Age times.

Just to the south of Wrexham is a glorious 2,000-acre estate and Country Park, also the setting for Erddig (National Trust), one of the most fascinating houses in Britain. The outbuildings here have also been restored and are the site of the award-winning working dairy farm known as Farmworld. The extensive Erddig Gardens were laid out in the 18th century and include walled gardens, a yew walk, woodland trails and acres of parkland. Erddig is also home of the National Ivy Collection.

The River Dee, which marks the boundary between Wales and England, runs through the village of Holt; its importance as a crossing point can be seen in the attractive 15th-century bridge. Bangor-is-y-coed, also known as Bangor-on-Dee, is in the area known as the Maelor, where the Cheshire Plains turn into the Welsh Hills. The Maelor Way is a 24-mile footpath linking Cheshire's Sandstone Trail to the Offa's Dyke National Trail. The village is well known to race-goers as it is home to a picturesque Racecourse, situated on the banks of the River Dee, which holds meetings during the National Hunt season.

The border village of Overton is home to another of the Seven Wonders of Wales – the Overton Yew Trees, 21 trees that stand in the churchyard of the village Church of St Mary. Towering some 126 feet above the River Dee and carrying the Llangollen branch of the Shropshire Union Canal, Pontcysyllte Aqueduct is a magnificent structure some 1,007 feet in length, built in 1805 by Thomas Telford.

Chirk Castle (National Trust), begun in the late 13th century, remains a magnificent fortress. The parkland surrounding the castle and gardens is equally impressive.

1 Alyn Hotel

Station Rd, Rossett, Wrexham LL12 0HE
☎ 01244 570368
Real Ales, Bar Food, Restaurant Menu,
No Smoking Area

2 Alyn Lodge

Pont-Y-Capel Lane, Gresford, Wrexham,
Powys LL12 8SA
☎ 01978 855811

3 Aqueduct Inn

Holyhead Rd, Froncysyllte, Llangollen,
Wrexham LL20 7PY
☎ 01691 772481
Real Ales, Bar Food

4 Australia Arms

Llangollen Rd, Trevor, Llangollen,
Wrexham LL20 7TG
☎ 01978 810441
Real Ales, Bar Food, No Smoking Area

5 Best Western Cross Lanes Hotel

Bangor Rd, Marchwiel, Wrexham LL13 0TF
☎ 01978 780555
Real Ales, Bar Food, Restaurant Menu,
Accommodation, No Smoking Area

6 Black Lion Inn

Park Rd, Newbridge, Wrexham LL14 3YS
☎ 01978 823878

7 The Boat Inn

Erbistock, Wrexham LL13 0DL
☎ 01978 780666
Bar Food, Restaurant Menu, No Smoking Area

8 Bridge End Hotel

Bridge St, Ruabon, Wrexham LL14 6DA
☎ 01978 822949
Real Ales, Bar Food, Restaurant Menu,
Accommodation, No Smoking Area

10 The City Arms

Wern Road, Minera, Wrexham LL11 3DU
☎ 01978 754550
Real Ales, Bar Food, No Smoking Area

The City Arms is an impressive and spacious inn serving great food and drink. Cosy and traditional, the interior features a large open fire, exposed beam and a wealth of warm woods that add to the inn's charm and friendly ambience.

Real ales from a local brewery are complemented by a good range of lagers, wines, spirits

and soft drinks – something to quench every thirst. The superb restaurant has very attractive furnishings and décor and seats 40; it is non-smoking. Guests can choose from the menu or a la carte Thursday and Friday evenings and Sunday lunchtime (when Sunday roasts are added to the main menu). Booking required on Sundays. The leaseholder, Ieuan, is also a professional chef with over 35 years' experience. Children welcome at all times.

☛ Turn off main A483 onto A525 Ruthin Road. Follow into Minera and turn left at main crossroads. The inn is about a mile further on the left.

🍺 Local Plassey brewery

🍴 Mon-Sat 12-9; Sun 12-6

🅿️ Car park, garden, children's play area, disabled ramp to restaurant

🚫 No smoking in restaurant

🕐 11.30-11 (Sun and Bank Holidays to 10.30)

🏛 Wern Lead Mines, Offa's Dyke Path

9 The Buck House Hotel

High St, Bangor-On-Dee, Wrexham LL13 0BU
☎ 01978 780336
Real Ales, Bar Food, Restaurant Menu,
Accommodation, No Smoking Area

10 The City Arms

See panel opposite

11 The Clayton Arms

Mosshill, Wrexham LL11 6ES
☎ 01978 756444
Real Ales, Restaurant Menu, No Smoking Area

12 Cross Foxes

High St, Pentre Broughton, Wrexham,
Powys LL11 6AW
☎ 01978 755973
Real Ales

13 Cross Keys Inn

Australia St, Ponciau, Wrexham LL14 1ED
☎ 01978 840458

14 Crown Inn

Top Rd, Summerhill, Wrexham LL11 4SR
☎ 01978 755788
Real Ales, Bar Food

15 Duke of Wellington

Llangollen Rd, Acrefair, Wrexham LL14 3SG
☎ 01978 820000
Real Ales, Bar Food

16 The Duke of Wellington Inn

Duke St, Ruabon, Wrexham LL14 6DE
☎ 01978 820381
Real Ales, Bar Food, No Smoking Area

17 Dymock Arms

Penley, Wrexham LL13 0LS
☎ 01948 830221
Real Ales, Bar Food, Restaurant Menu,
Accommodation, No Smoking Area

19 Fox and Hounds

Eyton, Bangor-on-Dee Road, Wrexham LL13 0YD
☎ 01978 822512
Bar Food, Restaurant Menu, No Smoking Area

Dating back to 1630, the Fox and Hounds brims with character. Real fires, polished wood floors and a wealth of brasswork adorning the walls add to the traditional and welcoming ambience. Keg bitters served include Mansfield Smooth and Camerons Creamy, complemented by a good selection of lagers, wines, spirits and soft drinks.

There's a very good choice of dishes from the daily specials board, with tempting hot and cold dishes. The inn has two separate dining areas (both non-smoking). Guests can also dine in the superb garden on fine days. On Sundays, roasts are on the menu – booking required. To the rear of the inn there's a recently-opened caravan and camping park with room for five tents or tourers.

☞ From the A483 take the B5426 signposted Bangor-on-Dee. The village of Eyton is a mile or so along this road. The inn is on your right.

🍴 Summer: 12-3 & 6-9 Winter: 6-9

🎵 Sun quiz from 9 p.m.; occasional food-themed evenings (ring for details)

🚗 Car park, garden, caravan and camping park, disabled access to bar area

🕐 Summer: Mon-Thurs 11.30-3 & 6-11; Fri-Sat 11.30-11 (Sun and Bank Holidays to 10.30) Winter: Mon-Thurs 6-11; Fri-Sat 11.30-11 (Sun and Bank Holidays to 10.30)

🏛 Bangor-on-Dee Racecourse 2 miles, The National Trust, Erddig Hall 1 mile

18 The Ffrwd

Ffrwd Rd, Cefn-Y-Bedd, Wrexham LL12 9TR

☎ 01978 757951

Real Ales, Restaurant Menu, No Smoking Area

19 Fox & Hounds

See panel on page 271

20 George and Dragon

Ael-Y-Bryn, Brymbo, Wrexham LL11 5DA

☎ 01978 758515

Real Ales

21 Glyn Valley Hotel

Llanarmon Rd, Glyn Ceirog, Llangollen,
Wrexham LL20 7EU

☎ 01691 718896

Real Ales, Bar Food, Restaurant Menu,
Accommodation, No Smoking Area

22 Golden Lion

Chester Rd, Rossett, Wrexham LL12 0HN

☎ 01244 571020

Real Ales, Bar Food, Restaurant Menu,
No Smoking Area

23 Golden Pheasant Hotel

Llwynmawr, Llangollen, Wrexham LL20 7BB

☎ 01691 718281

Bar Food, Restaurant Menu, Accommodation,
No Smoking Area

24 The Grapes Inn

Francis Rd, Moss, Wrexham LL11 6EB

☎ 01978 720585

Real Ales, Restaurant Menu, No Smoking Area

25 Gredington Arms

Cross St, Holt, Wrexham LL13 9JD

☎ 01829 270289

26 The Gredington Arms

Holt Rd, Llan-Y-Pwll, Wrexham LL13 9SD

☎ 01978 661728

Real Ales, Bar Food, Restaurant Menu,
No Smoking Area

27 Griffin Inn

Church Green, Gresford, Wrexham,
Powys LL12 8RG

☎ 01978 852231

Real Ales

28 The Hand and Heart

Castle St, Holt, Wrexham LL13 9YL

☎ 01829 270491

Restaurant Menu, No Smoking Area

29 The Hand at Llanarmon

See panel opposite

30 The Hand Hotel

Church St, Chirk, Wrexham LL14 5EY

☎ 01691 773472

Real Ales, Bar Food, Restaurant Menu,
Accommodation, No Smoking Area

31 The Hole In The Wall Bersham

Y Ddol Bersham, Wrexham LL14 4HN

☎ 01978 365588

Real Ales, Bar Food

32 Holly Bush Inn

Well St, Cefn Mawr, Wrexham LL14 3AE

☎ 01978 822154

33 The Holt Lodge

Wrexham Rd, Holt, Wrexham LL13 9SW

☎ 01978 661002

Real Ales, Bar Food, Restaurant Menu,
Accommodation, No Smoking Area

34 The Kings Head Inn

Ruthin Rd, Bwlchgwyn, Wrexham LL11 5UT

☎ 01978 755961

Real Ales, Bar Food, No Smoking Area

35 Llwyn Onn Hall Hotel

Cefn Rd, Wrexham LL13 0NY

☎ 01978 261225

Real Ales, Bar Food, Restaurant Menu,
Accommodation, No Smoking Area

36 Llyndir Hall Hotel

Llyndir Lane, Rossett, Nr Chester,
Powys LL12 0AY

☎ 01244 571648

Bar Food, Restaurant Menu, Accommodation, No Smoking Area

37 The Mile Stone Inn

Ruthin Rd, Bwlchgwyn, Wrexham LL11 5UT

☎ 01978 757571

Bar Food, Restaurant Menu, No Smoking Area

38 Mill Inn

Mill Lane, Cefn Mawr, Wrexham LL14 3NL

☎ 01978 821799

Real Ales

39 The Moors Inn and Restaurant

Ruthin Rd, Bwlchgwyn, Wrexham LL11 5YL

☎ 01978 755774

40 Moreton Inn

Ruabon Rd, Ruabon, Wrexham LL14 6PU

☎ 01978 846417

Bar Food, Restaurant Menu, No Smoking Area

41 Moreton Park Lodge

Gledrid Chirk, Wrexham LL14 5DG

☎ 01691 776666

Real Ales, Bar Food, Restaurant Menu, Accommodation, No Smoking Area

42 Mount Pleasant Inn

Croeshowell, Llay, Wrexham LL12 0NY

☎ 01244 570377

Bar Food, Restaurant Menu, No Smoking Area

43 The Nags Head

Ridley Wood Rd, Ridley Wood, Wrexham LL13 9US

☎ 01978 661314

Real Ales, Bar Food, Restaurant Menu, No Smoking Area

29 The Hand at Llanarmon

Llanarmon D.C., Ceiriog Valley, Llangollen LL20 7LD

☎ 01691 600666

🌐 www.thehandhotel.co.uk

Real Ales, Bar Food, Restaurant Menu, Accommodation, No Smoking Area

Set in a picturesque and rural location in the Ceiriog Valley, nestling beneath the Berwyn Mountains and alongside the sparkling River Ceiriog, The Hand at Llanarmon dates back to the 16th century. Stone walls and open fires add to the inn's traditional and welcoming atmosphere. The bar menu changes with the seasons, while the charming restaurant area is the setting for a range of superb meals, from grilled whole sea bass with lemon and tarragon butter to roasted vegetables with goats cheese and pesto cous-cous. Booking advised Friday and Saturday evenings and Sunday lunchtime. The guest bedrooms – located upstairs in the old farmhouse or in the former barn – are charming and beautifully furnished and decorated, commanding views over the village or surrounding countryside. Children welcome. Dogs welcome by arrangement.

☛ Llanarmon is on the B4500 13 miles southwest of Chirk (A483/A5)

🍺 Rotating guest ale

🍴 12-2.30 & 6.30-9

🛏 13 en suite rooms

🅿 Car park, terraced seating area, small lawned area for residents

💳 All the major cards

🏆 Welsh Tourist Board 3 stars

🚫 No smoking in restaurant or bedrooms

🕐 11.30-11 (Sun and Bank Holidays to 10.30)

🏛 Chirk Castle 13 miles, Llangollen 15 miles, Oswestry 20 miles

61   The Royal Oak

High Street, Bangor-on-Dee, Wrexham   LL13 0BU
☎ 01978 780289

Real Ales, Bar Food, Restaurant Menu, No Smoking Area

Renowned for its food, The Royal Oak boasts outstanding lunch and evening menus offering a good choice and variety of dishes. Specialities include locally-reared lamb and fish and chips cooked in home-made batter, together with fresh trout, Scottish haggis and a good selection of bar snacks and fresh sandwiches. Booking required at weekends.

Dating back to 1760, this former coaching inn is spacious and welcoming. Here in the picturesque village of Bangor-on-Dee, the inn's large garden is adjacent to the River Dee and there is terraced seating overlooking the river. To the rear of the inn, the Boathouse has been converted into a craft shop selling local crafts and open weekends and Bank Holidays from 11-5. Day tickets are available for fishing on the river.

- ☛ Off the A525
- 🍺 Old Speckled Hen and rotating guest ale
- 🍴 12-2.30 & 6-9
- 🎵 Weds quiz from 9 p.m., occasional food-themed evenings (ring for details)
- 🅿 Car park, garden, craft shop to rear, fishing on River Dee
- 💳 Not Amex or Diners
- 🕐 Mon 11.30-2.30 & 6-11; Tues-Sat 11.30-11 (Sun and Bank Holidays to 10.30)
- 🏛 Bangor-on-Dee Racecourse, Plassey Leisure Park

---

66   Travellers Inn

High Street, Johnstown, Wrexham   LL14 2SH
☎ 01978 842281
🌐 www.johnstown-travellers.co.uk

Real Ales, Bar Food, Restaurant Menu, No Smoking Area

Recently refurbished and sensitively redecorated, Travellers Inn is a welcoming place to enjoy great food and drink in the heart of Johnstown.
A sample from the menu includes hearty favourites such as beef and ale pie, gammon, mixed grills, steaks and more. Tenant Richard Lee is a qualified chef, and it shows in the quality of the meals served at lunch and dinner. On Sundays, traditional roasts are added to the main menu. Meals can be enjoyed in the bar or dining area/restaurant, or on the decked patio area to the rear of the pub. Banks Bitter is the permanent real ale, complemented by the occasional guest ale and a good selection of other thirst-quenchers such as lagers, cider, stout, wines, spirits and soft drinks. Children welcome.

- ☛ Johnstown is found on B5606 at junction with B5426, a short drive from A483
- 🍺 Banks Bitter and occasional guest ale
- 🍴 Mon-Fri 12-3 & 5-8; Sat-Sun 12-5
- 🎵 Thurs quiz from 9 p.m.; Fri live entertainment from 9 p.m.
- 🅿 Car park, disabled access
- 🕐 11.30-11 (Sun and Bank Holidays to 10.30)
- 🏛 Chirk Castle and Gardens 3 miles, Pontcysyllte Aqueduct 1 mile

44 The New Inn
Wrexham Rd, Johnstown, Wrexham LL14 1NU
☎ 01978 840481
No Smoking Area

45 Oddfellow Arms Inn
Chapel St, Acrefair, Wrexham LL14 3TB
☎ 01978 822135
Real Ales

46 Old Black Horse
Henblas Rd, Rhostyllen, Wrexham LL14 4AD
☎ 01978 357265

47 The Old Vaults Inn
Well St, Cefn Mawr, Wrexham LL14 3AE
☎ 01978 810316

48 Pant Yr Ochain
Old Wrexham Rd, Gresford, Wrexham,
Powys LL12 8TY
☎ 01978 853525
Real Ales, Bar Food, Restaurant Menu,
No Smoking Area

49 The Peal O Bells
Church St, Holt, Wrexham LL13 9JP
☎ 01829 270411
Real Ales, Bar Food, Restaurant Menu,
No Smoking Area

50 The Plough Inn
Chester Rd, Gresford, Wrexham LL12 8NE
☎ 01978 855010
Real Ales, Bar Food, Restaurant Menu,
No Smoking Area

51 The Poachers Pocket
Gledrid Chirk, Wrexham LL14 5DG
☎ 01691 773250
Real Ales, Bar Food, Restaurant Menu,
No Smoking Area

52 Queens Head
Glan Llyn Rd, Bradley, Wrexham LL11 4BA
☎ 01978 758151
Bar Food

53 The Railway
Smith St, Rhosllanerchrugog, Wrexham LL14 1AR
☎ 01978 840876
Real Ales, Bar Food, Restaurant Menu,
No Smoking Area

54 The Railway Tavern
Railway Rd, Brymbo, Wrexham LL11 5EA
☎ 01978 755599
Real Ales

55 Red Lion
Wrexham Rd, Marchwiel, Wrexham LL13 0PH
☎ 01978 262317
Real Ales, Bar Food, Restaurant Menu,
No Smoking Area

56 Red Lion
Marford Hill, Marford, Wrexham LL12 8SN
☎ 01978 853562
Real Ales, Bar Food, Restaurant Menu,
No Smoking Area

57 Red Lion Inn
Talwrn Rd, Coedpoeth, Wrexham LL11 3PG
☎ 01978 755680

58 Red Wither Inn
Red Wither Rd, Wrexham LL13 9RD
☎ 01978 661313
Bar Food, Restaurant Menu, Accommodation

59 Rollers Arms
High St, Southsea, Wrexham LL11 5PB
☎ 01978 755772

60 Rossett Hall Hotel
Rossett, Wrexham LL12 0DE
☎ 01244 571000
Real Ales, Bar Food, Restaurant Menu,
Accommodation, No Smoking Area

61 The Royal Oak
See panel opposite

62 The Stableyard Cottage

High St, Bangor-On-Dee, Wrexham LL13 0AU

☎ 01978 780642

Accommodation, No Smoking Area

63 Stanton House Inn

Holyhead Rd, Chirk, Wrexham LL14 5NA

☎ 01691 774150

Real Ales, Bar Food

64 The Swan Inn

Mount St, Rhostyllen, Wrexham LL14 4AU

☎ 01978 265900

Real Ales

65 The Telford Inn

Station Rd, Trevor, Llangollen, Wrexham LL20 7TT

☎ 01978 820469

Real Ales, Bar Food, No Smoking Area

74 Wynnstay Arms Hotel

High Street, Ruabon, Wrexham LL14 6BL

☎ 01978 822187

Real Ales, Restaurant Menu, Accommodation,
No Smoking Area

The Wynnstay Arms Hotel is a large and
impressive place offering food, drink and an ideal
touring base for exploring North Wales. Built in
the 1800s, it was originally a coaching house for
travellers. Now, brimming with character and
charm, it has an enviable reputation for the high
standard of the food and a homely, cosy atmosphere.

☛ Ruabon is on the A539, off the A483
southwest of Wrexham

🍺 Robinsons Unicorn, rotating guest ale

🍴 12-2 & 6-9; Sun 12-9

🛏 9 en suite rooms

🅿 Car park, good disabled access

💳 Not Amex or Diners

� RAC 2 stars

🚭 No smoking in restaurant

🕐 11.30-11 (Sun and Bank Holidays to 10.30)

🏛 Chirk Castle and Gardens 3 miles,
Pontcysyllte Aqueduct 1 mile

66 Travellers Inn

See panel on page 274

67 Trevor Arms Hotel

Marford Hill, Marford, Wrexham LL12 8TA

☎ 01244 570436

Real Ales, Restaurant Menu, Accommodation,
No Smoking Area

68 The Trotting Mare

Knolton, Overton-On-Dee, Wrexham LL13 0LE

☎ 01978 710743

Real Ales, Bar Food, Restaurant Menu,
No Smoking Area

69 Tyn Y Capel Restaurant

Church Rd, Minera, Wrexham LL11 3DA

☎ 01978 757502

Real Ales, Bar Food, Restaurant Menu,
No Smoking Area

70 The West Arms Hotel

Llanarmon, Dyffryn Ceiriog, Wrexham LL20 7LD

☎ 01691 600665

Real Ales, Bar Food, Restaurant Menu,
Accommodation, No Smoking Area

71 Westminster Arms

Ruthin Rd, Bwlchgwyn, Wrexham LL11 5UT

☎ 01978 753875

72 The Wheatsheaf

Mold Rd, Gwersyllt, Wrexham LL11 4AE

☎ 01978 755593

Real Ales, Bar Food

73 White Horse Hotel

High St, Overton, Wrexham LL13 0DT

☎ 01978 710111

Bar Food, No Smoking Area

74 Wynnstay Arms Hotel

See panel adjacent

75 The Yew Tree Inn

High St, Gresford, Wrexham LL12 8RF

☎ 01978 852566

Real Ales

ORDER FORM

To order any of our publications just fill in the payment details below and complete the order form. For orders of less than 4 copies please add £1 per book for postage and packing. Orders over 4 copies are P & P free.

Please Complete Either:
I enclose a cheque for £   made payable to Travel Publishing Ltd

Or:
Card No: Expiry Date:

Signature:

Name:

Address:

Tel no:

Please either send, telephone, fax or e-mail your order to:
Travel Publishing Ltd, 7a Apollo House, Calleva Park, Aldermaston, Berkshire RG7 8TN
Tel: 0118 981 7777   Fax: 0118 982 0077   e-mail: info@travelpublishing.co.uk

	PRICE	QUANTITY		PRICE	QUANTITY
HIDDEN PLACES REGIONAL TITLES			**COUNTRY PUBS AND INNS**		
Cornwall	£8.99	....	Cornwall	£8.99	....
Devon	£8.99	....	Devon	£8.99	....
Dorset, Hants & Isle of Wight	£8.99	....	Sussex	£8.99	....
East Anglia	£8.99	....	Wales	£8.99	....
Gloucs, Wiltshire & Somerset	£8.99	....	**COUNTRY LIVING RURAL GUIDES**		
Heart of England	£8.99	....			
Hereford, Worcs & Shropshire	£8.99	....	East Anglia	£10.99	....
Lake District & Cumbria	£8.99	....	Heart of England	£10.99	....
Lancashire & Cheshire	£8.99	....	Ireland	£11.99	....
Northumberland & Durham	£8.99	....	North East	£10.99	....
Peak District	£8.99	....	North West	£10.99	....
Sussex	£8.99	....	Scotland	£11.99	....
Yorkshire	£8.99	....	South of England	£10.99	....
HIDDEN PLACES NATIONAL TITLES			South East of England	£10.99	....
England	£11.99	....	Wales	£11.99	....
Ireland	£11.99	....	West Country	£10.99	....
Scotland	£11.99	....			
Wales	£11.99	....			

	PRICE	QUANTITY
HIDDEN INNS TITLES		
East Anglia	£7.99	....
Heart of England	£7.99	....
North of England	£7.99	....
South	£7.99	....
South East	£7.99	....
Wales	£7.99	....
West Country	£7.99	....
Yorkshire	£7.99	....

Value

Post and Packing

Total Value

Easy-to-use, Informative
Travel Guides on the British Isles

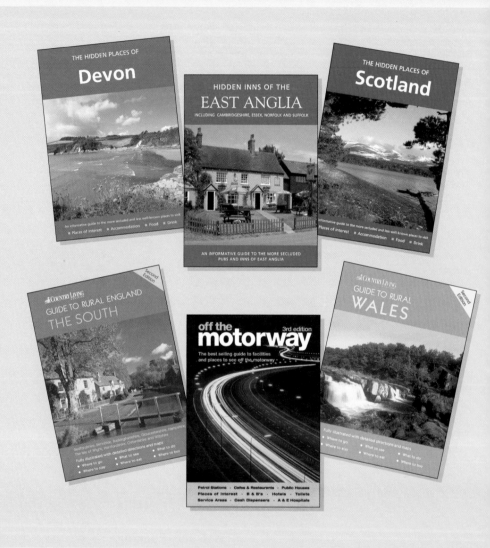

Travel Publishing Limited

7a Apollo House • Calleva Park • Aldermaston • Berkshire RG7 8TN
Phone: 0118 981 7777 • **Fax:** 0118 982 0077
e-mail: info@travelpublishing.co.uk • **website:** www.travelpublishing.co.uk

READER REACTION FORM

The *Travel Publishing* research team would like to receive reader's comments on any visitor attractions or places reviewed in the book and also recommendations for suitable entries to be included in the next edition. This will help ensure that the *Hidden Places series of Guides* continues to provide its readers with useful information on the more interesting, unusual or unique features of each attraction or place ensuring that their visit to the local area is an enjoyable and stimulating experience. To provide your comments or recommendations would you please complete the forms below and overleaf as indicated and send to:

**The Research Department, Travel Publishing Ltd,
7a Apollo House, Calleva Park, Aldermaston, Reading, RG7 8TN.**

Your Name:

Your Address:

Your Telephone Number:

Please tick as appropriate:

Comments ☐   Recommendation ☐

Name of Establishment:

Address:

Telephone Number:

Name of Contact:

Comment or Reason for Recommendation:

READER REACTION FORM

The *Travel Publishing* research team would like to receive reader's comments on any visitor attractions or places reviewed in the book and also recommendations for suitable entries to be included in the next edition. This will help ensure that the *Hidden Places series of Guides* continues to provide its readers with useful information on the more interesting, unusual or unique features of each attraction or place ensuring that their visit to the local area is an enjoyable and stimulating experience. To provide your comments or recommendations would you please complete the forms below and overleaf as indicated and send to:

The Research Department, Travel Publishing Ltd,
7a Apollo House, Calleva Park, Aldermaston, Reading, RG7 8TN.

Your Name:

Your Address:

Your Telephone Number:

Please tick as appropriate:

Comments ☐   Recommendation ☐

Name of Establishment:

Address:

Telephone Number:

Name of Contact:

Comment or Reason for Recommendation:

....

....

....

....

....

....

....

....

....

....

....

....

....

....

....

....